RECLAIMING THE PERSONAL

Reclaiming the Personal

Oral History in Post-Socialist Europe

EDITED BY NATALIA KHANENKO-FRIESEN
AND GELINADA GRINCHENKO

UNIVERSITY OF TORONTO PRESS
Toronto Buffalo London

Toronto Buffalo London
www.utppublishing.com

ISBN 978-1-4426-3738-2 (cloth)

Library and Archives Canada Cataloguing in Publication

Reclaiming the personal : oral history in post-socialist Europe/edited by Natalia Khanenko-Friesen and Gelinada Grinchenko.

Includes bibliographical references and index.
ISBN 978-1-4426-3738-2 (bound)

1. Oral history – Research – Europe, Eastern. 2. Social sciences – Research – Europe, Eastern. 3. Europe, Eastern – Historiography. I. Khanenko-Friesen, Natalia, author, editor II. Grinchenko, Gelinada, 1971–, author, editor

DJK50.R43 2015 907.2047 C2015-904603-3

University of Toronto Press acknowledges the financial assistance to its publishing program of the Canada Council for the Arts and the Ontario Arts Council, an agency of the Government of Ontario.

Canada Council for the Arts Conseil des Arts du Canada

Funded by the Government of Canada Financé par le gouvernement du Canada Canada

Contents

Acknowledgments

When we proposed to prepare this English-language collection about Eastern European oral history, we did not fully understand the challenge we embraced. Our intention was simple, we wanted to share with our English-speaking colleagues the best examples of oral historical work that has been conducted in Eastern Europe within the first two decades of post-socialism in Europe. At the same time, we wanted to show the important and oftentimes vanguard role oral history as theory and practice have been playing in post-socialist societies in times of post-socialist transition. To achieve this goal and to present this oral historical work to non-Eastern European audiences, we took the challenge of translating not just the texts but also the cultural and historical contexts within which the oral historical work has been pursued in the region.

First, and above all, we want to thank our contributors who shared our belief that such a collection, focusing on the achievements of oral history in the first two decades of post-socialism in Europe, is long overdue. It proved to be a time consuming project, and we are deeply grateful to all the contributors who patiently worked with us through all stages of this book's production. We have seen many drafts of this manuscript and if it had not been for this collective effort to better the volume, we might not have been able to produce it at all. Thank you for your fine contributions. We also want to thank many other researchers who responded to our initial call for papers but whose projects were not included in this collection due to the limitations of thematic and regional foci which we chose for this collection.

Besides the contributors, many other individuals and organizations have been instrumental in the preparation of this collection of essays for publication. We thank the Prairie Centre for the Study of Ukrainian Heritage (Saskatoon, Canada) and the Kowalsky Eastern Ukrainian Institute (Kharkiv, Ukraine) for sponsoring and hosting the international symposium, "In Search of One's Own Voice: Oral History as Theory, Method, and Source" that we convened in Kharkiv on the eve of 2010 and that later gave birth to this collection. We are very grateful for this support as it allowed a diverse group of scholars from both Europe and North America to convene and share the work done in the region. The symposium ultimately informed our decision to embark on the production of this volume as we realized that the dialogue and the exchange among various "camps" of oral history (in Eastern Europe and outside) needs to continue, not just within the parameters of independent projects in the region, but also in the format of such symposia and book collections as ours.

The preparation of this collection was supported through two publication grants and one subvention grant by St Thomas More College at the University of Saskatchewan (Saskatoon, Canada). This financial support has been truly instrumental in our work. The Prairie Centre for the Study of Ukrainian Heritage, through its support of the Oral History program that co-organized the aforementioned symposium, further insured that the project was actively pursued despite its being costly and labour intensive.

Translating texts and ideas and providing proper contextualization of historical circumstances for readers who may not be intimately familiar with Eastern European history were the most challenging dimensions of our work. All but one essay in our collection were written by non-native speakers of English who themselves speak and write in five different languages. Some essays we had to translate into English, others were submitted already translated and all required substantial language and context editing. We thank Andrei Vinogradov of Saskatoon, Canada, for his assistance with the translation of three Russian-language essays included in this collection. Natalia Khanenko-Friesen worked through these and all other translations to ensure that the original meanings were retained in all submissions before passing the manuscript on to the copy-editor. Matthew Kudelka, our capable copy-editor, spent countless hours working on and finalizing all the edits to make sure that all contributions finally made sense. We thank Matthew for his professionalism, patience, and attention to detail and for handling the challenge of editing our collection's essays so well.

We thank the University of Toronto Press team and especially our UTP editor Richard Ratzlaff for their efficient steering of this project towards its completion. Richard's consideration, kindness, and commitment to our project were amazing and beyond imagination. We knew it would not be easy to produce this book but thanks to Richard's earnest and timely attention to our project's needs we have this volume in our hands in the end. We extend our thanks to the anonymous reviewers who provided the critical feedback that helped us improve the scholarship of this book. We worked with all contributors to address the questions that the anonymous reviewers raised in their comments on the collection and are thankful for the opportunity to make this collection better. Our sincere gratitude goes to Nadya Foty, Yuriy Kirushok, and Oleg Tkhoryk, who in their capacity as graduate research assistants, were involved in the production of this collection as researchers and typesetters. Finally, we thank Timothy and Leonid, our spouses, for believing in the importance of what we do as scholars and for supporting us throughout the entire project. And while so many people have contributed to our work presented here, any of the collection's shortcomings or weaknesses are our own.

Reclaiming the Personal

Introduction. Reclaiming the Personal: Oral History in Post-Socialist Europe

NATALIA KHANENKO-FRIESEN AND
GELINADA GRINCHENKO

In mid-December 2009, scholars from eight countries convened in the Ukrainian city of Kharkiv for an international symposium, "In Search of One's Own Voice: Oral History as Theory, Method, and Source." Specialists in various fields of social studies and humanities from Ukraine, Russia, Belarus, Canada, Germany, Belgium, Finland, and Poland, all of whom apply oral history methods in their research, took part in this conference.[1] For two days they engaged in lively debate on the current state of oral historical research in their regions while sharing their own work with one another. We, the two editors of this volume, were the co-organizers of this symposium. Placed in different academic contexts, of Canada and Ukraine, working in different languages, and living on different continents, yet united by the same passion for the scholarship we pursue, some time ago we asked ourselves a question: Is there a unique post-socialist oral history that can be distinguished from various other oral historical discourses around the world? The year of 2009 also marked twenty years since the collapse of the Berlin Wall in Germany. Turning to the production of this volume and taking this anniversary as an opportunity to reflect also on the history of oral history in post-socialist Europe, we wanted to examine what defined and motivated oral historical research in the former socialist countries on the European continent in the first two decades of post-socialism. What role did oral history play in reconceptualizing the past in the societies that once lived under communist rule? What initially, in 2006,[2] seemed just a case of casual curiosity led to an active search for the answers to those questions. The Kharkiv symposium served as a platform for further exploring the meanings and directions of oral historical research in the first two decades of post-socialism in Eastern Europe.[3]

This collection brings the best examples of oral historical research in Eastern European societies to English-language readers and articulates the specific circumstances – historical, socio-cultural, political – in which oral historical scholarship has shaped itself in the region in the first two decades since the collapse of the Berlin Wall in 1989. Oral history altogether is a relatively young academic discipline that is still carving out a niche. In post-socialist countries, it also occupies a unique vanguard position in the social sciences and humanities (which themselves have been dealing with profound change since the collapse of socialism). At the same time, its role in national scholarly discourses is often overlooked and undervalued, for it often swims against the currents of mainstream scholarship. With this book, we bring to Western readers' attention the pioneering work conducted by oral historians as they continue to respond to and advance the socio-cultural changes that have been taking place in their regions, including changes in the social sciences of post-socialist countries. The individual contributors do not all discuss the relevance of their research for their societies, but as the editors of this collection, we believe that the findings they present here have both social and political implications for the societies where they do their work.

Oral history in post-socialist Europe has been actively promoting itself within national academies since the late 1980s. It is more strongly entrenched in some countries than in others. Overall, we can say that oral history's establishment in a given region has been a logical outcome of recent historical changes. With the end of socialism, which for many decades succeeded in controlling the West-to-East traffic in ideas, Western scholarship has become available for evaluation and critical interpretation by regional scholars. In the last two decades, oral historians of the former Socialist Bloc have been actively engaging with their Western counterparts, who first elaborated the oral history method and its theoretical foundations.[4] In terms of developing oral history as a method, the West may have led; but when it comes to oral history's content and applications, post-socialist oral historians have begun to develop and advance their own unique research agendas, which are specific to local or national situations, political discourses, and popular movements. Miroslav Vanêk, a Czech oral historian and recent president of the International Oral History Association, spoke of this in the context of Czech oral historical research at the 2008 IOHA meeting. He observed that Western oral history practices were not always applicable to the Czech situation stating that while oral historians in the West oftentimes focused on disadvantaged groups, Czech oral historians "could not pay attention to social, ethnic or minorities subjects, but to the main poles of Czech society – Communist functionaries and dissidents."[5]

Based on our scholarly engagements with other oral historians in Eastern Europe spanning more than a decade, we began to recognize several important dimensions of oral historical practice in the former socialist countries that in our mind distinguish it from how oral historical research is currently being applied elsewhere, specifically in Western societies. Here, we will focus on four such dimensions.

Oral History and Pluralization of Local Life-Worlds

The first dimension concerns the fact that oral history in post-socialist contexts became a very effective intellectual tool for accessing, assessing, and perhaps contributing to the rapid and ongoing pluralization of post-socialist societies. To better understand the choices, directions, and applications of oral history in times of post-socialism, one has to go beyond the specifics of various oral historical projects that have been undertaken in the region – indeed, beyond the historical period of post-socialism itself.

Overall, looking back to its beginnings, oral history as a scholarly discipline entered the global social sciences at a time of major civilizational transformations. The 1950s and 1960s saw the collapse of the centuries-old European colonial order, the appearance of new nations on the world map, and the emergence of worldwide cultural and ideological movements (for gender equality, human rights, global ecology, and so on), all of this coupled with technological revolutions in communications and transportation. Humanity, clearly, was entering a new phase of development. Much has been already said about this. Whatever it is called (late modernity, postmodernity, globalization, and so on), this new era has also been characterized by a growing recognition that the social worlds in which people find themselves are becoming increasingly pluralized. The compression of time and space so eloquently described by the geographer and anthropologist David Harvey (among others),[6] and the workings of what anthropologist Arjun Appadurai once called global ethnoscapes[7] – those ever expanding global circuits of goods, people, finances, cultures, and ideas – have been contributing actively to the pluralization of human experience, not necessarily in the sense of growing equality, but certainly in the sense of the diversity of human experience. This process is visible in global metropolises and on their peripheries. Recent movements for universal gender and sexual equality have resulted in a general recognition that differently gendered communities are legitimate subjects of history. The political movements in various nations since the second half of the twentieth century, transmitted by the media to the rest of the world, constantly remind the global community of the ethnic and cultural complexity that supposedly homogenous nation-states must deal with. This ongoing pluralization of the world, in tandem with awareness of the increasing social, cultural, and ethnic diversity of local worlds, enhanced by processes of modern reflexivity,[8] has deeply entrenched itself in nations, societies, and communities. All of these are subject to the global flows of various ethnoscapes.

In Eastern Europe, the pluralization processes that the world and especially the West experienced so richly in the second half of the twentieth century were delayed for several decades, until the end of socialism in the late 1980s and early 1990s. This delay happened for at least two reasons. First, socialist ideologies provided little space for thoroughly examining the increasingly dynamic nature of the world beyond the socialist domain. Socialist governments, to varying degrees, worked hard to block global flows of people, capital, goods, and ideas onto their territories. This impeded local awareness of the expanding plurality of the world outside of the Socialist Bloc. Second, socialist ideologies relentlessly asserted their own claims to egalitarianism and equality and prevented people from studying, acknowledging, and practising their own social and cultural complexity. Every socialist government buried the diverse spectrum of human experiences under official narratives of unity, classlessness, interethnic brotherhood, and so on. Governments relied on socialist understandings of the past and present to suppress alternative memories of socialism and pre-socialism, and this silenced the multitude of narratives of political and ethnic discontent while promoting an ideologically driven vision of socialist society as one homogeneous entity with shared (memories of) past, (understandings of) present, and (aspirations for) future.

With the collapse of socialism in the late 1980s and early 1990s, the former Socialist Bloc countries have been confronting external and internal pluralization processes. International corporations and media have all entered the region, bringing their capital and personnel with them. Legal migration and illegal human trafficking have affected all of the former socialist countries. Exiles have been on the move in large numbers; for example, Russian Germans have been "returning" to Germany, and Crimean Tatars have been resettling in the Crimean Peninsula after decades of internal exile in Russia's east. Private citizens have been reuniting with their families, as in the case of Hungarians in Romania or East and West Germans. All of this has led to changes in the population profiles of the former Socialist Bloc countries.

Internal factors have had an equally strong impact. The end of socialism also marked the end of egalitarianism as welfare systems disintegrated across the region. New economic classes began to form, with many people ending up destitute and a very few becoming fabulously wealthy. Cultural and ethnic minorities began advocating loudly for their rights. With the help of NGOs and other agencies, some groups of people began to differentiate themselves – single mothers, people with disabilities, asylum seekers, the semi-orphaned children of labour migrants, members of non-traditional faith communities, and pensioners whose savings have vanished during the upheaval, to name but a few.

In addition – and more importantly for the national projects of post-socialist states – social differentiation began to occur in the domain of historical imagination, as a result of a wave of revisionism that swept through all socialist societies in the 1980s and 1990s. Alternative memories and experiences of socialism that had once been suppressed were rising back into public discourse. This led to a profound reorganization of national memory projects based on the growing recognition that socialism in any given post-socialist country had "more than one past."

The alternative stories of recent history were never properly studied under socialism; but they never vanished either. People often kept them alive as a form of resistance to injustices that socialism had produced. Given how little coverage there had been of these alternative accounts during socialist times (setting aside governmental surveillance documents), the most effective means today to access and examine the histories, life-worlds, accomplishments, and identities of the affected groups is oral history, with its systematic and methodologically grounded focus on verbal communication, reminiscence, narrative, and personal memory.

Oral history has contributed a great deal to the "discovery" of multiple socialist pasts (and, for that matter, it is helping expose the complexities of the post-socialist present). Its core method – extended in-depth interviews of individuals – lends itself well to the study of alternative experiences of socialism (i.e., experiences that did not make it into official socialist discourses). The experiences of those who survived mass political repression or state mismanagement,[9] who participated in dissident movements,[10] who suffered through mass ethnic deportations or government resettlement schemes,[11] and so on, are all coming to light, and oral historians today find themselves actively pursuing the life stories of these people or their descendants while crafting new understandings of their experiences. Several contributions to this volume reflect this aspect of oral historical research (see Kurkowska-Budzan; Grinchenko).

Oral History as a Political Tool

The process of uncovering alternative pasts is inevitably political, profoundly so. This brings us to the second dimension of oral historical practice in post-socialist scholarship: the ease with which it has become a political tool. Throughout the post-socialist world, oral history has been used to expose the repressed histories of socialism. New national projects then use its findings to indict the previous regime. The earliest example of this comes from Hungary, where in the early 1980s an oral history project was established to gather eyewitness accounts and memories of the 1956 Revolution.[12] Research institutes and programs focusing on the study of totalitarianism have sprung up across the region, with oral history a primary tool in various projects to "indict totalitarianism." The Romanian Centre for the Study of Communism (founded in 1993),[13] the Polish Institute of National Remembrance (1998), the Memory Institute of the Slovak Nation (2002), the Romanian Institute for the Investigation of Communist Crimes (2005), and the Czech Institute for the Study of Totalitarian Regimes (2007) all devote themselves to the study of socialism's wrongdoings. Besides conducting archival research, they have recorded thousands of interviews with various "victim groups." These institutes routinely utilize oral history to unearth tragic memories and narratives of socialism as part of efforts to prove that socialism in Europe was a failure.[14]

These institutes are participating actively in the development of post-socialist discourses of trauma and tragedy, both of which were underlying conditions of life under socialism. Both had their roots in the wars and political conflicts of the twentieth century, which left a profound mark on Europe and especially on Eastern and Central Europe. Alexander von Plato, in this volume and elsewhere, points to the important accomplishments of oral historical work in Germany. In the post-Soviet

Baltic states, the oral historical research conducted by national academies, benefiting from strong diasporic involvement, has paid strong attention to the mass deportation of local populations to the depths of the Gulag system of penal camps after the Soviets annexed Estonia, Latvia, and Lithuania at the end of the Second World War.[15] One of the earliest oral history programs in Ukraine explored the Soviet persecution of the Ukrainian Greek Catholic Church after the USSR absorbed western Ukraine in 1939.[16] Also, the Holodomor, the Ukrainian famine of 1932–3,[17] which had been erased from public memory in socialist times, soon after the Soviet collapse became an important topic of inquiry for post-Soviet Ukrainian oral historians.[18]

In all of the former socialist countries, the Second World War occupies a prominent place in historical research. So does its aftermath. And it is especially significant in the former Soviet republics. Oral historians in Russia, Ukraine, Belarus, and the three Baltic states are pursuing alternative memories and narratives of the war and post-war years. Our Belarusian colleague Irina Romanova once told us, "All of us [in the former USSR] are nowadays rewriting the history of the war, yet out of this commonly shared past we construct very different national narratives of today." Russian political leaders today are seeking to reassert the Russian people's leading role in the defeat of Nazi Germany. Thus, many Russian nationals, including oral historians, continue to use the Soviet term "the Great Patriotic War" in reference to the events that unfolded on the territory of the former Soviet Union. By contrast, Estonians, Latvians, and Lithuanians in their newly free countries speak of the same war as the Soviet occupation. And in Ukraine, many people today have been using the more neutral term "World War II" as a means to reconcile the difference between Ukraine's predominantly anti-Soviet west from its pro-Soviet east and south. Belarusian historians focusing on the Partisan movement continue to speak of the war (at least on their territory) as the Great Patriotic War. Several articles in this volume reflect the importance of the war and its aftermath for the field of oral history research (Grinchenko; Golubev; Kurkowska-Budzan; Rozhdestvenskaya).

The oral history method has also been employed to record still-fresh memories of the collapse of socialism. Interviews with the politicians, protesters, and student leaders who brought about that collapse have been the basis for a new kind of contemporary historical research in Ukraine, Hungary, and the Czech Republic. This has involved extensive interviews with those who have shaped recent history.[19]

Given the different and constantly evolving political processes in post-socialist countries, there is much diversity with regard to how and why oral history is being used and practised in post-socialist Europe. The post-socialist countries that have joined the European Union have all officially renounced socialism as a failed and costly political experiment; the countries that were once Soviet republics present a far more complicated landscape in terms of political discourses and public opinion. In Belarus, Russia, and Ukraine, for example, one still finds sharply divided views of the Soviet past, with some citizens nostalgic for it and others very much the opposite.[20]

In such contexts, the political uses for oral history are not limited to official rewritings of national history. For many local non-elite interest groups and associations, oral history has long been a tool for self-advancement, and those groups have their own agendas, which are often highly political. Early on, academics in the oral history field were far removed from the histories they researched. Later, they began contributing to the production of grassroots epistemologies and understandings of socialist history. By the 1980s, refugees,[21] labour migrants, Indigenous populations, and other oppressed groups outside Eastern Europe were using oral history quite effectively in their struggles for better treatment.[22] Clearly, oral history has begun migrating out of academe and into the political arena. In post-socialist Europe, oral history has seen a similar development; interest groups are using it to advance themselves. This sort of appropriation may lead to the further politicization of oral historical research in local settings, especially where visions of the past conflict with one another. This is the case in Russia, Ukraine, and Belarus, with their competing memories of the Second World War. Alexey Golubev's chapter in this volume, about competing memories of the Second World War, illustrates well how politically far-reaching oral history work can be when communities adopt it for their own purposes.

When considering the political uses of oral history in post-socialist scholarship, remember that oral history has been an important tool in investigations that are *not* preoccupied with socialist and post-socialist politics. Chronological and regional perspectives help us see that oral history has followed a certain progression since it first came to be practised in post-socialist countries. Some observers of post-socialist oral history have noted that this research does not just serve new national political ideologies;[23] in line with ethnographic scholarship, it also examines the life-worlds of smaller communities and groups. But that being said, oral historical research in post-socialist countries about seemingly apolitical topics always eventually addresses the anti-socialist character of many everyday practices that developed in response to the daily impositions of socialism.[24] For example, researchers who studied the lives of the communist elite in socialist times (in Romania, for example)[25] certainly were doing so in response to the demands of post-socialist nationalist agendas. Those who studied local histories[26] inevitably participated in post-socialist revisionist projects.

In Poland and elsewhere in Central Europe, the oral history method has been used since the early days of post-socialism for the study of daily practices, local histories, and other non-political aspects of socialist life. In the former Soviet republics, this sort of research began to take root only in the 2000s, following an initial period that focused exclusively on revisionist projects related to the socialist past. In this volume, Romanova, Makhovskaya and Cherepanova illustrate this later phase in oral historical scholarship.

Oral history has also begun to explore the gendered dimensions of socialism and post-socialism. Indeed, this direction of research is well represented,[27] but in many ways, the oral history of gendered experiences is following the lead of Western scholarship of the 1960s and 1970s. In this volume, Pushkareva profiles the work in this direction.

Oral History and the Epistemological Shift in Humanities and Social Sciences

Intentionally or not, some post-socialist oral historians have been producing new kinds of historical writing that run counter to the scholarly practices developed under socialism. So the third dimension of oral history practice in post-socialist Europe concerns the impact of oral history on the humanities and social sciences of the former socialist countries over the past two decades. These decades have seen an important shift in focus, away from social classes and institutions (such as the history of Communist Party) and towards the lived experiences of people whose lives unfolded within or outside those institutions. In this volume, Rozhdestvenskaya, Curp, Khanenko-Friesen, Romanova, and Makhovskaya all provide examples of this new scholarship.

Oral historians, with their deep interest in "alternative" experiences of the socialist past and their reliance on individual memories, often find themselves contradicting the academy's old understandings of how to construct historical analyses and describe historical phenomena reliably and "objectively." But oral historians do not deal with the history of social classes or institutions, and they are not informed exclusively by archival and other written sources; their histories are of a qualitatively different kind. In the former socialist countries, oral history has evolved into a tool for deconstructing academic discourses long dominated by "class" and "collectivist" stances. Stances which, by the way, were imposed on scholars by the ruling socialist ideology of the time. Most often, and especially in the early years of post-socialism, oral historical research was viewed largely as an extracurricular activity for established historians and social scientists, who conducted these projects outside of approved research plans.

Examining personal memories of historical events inevitably brings the individual into focus. In the West, where oral history established itself as a scholarly discipline in the 1960s, individualism has long been acknowledged as a foundation of Western civilization. The roots of this go back to the birth of Protestantism in the early sixteenth century and the Industrial Revolution in the eighteenth. Also, history itself underwent a profound change in the second half of the twentieth century: it moved away from positivist paradigms of scholarship, with their focus on nations and states, wars and politics, and expanded into social history, the history of daily life, the history of ideas, the history of "humanity" whatever the context. These new research directions redeemed personal experience for historians. And all of this went hand in hand with another important change in the field in the second half of the twentieth century: the return of biography, narratives, and personal accounts as important tools of historical research.

In post-socialist Europe, the epistemological turn towards the personal and individual was delayed, and when it finally came, it was under different circumstances than in the West. The sustained focus on the individual, firmly grounded in interviewing methods, places oral history in the vanguard when it comes to paradigmatic changes in the post-socialist social sciences.

Oral History and the Legitimization of New Agents of History

This brings us to the fourth dimension of oral history practice in post-socialist times: its capacity to produce and legitimize – often retroactively – new agents of national histories. This particular impact of oral historical research is the direct outcome of oral history's participation in post-socialist revisitings of socialism. Throughout the 1990s and in some contexts even later, the practices of history writing established under socialism, rooted among other things in a positivistic belief in history's objectivity and ability to produce "truthful" accounts of how things have been, continued to objectify social groups, classes, and categories.[28] Viewed as both objects of historical research and subjects of historical processes, these groups and social categories were typically constructed as passive, voiceless receptors of history rather than as history's actual agents.

Oral history as a discipline allows its subjects to speak for themselves. It emphasizes the legitimacy and relevance of personal experience for the study of history; it also cuts across traditional representations of people's roles in historical processes. In this way, oral history endows its subjects with social agency and actively publicizes their views in the public domain, allowing them to be heard, better understood, and recognized as equally legitimate members of society. In doing so, oral history formulates new historical narratives and validates alternative lived experiences. Oral history's success in deobjectifying marginal groups and other categories of people – who were generally unknown in socialist societies – is contributing directly to the pluralization of post-socialist societies and successfully challenging positivistic scholarship in former socialist countries. The articles in this volume by Pushkareva, Khanenko-Friesen, and Grinchenko illustrate these processes quite well.

Oral History of Post-Socialist Times: Reclaiming the Personal

It is in light of all these considerations concerning the role of oral history in post-socialist societies that this volume focuses on oral history's intrinsic ability to reclaim and reposition the individual from and within the social processes of history. Over the past two decades of post-socialism, what role has oral history played in reinterpreting twentieth-century history and reclaiming individual agency from the collectivistic past? The chapters in this volume address that question. They address, reflect on, and exemplify this changing paradigm of scholarship from a variety of perspectives. To ensure depth of examination, besides those scholars who presented their research at the symposium in Kharkiv, we have invited a few others to participate. Thus, while the volume is more regionally focused than perhaps was originally intended and deals with oral historical research in contemporary Eastern Europe proper (in Belarus, Poland, Russia, and Ukraine), the authors amount to a broader cross-section. They include prominent authorities on oral history as well as young scholars at the outset of academic careers. They come from both East and West, if one can still evoke that twentieth-century political dichotomy, and they represent various fields of social sciences in which oral historical research has taken root – namely, anthropology, ethnology, history, and sociology. Together, the authors embody the existing and continuously growing blending of "Western" and local expertise in regional studies (in our case, Eastern European studies). Some of our authors live and work locally, others in Canada and the United States while pursuing their research in Eastern Europe. The picture is further blurred by the fact that several of our local authors were trained in the West whereas others were originally from the regions of which they write but are professionally based elsewhere.

In addition to the specific questions raised by the authors in their chapters, several thematic clusters emerge in this collection: the political uses of oral history in post-socialist times (Witeska-Młynarczyk; Golubev); the interplay of the personal and the social in oral history narratives (Rozhdestvenskaya; Pushkareva; Cherepanova); contested memories of the Second World War and its aftermath (Grinchenko; Kurkowska-Budzan); and alternative memories of late socialism (Curp; Makhovskaya and Romanova; Khanenko-Friesen). While we have chosen to organize the chapters along the above lines, each contribution speaks to a variety of other important issues regarding the intricate relations between the social and the individual in history, and in oral historical research itself.

By showcasing recent fine examples of oral historical work in Eastern Europe in times of post-socialism, this collection effectively highlights the unique place of oral history in Eastern European societies in the first two decades of post-socialism. Today, oral history in Eastern Europe continues to evolve and its own history is constantly unfolding. Sociocultural and sociopolitical context in the region also changes, at times rather abruptly. In lieu of these changes, oral historians in the region continue to respond to cultural, ideological and political needs of their societies while producing new oral historical accounts of past and contemporary affairs. As discussed in this introduction, the epistemological legacy of the first twenty years of post-socialist oral history deserves acknowledgment and recognition. This is also the case because oral historians, through their sustained attention to personal evidence in the study of history, were ahead of their academic peers in redeeming the individual as an active agent of history and individual experience as a worthy object of study. We hope this volume properly celebrates and recognizes this legacy.

NOTES

1 The symposium was organized with the financial support of the Prairie Centre for the Study of Ukrainian Heritage at St Thomas More College, University of Saskatchewan, and the Kowalsky Eastern Institute of Ukrainian Studies at the National University of Kharkiv. As conveners of the symposium, we acknowledge further support from the Ukrainian Oral History Association and the V. Karazin National University of Kharkiv, Ukraine.
2 In the spring of 2006, PCUH initiated and co-organized together with the Ukrainian Catholic University the first all-Ukrainian symposium on oral history, titled "Oral History and Sociocultural Change in Times of Transition." This symposium, held at the Ukrainian Catholic University in L'viv, Ukraine, between 19 and 22 May 2006, led to the founding of the Ukrainian Oral History Association later the same year. Selected papers from this symposium were published by Ukraine's leading academic journal in history, *Ukraiina Moderna* (Modern Ukraine) (*Ukraiina Moderna* 11 [2007]).
3 In some ways, our project builds on other scholarly reflections on oral history in post-socialist countries. See Obertreis and Stephan, *Erinnerungen Nach der Wende*; and Kurkowska-Budzan and Zamorski, *Oral History*. The first of these volumes is a collection of essays produced in Germany after a conference held in November 2005 in Wiesneck, near Freiburg. Most of its papers are in German, although some are in English. The second, co-produced in Poland by one of our contributors, does not focus on post-socialist scholarship in particular, although it includes a significant number of articles from the region. The present volume, with its focus on personal evidence in the production of collectively constructed knowledge of the past, offers English speakers a selection of translated works on oral history in Eastern Europe. Most of them were originally written in one of several local languages.
4 Oral historians in Russia and Ukraine, for example, acknowledge that the development of oral historical discourse in their countries is directly linked to the advance of large-scale "Western" projects onto the post-Soviet terrain; these brought into the region not only the research agenda but also research methods and resources. One such initiative was funded by the

German foundation "Remembrance, Responsibility, and Future," which helped launch a multinational study of the experiences of slave labourers who were forced to work for the Nazi regime during the Second World War. This project mobilized many researchers across Eastern Europe (the Czech Republic, Slovakia, Poland, Hungary, Slovenia, Croatia, Serbia, Bosnia, Bulgaria, Lithuania, Belarus, Ukraine, Russia, Moldova) after training them in the principles of oral historical research as practised by German researchers.

5 Vanêk, "The Development of Theory and Method."

6 Harvey, *The Condition of Postmodernity*.

7 Appadurai, "Global Ethnoscapes," 191–216.

8 *Modern reflexivity* is a notion introduced by British sociologist and philosopher Anthony Giddens. In his understanding, the reflexivity of modernity relies to a great degree on the "externalization" of specialized knowledge and its later dispersion through the domain of the everyday. In modern times, specialists' knowledge on any subject matter may become public knowledge. When such specialized knowledge is published and circulated, it becomes endowed with authority. Presented in the form of books and other media, it not only reports on aspects of social life but also routinely organizes and alters them. Giddens, *Modernity and Self-Identity*, 14.

9 Scherbakova, "The Gulag in Memory," 235–46; Noll, *Transformation of Civil Society*; Loskutova, *Pamjat' O Blokade*; Adler, *Victims of Soviet Terror*; Gheith and Jolluck, *Gulag Voices*; Alperin, Zhuravlev, and Ivashchenko, *My Pobedili Smert*; Liulkina, *Voina i Ukradennye Gody*; Borisova, Kozak, and Stuchinskaia, *Lager Smerti Osventsim*; Kozak and Balakireva, *Pravedniki Narodov Mira*; Grinchenko, *Nevyhadane*; Grinchenko, *"Proshu Vas Mene Ne Zabuvaty"*; Nahaiko, *Dzherela Pamiati*, vols. 1 and 2.

10 Long, *Making History*; Vanêk and Urbasek, *Vítězové? Poražení?*; Budeancă, *Prison Experiences*.

11 Uehling, *Beyond Memory*; Geisler, "From the Voice of the Deported."

12 In the early 1980s, Hungarian researchers András B. Hegedűs and Gyula Kozák launched "round table" discussions among participants in the 1956 Hungarian Revolution. Their reminiscences became a source of alternative, and still underground, memory of the 1956 events. Audio recordings of those meetings as well as more than one thousand pages of transcription were initially held in a private apartment. Eventually, with funds provided by the Soros Foundation, these oral historical documents became the basis of research into the wrongdoings of socialist regimes; Kanyo, "Zur Geschichte," 120. See also Kőrösi and Molnár, *"Carrying a Secret in My Heart."*

13 The Centre for Studies into Communism, founded in 1993, since its early days has been conducting oral history research on victims of communism and anti-communist resistance. Visit http://www.memorialsighet.ro/index.php.

14 Dobrochna, "Historia Mówiona w Krajach Postkomunistycznych."

15 Geisler, "From the Voice of the Deported."

16 The project, launched in 1992 by the Institute of Church History of Ukrainian Catholic University, continues to systematically gather and critically analyse oral testimonies about persecution and the religious life of Ukrainian Greek Catholics in the underground. See Hurkina, "Dvi Doli," 265–82; Gudziak and Susak, "Becoming a Priest in the Underground," 42–8.

17 From 1932 to 1933, the government engineered a mass famine in then Soviet Ukraine that took between 3 and 7 million lives – as much as 20 per cent of Ukraine's population at the time (editors' note).

18 Mytsyk, *Ukraiinskyi Kholokost 1932–1933*; Polischuk, "*Stolytsia Vidchaiu*"; Borysenko, *A Candle in Remembrance*; Lyman and Konstantinova, *Usna Istoriia Holodomoru 1932–1933*. See also a three-volume publication prepared in 1990 for the US Commission on Ukraine's Famine: Mace and Heretz, *Oral History Project*.

19 "An Oral History of Ukrainian Independence," a project on Ukrainian oral history, is being coordinated by Margarita Hewko (director, Ukraine) and Sara Sievers (director, US, and graduate student fellow of HURI). See "An Oral History of Ukrainian Independence," *Ukrainian Weekly*. See also Leviatin, "Listening to the New World"; Lass, "From Memory to History"; Kowal, "Dlaczego Doszło do Okrągłego Stołu?" See also Kenney, *A Carnival of Revolution*, a book that uses oral history to evaluate grand political changes and that considers all revolutions in the same monograph.

20 Ukraine's case is illustrative here. Under President Yushchenko (2005–2010), there was much political will to support research into the wrongdoings of socialism, in particular the Holodomor. This research has at times been rather rushed and not always methodologically sound according to our Ukrainian colleagues involved in various Holodomor projects. Under President Yanukovich (2010–2014), whose political agenda promoted a pro-Soviet view of Ukrainian history, the government stopped backing active research on the Holodomor and other tragic aspects of Ukrainian history under Soviet rule.

21 Westernman, "Central American Refugee Testimonies."

22 See Perks and Thomson, "Advocacy and Empowerment."

23 Dobrochna, "Historia Mówiona."

24 Dobrochna, "Historia Mówiona." An example of such research is Brzostek and Wawrzyniak, "Wiklina." See also Popa, "Understanding the Urban Past"; Ther, Królik, and Henke, *Polski Wrocław jako Metropolia Europejska.*
25 See *The Intellectuals and the Communist Regime.*
26 For example, the researchers at "Grodzka Gate – NN Theatre" Centre, a municipal cultural institution founded in 1998 by the City of Lublin in Poland. The oral historians associated with this centre follow its mandate to foster awareness of Lublin's rich multicultural history and develop a deeper sense of local identity. Visit http://www.annalindhfoundation.org/members/grodzka-gate-nn-theatre-centre-osrodek-brama-grodzka-teatr-nn.
27 Malysheva and Bertaux, "The Socialist Experiences"; Sheridan, "Women and Life History Work"; Pető, *To Look at Life*; Pető, *Hungarian Women in Politics 1945–1951*; Szpak, "Robotnice czy Chłopki"; Tóth, "The Cultural Identity."
28 Vanêk, in "The Development of Theory and Method," makes a similar claim.

PART ONE

From Subjects to Agents of History: Political Implications of Oral Historical Research

When we turned to the task of formulating the main directions and topics of this volume, we remembered and were guided by the gap that continues to display itself between traditional approaches to the study of socio-cultural processes within the framework of historical research and the methods of the oral historical approach. As we discussed in the introduction, the social sciences and humanities of post-socialist countries have only recently turned their attention to the roles that individual experience and personal agency have been playing in the history of their respective societies. This is not surprising, for under socialism, the academic domain was dominated by the state-informed scholarly paradigms of knowledge production and by the ideologies of the previous socialist regimes in these countries. The transition from studying populations, classes, and groups to studying history through the prism of diverse individual agents inevitably leads one to recognize that the deobjectification of human history has political implications and outcomes in regions that have been undergoing decades of sweeping political and cultural change. This has certainly been the case with oral history elsewhere, as the results of oral historical research find their way into public discourses. At the same time, as part of this process, oral historians have to develop an awareness of oral history's impact on and involvement in the ongoing politicization of public life in post-socialist countries. Is this the case with oral historians of post-socialist times? Some thirty-five years ago, Paul Thompson stated in his famous book *The Voice of the Past* that "the merit of oral history is not that it entails this or that political stance, but that it leads historians to an awareness that their activity is inevitably pursued within a social context and with political implications."[1] While not all Eastern European oral historians engage themselves in such conversations about their own role in their research, we believe that the contributors in this section illustrate well how some oral historians do reflect on the impact that oral history has on their societies (von Plato) or how their work furthers social and political differentiation in their societies (Witeska-Młynarczyk; Golubev).

Thompson's famous book invites historians to ask themselves what they are actually doing, and why; it also addresses the question of *whose* voice of the past is being projected in oral historical writings. This brings us to a second point: over the past two decades in post-socialist societies, we have been observing the rapid formation of distinct memory groups as part of the ongoing pluralization of their societies; their stories and narratives are shaping new competitive niches in the domain of public commemorative practices. This competition inevitably becomes political, for the socialist past is being actively re-evaluated by various memory groups that do not share the same vision of it. These new memory groups continue to gain strength and influence in their respective societies – albeit in various ways, as the contributors in this section illustrate. Having established themselves in some cases as public organizations of one kind or another, these memory groups, especially those that experienced socialism negatively, are actively competing for the right to rewrite national history and create new historiography. This is leading to new dialogues between the society, its memory groups, and the political establishment.

Today, there are many oral historical publications in the region that illustrate well the focus of this section; we discussed them in the introduction to this volume. In preparing this volume, with its focus on the return of the individual and personal to the humanities and social sciences of post-socialist societies, which we contend is to be achieved through oral historical work, we wanted to highlight that this process has political implications. We did not ask our contributors to report on how their research was informing or affecting local or national politics. Rather, we wanted to bring to the attention of Western readers some fine examples of how oral historical work is contributing to the ongoing pluralization of post-socialist societies by engaging in dialogue with the mainstream culture, the political establishment, and competing memory groups.

The discussion opens with the chapter by Alexander von Plato, a founder of the Institute of History and Biography at Fern University in Hagen, Germany, and former Vice-President of the International Oral History Association. Von Plato's contribution focuses on biographical research as a precursor to oral history in Germany. It provides us with a good overview of how oral historical discourse emerged in post–Second World War Germany. His reflections allow us to compare the questions addressed in the oral historical practice in the region today with those questions and concerns faced by German historians after the war. His discussion of different remembrance cultures in Germany helps us see how complicated the processes of collective memory formation and maintenance have been and that they can never be described by a single noun, "memory." "Memories" would serve the current European political climate better. Von Plato's assertion that there is no single shared collective memory of the past in any given European society nicely sets up the discussion in the following chapters.

The political implications of oral history in post-socialist societies inevitably raise another important issue: the impact of oral historical work in transitional times. Oral historians, while researching and documenting the experiences of once repressed populations in former socialist states, are contributing directly to new kinds of historical awareness of victimhood as well as to new kinds of discourses on traumatic memory. We wanted to include in this collection samples of work that highlights the complex dialogue between new post-socialist dominant national ideological representations of the socialist past and understandings by other memory groups who are lobbying for victim status (as victims of the socialist past, in the article by Witeska-Młynarczyk, or of the occupying enemy state, in the article by Golubev).

Witeska-Młynarczyk's chapter describes how the institutional politics of post-communist Poland continuously inform already established categories of victims. When the communist regime became publicly classified as a "second occupation," this new taxonomy generated the conditions for the emergence of a new category of people repressed by the communist regime. It was now possible for them to perform their identity in the public realm and to construct a life story nested in a new framework, that of a nation-state liberated from the violent Soviet occupation. Another important issue raised by this author (and discussed by others in this volume) is the inevitable interplay between the personal and the collective in individual accounts. Witeska-Młynarczyk talks about how biographical accounts gain coherence and a collective dimension through the use of publicly available storylines in the performance of individual accounts.

Another impact of oral historical work on political discourses in the post-socialist states of Eastern Europe relates the conflicts that can emerge among memory groups as they "compete for canonization." Alistair Thomson, in *Anzac Memories,* comes to mind in this context.[2] Thomson's book examines competing visions and narratives of the past that aim to represent the experiences and identities of the combatants who took part in the First World War as members of the Anzac forces (Australian and New Zealand Army Corps). The dominant memories of that corps as adapted by the mainstream culture in Australia for a long time excluded many other testimonies of Anzac experiences that did not fit the approved narrative. This led Thomson to label the dominant memory as a national legend. Thomson points out that the legend had little grounding in reality but that it became so dominant that many personal narratives and memoirs of Anzac veterans began to be moulded into the existing model so that the personal voices of the narrators could find public recognition as well.

A similar paradox, this one from Russia's north, is discussed here by Alexey Golubev, who examines competition between memories in the context of post-Soviet political, ideological, and social transformations. Golubev's article offers an intriguing ethnographic account of how, in Karelia, in the context of twentieth-century revisionism, oral history has been used by one grassroots group, the association of the young prisoners of Finnish concentration camps, to promote their own interpretation of the Finnish occupation of Karelia during the Second World War. Their interpretation glosses over the complexities of that period of Karelian history. Because their vision is congruent with the dominant political discourse of the Great Patriotic War, the group has enjoyed much support from the region's political establishment. This memory group works hard to publicize their shared experience. Individual voices and experiences that do not fit their narrative are being excluded from the public domain. The author cautions us that in times of social transformation and ongoing pluralization, various groups compete for "ownership" of the past. Personal voices and stories are edited and scrutinized to serve group political agendas.

NOTES

1 Thompson, *The Voice of the Past*, vi.
2 Thomson, *Anzac Memories.*

1 Political Changes and Personal Orientations: Germany and the European Remembrance Cultures

ALEXANDER VON PLATO

In this chapter, I focus on the complex nature of various remembrance cultures that emerged in Germany in the second part of the twentieth century. To contextualize my discussion, I first offer some observations on the dissynchrony of changes in political systems that German society has been subject to throughout the twentieth century and changes in personal orientations in the same historical period. Then I examine the role that biographical research and oral history concerning the Second World War, National Socialist persecution, and post-war times played in the formation of particular cultures of remembrance in Germany. Biographical research and oral history work that explored these dimensions of German history in the twentieth century focused especially on how political disruptions affect personal attitudes and orientations, biographies, and life-story narratives of various elites and other groups within German society. The discussion here centres on two periods of political transformation that German society underwent after 1945: the post-war years after the end of Nazi rule; and the post-1989 years after the fall of the Berlin wall, which ended Communist rule in Europe. In a certain sense, the German case serves as an example of how countries that undergo changes in their political systems develop cultures of remembrance. Third, I compare different national remembrance cultures in Europe East and West as they relate to the Second World War, forced labour, and the Holocaust. The discussion here draws from two international life-story projects: the first concerns the Nazis' use of forced labour during the war and was conducted in twenty-seven countries; second is the International Mauthausen Documentation project, pursued in over twenty countries. I also refer to other research conducted in both East and West Germany.

The Dissynchrony of Personal and Political Changes

Looking back on the twentieth century, one can say that over just two generations, not just in Germany but in many other societies, people lived through more than five changes in political systems. How did "the people" – or more specifically, the different generations, sexes, classes, and groups – deal with these political transformations? How did they judge the new political system and its new orientations, ideological and otherwise? How did individuals and groups work through their own orientations that had been formed under the previous political regimes?

In general, one can say that changes in personal predispositions and orientations follow changes in political orientations. So stated the philosopher Ernst Bloch in his "dissynchrony" thesis. European societies have been experiencing frequent political transformations since the mid-twentieth century, and this has had a strong impact on the personal lives of Europeans. Bloch showed that this "dissynchrony" generated a number of problems, the main one being that the past was not "done" in a personal sense – it was not yet finished. There were, for example, plans that could not be carried out; there were losses of competence and of the security that the old systems had provided. This led to anger and frustration and to an irrational defence of the past against the present.[1]

When we look at both Germanys of the post-war era, the Federal Republic in the West and the Democratic Republic in the East, we see that Bloch has provided us with a strong lens through which to examine the individual consciousness and orientations that develop in societies after a political rupture. In Germany, most Germans did not throw away the old systems (of personal predispositions and orientations), not after 1945, and not after 1989. The old systems continued to be attractive to many, and many members of society did not accept the new systems. Perhaps this explains why only a few Nazi war criminals were ever prosecuted and why most of the victims of National Socialism have not been recognized as such.

In post-war West Germany, it took about fifteen years for the perpetrators of war crimes to be sentenced for their role in the Holocaust. It took more than forty years for the Roma to be recognized as victims of the Nazi regime, and it took more than fifty years for the forced labourers who were shipped to Germany from the occupied territories to receive compensation from the German government. One or two generations had to come of age for German society to see the criminal character of the Nazi dictatorship.

In both post-war Germanys, society's recognition of various victim groups changed over time. The trajectories of acceptance crossed over, with some groups gaining status and some losing it. This process was determined more by the Cold War than by constitutionality or pity.

After the war, the Holocaust survivors were subjected to humiliating experiences, which for some of them amounted to a second trauma. Yet the victims of Stalinism were recognized in West Germany during the Cold War for having suffered in the Soviet Gulag system. Beginning in the 1970s, with the politics of détente, it was the other way round. As a result of these changes in the trajectories of acceptance, different victims' groups were offered public opportunities to express their memories at very different points in time.

These patterns of judgment and acceptance shed light on the changing German societies; having produced different "victim hierarchies" in East and West, they also have influenced the ways in which the victims have worked through their experiences. For example, for both groups of former inmates, those of the Nazi camps and those of the Soviet special camps in East Germany after the war,[2] the trajectories of public recognition have influenced the ways in which they remember and narrate their life stories. Both groups were traumatized, but their acceptance (or rejection) by their respective societies and their immediate social environments were crucial for their coming to terms with the past that had so brutalized them. Their life stories point to a prominent difference between these two groups: in contrast to the inmates of the Soviet special camps in Germany, the Holocaust survivors, besides being persecuted, had lost their families. Given the importance of family, this means they had limited help in working through their trauma. In West Germany, it must have been a very bitter experience for them to watch their former perpetrators being accepted by society, receiving restitution money, and being portrayed as victims of communism, while they themselves were struggling to receive even a modicum of financial restitution. In West Germany, this all changed at the end of the 1960s and the beginning of the 1970s. Meanwhile, however, in the German Democratic Republic, the former inmates of the Soviet camps had to remain silent.

As a result of these different trajectories of recognition, various groups of victims have found themselves in a kind of competition for recognition and acceptance. That competition reached new heights after 1989, when the Berlin wall finally fell, clearing the way for the reunification of Germany. This competition tells us that it is very important for people to "digest" the past, which can destroy them if they do not process it properly. That is a challenge, however, for in Germany, the experiences of these various competing victim groups originated in and have been unfolding in three different political systems: two dictatorships and a democracy.

Germany thus provides compelling evidence that there is no such thing as a single culture of commemoration pertaining to the post-war period that is accepted by the majority. Divergent, hotly disputed, and even irreconcilable cultures of commemoration have driven a wedge between East and West as well as between different generations and political camps. These divisions persist, albeit in diluted form, and have manifested themselves most recently in debates over the comparability of the crimes perpetrated by the Nazis before and during the war and those perpetrated by East Germany's Socialist Unity Party (the GDR's ruling party) between 1949 and 1989.

The German example shows that victims encounter different possibilities for influencing historiography and remembrance cultures; it depends on the political system, the opportunities that governments or societies provide them, and the patterns the specific culture offers.

The Development of Biographical Research and Oral History in Germany

How did historians deal with these challenges? When and how did they turn their attention to people's "consciousness" and the dissynchrony of political and personal changes? In the first decade after 1945, most German historians focused on the Third Reich's political and institutional systems; the "consciousness" of the people was for journalists, not historians. A decade later, scholars turned to the study of the fascist ideology and the fascist elites, and after that to the resistance movement and the victims of fascism.

It was more than thirty years before large-scale in-depth research projects were launched to examine the consciousness of the people. Lutz Niethammer, a renowned historian of post-war Germany, made the following point when introducing one of these projects: "We asked about the continuity and the discontinuity of political parties, institutions, and administrations after 1945. However, we forgot to ask about the main reason for [such] continuity – the people."[3]

These qualitative changes in historic research in West Germany led to the first large-scale oral history projects in West Germany presented in the books *Bavaria under National Socialism* (1977) and *Life Histories and Social Culture in the Ruhr: 1930–1960* (1983–1986).[4] In East Germany, meanwhile, oral history continued to be suppressed and was not allowed at the universities.

Quantitative Biographical Research

By the 1960s and 1970s, biographical research about the German elites was already being conducted.[5] This largely entailed statistical analyses of certain social strata, which turned out to be an important percursor for oral historical scholarship in Germany. Statistical biographical research concerned above all questions about the continuity and discontinuity of different "functional elites" in German society, before and after 1945. As these elites were very differently affected by the political changes, this was an important direction for historical research to take. When we consider the changes brought about by the collapse of the Berlin Wall in 1989, we can make an interesting comparison between the levels of continuity and discontinuity within the German elite. Let us consider what happened to three German elites: teachers, entrepreneurs, and journalists.

With the end of the war in 1945, in the Soviet Occupation Zone, 88 per cent of teachers were fired and replaced.[6] By contrast, in the 1990s after East Germany's collapse, only 18 to 25 per cent of teachers lost their positions and were replaced, and only 1 or 2 per cent had to vacate their positions because of their cooperation with or membership in the GDR's security police.[7]

Let us turn to the entrepreneurs. After 1945, in West Germany, only 8 to 15 per cent of the heads and senior managers of industrial organizations were "exchanged," whereas in East Germany, the proportion was significantly higher – about 60 per cent.[8] However, in the 1950s, between 30 and 40 per cent of company managers in East Germany, who had been members of the Nazi Party (NSDAP), regained their leadership positions, for the socialist state badly needed their expertise to rebuild the economy.[9] After 1990, these managers encountered difficulties in their employment, but this was less for political reasons than for economic ones.

Regarding the journalist profession, remember that after 1945, in all occupation zones, the Allies shut down all newspapers, radio stations, and publishing firms and established new ones. Nearly all the new editors-in-chief and most other editors were returnees or had been opponents of the Nazis. More precise are the results of research about broadcasting companies. Although these were founded by the Allies as well, about 63 per cent of the more junior journalists had been in the same or similar positions during National Socialist times. It is plausible that the same situation developed with publishing houses and newspapers. At the same time, most sports journalists were able to keep their positions.[10]

We can extend this analysis to other professions across both Germanys. For example, the strongest employment continuity was among the generals of the Federal Army, founded in the 1950s. About 90 per cent of the high-ranking officers had been active during the war. In the GDR, the Socialist Unity Party tried to find former officers for the new People's Army, but with less success. The lowest levels of continuity were among trade unionists and shop stewards. Of the five thousand shop stewards in 1945 and 1946 who had been *Vertrauensmänner* of the *Deutsche Arbeitsfront* during the Third Reich, I found only one. And he had had to withdraw his candidacy.[11]

Oral History: Researching People's Mentality

Quantitative biographical research can shed new light on historical and social processes. Statistics about the continuity and discontinuity of membership in various elite groups tell us a lot about the development of the new political system, the fate of the old "functional elites," and changes in leadership after a political rupture. However, they do not show whether people changed their minds, their orientations, and their attitudes. It is in this context that oral history offers useful findings and even plausible theses. Let us turn again to the same elites considered above.

Oral history studies found that senior managers and entrepreneurs who had been members of the Nazi Party had to defend themselves against war crimes accusations after 1945.[12] Some of them were interned in Allied camps. These studies also found that these former Nazis had changed their orientations and attitudes regarding trade unions and the role of the state. Now they tried to get along with the trade unions – just the opposite of those German nationalists and conservatives who tried to bar shop stewards and union reps from their companies before *and* after 1945. Indeed, it was former Nazis who in 1953 developed "workers' participation" with the trade unions.[13]

After 1990, most of the teachers in the former GDR were enthusiastic about the Federal Republic's school system. But within a few years they had grown disenchanted with the Western system and remembered the Eastern one with more fondness. Most of our interviewees were critical of the West German model, which had three types of schools.[14] Those who were not members of the Socialist Unity Party[15] now stand with the former diehard socialists. This is quite easily explained by their experiences in the unified Germany, where there is very high "elite reproduction" – that is, upper-class parents are better able to send their children to universities (much more than in the United States or the Scandinavian countries, for instance) while lower-class children remain in the lower schools.

The journalists who were active in their professions before and after the end of the war made clear in their life stories that at least twice, in 1945 and around 1949, they had had to adapt themselves to political changes and to look for new jobs and orientations. The end of the war affected the former Nazis, and the beginning of Cold War in 1949 affected the communists and leftists. Our core group of interviewees tried to find their way to the "middle," whatever that meant, having learned the hard way that adhering to political extremes was dangerous. Many of our interviewees were impressed by the democratic attitudes and the professionalism of the British and American press officers. Some of them attended re-education seminars or even journalism schools in Great Britain.

Overall, oral history interviews are excellent tools for accessing and understanding how people's mentalities, attitudes, and political orientations evolve in a changing society.

Remembrance Cultures in Europe East and West after the Second World War

Recently, researchers in historiography and especially in oral history have raised two very important questions concerning the presence of remembrance cultures: How far have those cultures developed in Central and Eastern Europe since the war? And what has their impact been on individual ways of working through personal war experiences and the narrations about them? Allow me next to discuss recent international research projects, conducted between 2002 and 2006, concerning both forced labour and National Socialist persecution.

Ways of Narrating

Narratives of German occupation, Nazi persecution, and slave and forced labour differ from one another in terms of the extent of persecution and the nature or type of work these individuals were forced to do. They are also marked by the cultures from which these individuals came or to which they returned. Our interviews uncovered marked differences among individuals with regard to narrative style, but there also seemed to be narrative or literary patterns specific to the cultures from which the speakers came – for example, in the balance between the visual and the verbal, the specific and the general, example and precept, delight in the vivid plasticity of the narrative and commitment to a didactic intent. In the context of a summary like this, we can only point out that the biographical narratives we have collected are also a treasure trove for literary studies, linguistics, autobiography research, and ethnology – not just for the historical sciences.

Among our interview partners there were real storytellers who sometimes made it difficult for the researchers to determine whether they were more interested in the art of storytelling than in conveying accurate information.

The cultures of origin of our interviewees possessed their own literary forms. These included epic tales of heroes and victims as well as myths of national defence, such as stories from the Jewish Diaspora or (completely different) from Russia's Patriotic War against Napoleon. These furnished templates for narratives from the time of Nazi persecution and forced labour. Beyond this, slave and forced labourers who returned home, or who had been forced to emigrate and then been liberated, were offered very different ways of coming to terms with their experiences by the societies and governments of their home countries. These ranged from fundamental support, special access to material assistance and health care, and special institutions of solidarity, which also collected testimony; through indifference amidst the general post-war suffering; to rejection arising from the general suspicion that all forced labourers had been collaborators or traitors.

Compassionate recognition or brusque rejection elicited explicit and implicit reactions from those concerned. Thus, for example, in the context of interviews with former Soviet prisoners of war in Germany, a pattern came to my attention: interviewees would speak of somehow being unable to fight – of being half buried or unconscious – at the moment of being taken prisoner, so that they were unable to use their pistol to commit suicide. Some explained elsewhere during the interview that there was a standing order, at least for officers, to save one bullet for oneself, to die rather than be taken prisoner.

As is well known, victims' groups developed during the post-war period, where people talked about their own experiences, learned the fate of others, and compared their own stories to those of others. This certainly influenced their own narratives, and some even took over other people's stories (which, by the way, does need not mean they were reporting something "untrue"). Moreover, there was and still is competition among the various victims of the Nazi dictatorship,[16] and especially between the victims of Nazism and the victims of the Soviet dictatorship. This competition among victims has taken very different forms in different countries, depending on the political system but especially on the degree of rejection or acceptance experienced by forced labourers in society and politics. It also reflects the country's status as enemy or ally of Nazi Germany.

For Germany, one can say that "Auschwitz" became the touchstone, the symbol of the most terrible degree of persecution, and this had the effect that everyone compared themselves to Jews who had survived the extermination camps. Those who had not experienced those camps sometimes felt like "second-class victims." Examples include deserters who had been condemned by *Wehrmacht* tribunals, or those who had been imprisoned in Soviet special camps after the war without having been Nazis. The touchstone of Auschwitz had the effect that stories about one's own persecution were and often still are implicitly and sometimes even explicitly compared to the threat of being gassed.

The State of Israel and the memorial centres and historical institutes there have provided space for the survivors of the Holocaust, who often had to do slave labour, to give testimony on their persecution. They have done this among other things for the purpose of researching the Holocaust, to keep the memory of the murdered alive, and to raise a monument to them. Moreover, many survivors had remained silent about their sufferings and humiliations and about the loss of relatives. Others encouraged them by example to tell their stories. For more than thirty years, Yad Vashem in Jerusalem has been collecting stories. In the United States, a great number of interviews have been conducted over the past three decades. Examples include those held by the Fortunoff

Archives at Yale University, by the Holocaust Memorial Museum in Washington, and by Steven Spielberg's Shoah Foundation in Los Angeles. All of this has surely increased the victims' self-confidence and thus also their readiness to speak about their own fate. In Germany, at every memorial and every history workshop, interviews with Holocaust survivors have been conducted; many historical institutes (including ours at the Fernuniversität Hagen) conducted them as well; and private individuals like the filmmaker Loretta Walz have created significant video archives, in this case about former female inmates of the Ravensbrück concentration camp.[17]

A Rag Rug of Remembrance Cultures on the Second World War

In the cultural memories of the nations of Eastern and Western Europe and of Israel, forced labourers played a very different role in the post-war period. Depending on the possibilities they were offered to express themselves, on the degree of acceptance or rejection they experienced, and on how their experiences were mixed up with those of others or were dominated by them, there was a shift in emphasis with respect to the memories of contemporary witnesses and their retrospective judgment of forced labour under Nazism.[18]

In the countries of the former Soviet Union,[19] for decades the state-determined "policy on the past"[20] was predominant. That policy emphasized the heroism of the Red Army, the Communist Partisans, and the political leaders of the Communist Party of the Soviet Union and their allies during the Great Patriotic War. This attitude was understandable after victory over an aggressor widely perceived to be stronger, but the effect was that less heroic elements of the war went by the board – for example, Stalin's dictatorial rule, the terrible losses suffered by Red Army, and the crimes its soldiers committed during their advance into other countries, most of all in Eastern Europe. Furthermore, the extermination of European Jews came to be subsumed under this account of heroism, and the sufferings of Soviet prisoners of war[21] were as neglected as those of forced labourers, when the latter were not actually treated as traitors.

Forced labourers were refused any sort of recognition by Stalin's regime. After returning, almost all of them went through so-called filtration camps, where they were investigated for possible collaboration with the enemy. Some were released soon after; others were assigned to forced labour again and came home later; still others were inducted into the Red Army, sometimes for years, or were sent to detention camps. The director of the State Archive of the Russian Federation in Moscow, Sergey Mironenko, estimates that no more than 10 per cent of forced labourers had to stay longer than three months at filtration, labour, or detention camps; the period was probably longer for those who were inducted into the Red Army or who were sent to forced labour far from home.[22] Most of these returnees were profoundly hurt by the insinuation that they were collaborators or traitors and were deeply disappointed and fearful.

Those countries in Eastern Europe that did not persecute forced labourers (or at least did not suspect them of collaborating) marginalized them through remembrance cultures that raised Communist fighters and Partisans to the status of heroes. Thus, in contrast to the Soviet Union, returning Polish prisoners of war and forced labourers were not treated as possible traitors and collaborators.[23] Much the same in Czechoslovakia (and thus also in the former Slovakian Republic,[24] the former ally of the German Reich, which had been dissolved again in 1944). In Yugoslavia, some forced labourers were even equated with the Partisans in several respects; however, this was different in Slovenia during the early post-war period: during the Dachau trials there, the liberated forced labourers were sentenced as collaborators or war criminals.[25] But except for that, in Yugoslavia a certain pride developed after the victory over Germany, so that former forced labourers were viewed as victims of the Nazis. In the Soviet Union, by contrast, the sense of pride that was promoted in the Soviet society with respect to the soldiers who had fought against Nazi Germany excluded prisoners of war and forced labourers, who were viewed as collaborators.

After the war, countries that had fought the Soviet Union on the Axis side – Bulgaria, Slovakia, Croatia, some others – entered the Soviet orbit.[26] It is astonishing that for decades in these countries, the image of the heroic Soviet Army and Communist Party would determine official history. The success of this Communist "master narrative" in Croatia and Bulgaria and in occupied and divided Slovakia cannot be explained solely by the fact that in those countries the parties that took power after 1945 were the allies of the Soviet Union. Another factor was that after a short but harsh period of punishment, there took place a largely covert amnesty of former enemies. Thus, former enemies in these states were permitted to settle into their post-war lives provided that they did not openly promote another view of history. As a consequence, the predominant image of history as belonging to heroic soldiers and Communist Partisans made internal peace possible in these former enemy states – at least for one or two generations.

And it was not just in Eastern Europe that the heroism of those who had fought against fascism dominated Second World War history in the early post-war years. In most Western European countries, similar attitudes predominated. In France, for example, for decades, images of Resistance fighters and of de Gaulle's government in exile dominated French remembrance culture. Yet most of the French had been compelled to live under German occupation or in Marshal Pétain's Vichy France and had struggled to adapt, and only a tiny number of them had been Resistance fighters. Acknowledgment of this was hardly a path to rebuilding a national identity;[27] the same, obviously, with acknowledging complicity in the extermination of French Jews. Intentionally or not, the master narrative of the Resistance and of de Gaulle's government in exile benefited those who had collaborated with the German occupiers, had committed crimes against humanity, or had adapted. Only later was there a debate about collaboration in France. To this day, distinctions are drawn between those who were transported to Germany from occupied France and those who were taken to Germany from Vichy France while carrying French passports. The former are treated as victims of the Nazis or as members of the Resistance; the latter are not.

Similar contradictions are found in other countries of Western Europe. Some Danes and Norwegians cooperated with the Nazis, as did some Belgians. Especially remarkable is Italy, which was an ally of the German Reich until it signed a separate truce on 8 September 1943, but which after the war emphasized Italians' resistance and the overthrow of Mussolini's fascist government (although resistance had been rather weak and King Vittorio Emanuele III and the new government initially had to flee from the Germans). Truly heroic were those multitudes of Italian soldiers who refused to side with the *Wehrmacht* when offered the chance and instead chose forced labour in Germany and the occupied zones. Their history has been marginalized.[28]

Only recently has Spain begun addressing the history of victims of the Franco regime during and after the civil war, decades after Franco's death and the return of democracy under a constitutional monarchy. Since the Remembrance Act was passed by the Spanish Parliament on 12 December 2006, this has begun to change.[29]

Austria is mostly forgotten in this context, although one in ten forced labourers were sent there[30] – at least one million.[31] The Mauthausen complex, with its notorious quarry, was one of the harshest slave labour camps in the German Reich. Also, many institutions of persecution were headed by Austrian members of the SS, including the Nazi euthanasia program known as Action T4.[32] For decades, Austria hid behind the story that it had been the first victim of Nazi expansion. This view was challenged only in 1986, when it came to light that Kurt Waldheim, the UN Secretary General from 1976 to 1981, and President of Austria from 1986 to 1992, may well have at least known about war crimes.

In Germany itself, for decades slave and forced labourers were not recognized. They fought for compensation even longer, just like the "politicals" and the sentenced deserters, who also had to do forced labour. It was almost one generation before changes began to be made in this respect and two generations before the government began addressing issues of recognition and compensation.[33]

In contrast to all of this, there was a high degree of recognition in Israel and the United States and – to some degree – in other immigration countries like Australia or Canada, which had their own remembrance policies.

Today, when one examines memories of the war, the Holocaust, and the resistance movements, and memories of prisoners of war and forced labourers, Europe begins to resemble a multi-coloured quilt: the different political systems and post-war societies have developed different remembrance cultures in different regions, and these patterns have only intensified since the end of the Cold War. Also, governments have used the history and memory of the war for their own unique "policies on the past." Remembrance cultures in Western Europe are much more split than is suggested by such policies. Their master narratives have been highly successful, largely because they have included the less heroic aspects of the war (including collaboration and participation in war crimes) and thus made at least superficial reconciliation possible. But underneath this, other, more informal memories continue to exist and now conflict with the official ones – especially in Eastern Europe, but not only there. And it is unclear which "alliances of remembrance" are being made in politically united Europe by new generations at the beginning of the twenty-first century.

Internationalization of the Holocaust – Nationalization of Forced Labour?

As a result of the project on slave and forced labour (discussed above), it became obvious to the researchers that in the post-war period, two processes could be observed: an astonishing internationalization of depictions of the Holocaust; and a remarkable "nationalization" of the experience of war and forced labour. The models of Yad Vashem and the Holocaust Memorial Museum in Washington are being applied at museums and exhibitions in Eastern Europe. Also in this context, some national particularities are evident.[34] The representations of forced labourers are especially unique. Constructed in very specific ways in public presentations at the national level, the forced labourers are seen as having been persecuted by the Nazis, not unlike the Communist resistance fighters. In some museums in the Baltics and in Hungary, the Stalinist dictatorship is sometimes condemned just as strongly as the Nazi one, if not *more* strongly.[35] With respect to the Holocaust, this sometimes results – for example, at the Budapest museum "House of Terror" – in the sentencing of Nazi collaborators in the post-war years being treated as a Stalinist judicial crime.

Setting aside the "big politics" in East and West after 1945, those who had been condemned to slave or forced labour during the war felt a profound need to be acknowledged as victims. It mattered greatly to them that they be recognized as victims of the Nazis instead of being left to cope with their past on their own. Being recognized as a victim alleviates one's own suffering as well as one's mourning for fellow sufferers. Recognition offers the possibility that one's suffering was not in vain and that societies will perhaps learn from the past. Recognition also extends significance to their personal biographies if historians, politicians, memorial centres, and teachers show interest.

Instead of Conclusions: Turning to Eastern and Central Europe

There has been rising interest in biographical research and oral history methods in Eastern Europe over the past ten years. This book is a strong example of this development, especially with regard to the countries of the former Soviet Union. However, there are some astonishing peculiarities related to my main arguments here.

First, it puzzles me that I have been unable to find any quantitative biographical research on national and professional elites in the Eastern European countries that have undergone major social transformations over the past two decades. I wonder why. Is it because there have been no changes among the elites? Or is it because those elites do not want to support such research or even discuss the subject because it might endanger them or their country's supposed national identity? Or are there other reasons?

Second, in Central and Eastern European countries, many oral history research projects have been launched using qualitative methods. This book provides a number of examples, as does the bilingual volume *Remembering after the Fall of Communism – Erinnerungennach der Wende*.[36] Even so, it is strange that the vast majority of these projects deal with the Second World War or the German occupation. This may be understandable, given that the war was the core experience of the older generations and brought about radical changes in their lives. In addition, the "Great Patriotic War" has been deeply incorporated into the Soviet identity. Nevertheless, there are "missing themes" that could also be of interest: the relationship between the war and suppression by one's own government; the less heroic aspects of the war such as fear and desertions; the war's impact on family life; the treatment of homecoming prisoners of war in the former Soviet Union; the high rate of execution of Red Army soldiers; the experience of losing comrades and friends, partners and children; the suppression carried out by the Red Army and the GPU[37] in other countries during the Soviet advance; collaboration with the German army and administration in the occupied zones (especially collaboration with the German authorities in persecuting opponents or Jews, Gypsies, and others in various Eastern European countries); the treatment of forced labourers on their return home ... the list could be endless.

Some research on one or another of these topics was published during the 2000s, mainly by societies such as Memorial (Russia)[38] and KARTA (Poland).[39] But it is astonishing that only a handful of oral history research projects focus on these topics; and it is astonishing, too, that those few projects started so late. The same applies to other important themes about the post-war years, such as everyday life after 1945, the difficulties acquiring food, the disruption of families, the experience of post-war suppression, the difficulties faced by homecoming soldiers and forced labourers, the consequences of the post-1956 political thaw, the consequences of the political changes after 1985 in Eastern Europe for private life and personal orientation and even for "national identity," to mention only some.

Third, we have yet to see research projects in oral history that deal directly with remembrance cultures, the consequences of past government policies, the relationship between family memory and official memory, the cross-national comparison of memory cultures in different countries, and so on.

If I understand correctly my discussions with Eastern European colleagues during various international conferences, it seems they are aware of all these themes. However, they explain, they have only limited funding to conduct research projects that deal with some of these subjects. A second and related reason is that, while oral historical work is being actively carried out in the region, as a scholarly discipline it has not been given much institutional recognition and is only partly accepted as a field of study at universities. Third, there are only a few possibilities for international exchanges; congresses and conferences are expensive, and joint projects are often difficult to undertake with the universities of the former Soviet republics. Fourth, my Eastern European colleagues understand that the old generation who experienced war is dying out, so we have to focus our work on these very old people. In my view, this argument is not convincing; post-war experiences should also be given attention.

To summarize, despite all the difficulties mentioned, international contacts, networks and exchanges are all necessary. It is important to continue organizing European and broader international projects and conferences, and these should be supported by the European Union or international foundations. Western and Eastern European scholars should support one another by organizing both national projects and international conferences to discuss their work. It is equally important to exchange and publish project findings and essays in various national journals. And not to forget: we should build up a "public history," and we should consider publicizing our research findings through newspapers and magazines, for in today's Eastern Europe, such venues are perhaps more interested than the academic establishment in oral history work and its results. The ongoing effort to build new public history might change attitudes towards oral history and biographical research in the universities and research institutes. I know these are only unsatisfactory answers to the mentioned problems. However, as this book demonstrates, we continue to work in this direction, and this is a hopeful sign.

NOTES

1 Ernst Bloch's *Erbschaft dieser Zeit* was first published in Switzerland in 1934 and again in 1962. Bloch, a philosopher who had to emigrate after the Nazis came to power, lived from 1885 to 1977 and was highly influential among European student movements.

2 The Soviet authorities in their occupation zone established *SpezLager* (special camps) to intern Nazi prisoners. These camps also held various other "enemies of the Soviet Union," including communists. The Soviets also

used former concentration camps such as Buchenwald, Sachsenhausen, and Jamlitz as *Spez Lager*. See von Plato "Zur Geschichte," 19–75.

3 Niethammer, *Die Jahre Weiß Man Nicht, 7.*

4 Broszat, Fröhlich, and Grossman, *Bayern in der NS-Zeit*; Niethammer and von Plato, *Lebensgeschichte und Sozialkultur im Ruhrgebiet: 1930–1960.*

5 Pioneering research in West Germany was conducted by Wolfgang Zapf. See Zapf, *Wandlungen der deutschen Elite.*

6 See Gruner, "Nun Dachte ich."

7 von Plato, "'Entstasifizierung.'"

8 von Plato, "'Wirtschaftskapitäne.'"

9 von Plato and Leh, *Ein unglaublicher Frühling*, 89.

10 Möding and von Plato, "Nachkriegspublizisten."

11 See the author's early research about trade unionists and shop stewards. See von Plato, "*Der Verlierer.*"

12 von Plato, "Wirtschaftskapitäne."

13 This political attitude can be called "corporatism." My thesis is that the West German government and trade unions used some aspects of Nazi corporatism when fostering "worker's participation" in the 1950s. See von Plato, "Wirtschaftskapitäne," 154.

14 Neumann, "Die DDR"; von Plato, "Elternhaus und Schule in der DDR," *Ergebnisse eines wissenschaftlichen Filmprojekts.*

15 *Sozialistische Einheitspartei Deutschlands*, SED.

16 See von Plato, "Opferkonkurrenten?," 74–92. Translated into English as "Victims Competition?," *International Journal on Audiovisual Testimony*, December 1998, 7–14.

17 See Walz, *Und Dann Kommst du Dahin*; see also her film *Die Frauen von Ravensbrück*, which received a Grimme-Preis in 2006.

18 On this, see Scherbakova, "Oral Testimonies from Russian Victims of Forced Labour"; Reznikova, "Presenting Life in Captivity"; Dalhouski, "Belarusian Forced Labourers."

19 On Russia for this context, apart from other contributions in *Hitler's Slaves*, see Osterloh, "Die Lebensbedingungen und der Arbeitseinsatz. See also *Ostarbeiter*; and Gerlach, *Kalkulierte Morde*. On Russia, see Polian, *Zhertvy Dvukh Diktatur*; and Polian, "Die Erinnerungen." In this volume, see also Penter.

20 This term, coined by Norbert Frei, is suitable for expressing how politics dealt with history. See Frei, *Vergangenheitspolitik*.

21 On Soviet prisoners of war see the pioneering work by Streit, *Keine Kameraden*. On forced labour, see Herbert, *Fremdarbeiter*; Spoerer, *Zwangsarbeit unter dem Hakenkreuz*. On the compensation debate, see Niethammer, "Von der Zwangsarbeit."

22 Sergey Mironenko, in personal communication with the author on several occasions during the project "Soviet Special Camps in Germany 1945–1950," Moscow, Essen, and Weimar, 1991–1996.

23 In general, on the subject of returning from slave and forced labour, see Thonfeld, "Former Forced Labourers," and the report by Filipkowski (KARTA) on Poland, "Daz Zentrum KARTA."

24 See Jarská, "Czechs as Forced and Slave Labourers," and Jakshova, "Slovak Republic (1939–1945)."

25 Further to this, see Kocevar, "Mother"; Schölzel, "Of Silence and Remembrance"; Wiesinger, "If You Lose Your Freedom."

26 Further to this, see Luleva, "Forced Labour in Bulgaria, 1941–1944"; Jakshova, "Slovak Republic (1939–1945)"; Schölzel, "Of Silence and Remembrance."

27 See Granet-Abisset, "The French Experience"; Granet-Abisset, "Témoins et Témoignages"; Bories-Sawala, *Franzosen im "Reichseinsatz."*

28 Sommaruga, "Cifre Della Resistenza"; Hammermann, *Gli Internati Military Italiani*. See also Felsen and Frenkel, "The Deportation of the Italians."

29 Further to this, see Bernecker and Brinkmann, *Kampf der Erinnerungen*; Vilanova, "Work, Repression, and Death."

30 Karner, Ruggenthaler, and Stelzl-Marx, *NS-Zwangsarbeit in der Rüstungsindustrie*, 8; Rathkolb, Fallend, and Gonsa, *NS-Zwangsarbeit*. The second volume, organized by Fallend, deals with "(Auto)Biographical Insights."

31 Perz, "Labour and Extermination."

32 The decisive leadership positions of the National Socialist Euthanasia Program were occupied by Austrian SS members; the headquarters were at Tiergartenstaße 4 in Berlin (thus "T4").

33 See the introduction by the editors of this volume.

34 At the Holocaust Museum in Budapest, for example, remarkable consideration is shown for Horthy and his governments.

35 For example, at the national museums of Riga and Tallinn.

36 Obertreis and Stephan, *Erinnerungen nach der Wende*.

37 *Gossudarstvennoe Politicheskoe Upravlenie*, the Soviet Security Police (GPU).

38 Memorial: Russia's historical and civil rights society, which records, documents, and publicizes the totalitarian legacy of the Soviet Union.

39 "The KARTA Center Foundation (Polish: *Fundacja Ośrodka KARTA*) is a Polish non-governmental public benefit organization, documenting and popularizing the recent history of Poland and history of Eastern Europe." Visit Karta Center, http://en.wikipedia.org/wiki/KARTA_Center.

2 Empowering Files: Secret Police Records and Life Narratives of Former Political Prisoners of the Communist Era in Poland

ANNA WITESKA-MŁYNARCZYK

My dress and the photograph are a tiny part of a grand ceremony of affirmation, of commitment to a larger identity: a sense of national belonging.

Annette Kuhn, *Family Secrets*

The year 1989 was a turning point in the lives of Eastern Europeans. With the collapse of communism, there developed an urge to define what the communist past *meant* for the recently democratized societies. Political processes of symbolization, myth making, and settling accounts with the past took various trajectories in the post-communist societies of Eastern Europe;[1] and as evidenced in Poland, during the transition from communism to post-communism, those processes influenced individual modes of remembering and self-understanding.[2] For past victims of communist repression, state-led memory and retroactive justice projects have constituted what Jaber Gubrium and James Holstein refer to as "local conditions of storytelling."[3] This chapter explores the structuring effect that such conditions have had on the life narratives of communist-era political dissidents. It focuses on the links between the resources and challenges produced by the bureaucratic machinery of the two Polish states (communist and post-communist) on the one hand, and the life stories performed by Stalin era political prisoners on the other. Following Gubrium and Holstein, who consider the interplay between state discourses and private narrative practices,[4] I also examine the *narrative linkage* between state-controlled discourses and practices and individual life accounts (i.e., storytelling).

Focusing on post-communist Poland, I discuss how the life stories of former dissidents have been shaped by and incorporated into public collective representations of the recent past. At the core of this process has been a public institution established in post-communist Poland in 1998, the Institute of National Remembrance – The Commission for the Prosecution of Crimes against the Polish Nation (INR).[5] Last but not least, I consider the special role that the communist secret police files, now accessible to the public, have played in the production and performance of my informants' life stories. Following Marianne Hirsh and Leo Spitzer,[6] I approach the files as unique "points of memory" that in the post-communist era have profoundly shaped public memories.

Memory Politics and State Bureaucracy

During the round table talks in 1989 between the Polish government and the opposition groups, it was discussed how transgressions committed by the communist authorities would be addressed. The idea of "forgiveness through oblivion" (*przebaczenie przez zapomnienie*) prevailed during those talks. This approach to dealing with communist wrongdoings was advocated by the former communist elite as well as by some activists in the Solidarity Movement.[7] Consequently, the first prime minister of democratic Poland, Tadeusz Mazowiecki, advocated a "thick line" (*gruba kreska*) – that is, the new government would not take responsibility for the actions of the previous regime, and the state would not support policies of vengeance or retribution. A number of tepid condemnations of the previous regime's activities appeared, such as an official condemnation of the martial law of the 1980s, passed in 1992. Various compensation programs for victims of the communist state were gradually implemented by later governments. When the post-communists formed a government in 1993, they adopted a strategy of non-involvement in retributive justice and lustration[8] projects and openly protected the privileges of former communist functionaries, including security officers. When Solidarity Electoral Action (*Akcja Wyborcza Solidarność*) came to power in 1997, it accelerated the creation of the INR, a body that would become central to the "history policy" implemented by post-communist politicians.

Established eight years after the collapse of the communist state, the INR performs a number of important functions in the Polish society. Its principal task for some time has been to manage the files the secret police generated during the communist regime in Poland (22 July 1944 to 31 July 1990), as well as those of the Nazi and Soviet security forces. The INR maintains a number of regional offices throughout the country. In the city of Marianowice,[9] for example, where I conducted my fieldwork for this chapter with former political prisoners of the communist state, the INR's local office oversees around 2,786 metres of files.[10] Citizens who wish to view the secret police files documenting their lives must apply to the INR by filling out a special request form.[11] Until recently, applicants could also apply for "grieved party" status[12] – that is, for certification that they had been repressed by the previous regime. In addition to this, the Act on the Institute of National Remembrance (1998) established the concept of "communist crime," thereby providing legal grounds for prosecuting transgressions committed during communist times by the functionaries of the communist state.

The INR does not simply manage files. Its Prosecution Branch was created to pursue Nazis and Communists who had committed war crimes as well as crimes against peace and humanity. Its Educational and Historical Research Branch was founded to build and disseminate knowledge about the country's recent history, encompassing the Second World War and the years of communist rule. Its employees pursue historical research, prepare educational programs for schoolchildren, publish their findings, and organize public exhibitions. The 1998 Act and the 2006 Act on the Disclosure of Information outlined the rules of lustration with regard to public servants who had possibly cooperated with the communist regime. The INR's Lustration Branch, created in 2007, documents and catalogues these people, as well as those who were employed in the security services; it also analyses and verifies lustration statements.

The interviews I conducted with INR staff between 2006 and 2008 led me to conclude that the institute, being a public institution, had been sensitive to changes in government over the course of its existence. As such, it had gone through different periods in its work, some were more active, some probably less so. Much depended on who was in power at a time. When the conservative Law and Justice Party (LJP) won the 2005 parliamentary elections, the institute's standing and position in Polish society was strengthened and its work was further supported. The LJP stated openly that one of its goals was to establish a clear policy of disclosing crimes and those who had committed them. They also called for public education in a spirit of patriotism, for a full accounting of communist crimes, for reconstitution of the true national heroes, and for compensation for victims for their suffering.

The Association of Former Political Prisoners

The mere act of founding the INR helped many people reposition themselves in the transition from communism to post-communism. Some achieved new roles in Polish society, and various legally defined categories of citizens emerged. Those who had been imprisoned during the Stalin era involved themselves in the INR's work and became the principal users of the secret police files, which by then were available to the public. My attention was drawn to former political prisoners who were actively pursuing their past and no less actively seeking public recognition of their victimhood. Between 2006 and 2008, as part of the doctoral dissertation I was writing at University College London, I examined the work of the Association of Former Political Prisoners of the Communist Period in the city of Marianowice. I chose to conduct my study there because most of the association's members, former Stalin era prisoners, were from a single voivodeship (district) and were actively engaged in memory work.

This association was founded in the early 1990s through the initiative of members of the Association of Former Political Prisoners of Marianowice's Tower.[13] Their original efforts brought together those who had been imprisoned in the tower for political reasons during the Nazi occupation. When the communist regime became publicly classified as a "second occupation," new understandings of the communist past led to the emergence of new categories of Polish citizens. Those who had been repressed by the communist regime now had an opportunity to reclaim their position in society, to reconstitute their own life histories, and to reconstruct their broken identities, as well as to organize themselves in public associations based solely on their experiences of repression. Hence, in the 1990s, the political prisoners of communist times were able to group themselves into new associations and build a distinct political identity, relying on resources offered by the post-communist state. The Marianowice Association is one of them.

In Marianowice, the idea of singling out the political prisoners of the communist period in a separate association was raised in 1990, during a gathering of the Association of the Former Political Prisoners of Marianowice's Tower. In 1991, after a Catholic mass conducted in a garrison church, the first meeting of the new association was held at a local municipal building. Those gathered decided they should not restrict membership to prisoners of the Stalin era, although most of the founding members had been imprisoned under that regime. Rather, they would allow *all* communist-era political prisoners to join the organization. After all, as one of the association's members told me, "the communist repressions ended only when the new Poland was born – in 1989." As a result, the association comprises several subgroups: those involved in both anti-Nazi and anti-communist resistance as underground partisans and members of the civil population in the 1940s and 1950s; the members of pro-independence youth groups active in the 1950s; those persecuted for their religious beliefs; prisoners of the Soviet Gulag in the 1940s and 1950s; and those interned under martial law in the 1980s.

The association's membership reached a peak of 965 in the late 1990s but has since been steadily decreasing. Today, its members are mostly elderly men of various backgrounds; most are from peasants' and workers' families and were imprisoned by the communists for activities ranging from serious military engagement in the underground army to telling a joke about the communist authorities, for which they were sentenced to a short spell in prison. Early in its existence, the association focused on expanding its membership and on vetting prospective members; it was believed that many applicants were motivated to join in order to gain access to social benefits, such as pensions for war veterans and for victims of repression. The association operated as a go-between, carrying out authentication procedures and linking those who "passed" to appropriate government authorities. After documents were verified and membership in the association was approved, they qualified for social benefits.

Out of nearly one thousand members, only a handful were actively engaged in the association's work. During my fieldwork, I focused on interviewing and exploring the work of those members who were actively engaged in the association, attending its meetings, maintaining its documents, and managing its affairs on the weekly basis. These individuals, whose number I estimated to be no more than twenty-five, were the association's backbone. Its most avid supporters and promoters, they regularly visited its office and helped the board members with their work.

Narrative Linkages

The collective discursive landscape on which the life stories of my informants are being mapped is the landscape of public memory of the post-communist Polish state. That landscape is also being shaped by work of the INR, a powerful agent of the state in Poland's present-day memory politics. The same landscape is also informed and shaped by local discourses of the communist past produced by regional and local organizations such as the Marianowice Association. For the elderly members of the association with whom I worked, public recognition and legitimization of their past actions as heroic was vital to rebuilding their sense of self, which had been violated and broken by the security police. Membership in the association provided them with a means to share their stories with others and to watch those stories enter the post-communist public narratives on communism.

Their individual accounts buttress public narratives, which are disseminated through institutional channels. This mutual informing of both vectors of narrativization of the past constitutes the "narrative linkage."

Like Gubrium and Holstein, I use the term narrative linkage to highlight the impact that cultural resources, such as public practices and orientations informed by the ideologies and bureaucratic machinery of the communist and post-communist Polish states, have had on individual stories. The state's ideology and discursive practices produced within the bureaucratic domain together generate "guidelines" for individual life narratives but do not determine those narratives. Gubrium and Holstein assert that telling one's experience in, say, a group that shares a relatively crystallized repertoire of storylines presents one with a bundle of discernible plots, which in turn offer ways of giving shape and substance to experience.[14] As each individual story is told, the biographical accounts gain a coherent collective dimension through "public" storylines that circulate in the public discursive domain. This utilization of the public in the performance of private stories is one example of the narrative linkage between the public and private narrativizing of the past.

Pierre Nora in his reflections on memory and history sees the nation-state as a means for articulating and legitimizing memories.[15] The post-communist state has authenticated my informants' memories, and in turn, my informants have authenticated the myth of national community promoted by the LJP. The interpretation of the past and the legitimization of an interpretative frame both happen through cultural resources such as commemorative rituals, acts of symbolization of the past, acts of recognition such as giving out medals and issuing veterans' and victims' ID cards, the provision of privileges such as special pensions, and the fostering of historical research and publications concerned with communist repression and anti-communist engagement.

Below I focus on how my informants' life stories acquired a certain structure in the context of state politics and historical research. Both provided legitimate forms of objectification and representation and thereby influenced identity formation. Here I present some of the ways in which a particular symbolic system of bureaucratic memory production influenced individual narratives.

One goal of the Marianowice Association was to help its members gain access to the social benefits earmarked for Poles who had encountered repression under communism. Those benefits included special pensions, official recognition that they had been victimized by the communist regime, and recognition by the broader community. From the outset, the former dissidents had to find effective ways to "show" themselves to the state. And this self-objectification had to follow a particular route, owing to pre-existing bureaucratic protocols for constructing new categories of Polish citizens – veterans, for example, and victims of communist repression. The association's members formed their own verification commission (*Komisja Weryfikacyjna*), which developed criteria for membership as well as a system for vetting applications. The commission, with the help of state bureaucrats, established the application protocol and developed forms that applicants had to fill out. This led to a new genre[16] of writing, one based on protocol requirements, which informed what Jerome Bruner once referred to as the "local conditions for storytelling"[17] and contributed to the "genericness" (Bruner's term) of individual life narratives.

An application for membership had to include a Member's Declaration (*deklaracja członkowska*), a Life Story (*życiorys*), and an Information Card (*karta informacyjna*), among other documents (*dokumentacja*). These documents prescribed the form in which individual life stories were to be presented to the association. When applying for membership, the candidate had to state in writing that he or she wished to join the association. When preparing a life story, the applicants turned to the association's members for advice on how to write it. The board members advised the applicants in the following manner: "write about the kind of repressions you suffered from," "where you were imprisoned," "keep it short and to the point," "support your statements by pointing to official and legal decisions," and so on. In this way, the application procedure became an interactive endeavour through which people oriented themselves towards the established genre of application writing.

As a consequence, the life stories often looked similar, as if structured around the same events, and the specifics of individual lives were omitted or glossed over.

Because they were routinely exposed to the life stories of other members formulated and expressed in terms similar to their own, the storytellers tended to develop a sense of shared life experiences and a strong sense of community. This, even though all the association members had their own unique pasts. They had been imprisoned in different detention centres throughout Poland, and they represented a dozen different political groups, so one would have expected them to have formed their own unique memories. On the other hand, they had been sentenced under similar conditions and had faced repression from the same regime, which had consistently applied the same methods of repression. The Marianowice Association's members knew that their stories varied – for example, they knew when and where the other members had been imprisoned, and why, and even who interrogated them. When describing to me the other members, they routinely used the same referents with respect to other individuals: "Marek is a man who got a death sentence"; "Marian, who recently got a medal from the president himself"; "You have to talk to Mietek, he faced a show trial"; "Alfred, who gave an interview to the local newspaper." Specific facts of repression and acts of recognition, used when describing others, served the tellers as important identity markers. Describing others, my informants focused on select facts from their lives. Importantly, when discussing their own lives, the members relied on the same tactics. Including in their life stories only select features, such as their experiences in resistance movements or their political repression, helped them constitute and legitimize themselves as heroes/victims. A life story written by one member of the Association, Jan, illustrates this:

> I was born on the 6th of July 1934 in Potok. I graduated from a primary school (7 grades) in Mlyn and I started a vocational training in Tarok, where I was arrested on the 20th of August 1954. I was under investigation for five months. After the investigation I was judged in a Marianowice court and, as an enemy of the People's Republic of Poland, I was sent to Silesia to work in a mine. After serving my sentence, I came back home and there a call-up was already waiting for me. After two days of being home, I was taken by a military escort to Silesia to another mine where I worked for two years as a soldier. In 1957, after I came back home, I wanted to finish the school but, as an enemy of communism, I was not

allowed to. Caught in a deadlock, I finished a course for drivers, where I worked till I retired in 1982.[18]

One can argue that such self-positioning and self-identification as a hero/victim was informed by the association's practice of creating files and was rooted in both bureaucratic management and the authority of contemporary Polish historiography. Importantly, adopting such an identity helped the narrators objectify their individual experiences of repression.

When I started my research, I was astonished by the seeming automatism with which my informants recited to me their life stories and how faithful these accounts were to the genre of life story presentation as practised within the association. Often, I did not even get a chance to explain what my research was about and what interested me; I was given the account these people imagined was relevant and important for my research and in the context of their membership in the association. As part of my fieldwork, I planned to carry out in-depth open-ended interviews with a number of the association members. I wanted to meet with them in various contexts and to conduct follow-up interviews. I wanted to combine recording their life stories with visiting the places where their past had unfolded. The first months of working with the association members left me with little hope for this kind of in-depth fieldwork. My informants, when we sat down for an interview, would quickly recite to me what seemed to be rehearsed accounts of their lives. They did so in a low voice, in a corner of a crowded room, and they always suggested that I see their files at some point. I was disappointed by these compact accounts, which mimicked the official documents, for I had hoped to hear fuller and less generic life stories. In time, I managed to establish better rapport, and some of my informants opened up, abandoning the "official" genre and holding dialogues on many other topics. Yet the established genre of document writing with its sharp narrative framing seemed to maintain a strong grip on the personal narratives performed for me. That genre was always tangibly present.

That narrative framing was informed by one particular document that the applicants had to fill out: the Information Card. That card, which the board members had composed, asked specific questions concerning the imprisonment history of an applicant. It had the effect of imposing rigid parameters on future recitals of life stories. The form required the applicants to provide their date of arrest, their place of interrogation, the duration of that interrogation, their sentence (including the court, the penal code, and the articles), the date the sentence was handed down, how many years the sentence was for, the names of detention centres and camps in which they had served time, the date of and reason for release, whether the sentence was overruled, whether they had belonged to clandestine organizations, area of operation, rank and duties in clandestine organizations, and, finally, a current military rank. This information was sufficient to legitimize one as a victim of communist repression. Those who failed to provide it could not be accepted as members of the association.

Clearly, as Coronil and Skurski have observed, the protocol for authenticating the submitted documents and claims to the association was informed by the state bureaucracy's practices and by state-formulated categories and narratives.[19] I would add that this authentication reflected, and cannot be conceived without, particular artefacts of the state bureaucratic machine – the paperwork itself, including the files produced in both communist and post-communist times. The categories of *veteran, victim of repression,* and *grieved party* had previously been legally defined, and now they were being used routinely both in historical writings and in the state's commemorative practices. One could be assigned the status of veteran or victim of repression only by adhering to the law and by engaging with the institutions devoted to its implementation, such as the Office for Veterans and Repressed Persons or the INR. Having formulated the regulations and having produced the forms to be filled out by those who wanted to fit into a particular category, these institutions prescribed narrative genres through which people were expected to represent their past experiences. Also, the claimants relied on a variety of files generated by state bureaucrats in the communist and post-communist eras. For their purposes, the most important of these were the files generated by security officers, which today are managed by the INR.

Security Police Files as Points of Memory

The INR's employees search for and analyse files only after a request is made. Those files are kept in the INR's cellars, and many kilometres of them still wait to be read and used. At times, various members of the Marianowice Association have requested access to the files compiled on them or on other association members. This has been for various reasons – in some cases, support documentation is needed to complete a membership application; in others, members are applying for grieved party status; in still others, they are attempting to gain a broader perspective on one or another aspect of past persecutions.

What these files mean to people has changed over time. Earlier, they were a source of information for the applicants; today, housed in the INR, they have become important "points of memory." Let me elaborate on what I understand points of memory to be. Hirsh and Spitzer, writing about material remnants from Nazi camps, use Roland Barthes's notion of points of memory to highlight productive intersections of past and present, of the cultural and personal domains of human existence.[20] Focusing on artefacts such as a tiny cookbook written by female prisoners in a Nazi concentration camp, scholars have argued that even the smallest material objects can be important for generating remembrance. As points of memory, these material objects of the past testify to subjective experiences and to the self-positioning of those who lived through that past; they allow one to access the culturally and historically specific context in which the individual story unfolded. Yet such objects are also viewed and discussed in the present; and as such, argue Hirsch and Spitzer, by carrying within themselves that past and the memories of it, they contribute to the process of its transmission.[21] In a peculiar sense, they directly inform the personal narratives of the people who are using them. In their search for personal integrity and moral order, my informants did not distance themselves from the language of the security files. Instead they embraced it in an effort to legitimize their hero/victim status.

In her work on the opening of the KGB files in Latvia, Vieda Skultans argued that the language of the files and the language of her informants – people on whom the KGB kept files during communist times – belonged to different orders of purpose and allegiance. "The allegiance of the language recorded in the archive is to social structures and institutions"; that of her "informants is to preserving a sense of moral and personal integrity."[22] Skultans interviewed her informants in relation to the KGB files collected on them. She found that her informants felt a need to challenge those files, which bore no resemblance to how they recollected their experiences. That challenge was performed through personal narrative, which, Skultans argued, constituted an authentically individuated moral practice in the face of "a dishonest society" that did not provide justice in the aftermath of communism.

My work with the members of the Marianowice Association demonstrates the links between public and private discourses on victimhood in post-communist Poland, between the genre of communist Poland's security files and the language of the personal narratives of the former political prisoners. Unlike Skultans's informants, Poland's former political prisoners, as they communicated their experiences, used and indeed relied on the language of the files in their private testimonies of the injustices they had suffered under communism. In retelling their life stories, as they routinely referred to the files, they regained the moral and personal integrity they had been deprived of under the previous regime.

In practical terms, the security files and their language directly helped the former political prisoners authenticate their new status as both victims and national heroes. Individuals wishing to obtain such a status for themselves engaged in reproducing and disseminating the files. The application process required the applicants to prepare multiple hard copies of a variety of documents from their own security files proving the act(s) of repression committed against them. Copies of these documents then had to be submitted to various offices. These documents typically included a sentence handed down to the person by a communist court (or, if the sentence was not given, an attestation issued by the court) as well as a statement from the present-day security office (*Urząd Ochrony Państwa*, UOP) or a similar statement from the INR confirming the existence of one's security files along with the protocols of interrogation. In this way, the security files became the primary source for confirming the repression against the applicant; thus, the hero/victim had no choice but to engage with them to ensure that their contents were not dismissed. That an institution, the INR, had been founded specifically to archive and study these files lent them symbolic and pragmatic weight. No wonder those files and their lingering authority have evoked conflicting sentiments in post-communist Poland. Some members of the Marianowice Association even felt disappointed if their files were not thick and substantial. They had become attached to the idea of the security forces' interest in them, expressed in the tangible form of the files. This attraction to such forms of objectification of their sufferings has had consequences for how they enact their heroic and victimized selves.

In the fragment below, Roman, who had recently examined his files in the INR, talked to Leszek, who had not yet received permission to "view his files" (although he had read parts of them from different sources).

LESZEK: He [referring to another hero/victim] is currently sitting in the INR reading his files and he told me: "imagine, fifty-eight pages!" So, I replied: "fifty-eight pages is nothing!" [laughing]

ROMAN: To produce such follies, it is a lot!

ME: What interesting things did you see in the files?

ROMAN: What interesting things?

LESZEK: Interesting ... that he has friends who are still alive, whom he treated with beer and vodka [laughing], and they in turn sneaked on him!

ROMAN: Like that someone arrived – these sort of descriptions, about family, about people with whom I contacted, about that time when they arrived, and when Michal arrived.

LESZEK: Yet, nothing concerning me ... When I visited you ... because it was at night and they were sleeping [laughing].[23]

In this conversation, Leszek overemphasized the significance of the files. He sought legitimacy in them, noting how the size of the files mattered for association members' identity. By answering my question for Roman, Leszek was asserting his status by suggesting that people had informed on him (being surrounded by snitches points to "authentic" status as a hero or a victim). This strategy of alignment[24] has strengthened the solidarity that binds association members. Leszek then created a "participation framework"[25] for himself, for he felt obliged to explain his absence from the files, even though no one had raised this matter. Apparently, it disappointed him that there was no mention in the files of his visit to Roman's place. So he took the opportunity to self-represent, shifting the focus of the conversation from Roman to "I" while staying within the framework of Roman's files, bringing into the conversation a sense of shared experience. In his representation of that absence, Leszek highlighted his own cleverness: it was not the case that he was unworthy of being mentioned in the files – rather, he had come in the night to avoid being observed.

Reading one's files was an important and almost ritualistic undertaking. It was an activity subject to further discussion with others who had shared the experience of reading their files. Those files brought to life a past that had been shifted away from active memory. Minute details in the files were discussed among a close circle of peers seeking the same status, and questions like "Why did they write this?," "Who could that be?," and "Do you remember such an officer?" were regularly asked in conversations with others. By reporting to one another about the files' contents, the former prisoners created a community. They shared not only the past but also, now, a specialized knowledge about it. In sharing their experiences of reading the files as well as their experiences of persecution, the former prisoners found many links among their own life stories. By providing the opportunity to create links between their life stories and experiences, the security files served my informants as points of memory. By turning to others' stories in search of details relevant to their experiences and by sharing their own stories, my informants not only upgraded their own accounts but also, eventually, altered the life narratives of their peers. Since they were allowed to take copies of the files, they also lent those copies to one another. The files were an important dimension of the conversations among my informants, especially among those who once conspired together. Often, they carried with them their own photographs taken by the security service to show them to others. The files and their contents empowered them, legitimizing their claims to a heroic and victimized identity and providing the means to express that identity.

When I visited my informants in their private flats, I was often welcomed with a cup of tea. Next to tea there would be a stack of files, set aside, photocopied, and waiting for me to look through. It was as if, even in their own homes, the official documents continued to exercise control over their lives. They offered as well a sense of closure – the past, once denied, had finally been returned and reclaimed. Yet these documents, casually lying on the table, simultaneously allowed the past to rise again, as if forcing itself into my informants' present-day lives. One evening in the fall, when I visited Andrzej, a member of the association, we looked through his files, as I did with everyone else. After we had gone through his family album and covered a part of his life story, he started to search for one document – "You ought to see it," he told me. Eventually, he pulled out a piece of paper with a copy of an enlarged photograph of a man's face. Keeping it exposed for me, almost covering his own face with it, he informed me in a shaky voice, "This is my persecutor," that is, the judge who had sentenced him. A vivid imposition of an image of someone who had been an antagonist in his broken life story made the inherently intimate experience of repression, which had long been veiled in secrecy, obvious. The photo was part of the security files.

For members of the association, the security files now housed in the INR served as both containers and vehicles of memory, directing the process of their transmission. In this sense, they served as points of memory that facilitated and structured their life testimonies. As I was recording the association members' life histories, I realized that every life story I heard relied, in both content and framing, on the security files. It often happened that people almost cited the files when narrating their life stories. Thus seventy-three-year-old Adam, while describing his anti-communist political involvement, recited protocols from his interrogation. How else could he have brought back the details of what had happened over fifty years ago, recalling questions and answers, articulating them in a jargon specific to the communist period? Normally, when I visited a person for an in-depth interview or to record a life narrative, apart from a pile of copies of the files prepared by the security forces in reference to that person, I was also presented with documents certifying my interlocutors' status, issued by the post-communist state. People often commented that "it is all written here" or "you should read this" or "this is my ID" or "here it says when I got the pension" – as if asserting that their life stories could be easily verified thanks to the security files and the documents contained in them.

Conclusion

The testimonies of my informants, who have participated actively in Poland's production of public memories of socialism, both as subjects and as objects, are playing an important role in reinterpreting socialist repression in Poland. Having gained, in the post-communist period, access to an extended pool of resources – material, textual, interactional – they have focused on reclaiming their own pasts and lives. In doing so, they have been able to contribute to the production of a new ideological metanarrative of Polish suffering and perseverance under the previous regime.

Having researched the mechanisms of public (re)presentations of the Holocaust, Lawrence Langer has argued that for today's audiences, the only real point of entry into how it was "back there" is documented witness testimonies, especially video testimonies.[26] According to Langer, "information about life behind barbed wire does not come from German documents."[27] Rather, it is the victims' testimonies that inform our understanding of the experiences and meanings of the Holocaust. In other words, for contemporaries to understand what the Holocaust was really like, it is best to rely on survivors' testimonies, for those testimonies are the most real, the most true to how it was "back then." The assumption here is that the survivors' testimonies have somehow remained true to the Holocaust, unaffected by later developments in the survivors' lives. But is this the case?

Although I do not research experiences of the Holocaust, my work with the survivors of socialist repression in Poland points to a very different scenario of memory production. Constructing their own memories of the past on the basis of what they have found in the security files, drawing on frameworks and paradigms in scholarly discourses concerning the history of totalitarian crimes against Polish society, my informants actively engaged in dialogue with those external resources, internal to their own personal lives. All of this speaks to novel conditions of personal reminiscing about the socialist past in Poland, at least in the context of the life experiences of my informants who directly experienced socialist repression.

This dialogue results in the emergence of a collective identity and a repertoire of performance for individual selves, which in turn moves my informants away from what Langer has called "back there." Through interaction with what communist functionaries wrote or photographed, and with INR historians' interpretations of these things, their personal stories have become deeply entangled with the official documents, and the "back there" has become more difficult to find.

NOTES

1 Borneman, *Settling Accounts*.
2 Witeska-Młynarczyk, "Landscapes of Polish Memory."
3 Gubrium and Holstein, "Narrative Practice."
4 Gubrium and Holstein, "Narrative Practice," 166–72.
5 In Polish, Instytut Pamięci Narodowej, Komisja Ścigania Zbrodni przeciwko Narodowi Polskiemu.
6 Hirsch and Spitzer, "Testimonial Objects."
7 Roszkowski, *Najnowsza Historia Polski*, 129. The independent trade union "Solidarity" emerged on 31 August 1980 at the Gdańsk Shipyard as a non-communist federation of trade unions. In the early 1980s it united approximately 10 million Poles. Solidarity was a social movement fighting for workers' rights and social change.
8 Lustration laws in Poland make it mandatory for certain categories of public functionaries to declare whether they cooperated with or worked for the security forces. These statements were later verified by the lustration

branch of the INR, and the names of those who cooperated and worked for the regime have been published in special registers, which are easy to access online.

9 Marianowice is an invented name for a real place.

10 Source: INR.

11 In Marianowice between 2001 and mid-March 2007, out of 4,464 applications, 3,036 people were allowed access to the files collected on them; 1,127 people gained the status of a grieved party and 141 were denied access because they had hidden the fact of their cooperation with or employment in the security services. See INR.

12 Under the 1998 Act, a grieved party is a person about whom the state security organs secretly collected information. A person who later became a functionary, employee, or collaborator of the state security organs is not deemed a grieved party. See INR, "The Act on the Institute of National Remembrance."

13 Marianowice Tower is one of the town's historic buildings.

14 Gubrium and Holstein, "Narrative Practice," 166.

15 Nora, "Between Memory and History."

16 I use here Pam Morris's definition of a genre as "typical forms of utterance associated with a particular sphere of communication (e.g. the workplace, the military, the sewing circle), which have therefore developed into *relatively stable types* in terms of thematic content, style and compositional structure." Morris, *The Bakhtin Reader*, 80.

17 Bruner, "The Narrative Construction of Reality."

18 Jan is not a real name. The names of all of my informants and places have been changed.

19 Coronil and Skurski, "Introduction: States of Violence and the Violence of States," 2.

20 Hirsch and Spitzer, "Testimonial Objects," 358–60.

21 Hirsch and Spitzer, "Testimonial Objects."

22 Skultans, "Arguing with the KGB Archives," 323.

23 Matyjaszek and Kaniowski, personal communication.

24 Schiffrin, *Approaches to Discourse*, 109–31.

25 Schiffrin, *Approaches to Discourse*, 102–5. I draw here from Goffman's notion of the "participation framework," understood as a linguistic structure that organizes and is organized by talk and interaction in the making. Goffman, *Forms of Talk*.

26 Langer, "Hearing the Holocaust."

27 Langer, "Hearing the Holocaust," 303.

3 Memory Silenced and Contested: Oral History of the Finnish Occupation of Soviet Karelia

ALEXEY GOLUBEV

Introduction

In 2004, the Karelian Union of Former Young Prisoners of Fascist Camps[1] sent a petition to the President of Finland, Tarja Halonen. In that document, the union's board asked the Finnish government to pay compensation to former prisoners of Finnish concentration camps located between 1941 and 1944 on the territory of Soviet Karelia (then a republic of the USSR), similar to what was being paid by the German foundation "Memory, Responsibility and Future" to former prisoners of Nazi concentration camps. The German foundation had previously refused to pay compensation to former prisoners of concentration camps in Soviet Karelia, justifying its decision by the fact that the territory of this Soviet republic during the Second World War was occupied by Finnish, not German troops. The answer of the Finnish authorities was negative as well. In a letter signed by President Halonen herself, it was pointed out that under the Paris Peace Treaty of 1947 between Finland and the Allies, the Finnish government had no obligation to compensate Soviet citizens directly. The reparations paid by Finland to the Soviet Union immediately after the war already included compensation for personal losses, and therefore the current Finnish government was not liable for any personal claims. Whatever Russian citizens wanted to demand for war damages, they had to demand it from their own government.[2]

Yet in the Republic of Karelia, today a federal unit of Russia, former prisoners of Finnish concentration camps have had a hard time securing compensation from Russia. In the early 2000s, local Karelian authorities tried to cancel payments to former prisoners of Finnish camps on the grounds that their imprisonment was often poorly documented and that the definition of "concentration camp" was applied too broadly. The reinstatement of these compensation payments required a great number of painful legal hearings in local courts, and the resulting payments were meagre.[3]

The financial disputes that former prisoners of Finnish concentration camps in Karelia were involved in during the 2000s embodied and expressed a complex relationship, one in which personal wartime memories engaged with pressing issues of post-socialist Russian society such as ethnicity, age, social authority, historical voice, and the making of new post-Soviet identities. To address this relationship, I will focus on the activities of the Karelian Union of Former Young Prisoners of Fascist Camps (hereafter KU, or union). I will argue that the KU uses the individual memories of its members as a symbolic resource for creating a collective vision of the Finnish occupation of Soviet Karelia during the war; also, that appeals to their wartime experiences are intended to buttress the KU's claim that its members have an exclusive right to form the social memory of the wartime suffering of the Soviet Karelian population. The oral histories provided by its members regarding the wartime occupation of Soviet Karelia have given them a voice in the making of history; simultaneously, their collectivized experience has become a social force that has silenced other experiences of the Finnish occupation, which offer interpretations that differ from the picture of wartime sufferings that the union has developed for the public.

One particular Soviet and then Russian region is the focus of this chapter: Soviet or Russian Karelia, which during the war was officially named the Karelian-Finnish Soviet Socialist Republic. Today, its official name is the Republic of Karelia. Located in northwestern Russia along the Soviet–Finnish border, Karelia had a long history of cross-border contacts and conflicts, first between Sweden and Russia (in form of Novgorod, Muscovy, or the Russian Empire) and then between Finland and the Soviet Union. Most importantly for this study, owing to its large ethnic Karelian population, which spoke dialects close to Finnish, Russian Karelia has since the nineteenth century been part of the Finnish imagined cultural and political space.[4] After Finland proclaimed independence in December 1917, following the Bolshevik Revolution, Finnish nationalists made several attempts to incorporate parts of the territories inhabited by Eastern Karelians by military and diplomatic means. All of these failed.[5]

In 1941, an alliance with Germany allowed Finland to finally establish real control over most of Soviet Karelia. After this, the Finnish authorities developed a policy that would eventually incorporate this region into Finland if the Soviet Union were defeated. Ethnicity became the main criterion in Finnish occupation policy. Finnish authorities divided the population of the occupied territories into two approximately equal groups: privileged "kindred" people, including Karelians, Finns, Ingrian Finns, Vepsians, and Estonians (all Finno-Ugric peoples), and "non-national" people, including Russians, Ukrainians, and representatives of other non-Finno-Ugric groups.[6] The Finnish leadership planned to cleanse Karelian territories of "non-nationals" after the war, and the dominant approach taken by the Finnish occupation authorities towards non-nationals was to treat them as a source of cheap labour.[7] Living conditions for Karelians, Finns, and Vepsians under the occupation regime were substantially better; their communities enjoyed better food supplies, educational opportunities, and medical care as part of an explicit effort to turn them into loyal Finnish subjects.[8]

The Red Army freed the occupied territories of Soviet Karelia in the summer of 1944. This was the point at which the experience of the Finnish occupation became memory; however, post-war political and cultural conditions would not favour the "socialization" of that memory for many decades.

Unspoken Experience of Wartime Memories

Throughout the Soviet period, the wartime experiences and memories of the occupied population of Soviet Karelia were not simply silenced and ignored – they were actually excluded from the Soviet social memory. Immediately after Soviet Karelia was freed, a special investigation committee staffed by NKVD officers started its work in the republic. Its primary purpose was to collect evidence of crimes committed by the Finnish occupation regime.[9] After several years, however, Moscow and Helsinki built a "special relationship" through Cold War diplomacy, and all negative aspects of the Finnish occupation of Soviet Karelia were "put to sleep" in favour of renewed Soviet–Finnish relations. Historical studies of the Finnish occupation were now restricted to the activities of Partisan units and underground groups; the life of the civilian population in the occupied lands – except for the most general descriptions – remained completely outside the scope of these works.[10]

Setting aside foreign policy considerations, this outcome was generated by the fact that even a superficial study of this topic would have revealed facts about the interactions between the local Karelian population and the Finnish occupiers that would have destroyed all notions that the Soviet people had unanimously resisted the enemy. Soviet society accepted the demand for silence imposed by the Soviet master narrative – a narrative that was expressed most emphatically by an episode in the 1977 novel *Za chertoi miloserdiia* (*Behind the Edge of Mercy*) by Soviet writer Dmitry Gusarov. In that episode, an eighteen-year-old Partisan is sent out to reconnoitre his home Karelian village. On his return, he invents a story that he strangled his own sister because she was dating a Finn. In his Partisan group, this invented story makes him a hero, and the political commissar uses his account to prepare a lecture titled "No Mercy to Traitors."[11] What is important here is not the character's reaction but the author's position: he does not criticize his character and indeed is rather sympathetic to him – the latter wanted to commit a "heroic" deed, even if that deed was the murder of his own sister. The author's position reflected societal views of these problems in post-war times. All interactions with Finnish (as well as Nazi or any other) occupation forces were viewed as so shameful that they had to be silenced or, if word of such an interaction spread through the community, eradicated. In this respect, the strangling of a woman in Gusarov's novel can be interpreted as a metaphoric action, as silencing a "shameful" experience by means however brutal.

Another proof of this statement involves the post-war fates of children born to local women from Finns. The social pressure on these children and their mothers was so strong that tragedies inevitably followed. One of my informants mentioned a woman who strangled her newborn child.[12] Another mother of an "illegal" child was harassed until she killed herself.[13] Illegal abortions that sometimes resulted in the death of the woman were common.[14] Given all this, it is no wonder that people who lived in Finnish-occupied territory between 1941 and 1944 preferred to remain silent about their wartime experiences. Only in the second half of the 1980s did societal attitudes change so that personal and group memories of life under the Finnish occupation began to emerge into society. Former young prisoners of Finnish camps led the way when in 1989 they assembled in Petrozavodsk and founded the KU.[15]

Liberalization of Memory and History

The socialization of memory about the Finnish occupation of Soviet Karelia occurred in the context of, first, fast-deteriorating living conditions during the late 1980s and 1990s, and second, a newly forming pluralist social environment. During this period, old people became one of the most vulnerable social groups in Russia, and the former young prisoners began to use their wartime experiences as a resource for acquiring financial compensation. Equally important, they desired to secure their version of history. After decades of silence, they now had an opportunity to tell Karelian society about the crimes and cruelties of the Finnish occupation regime as they saw them. These "enlightening" activities – in the form of lectures in schools, public speeches, TV and radio interviews, and newspaper articles – became the union's main focus, as its conference resolutions demonstrate.[16]

However, in the liberal social context of the 1990s, the image of the Finnish occupation of Soviet Karelia imposed by the former young prisoners was not the only one in circulation. Contested histories of this period emerged, influenced largely by Finnish scholarly works. In Finland, assessments of that country's participation in Nazi Germany's aggression against the Soviet Union remain a topic of heated debates. Most Finnish historians try to differentiate between the Nazi and Finnish occupation regimes so as to demonstrate the more "humane" nature of the latter,[17] although a few scholars see little difference between the two.[18] The liberalization of social life in the Soviet Union during *perestroika* gave the former prisoners of Finnish camps an opportunity to recount their experiences, but it also injected scholarly views of the Finnish occupation into the Russian academic community.[19] Moreover, the alternative views of the Finnish occupation regime as more "humane," especially compared to the German one, could be supported by wartime experiences of large population groups, mainly of non-Russian ethnicity.

This led to yet another problem – that of suppressed ethnicity. Soviet Karelia was established as an autonomous administrative region only in 1920, under the leadership of Finnish émigré communists who after their defeat in the 1918 Finnish Civil War fled to the Soviet Union. Three Finno-Ugric ethnic groups formed the "national" basis of Soviet Karelia: Karelians, the most populous group; Finns, most of them recent immigrants; and Vepsians, another Indigenous ethnic group. The latter two were rather insignificant in terms of their proportion of the Soviet Karelian population; it was Finns who constituted much of Soviet Karelia's political, economic, and cultural elite. Soviet Karelia was intended to serve as a bridgehead for the "export" of proletarian revolution to Scandinavia and as a model of ethnic autonomy, a sort of "alternative" socialist Finland that would arouse revolutionary aspirations among

Finnish workers and peasants.[20] From the very beginning, however, Soviet Karelia included large territories with predominantly Russian populations, and as a result of migration from Russian, Belorussian, and Ukrainian territories, the proportion of Finno-Ugric groups within the Soviet Karelian population decreased throughout the Soviet period.[21] The histories of Karelians, Vepsians, and Russian Finns are, therefore, histories of loss – loss of language, loss of culture,[22] and, finally, loss of their own voice and representations in history. So I will demonstrate later in the case of contested memories of occupied Karelia.[23]

This is the background of my oral history research on memory work about the Finnish occupation of Soviet Karelia. This background is extremely politicized on both sides of the border and is complicated by different historical experiences and historiographical perspectives, by unequal access to power (including, in particular, the power to produce knowledge), by varying abilities of social agents to find public support for their cause, and, finally, by practical considerations.

Collectivization of Memory about the Finnish Occupation

The KU is the most active player in the contemporary Republic of Karelia in terms of writing down its wartime history, and its members perceive alternative visions of the Finnish occupation as a threat to their newly found position in society, which offers them authority over their own past. They have positioned themselves as the only true source of information about civilian life under the Finnish occupation. They use their size advantage in the battles for historical memory that have been waged in Karelia over the past two decades. The KU is large enough to have monopolized first-hand information about daily life in the occupied territories. Almost all documentary sources were generated by the Finnish side and are stored in the archives of Helsinki, which makes access to them complicated for students, journalists, and other people involved in researching the Finnish occupation regime and resolving disputes related to it. Soviet documentary sources were created only after the liberation of Karelia, and as was mentioned before, these cannot be characterized as objective. In this situation, the KU's board has been able to socialize the childhood memories of its members so as to create a settled negative image of the Finnish occupation regime in contemporary Karelian society. My students who wanted to use oral histories about the Finnish occupation in their term papers visited the union offices several times to request contact information for possible interviewees. The union's board was always very friendly to them and happily gave them phone numbers and other contact information. However, visits to the union office invariably ended with promises taken from my students that they "would not write that the Finns fed [the] local population with candies."

This phrase, repeated almost word for word by my students, is highly symptomatic, for it is based on two logical assumptions. First, the union's board believes it has the right to impose on researchers (even those in the early stage of their careers) semantic constraints, which the latter should follow when studying the Finnish occupation of Soviet Karelia. Second, the board fears that if given freedom of choice, students might depict the Finnish occupation in a "wrong" way, one that emphasizes the "humane face" of the occupation regime and omits its negative side. This strongly suggests they are aware of competing discourses about the Finnish occupation and are trying to convince students to ignore them. In this sense, students are only part of the audience targeted by the KU's activities. Through books and newspaper articles, public speeches, and television appearances, the board disseminates the oral histories of its members with the goal of constructing a more appropriate version of social memory of the Finnish occupation. Oral histories and memoirs published by the union represent memories about hunger, filthy conditions, tortures by camp guards, executions, cruel punishments, and so on.[24] Some episodes presented in these books arouse serious doubts as to their credibility – for example, stories that people ill with typhus were incinerated in ovens,[25] that Finns set dogs on children[26] and beat them to death,[27] and that prisoners (including children) were used as subjects of medical experiments.[28] Here, knowledge about Nazi concentration camps has been an obvious influence.[29] But even when we set aside these extreme descriptions as unreliable, the overall picture of life in the Finnish camps as represented in the stories of former young prisoners is hardly less cruel and inhumane than that of the Nazi concentration camps.

Ethnic Aspects of Remembering the Occupation

There is an alternative layer of memory about the Finnish occupation of Soviet Karelia. It is represented, first, by the memories of Finno-Ugric ethnic groups living in Karelia, namely, Karelians, Vepsians, and Russian Finns. As I mentioned earlier, one of the most important features of Finnish occupation politics was the ethnic division of the local population of Soviet Karelia into two groups: the privileged, who included Karelians, Vepsians, and Soviet Finns; and the non-privileged, who comprised all others, including Russians, the ethnic majority. The former group had better jobs and salaries, received more generous food rations, and enjoyed more rights and privileges.[30] As a result, the oral histories of representatives of this group depict the Finnish occupation regime in a very different way than what we find in the stories published by the KU. The board of the latter probably implied as much when it asked my students not to mention that "the Finns fed local population with candies."

Available interviews make it obvious why Karelian or Vepsian versions of historical memory are perceived by former prisoners of Finnish camps as dangerous. This is demonstrated in a statement from an interview with a Vepsian woman, which by the way is typical: "Under Finns ... we were well-fed. I had footwear and clothes. [After the restoration of the Soviet power] there was nothing left. I was naked and barefooted."[31] Another informant quoted a Belorussian woman who lived in the territories occupied by German troops and who migrated to Karelia after the war. The latter directly compared the Finnish and Nazi occupation regimes: "God forbid, here with Finns you lived a thousand times better than we with Germans."[32] Information of this kind, of course, directly contradicts the wartime experiences of former prisoners of the Finnish camps.

Even oral history interviews with Russians who lived in occupied Karelia present a different picture of the Finnish regime if they are taken from respondents who did not associate themselves with the KU's activities. In an interview taken as part of my project of collecting wartime oral histories of the Finnish occupation of Soviet Karelia, my Russian interviewees mentioned hunger, hard physical labour, and physical punishments, but in general their evidence did not suggest a harsh occupation policy that verged on genocide, as reflected in KU members' memories. Here is a range of opinions expressed by Russian respondents whose oral histories were collected as a part of my project: "Finns treated us not bad at all, as those say who lived under Germans";[33] "Finns did not do anything bad to us";[34] "It's good that they did not taunt us as Germans did. Finns were, after all, kind people";[35] "[Finns] did not oppress anyone, they supplied food, not extremely nourishing, but nevertheless";[36] and others.[37]

This evidence does not contradict but rather supplements the personal memoirs and oral histories that the union has disseminated through its publications and activities. There is no question that Finnish occupation policies were implemented differently under different conditions, especially given that the Finnish leadership had made it their project to cleanse Karelian territories, albeit without resorting to extermination.[38] A lot also depended on low-level Finnish military officials in occupied villages and towns. These days, Russian scholars could combine Finnish and Soviet/Russian historiographical traditions, as well as documentary sources and oral evidence from both sides, to offer Karelian society a pluralist history of the Finnish occupation of Soviet Karelia. This has not happened, however, to a certain extent because of the KU's uncompromising position with regard to those views of the Finnish occupation of Karelia that do not coincide with its own version of these historical events.

A Civil War of Memory

The union's uncompromising position is evident in several public debates in the regional Karelian press. The most heated of these was in January 2005, when a local newspaper published an article by a well-known Karelian journalist who expressed – very cautiously – reasonable doubts as to the credibility of some (not all) memoirs and oral histories published by the KU.[39] The author criticized obvious exaggerations of this sort: "hundreds of dead bodies taken out daily [from Finnish concentration camps]" (which would have meant a prisoner death toll of 90,000 – three times the total number of civilians who passed through Finnish camps). He also raised doubts about mass tortures, the deliberate extermination of prisoners, and so on. He agreed that the occupation of Karelia had overall been a harsh one that had led to great sufferings and many innocent deaths. Yet even this moderate position did not save the author from KU accusations that the article had been commissioned by Finnish political groups and that its author was unprincipled.[40]

Some former young prisoners of Finnish camps tried to write their own historical narratives about the occupation of Karelia. While declaring that their aim was to create an "objective" history of the occupation, they nevertheless followed the same harsh anti-Finnish discourse and ignored primary and secondary sources that offered an alternative or at least a broader position. In his speculations about the events that led to the Finnish occupation, Nikolai Denisevich accused Finland of provoking the Soviet–Finnish (Winter) War of 1939–40. This argument had been invented by the Soviet leadership to justify the war and had long been accepted by Soviet historiography, although it would be abandoned in the late 1980s.[41] An essay by V. Mikhailov, which he characterized as a "historical investigation," obviously extrapolated separate, mostly harsh episodes of life in Finnish concentration camps to the entire occupation regime.[42]

In this struggle for historical memory about the Finnish occupation of Karelia, the version represented by the KU has undoubtedly had the upper hand. Until recently, there were no attempts at all to collect the wartime stories of Karelians or Vepsians, who had been the "privileged" groups during the Finnish occupation.[43] As a consequence, history has been written without their voice – a situation that obviously owes less to the KU's activities than to the general social tendency to repress the ethnicity of these Indigenous groups. In recent years, the version of the Finnish occupation represented by the union has become even more dominant, so much so that it has succeeded in substituting all alternative versions in the public discourse and, consequently, social memory. This has become especially obvious every year in the wake of the Victory Day celebrations on 9 May, during which the Russian media are flooded with all kinds of materials related to the Russia's role in the defeat of Nazi Germany. Stories of former prisoners with their black-and-white assessments perfectly fit the new image of the Great Patriotic War created as part of new Russian ideological project; alternative stories have again been forced from the social memory.[44]

The dominance of this extreme position that the Finnish occupation was "fascist" is evident even in academic research. The essays written by students who use the oral histories of former prisoners as their primary sources (and who also regularly skip consultation hours) reproduce the dominant discourse about the Finnish occupation of Karelia – so much so that the results can serve as typical examples of popular postmodernist theories about historians' inability to rise above their sources. Even established scholars demonstrate this tendency.[45] The last work mentioned in the endnote, for example, claims to address the entire "memory of the generation which lived through the Finnish occupation of Karelia" (as seen from its title). Yet for primary sources, the author restricted herself to children's memories of life in Finnish concentration camps published by the KU; all other layers of memory about the Finnish occupation remained outside the analysis, if she consulted them at all. Once again, Karelians, Vepsians, and Russian Finns have become invisible and unheard in their own history, and their loss of voice has now been legitimized by the authority of Russian academe.

Conclusion

The Karelian Union's success in this "competition" for historical memory about the Finnish occupation of Soviet Karelia evidently comes from the moral power of their argument. This is their most critical advantage, for any person who addresses these events must inevitably pass a moral judgment on the Finnish occupation regime. In this respect, the position of the KU board is very logical: the crimes of that regime as represented in the stories of former prisoners are a sufficient basis for characterizing it as "fascist." Questions about how widespread those crimes were, and whether they were committed with respect to other population groups, are not considered. All attempts to introduce into the social memory in the Republic of Karelia any alternative interpretation of the Finnish occupation are regarded as revisionism. This one-sided position gains moral weight through argumentation of the type "I was there while you were not." This places scholarly approaches to the history of the Finnish occupation (however strong their claims to objectivity) in a vulnerable position, for the former young prisoners of Finnish camps appeal to their moral right as victims and witnesses to promote their black-and-white interpretation of the Finnish occupation as the only true one.

When we place this situation in the context of the current volume, the obvious conclusion to be drawn is that all personal memories (be they Karelian, Vepsian, or Russian) that do not fit the conventional social image of the Finnish occupation will not be reclaimed within the remaining lifespans of their bearers. The KU's uncompromising position is an attempt to exclude from social space alternative memories of the Finnish occupation of Karelia – the memories of Karelians, Vepsians, Russian Finns, and those Russians who did not witness the crimes of the Finnish occupation regime. The moral right of victims to an exclusive role in constructing and representing their past is invoked – a right that allows their evidence to be more "right" than the evidence of other people who suffered. The irony is that the current dominance of the anti-Finnish narrative is equally negative for representations of the personal memories of the former young prisoners themselves. It has led to substitution of all separate personal memories of the Finnish occupation of Karelia by one unifying narrative, to a symbolic collectivization of memory. Where the interests of a social group are at stake, no place for the personal is left, whether the personal belongs to this social group or to somewhere else.

NOTES

1 This is the organization's official title. In Russia, "fascist" refers to everything related to Nazi Germany and its allies during the Second World War.
2 Correspondence between the KU and the administration of the President of Finland was published online: Karelskii Soiuz, "Pisma KS BMU Vlastiam i Nekotorye Otvety."
3 Ukkone, "Kak Zashchititsia ot Sotsialnoi Zashchity"; Ukkone, "Uzniki Chuzhoi Sovesti"; Kuznetsov, "Uzniki Biurokratisma." In 2005, the monthly payment from the Russian government to people recognized as former prisoners of Finnish concentration camps amounted to roughly 3,000 rubles, or $100 at the current exchange rate.
4 Sihvo, *Karjalan Kuva*.
5 See, for example, Niinistö, *Heimosotien Historia 1918–1922*.
6 Laine, *Suur-Suomen Kahdet Kasvot*, 106.
7 Laine, *Suur-Suomen Kahdet Kasvot*, 105.
8 Vehviläinen, *Finland in the Second World War*, 104–5.
9 Some materials collected by this committee were published in Sulimin, Truskinov, and Shitov, *Chudovishchnye Zlodeianiia*. The very name of this book – *Monstrous Crimes of Finnish Fascist Aggressors on the Territory of Karelian-Finnish SSR* – is symptomatic. It was rendered obsolete in the Soviet historiography almost immediately after its publication and is now available only as a bibliographic rarity.
10 See, for example, Morozov, *Kareliia v Gody Velikoi Otechestvennoi Voiny (1941–1945)*; Mashezerskii, *Ocherki Istorii Karelii*.
11 Gusarov, *Za Chertoi Miloserdiia*, 20–3.
12 Kemliakova (born 1927), Interview, 55.
13 Yarshin (born 1929), Interview, 91.
14 Koshkarova (born 1927), Interview, 179.
15 General information about the union and its charter and resolutions of its regular conferences are available on the union's website: Karelskii Soiuz, "Sozdanie KSBMU."
16 See, for example, resolutions of the union's sixth conference: Karelskii Soiuz, "Rezoliutsiia VI."

17 For this perspective, the basic reference is the final volume of a six-volume study on the history of the Finno-Russian War of 1941–44, which in Finland is considered to be a separate war, the so-called Continuation War, or Jatkosota: *Suomen sota 1941–1945*, vol. 6: *Toim. Puolustusvoimien pääesikunnan sotahistoriallinen toimisto* (Helsinki: Kustannusosakeyhtiö Sotateos, 1956). None of these works was ever translated into Russian.

18 See, for example, Seppälä, *Suomi Miehittäjänä 1941–1944*.

19 Seppälä's monograph was translated into Russian; see Seppälä, "Finlandiia kak Okkupant." So were research works written by Johan Bäckman, who argues that the Finnish occupation of Soviet Karelia had a "fascist" character: Bäckman, "Fashistskaia Okkupatsiia Sovetskoi Karelii." There is no Russian translation of the most objective – as is commonly accepted – research on the Finnish occupation of Soviet Karelia written by Finnish historian Antti Laine (Laine, *Suur-Suomen Kahdet Kasvot*), who does not adhere to either of the extreme positions. Yet despite a one-sided approach to the translation and publication of Finnish research about the Finnish occupation, Karelian historians are quite familiar with the whole spectre of Finnish historiography, and as a consequence, disputes about the nature of the Finnish occupation have been transferred to the Russian academic community and through it to Karelian society.

20 Regarding the rationale behind the establishment of Soviet Karelia, see Butvilo, "Formirovaniie Territorii Karelskoi"; Baron, *Soviet Karelia*; and Kangaspuro, *Neuvosto-Karjalan Taistelu Itsehallinnosta*.

21 The Institute of Demography of the Higher School of Economics (Moscow) provides the following figures for the population dynamics in Karelia: in 1926, the combined number of Finno-Ugric people (Karelians, Finns, Vepsians) in Soviet Karelia was 111,912 people, or 42 per cent of the total population: *Demoskop Weekly*, "Vsesoiuznaia perepis naseleniia 1926 goda." According to the most recent census of 2010, this combined number had dropped to 57,570, or 9 per cent of the current population of Karelia: *Demoskop Weekly*, "Vserossiiskaia perepis naseleniia 2010 g."

22 Younger generations of Karelians and Vepsians have only passive knowledge of their native languages, and the traditional cultures of their ethnic communities exist only in the form of relics, as I saw during my field trips to Karelian and Vepsian settlements. Golubev and Osipov, *Ustnaia Istoriia v Karelii*, 74–85. See also Suutari and Shikalov, *Karelia Written and Sung*.

23 See, for example, official histories of Soviet Karelia written during both Soviet and post-Soviet times, where Karelians and Vepsians exist only as passive subjects devoid of any agency or stake in their own past. Mashezerskii, *Ocherki Istorii Karelii*; Korablev et al., *Istoriia Karelii*. Russian Finns

are more visible in the writing of Soviet Karelian history for a number of reasons: first, they formed the political and economic elite of Soviet Karelia during the 1920s and early 1930s; second, as urban residents with a higher than average educational level, they have been and are highly visible in the public and academic space of Karelia, and this stimulates historical representations of their ethnic group; finally, their histories are written and thus supported by Finnish historians. See, for example, Kangaspuro, *Neuvosto-Karjalan Taistelu Itsehallinnosta*.

24 Apart from numerous newspaper and journal publications, at least four books have been published that were written or edited by members of the union or representatives of similar veterans' organizations: Kostin, *Sudba*; Lukianov, *Tragicheskoie Zaonezhie*; Kostin and Niuppieva, *Plenennoe Detstvo*; Denisevich, *V Finskom Kontslagere*.

25 Denisevich, *V Finskom Kontslagere*, 137.

26 Lukianov, *Tragicheskoie Zaonezhie*, 64.

27 Kostin and Niuppieva, *Plenennoe Detstvo*, 12–13.

28 Kostin and Niuppieva, *Plenennoe Detstvo*, 72.

29 The information about cruelties mentioned above is not supported in scholarly research about the Finnish occupation regime or in other written and oral primary sources. Moreover, in some of the cases cited, information about the Finns' crimes is noted with reservations ("people said," "rumours circulated," etc.).

30 Laine, *Suur-Suomen Kahdet Kasvot*, 92–156 (esp. 105–6).

31 Maksimova (born 1930), Interview, 81.

32 Kemliakova, Interview, 49–59.

33 Kochanova (born 1929), Interview, 133.

34 Rogozina (born 1932), Interview, 136.

35 Osipova (born 1935), Interview, 149.

36 Agapova (born 1937), Interview, 158.

37 These opinions were presented in interviews published in Golubev and Osipov, *Ustnaia Istoriia v Karelii*. The number of positive assessments of the Finnish occupation regime was – surprisingly – higher than the number of negative assessments. Possibly, this is partly because the interviewees came to realize after the war that the Nazi occupiers in other Soviet territories were much worse. To avoid accusations of bias, I stress that we published all the interviews we conducted. Also, there was no preliminary selection of interviewees – we interviewed everyone who was physically available as a witness to the Finnish occupation.

38 Laine, *Suur-Suomen Kahdet Kasvot*, 64.

39 Vladimir Mashin, "Tiazhelyi Plen Vospominani."

40 Ivan Kostin and Klavdiia Niuppieva, "Nas Zharili v Bane i Travili Izvestiu," 101–5.
41 Denisevich, *V Finskom Kontslagere*, 45.
42 Kostin and Niuppieva, "Nas Zharili v Bane," 35–8.
43 The first attempt of this kind was undertaken by me and my colleague Aleksandr Osipov, both from the Faculty of History of Petrozavodsk State University. See Golubev and Osipov, *Ustnaia Istoriia v Karelii*, in which we have published eight interviews with representatives of Finno-Ugric minorities of Karelia.
44 Over three years, especially in 2010, which marked the 65th anniversary of Victory Day, I carefully followed local TV programs on both commercial and state-owned channels, in which interviews with veterans of the Second World War were broadcast. There were at least seven interviews with former prisoners of Finnish camps, and all of the interviewees were members of the KU. Either representatives of other social groups were not interviewed or their interviews were not broadcast.
45 Baryshnikov, *Mannerheim without the Mask*; Makurov, *Voiennaia Letopis Karelii*; Iusupova, "Voiennoe Detstvo v Pamiati Pokoleniia."

PART TWO

Reclaiming the Personal: Beyond the Collective Vision of History

An important dimension of the socio-cultural changes in post-socialist Central and Eastern Europe has been the re-evaluation of the relationship between social processes and their human agents. At the core of this paradigmatic transition from socialist conceptualizations of society to post-socialist ones has been the shift in how history and society are studied. In socialist times, priority was given to the study of social processes, and those processes were understood as bringing changes to social or corporate bodies (social classes, ethnic and social minorities, rural or urban populations, etc.). The imminent collapse of socialism inspired scholars and activists to turn to examining the human dimension of these social processes. The reasons for and outcomes of this transition were discussed in the introduction to this volume. This interest in the human dimension of history led to the formulation of new goals in the humanities and social sciences of post-socialist societies. Thus, priority has been given to re-evaluating the roles that both personal and collective subjectivities have been playing in national histories. Oral history has been at the forefront of this paradigmatic change.

Post-socialist oral history is uniquely positioned not just to inform but to enable this paradigm change in post-socialist re-evaluations of the past. First, as mentioned in the introduction to this volume, its focus on individual pasts and stories, adopted from well-established oral history scholarship in the West, has legitimized those individuals as new subjects of history. That legitimization has taken place among scholars, who have adopted oral historical methods in their research, and, importantly, in the eyes of the interviewees themselves, who, rather unexpectedly for them, began to be granted more and more attention as agents of history. With the growing expansion of oral historical methods in the region among established academics, local historians, and community activists, this focus should further legitimize various alternative pasts, memories, and stories in the society at large, even though at this current juncture in history, such ongoing legitimization is being actively contested on the ground by competing ideologies (see Golubev in this volume).

Second, the collaborative nature of oral historical research, which relies on the input of both researchers and the interviewees, has allowed the latter to emerge in the writings of post-socialist oral historians not only as agents of socialist history but as active collaborators in its new representations (see Kurkowska-Budzan in this volume). This emerging trend in social sciences and humanities in the region has strong potential to change the overall culture of academic representations of history in the national academies of post-socialist states. This is because historic research in many ways continues to display a tendency towards "consumptive" scholarship, which views the living agents of social change and history more as donors of information than as research collaborators. The chapters in this section reflect the gradual emergence of this new trend in scholarly discursive practices in the region. This trend concerns the transition from purely extractive scholarship, in which the researcher takes in the interviewee's information and then produces a single-voiced researcher's narrative, towards more engaged and interactive ways of presenting research findings in which researchers' and informants' voices collaborate.

Third, with the expansion of oral historical methods into the region, new possibilities have emerged for scholars to register and differentiate between the individual and collective subjectivities that have been actively informing, through their own evolution and interplay, the narrators' views on their own lives as well as their understandings of their place in society. How do individuals born and raised in times of socialism, who are now living through profound socio-cultural transformations, construct their own accounts of their pasts and/or their own social roles in society? On what narrative means do they rely in their accounts? Given the ongoing transformations in social and cultural values, is there one particular "cultural grid" or system of cultural references and societal values responsible for sustaining collective subjectivities in their society, that underlies and holds their narratives together?

This interrelationship of private and public in personal narratives has been of interest to oral historians since their early days of practice. Inspired by the work of other social scientists on private and collective memory – and above all by the work of Maurice Halbwachs,[1] the studies of the narrative structure of the human mind offered by Jerome Bruner,[2] and the narrative principles of historic representation as discussed by Hayden White[3] – many oral historians beyond Eastern Europe have documented the relationship between individual perspectives on one's past and the narrative structures characteristic of a particular culture that inform and frame individual accounts.[4] How do oral historians in post-socialist countries explain the relationship between personal and collective subjectivities when the latter are undergoing dramatic transformations, given the ongoing cultural change in the region? How does the movement from socialism to post-socialism, however defined, inform personal narrativity and personal stories of former socialist citizens in this region? Are there any unique characteristics of this relationship in the context of post-socialism on the European continent?

The authors of the chapters in this section are united in their search for answers to the above questions, and their work serves as a superb illustration of how oral historians in Eastern Europe are seeking to document and explain post-socialist ways of narrating and reminiscing. All three scholars, while drawing from their own distinct scholarly disciplines, focus specifically on narrative means of constructing one's biography and life story, understood here as "biographic work," which they see as informed by a complex interplay between individual and collective subjectivities. Biographic work is widely used in oral historical research in Europe, informed by the work of German scholars Gabriele Rosenthal[5] and Fritz Schütze.[6] The use of this analytical tool in their own interpretations of stories unites these writers.

Yelena Rozhdestvenskaya, Russian sociologist and a leading specialist in the study of biography as social phenomenon and object of sociological analysis, lends her powerful voice to such discussion in her chapter on how Russian seniors who once were forced labourers (*Ostarbeiters*) navigate their life stories in their efforts to compensate for "biographical traumas" and "biographical gaps." Like other authors in this volume (von Plato, Witeska-Młynarczyk), Rozhdestvenskaya touches on trauma but focuses mainly on the narrative means her informers use to overcome biographical traumas. In doing so, she advances an interesting thesis: "the overcoming of trauma depends largely on the discursive accessibility of the trauma narrative and its rotation within a culture, and also on the possibility of narrator's acquisition of the status of the expert witness." Analysing interviews with former *Ostarbeiters*, she explores the narrative strategies used by her informants in their descriptions of their traumatic experiences of war and post-war times as well as their narrative efforts to create a coherent social identity for themselves. She concludes that while narrative strategies are being developed, the social rehabilitation of the former forced labourers in Russia is far from complete.

Natalia Pushkareva, a leading Russian anthropologist and a gender studies specialist, continues the discussion on the interplay of personal and collective subjectivities in oral historical interviews. Pushkareva turned to exploring this matter because she was intrigued by the question of why successful and established female academics routinely downplayed their professional successes and achievements – in other words, why their personal projections of who they are come into conflict with public understandings of who they are. Exploring the "biographical work" of Russian and Belarusian female academics, she devotes her attention to women's choices to project themselves as successful citizens of their societies or as just regular members. Analysing the narrative organization of personal life stories of female academics in Russia and Belarus, she seeks to understand what motivated female scholars to succeed in life. She also compares, however briefly, women's to men's narratives, emphasizing that in their biographical work, women do not centre their stories around their own egos as much as men normally do and that women more commonly cite other social networks and relations as important sources of their advancement in life. Of value to us is that Pushkareva's project was designed to challenge established understandings of the past as dominated by the male perspective.

Rozalia Cherepanova, a cultural historian based in Chelyabinsk, Russia, in her reflections on a recently conducted oral historical project with Russian intelligentsia, contemplates the intersections of personal and public in the life histories of her informants. She advances the claim that the public in oral historical accounts "in the end turns out to be nothing but the background for the 'cultivated the hard way' and thus deeply intimate and treasured *personal* history of oneself as a winner or a loser, a happy person or a sufferer, a hero or a victim." Informed by the debates in humanities and social sciences about the validity of subjective voices in the construction of historical and other scholarly accounts, she argues that narrators, as they narrate their stories, tacitly create for themselves new and active identities. Creating a character in a life story out of themselves, they cease to be the "ordinary," common, average citizens whose perspective was sought by the researchers in their project on how the twentieth century has been understood by ordinary Russians. Instead, they emerge as actors and agents in their biographical lives. While this claim may resonate with very many researchers outside of Eastern Europe, it is worth pointing out that such analysts' emphasis on human agency and respect for the informant's narrative self-positioning vis-à-vis "large" history is an important contribution to the historical discourse and public debate on the recent past in the Russian Federation.

NOTES

1 Halbwachs, *On Collective Memory*.
2 Bruner, *Acts of Meaning*.
3 White, *Metahistory*.
4 Vansina, *Oral Tradition as History*; Tonkin, *Narrating Our Pasts*; Cruikshank, *The Social Life of Stories*; Grele, "Movement without Aim."
5 Rosenthal, "Reconstruction of Life Stories"; Rosenthal, "Biographical Research."
6 Schütze, "Prozessstrukturen des Lebensablaufs"; Schütze, "Biographie Forschung"; Schütze, "Kognitive Figuren."

4 Restoring the Meaning: "Biographic Work" in *Ostarbeiters'* Life Stories

YELENA ROZHDESTVENSKAYA

This chapter analyses the life stories of former *Ostarbeiters*, forced labourers in Nazi Germany during the Second World War. I explore how, as they tell their life stories, they resort to unique narrative strategies directed at both narrative trauma compensation and the restoration of meaning in their lives. Such narrative "working" at one's life story often generates a sense of "non-connectivity and incompleteness." This appears to be a defining characteristic of the *Ostarbeiters'* life-story narratives, so I focus here on these narrative experiences of non-connectivity and incompleteness, my term for which is "biographical trauma." My analysis of their life stories demonstrates the destructive effects of social and historical developments on their life stories. It also reveals the biographic ruptures produced by the social and historical circumstances of narrators' lives. Finally, the analysis presents how the narrators overcame these ruptures by narrating their life stories.

The following discussion is based on in-depth interviews with former forced labourers who had been transported to Germany during the Second World War to meet the Third Reich's demand for labour. These interviews were conducted by Russian researchers as part of an international documentary project, "Forced and Slave Labour," mentioned earlier in this book by Alexander von Plato.[1]

As a part of this work, my colleagues Viktoriia Semenova, Chief Researcher at the Institute of Sociology, Russian Academy of Sciences, and Olga Nikitina, an independent researcher in Paris, along with myself, recorded thirty in-depth interviews with former *Ostarbeiters* in Pskov *oblast*, which was occupied by the Germans for over three years.[2]

The oral biographies of *Ostarbeiters*, recorded and collected using oral historical methodology, are beginning to occupy an important position in the discursive field of symbolic memory of the war in

Russia, however uneven and discordant this discursive field may seem in Russian society today. The main tasks that united the various projects conducted in different countries under the umbrella of "Forced and Slave Labour" were, first and foremost, to document the *Ostarbeiters'* experiences and, second, to archive the gathered audiovisual data. Our research team focused on three categories of former *Ostarbeiters*: (a) civilians in the occupied territories who were forcibly transported to Germany to work; (b) military personnel who became prisoners of war (POWs) and were assigned to forced labour; and (c) people who were compelled to work during the occupation where they lived.

The sociological approach required us to treat the life stories of our interviewees not only as sources of oral historical knowledge and "testimony" but also – and more importantly for our research team – as parts of life trajectories. We followed the entire lifespans of our interviewees.

A significant analytical achievement of this international project has been that it not only has documented the shared trauma of the war generation as experienced in all European societies affected by the war, but also has revealed the different social and narrative trajectories of the interviewees, who live in different societies and participate in different national histories. Not all of them could talk openly about the past, and in the former Soviet Union, the strong possibility of repression (both by the Soviet government and by society-at-large) on their return from forced labour prevented them from integrating their experiences into a collective memory. This was so until the 1990s, when former *Ostarbeiters* were able to form a socially recognizable group in post-Soviet Russia, as part of a campaign for compensation from German institutions.

The Transformation of a Subject

Let me turn to the topic of the "transformation of a subject." The collected life stories of the Russian *Ostarbeiters* are of interest to researchers because of their unique testimonial character. As such, they have much to contribute to the ongoing rewriting of the history of the war in Russia. Furthermore, from the philosophical point of view, to evoke Michael Foucault's notions of biopower and biopolitics,[3] these life stories document "biopolitical experimentation with the conditions of existence" that changed the subjects themselves by depriving them of their subjectivity, or sense of self. This process of desubjectivization is well described by the paradoxes of Primo Levi, a Jewish-Italian writer and philosopher best known for his accounts of life in the Auschwitz concentration camp. His first paradox states that "a *goner*[4] is a born-again witness," but that his/her subjectivity as a witness is split. A witness, as an ethical subject, states Levi, is a "subject without subjectivity." Levi's second paradox is that "a human is the one who can survive the human." Here Levi also offers a statement on double surviving, or outliving, which is expressed in the idea that a non-human outlives the human, and a human outlives the non-human. In other words – and this is relevant to my discussion here – the witness in *the goner* can outlive the *goner*. "What can be endlessly destroyed, can endlessly survive."[5] The fact that a witness as an ethical subject can outlive the real person of a witness is an important observation for my analysis here.

Such double survival is a sociologically important phenomenon that calls for study. According to Levi, double survival results in identity rupture. One difficulty (among many) in studying identity ruptures is related to the fact that the fear, suffering, and privations that the narrators experienced in their lives caused them to create and use "new language"[6] when they tried to relate their experiences. To understand what is being said in such life stories, one must understand the unique semiotic coding that defines the new language system as well as the psychotherapeutic nuances that accompany it. The process of narrating thus becomes a challenging act, a work of its own kind, and I refer to this act as biographic work. The biographic work the narrators perform is aimed at overcoming the experience and memory of trauma and its accompanying stigmas; these are felt by the narrators, who realize intuitively that their life stories and life trajectories are deviations from the biographical "norms" of their generation. The peculiar "repair work" of biographies can be traced at two levels – on the plane of the reconstruction of a "life path"[7] in an attempt to bring it closer to the biographic norm,[8] and on the plane of telling one's life story, as a narrative strategy for representing life events.

The Trauma and Catastrophic Experience

Allow me at this point to return to the concept of trauma. First of all, it is important to mention a terminological conflict that often arises between sociology and history. Thanks to the work of the Polish sociologist Piotr Sztompka, Russian sociologists have adopted the concept of cultural trauma for their own work.[9] Cultural trauma, as understood by Sztompka and interpreted by others, is the outcome of the collision between the values of different and incongruent social worlds. It is a massive socio-cultural crisis of basic cultural values and meanings. The previous social order and its values are subject to re-evaluation, and this leads to the loss of individual and group identities.

According to Andrei Zdravomyslov, a society can and does find in itself the strength to overcome trauma, notably by finding ways to repattern its social actions in response to the trauma; eventually, this serves as a social basis for overcoming the traumatic consciousness.[10] I would stress, however, that in addition to these cultural means of curbing the experiences of trauma, the overcoming of trauma in the society depends heavily on the ready accessibility of trauma discourses and narratives and their circulation within a culture, as well as on the possibility for the narrator to be granted the status of an expert witness. Thus, *Schindler's List*[11] is inaccessible to external analysis, in the sense that such analysis is reserved for the cultural memory of the ethnic community that survived Shoah. That is the group that can use the book for the purposes of collective identification. This overcoming of a trauma – a kind of counter-trauma – poignantly illustrates the ambiguity of the trauma itself. It preserves the information about the trauma – or, rather, the collective narrative about the trauma – together with the inevitable victimization.

The sociological view of group trauma takes into account the post-traumatic social situation. That situation reveals itself as the plane of future actions (which are either possible or impossible in the aftermath of trauma), that is, as the presence (or marked absence) of a shared collective narrative about the trauma. The post-traumatic situation enters the structure, together with narrative methods of its delivery; it also mobilizes the biographic resources for overcoming traumatic experience.

I share the position of Sztompka and Zdravomyslov, especially their emphasis on the importance of biographic material, qualitative data gathering (including interviews), and the analysis of life stories about socially constructed trauma and its overcoming. But in the context of sociological research, the concept of trauma needs some further decoding and deciphering. Current understandings of trauma *can* be satisfactory if we ignore or distance ourselves from the inevitable subjectivity of the narrators – a subjectivity that is usually concealed by their own narrative rationalizing. Those concealed aspects include the loss of meaning (e.g., a crisis of the relations between the past and the present that devalues the past, or a particular experience that destroys the very possibility of its interpretation) and the loss of semantic coherence of constructed biographies.[12] These issues, as empirically accessible phenomena, reveal themselves in biographic gaps, that is, in the narrators' inability to tie together all phases of their life path in one coherent space; this brings about the collapse of the narrative, with its subsequent and inevitable fragmentation, lacunae, figures of silence(ing), and other narrative strategies. In this sense, narrative identity, within which the "repairs" of a biography are taking place, is an important field of analysis of the resources used by the narrators for the most important task in their lives – assembling and putting their selves together.

As I pointed out earlier, the concept of trauma is linked to the catastrophic experience. What is meant by this? In the following analysis of *Ostarbeiters'* biographies, I rely partly on the cultural anthropological approach of Jörn Rüsen to the study of the crisis of historic memory, a crisis that emerges when the historic consciousness collides with an experience that goes far beyond the boundaries of the idea of the socio-historic norm and hence is labelled a catastrophic experience. For Rüsen, the emergence of the interest in microhistory – and of localized experiences and biographies in particular – demonstrates that both academics and non-academics are paying increasing attention to how people perceive and interpret their own worlds and socio-cultural environs. This attention involves what he calls "the penetration into the consciousness of the studied people," which scholars undertake in an effort to restore people's own cultural autonomy with respect to their own perceptions of their world, distinct from the world of the researchers and other outsiders.[13] Asserting the methodological rationality of such an approach, he writes that "there is no memory that absolutely does not aspire to be truth-like, and this aspiration rests on two elements: the trans-subjective elements of the experience and the intersubjective element of the consensus agreement."[14] If memory is a fixed and reproduced experience transmitted in group and family narratives, then intersubjectivity is yet another dimension of history and historical meanings. History is unthinkable without its acceptance by those to whom it is addressed. However, Rüsen continues, history's truth-likeness does not depend solely on how it relates to real experiences. It also depends on how it treats norms and values shared in the community to which this history is addressed."[15] Thus, history depends on discursive rules that inform the intersubjective agreement.

So I approach the collected biographies of *Ostarbeiters* as a space of the traumatized and, may I add, of ruptured and incoherent social identity. On the one hand, these biographies are under the imminent pressure of the crisis of meaning imposed on them by the discursive norms and rules of the society-at-large. These discursive rules gloss over and ignore the intersubjective agreement achieved by other social groups of former Soviet society regarding the social place and role of *Ostarbeiters* and the evaluation and acceptance of their post-war narrative. On the other hand, from the point of view of the narrators themselves, the catastrophic experience they lived through cannot be assigned any meaning.[16] As such, they must disown it through (a) escape into various forms of group or collective narrating, (b) story fragmentation, and (c) omission and silence.

Ostarbeiters' Biographies: Collective and Individual Experience and the Category "We"

The above reference to escape into a form of group or collective narrative means that the narrator chooses to speak about his or her experiences in terms of their being not just part of a group experience but *only* a group or collective experience; there is no personal story, there is a story about *us* and what happened to *us*. The collective or group experience is then typically conveyed through the constant use of the collective pronouns *we/us*. These pronouns identify the collective protagonist of stories and act as figurative language scaffolding, projecting a particular image of the social environs of the narrator and establishing the boundaries of his or her social self. Consider the narrative of Nikolai Zaitsev. Mr Zaitsev received the Order of Glory medal for his actions in the war, and after the war he enjoyed a successful career as a civil engineer reconstructing the Soviet economy. Having fallen in love while in the labour camp, he attempted to escape; he was caught and sent to another camp, from which he also managed to escape. He was reunited with his wife and her child after the war. In the following extract from an interview with Nikolai, "we" semantically transforms itself into "us" through the use of subjective verbs.[17] This creates an image of repressive social order, of the faceless, machine-like nature of the events.

> They led us to the entrance of the concentration camp Gross Rosen. Over the gate there was a big poster: "to each – his own." They counted us, one team of guards handed us to another and we were convoyed across the territory. So we reached the first barrack. It was called the sanitary barrack. There was a hall, we were undressing ourselves until we were naked and throwing our clothes into a pile ... They shaved us and cut our hair. And when we had go to the washing rooms, there were controllers, already standing and watching, checking on us, how we were shaven, and how our hair was cut. And if these controllers did not like something, they beat us up right there and sent us back to the barbers. They would come and say that something is not shaven well enough. They would also throw a tantrum and beat us up, but after that they would finish cutting hair and shaving ... We waited for a very long time for them to turn on the water, then suddenly they turned it on, everybody started washing, soaping themselves and momentarily that water was turned off. And those who hadn't finished washing themselves, went to the dressing room not entirely washed, and there we were given white long underwear with black and blue stripes and a robe. So, in such a condition, in the cold, they took us to Block #9. There we lay on our sides, then the drover would beat, with a stick, those lying so that they would move. And when he was beating the last person, a certain territory was freed, vacated, and those who did not have any space at all were ordered to lie down in that space. And so we were lying, all squeezed up, one by another, and at 5 a.m. there was a wake-up.[18]

The following stories narrated by three women demonstrate the difference between collective and individual kinds of narration. Collective experiences facilitate the output of collective grand narratives. Deviations from these produce difficulties of narrativization and appropriate legitimization of experiences.

Raissa Kriukova: "I just wouldn't remember my number ..."

Raissa Kriukova was born on the outskirts of Pskov in 1926 and deported to Germany in March 1943 when she was seventeen, together with her parents and a younger brother. On their arrival, after two weeks in the barracks, the family was placed in prison. Sometime later, they were transported to Lauterwerk, 60 kilometres from Dresden, to an aluminium plant. They all worked there, except for her three-year-old brother, who stayed in the barracks. She remembers permanent hunger and weariness:

> The place was called Lauterwerk, and there was an aluminium plant nearby. Lots of people died there. The aluminium was heated up and was flowing along the gutter. So, my father would stand on a very narrow platform, and since everybody's hungry, if your head spun, you'd fall down into this aluminium. And would get boiled there ... As for me, I was sitting at the little table, there was a circular saw on it ... We sawed aluminium plates and then stamped what we got. They said it was for planes, but I don't know exactly, they'd just have us do it ... My finger ... I fell asleep at the table, and it was caught into the saw ... They gave us clothes at the plant, to those who dealt with the fusion, such rough tarpaulin grey pants and a jacket. We also had chains with metal plates with our numbers on them. On the sleeve, there was the sign "Ost" in blue. Eastern workers. I just wouldn't remember my number. My father's number began with one thousand, and then I don't remember. When we had to go to work we put these plates on the chest, when we came back, it was according to our numbers.[19]

Mrs Kriukova told her story without much emotion, so there was an impression that she had chosen a form for the story that would be least traumatic for her. Her past is closed in terms of feelings. She answered questions about her present-day life more eagerly. This form of story is typical of a collective narrative told with the help of the first person plural "we." All the residents on their street were deported, forced to work, then liberated. Shared hardships and material losses all find a place in such stories.

Ostarbeiters' narratives include another kind of story, which I refer to as the "constructed" collective narrative. In these, there are hidden individual meanings, with the "hero" playing some active role that involves confronting or overcoming challenges presented to her. These constructed narratives developed during the post-war years, when *Ostarbeiters* returning to the Soviet Union were forced to tell their stories to KGB agents. Later, these constructed narratives were rewritten and reconstructed in a new social and cultural context. In such stories, even the ones shared with our researchers only recently, one can track earlier models of self-justification.

The Story of Liubov Terekhova, a Teacher in the Occupied Territory

During the occupation, Mrs Terekhova, born in 1921, stayed as a teacher in the same village near Pskov but was also asked to work as an interpreter, because she could speak German. She had to accompany a person who recruited workers to be sent to Germany. She visited those workers' homes. As for herself, she persuaded the Germans not to deport her, because of her health problems. In fact (and this was the beginning of the conversation), she suffered from long, heavy, and painful menstruations, during which she had to stay in bed. She managed to remain in the village until 1944. When the Russian army was about to come, she and other teachers were put on a truck, which was in the middle of a motorized column. "We were hostages, maybe to scare away the partisans," she remembered. In her version of events, the commandant was saving those whose houses he had stayed in, although this is doubtful. For after they left, the remaining villagers were marched in a column out of the village, ordered to run away, and when they did, were shot in the back. Thus, Mrs Terekhova, although she knows she is not at fault, feels guilty and suffers from her inability to find vindication:

> I can't explain to everyone in the village that I did not leave by my own will. That commandant, he took everybody ... because he knew there would be a catastrophe after they left. So he was saving those people, maybe trying to soothe his conscience or something like that.[20]

Mrs Terekhova's story also illustrates how a person in her position had to make difficult individual decisions and how unique one's own destiny can be:

> Well ... I don't want to tell about certain things ... In a nutshell, our way back was hard ... I don't want to remember it ... Our soldiers gave us a lift, they saw we were walking at night in a forest and they had a car ... But then they started to behave badly towards us. So we got from the car and said, "No, we won't go with you," and walked on in the forest all by ourselves ... [Later, during the filtration period,] they tried [to sexually harass us] ... Oh they really tried ... those in command, at that. No soldier would propose that, not a single one.[21]

Mrs Terekhova's story, then, revolves around her own experiences and as such does not have the support of a collective narrative. So she has constructed her own interpretations of past events. She and others came across Soviet soldiers several more times, and these, by contrast, were empathetic. But when she returned to Pskov, she was often interrogated by the NKVD, and there she had to give in to the officers' sexual harassment. After the war, Mrs Terekhova never worked as a teacher again, for teachers in the occupied territories or who had been prisoners of war were all removed from their positions by the Soviet authorities. In 1945 she married a war veteran who worked as a driver. They had four children, two of whom died at a young age.

The Story of Ekaterina Shipova, a Former Prisoner of War

Ekaterina Shipova's reflections on her life during and after the war offer another example of how *Ostarbeiters* do biographic work and construct their narratives. Mrs Shipova was born in 1924. After being transported to Germany, she worked in a rubber factory in Trier. Eventually, she was taken as a prisoner of war and placed in the infamous POW camp of Sychevka, which the Nazis had built in the occupied Smolensk *oblast*. At one point in her life story, she focused on one incident that remained vivid in her memory and proved to be of great importance when it came to her life story. The story, presented below, is an example of how a gesture of charity coming from a German woman was interpreted as God's Providence:

> But once ... You know, I got to believe in God after that. Once, after a long working day I felt really bad, thought I wouldn't survive ... When it finished, everybody went to toilet rooms, and I stayed with my back to the wall. I had no strength to move, thought I was dying. Please, help me, God! At that point, a German woman working by one table passed by, the one who worked at the table with me. She rarely talked with me, probably it wasn't permitted. But there she says, "I left you a sandwich, did you take it?" I said, "No. Where?" She says, "Here," and I see the sandwich, a German one, small. I hadn't seen it! And this sandwich helped me. That's a destiny.[22]

After the camp was liberated, she was constantly on the move, running from offers to combine work with the role of an informer. She had attracted the KGB's attention several times in her life. She does not have a family, as she could not overcome the deep trauma of a failed relationship with a Soviet officer back in Germany, who left her because he was afraid of jeopardizing his military career by attracting "bad biographical data" (i.e., about a wife who had been a POW).

Contextualizing Individual Experiences

Each particular experience that constituted a separate story, or a fragment of the overall life story of an *Ostarbeiter*, must be seen and understood in the context of its time and place. *Ostarbeiters'* experiences are often comparable to the experiences of those who were forcibly transported to labour camps, where workers faced hunger, exploitation, and high levels of control. In addition, poverty and survival practices were comparable across the prewar, war, and post-war years, almost merging these distinct periods into a single extended one. Against this background, the devaluing of human life was not sudden; instead, it was constant and "habitual." Ekaterina Aleksandrova remembered:

> When our liberators came, they right away started to treat us like bullies. Well, we were in one house. So once, at night, they came to our room. Our one bed stood here, like that, there were two guys sleeping, and on the other one slept me together with that one woman, there was one woman there. So they go: "Hey," they say "Move!" to us, "Move! Here, with Germans, did you not have a good time? And what about us, you're pushing us away?" We jumped off the bed. The guys are still lying there, not even moving. They know that those men are armed. Well, so we stayed like that for a while, they were shy, probably, of the guys, so they left later. "Alright! We'll arrange for you … a queue …"[23]
>
> And so when we came home, here a different kind of work began. This was September, when vegetables begin, barges. That is, they began to send us to unload the barges. And when winter came – to the forest to saw wood. Because everything had to be rebuilt. In the forest, I got a cold, fell ill, I had boils, fever – nothing, they didn't recognize [these things], go, go and work! And the doctors didn't recognize either, that there was fever – go to the forest and work! In my opinion, even the livestock was not treated like we were … They considered us traitors, enemies.[24]

Mrs Kriukova, whose story was cited earlier, spoke in the following terms about returning home from the camp:

> And in our house there were some people living already. And when we came, we warned them that we were coming, so [they would] vacate our space. "What [do you mean, that] we go to a shed or something? You had no business kicking around in Germany!" [pause] Russian people. The compassionate ones [with bitterness].[25]

Another narrator, Nina Danilova, talked about how she returned from the camp to her home village after the war:

> And when we came home, there wasn't a single house, everything was laced with landmines. Several people blew up while we walked somehow those seven kilometres to our Kuprovshchina, and we moved into the *sel'sovet*[26] – ten families or however many, in one room, we were. So we're sleeping and huge rats are biting us, we're crying, we're scared ... But, glory to God, we're home, we're in our motherland. So we started living like that. Papa was still in the hospital ...
>
> Later, after six months, papa came home. And we, my brother, myself, started working at a collective farm. But it was impossible, all fields were land-mined, later we learned ... They ... showed us how to defuse the mines, and we defused them on our own. We collected dynamite ... in our village, eh ... By Germans ... were built some bunkers. We needed logs to build some sort of a little house. So we would blow everything up, dig out with shovels, tie a rope, and pull those logs ... to the house. Well, we hadn't built a house, but brought a lot of logs ...
>
> No shoes to put on, no clothes – nothing! And we had to attend school ... We had to walk two and a half kilometres there. Mama gave us long johns. She would roll some rags, then – these felt boots, so that was the only clothing ... So. I am reaching the Isakovshina village, and there my brother meets me, takes off my shoes ... And I run just in these foot wraps ... And it was cold – thirty degrees and colder. And one time I wasn't able to run to the village, fell in the snow. So, there was a woman going by, from that same village, she picked me up, she saved me.[27]

Testimony

Primo Levi, Giorgio Agamben, and others have postulated with regard to the survivors of the concentration camps that a correlation exists between the determination to survive and the willingness to offer a witness account.[28] Scholars have pointed out that witnesses' narratives of what happened has an important function, which is to give value and meaning to their experiences. The survivor's calling is to remember – indeed, he is unable *not* to do so.[29] Addressing this task through narration, former prisoners, who had been degraded to the level of objects of violence, partly regained their selves, their own subjectivity. One must remember here that deniers' and revisionists' discussions of the

Holocaust unfold against the background of established legal discourses regarding the past and memories of the Holocaust that have already established the range of legal responsibilities as well as the spectre of evaluations of Holocaust crimes. In the context of such developments, what is the function of a (former) Soviet *Ostarbeiter*'s story about his or her own past? It is not easy to identify this function. Neither Soviet nor (later) Russian official discourses in history and humanities acknowledged those who worked for the "nation's enemy." This setting apart of an entire category of people was never reversed in Soviet times. Having fallen through the cracks of official scholarly discourses on history of the war, *Ostarbeiters'* stories could never be integrated into the post-war Soviet Union's grand narratives on "how we (the Soviet people) forged the Victory" or "how we heroically worked on the home front for the Victory." As a consequence, silencing, biographic gaps, and the disownment of important segments of one's earlier life that would have otherwise been important resources of self-identity were the primary means by which the narrators communicated their own stories of living through the war and beyond. This is how Ekaterina Aleksandrova, whose story we referenced earlier, described her strategy of silence:

> [I] didn't tell. My girlfriend knew, of course, but in general, I told nobody that I was in Germany. Later, they began to talk about that. But before – not a sound to anyone.[30]

Most of the narrators began talking about their experiences of forced labour only in the 1990s, with the onset of the compensation campaign launched by the German government at the time. Prior to this, they had not spoken about their experiences even to their close relatives – husbands, wives, and children. This non-sharing affected the interviews we recorded for our research project. During those interviews, narratives often underwent a degree of inversion, manifested by the narrators' attempts to tell only about the war and the camp while omitting descriptions of childhood and post-war life. All this speaks to the narrators' inability to connect normal life *before* the traumatic event with life's normalization *after* the event. From the interview of Mr Zaitsev:

INTERVIEWER: Please, Nikolai Dmitrievich, I'm listening. When were you born, where, how old are you?

RESPONDENT: I was drafted into the army on the 20th of June 1941 …

I: Nikolai Dmitrievich, when were you born? Let's start from the moment of your birth, from your childhood. Before the army, there had been life, yes?

R: I was born on the 26th of July 1922 in the village of Lokhnovo in the Pskov region. When I was two years old, my parents moved to the city. Father worked as a shoemaker … We lived … by the hotel Oktyabr'skaya on the first floor. There was a bookstore and we were right by, we were friends … There were four of us, friends-comrades. So two of us were drafted into the army on the 20th of June 1941.[31]

From the interview with Mrs Kriukova:

> What about childhood? Well, in childhood I … But I really don't remember much, remember just school. Over there, where the post office is now, there was a school, four grades. Later, I had to transfer over there, near the train station, there was the School #9, there I studied till the beginning of war. Exactly in June the war began, when I had my finals.[32]

Problems of Narrativization

Scholars, analysing interviews with the survivors of traumatic events (Shoah, the concentration camps, the repression) long ago noticed that victims of oppression find it hard to assemble and articulate their life stories or to make sense of the events in their lives related to oppression.[33] Also, as narrators they rarely use strategies of distancing themselves from the terrible experiences. Many speakers rely on silencing, on omissions, yet still have the desire to tell their stories anyway, to share them. The difficulties they have telling their stories after many years of silence create lacunae determined by the experiences of traumatization. Their difficulty in telling their stories is also related to the fact that they have not yet formed a complete understanding of what they experienced.

As we have seen so far, the fragmentation of their stories is a consequence of their traumatic experiences and their shattered integrity and continuity. Their experiences have shattered their consciousness as well as their sense that the different phases of their lives are connected. As a result, whole periods of their lives may go mute. Storytelling, itself is a form of expression, may be bypassed altogether. A "saving" structure of presentation is often invented in its place. First, the narrators describe the beginning of the war and the traumatic time itself. Then they move on to talk about the liberation period. The post-war years are presented as relatively uneventful. However, omission or silencing may affect all temporal modalities of the story: the times of "before," "during," and "after" the trauma. Their difficulty in recounting their childhood derives from their difficulty in trying to integrate stories from that time into their biographies, since they view their earlier lives as broken, or shattered. In terms of Gestalt, they cannot integrate the form, content, and pattern of their prewar experiences with the form, content, and pattern of their post-war lives, because nothing connects the two, no connective lines exist. Another reason for the loss of complete life stories is that the time before the trauma has been idealized, so that all emotions, acts, and thoughts related to that time have been distorted.[34] Idealizations of happy times, of wonderful, loving parents and siblings, may lead the narrators to avoid stories that might destroy those idealizations. This is evidenced in the interviews we conducted that touched on prewar childhood. From the interview with Nina Danilova:

> We were six children, there ... Our parents were very good, especially papa and mama ... in general, very good parents ... We had a very good house. A *piatistenka* house.[35] There were nine of us children, three died ... Because we didn't have time to look after them, we had to work, because there were a lot of children and we had to do many things at home. We did everything, they made us do everything, made us wash clothes, we did all ... Well, in general, my childhood, really, I cannot ... And so in the evening, what parents gave us, we would do – so we earned right to go sometimes for a walk, here ... And if we haven't done what we were told, then we'd be doing it until it's done. It is because we had to help our parents.[36]

Incoherence of Biographies as the Problem, Solved by Narrators

Not all narrators failed to integrate their prewar lives with their post-war life experiences. Those who did achieve that integration in their life stories had developed and established in their narratives effective links and threads between their prewar and post-war life experiences. Thus, in the preceding narrative and the one that follows, both contextually (i.e., in context of work and making a living) and intentionally (i.e., oriented towards achieving the common good of the family with many children), the narratives have been tied together to achieve a certain coherence of meaning. That connection emphasizes the continuity of traditional peasant values such as respect for parental authority. At the same time, there are examples of discontinuity. The following interview segment reflects the weakening of parental control over the lives of adult children caused by improved education, urbanization, and work migration. From the interview with Mrs Danilova:

> Well, I was already reaching many years, I was pushing twenty-five, yes … Also, I had absolutely no clothes to get married. What was I earning? And whatever kopecks I made, right away: "Mama … Mommy, take all the money, to the last kopeck" … For the first time in my life, my … parents allowed. I wanted a watch, so much … So I am saying: "Let me buy a watch." And so they let me. So, when I bought the watch, "Zaria," I remember still, they served me for a long, long time. I admired them day and night … So, well, such was our life …
>
> I [was] thinking: "My Lord, when I finally have children, when will they start earning? They will bring me money, I'll have so much money … Like that. And I waited for nothing. Everyone flew away – one daughter got married, the other one …[37]

Allow me to elaborate on several narrative solutions the narrators used when building their biographies. Typically, the interviewees chose the following narrative methods to deliver their traumatic biographies: complete silence about the past sustained for an extended period; partial omission of its parts; and dechronologization of their biographies to the point of eliminating entire periods of their lives. Although they came across as passive withdrawal from their biographies, these narrative solutions presented an important set of social acts.[38] Those acts relied on *anonymization*, *compensation*, and *hyper-compensation*, all directed at normalization and the overall restoration of the biography's integrity. Let us consider those strategies.

Normalization is the effort to realign the individual biography with the imagined social biographic norm. In male biographies recorded for our project, normalization was realized through the narrator's efforts to "add on," that is, enhance his or her war/military and employment experiences. In female biographies, the life story emerged as a story of marriage, revolving around a change in surname and the birth of children. Commonly, the story was "stained" by the fact that the narrator had worked in Germany and experienced state-imposed restrictions on future employment after returning to the Soviet Union.

Two men's biographies, one of which we considered earlier (Mr Zaitsev), relied on the strategy of normalizing one's military heroism during the war.[39] This presentation "overwrote" the stigma of captivity. As a soldier, Zaitsev had committed a heroic act and had been awarded the Order of Glory, 3rd Class. In his biography, he recounted many important "normative" threads in the standard biography of his generation: the taking of Berlin, a career in *Oblkomkhoz*,[40] reconstruction work. Yet even his military achievements did not protect him from reproaches: "[I was] reproached by my own employees, because of envy, probably, because I was a POW and now suddenly I have such a position – I don't even want to recollect this."

The second "male" biography, of Mrs Kriukova's father, provides another example of normalization. It revolves around conscription into the army, which can be viewed as participation in the military, even if as a home front worker. The status of belonging to the military allowed Mrs Kriukova's father to reach the end of war while still in military service, as opposed to being a forced labourer. As such his biography ends with military (normative) rather than labour camp experience.

The following segment from Mrs Kriukova's interview deals with her return to the motherland and her father's conscription into the army:

> Two lieutenants drove to us, one was so mean, said that "Hey, [you] went to work for Germans?" The second one began talking to father, said, "You know what, daddy, leave," he says, "go as far as you can. Because," he says, "we'll retreat, and you'll be again under the Germans." So we went for a kilometre or so along the road, because here people walk on the shoulders without end. And then one military man approaches us and says "Daddy-o, what is your year of birth?" He told him what his year of birth was, and so he says, "You will have to walk under a yoke for a while ..." And he was drafted to the army. And so the three of us remained.[41]

Women's biographies, exemplified here by the interview with Liubov Terekhova, often refer to the experience of dealing with the prohibition against professional employment[42] and with marriage and children as a strategy of carving out a life for oneself. From the interview with Mrs Terekhova, a teacher in an occupied village:

> We did not even take each other's addresses, because after the war we did not try to look for one another ... The war had to end and do not remind us anymore ... Later, how to say, everyone who was in occupation, all teachers were fired, so I was kicked out on account of that occupation. Of course,

> they made up a different reason: they did not put it down straight. Well, after that I did not pursue a teaching career anymore. Later, I got married here, and later yet I went to work as a secretary in various offices.[43]

The strategy of *anonymization*, too, was well represented in our project interviews. *Anonymization* here relates to various means of avoiding possible repression in Stalin's Russia. These included labour migration, the manipulation of documents (i.e., their "loss" and replacement), hiding or omitting biographical facts, and, again, "marriage." Consider the following fragment from the interview with Yevgeniia Mikhailova about her work biography and migration:

> In the city, of course, it was easier, you lay low, nobody was asking ... You don't talk – so you don't talk about that ... Four grades I have finished, that's it, afterwards one must work, had to help mama, we had to pay taxes for everything. Such were the taxes that ... whether you keep a hen or don't – you have to bring eggs, a specific number, wool you had to bring, milk from a cow ... So much potatoes, so much garlic ... And monetary tax on top of that ... It was a nightmare. And so I went to work in a brick factory, still a girl. Turned fifteen, worked the second season – they gave me a certificate, and I got a worker's passport. Later, I got recruited to Leningrad, to a construction site. I worked there for three years, then, when the recruitment contract was over ... I went to a factory.[44]

The strategy of *compensation* is exemplified by the search for a cultural niche either through employment and a career or simply through status that would allow one to maintain a sustained dialogue about one's past experiences. Compensatory strategies can be direct, from organizing a cultural association of people of similar experiences (e.g., a society of camp inmates) to organizing a literary-historical society, or they can be indirect.

One of our respondents was Georgii Kozhevnikov, a chairman of the Pskov Society for the Inmates of Concentration Camps. While still a child, he was transported to the Sachsenhausen camp. These days, with his wife, he does community work, organizing meetings and helping his comrades. His activities are ultimately commemorative ones of the sort that occupy an ambiguous niche in the public discourse on war in Russia, especially when compared to the work of the government-endorsed Society of Veterans of the Great Patriotic War. The members of the Pskov society include poets, essayists, historians, and ethnographers. These people are able to translate their biographic experience into literary forms, which serve to distance them from what they experienced and thereby allow them to achieve symbolic acknowledgment.

Hyper-compensation, another normalization strategy, involves reprocessing the past, adopting a different social role in one's life course and biography, and identifying with the oppressive structures. An example of this strategy was discovered by accident. From one of our female respondents, a member of the Pskov Society for the Inmates of Concentration Camps, we learned about her neighbour, a woman with a life experience similar to that of an *Ostarbeiter*. After telephoning her to arrange an interview, we visited her house to conduct it. An elderly woman, she had recently suffered a stroke and a broken arm. After she filled out the consent form, we got ready to start, but she refused to continue and attempted to give back the modest gifts we had brought with us. No interview was conducted, and no narrative was recorded, but we managed to gather a certain biographic construct, a life course, that partly explained her unwillingness to cooperate. We learned that Mariia Ivanova had been transported to Germany at the age of nineteen, where she worked for three years as a welder at a military plant near Dresden. After Germany's "liberation" by Soviet forces, she did not return to Pskov; instead, she wrote to her girlfriend from the camp and went to the gold mines in the north of Russia, where she worked as a security guard, guarding the inmates who extracted gold. While there, she met her husband, who was also a guard. They never had children. Nearing her retirement, after the death of her husband, she finally returned to her hometown. Her reluctance to talk about her life experiences confirms that an inversion of roles (victim/oppressor) and personally pursued devictimization had indeed taken place.

To summarize: silencing, partial omissions of the past, dechronologization, and fragmentation all served our narrators as narrative solutions to "delivering" the traumatized biography. These strategies of normalization represent the "realized trajectories" of narrators' life courses. In Rüsen's set of strategies of detraumatization,[45] we find another discursive means of overcoming the consequences of traumatic experience: the placing of traumatic events in a different historical context. These approaches include anonymization of the perpetrator of violence, moralization, aesthetization, teleologization, historical reflection, and specialization (understood as segmentation of the issue according to the interests of different interpreters). The results of our research partly point to the presence of the strategy of categorization when the trauma, shared by many, is discursively converted into the category of "privation." Our narrators relied on normalization understood in a such a way that they perceived traumatizing events as inevitable and repetitive. In general, I agree with Rüsen that historical research is a cultural practice of detraumatization, in that it converts trauma into history,[46] but this concept is viable only within the domain of public discourse and is less applicable, if at all, to the internal discourses of closed social groups who have had traumatic experiences. By contrast, the narrative strategies of our narrators have evolved over the course of my exposure to their narratives (between 2000 and 2006),[47] from silence to partial omission to partial articulation. This indicates the narrators' partly restored self-identity. The collective narrative of the *Ostarbeiters* is being circulated *within* their community as part of commemorative practices; they are unable to overcome the public's apathy towards their stories in Russian society today.

The conversion of our respondents' wartime suffering into monetary compensation could have opened new possibilities for their efforts to overcome, narratively and otherwise, the stigmas and injustices of the past. But the process of documenting the past experiences of *Ostarbeiters* that took place in Russian society was not the same as in other places. It did not extend beyond the creation of personal files that confirmed the identity and the fact of being subjected to forced labour in Germany, and it did not lead to new, normative public interpretations of the past. If this had happened in Russia, it might have led to the public rehabilitation of *Ostarbeiters* in the minds of Russians. But as we heard in our interviews, the compensation for forced labour was never transformed into broader social rehabilitation; it remained strictly monetary. In Pskov, where the interviews were recorded, only one social outcome grew out of the compensation process: a small parcel of land was set aside by the city administration for the Society of Former Young Prisoners of Concentration Camps.

Our respondents were dissatisfied with the amount of compensation to cover the losses and sufferings they experienced as forced labourers, and they held the Germans responsible for all those injustices. Interestingly, through their silence, the respondents seemed to be assigning the guilt for their post-war stigmatization and marginalization to those who were compensating them now. Since no public discourse has accompanied the compensation process in Russia, so as to identify the individual and collective responsibility of states and their agents, that compensation has not been processed in Russian society in symbolic terms and is not experienced as social rehabilitation, especially considering that the monetary sums are minimal and the problems these monies could have helped address are extensive.

One reason for this is that official discourses that have evolved in Germany over many years in relation to war compensation have served an important cultural and political purpose in post-war German society. The compensation discourse in Germany has contributed directly to public re-evaluations of that country's Nazi past. That discourse, with its orientation towards *German* society and the problems of *German* history, simply did not have comparable grounds to evolve in the *Russian* context. As a result, in Russia, the discursive "discovery" of the category of Russian *Ostarbeiters* has not translated into the discovery of new subjects of history. The oral history interviews we have recorded in Russia have not become public documents of the past, at least not yet.

NOTES

1 This international project, organized and coordinated by the Institute of History and Biography of Hagen University (Germany) with the support of the foundation "Memory and the Future," is discussed in von Plato, Leh, and Thonfeld, *Hitlers Sklaven.*

2 Owing to its somewhat fringe location (it borders Estonia and Latvia in the West and Belarus in the south), the Pskov region was occupied soon after the war began, on 9 July 1941. The occupation continued until 22 July 1944.

3 Foucault, *Society Must Be Defended.*

4 *Goner* is used here to represent the original Russian terms "dohodiaga" and "musulmanin." In her dissertation on Gulag terms in Solzhenitsyn's writing, Elena Kharitonova translates *dohodiaga* as "goner, last-legger" ("Perevod Russkoi Lagernoi Leksiki"). However, both Russian terms have a much more precise meaning than the English term. Both refer to the context of the "not quite" death camp, where mass executions were rarely conducted but where the basic needs for life were grossly insufficient for survival, so that a significant part of the camp population died out, to be replenished by new arrivals. Thus the term "dohodiaga" referred to the part of the camp's population that was dying or likely to die soon. These people, however, received no medical care. Like everyone else, they did hard labour, etc. (translators' note).

5 Quoted in Dubin, "Chto Ostaetsia ot Aushvitsa."

6 *Novoiaz* in Russian (editors' note).

7 *Zhyznennyj put'* in Russian (editors' note).

8 The reconstruction of the biographic norm results from the narrators' efforts to articulate their biographies for the purpose of either giving the sequence of biographic events a typical/standard character or attempting to camouflage events in their lives that are impossible to convert. Thus, the structure of the ethno-methodological order becomes transparent once we discover the strategies of its restoration. Using our representational sample, we can reconstruct the biographic norm as being settled, as loyal to a chosen and common profession, as stable relative to the social context, as mediocre (in the sense of being "in the middle of the Bell curve"), as having a complete/standard and ethnically homogenous family, and as following norms of health, well-being, and behaviour. See Meshcherkina, "Struktura Zhenskoi Biografii."

9 Sztompka, "Sotsialnoe Izmenenie kak Travma."

10 Zdravomyslov, "Troistvennaia Interpretatsiia Kultury," 10.

11 *Schindler's List* refers to the list of people saved from the Holocaust by Oscar Schindler, a German businessman who employed the Jews in his factories in an effort to save them from death (editors' note).

12 "Coherence" is understood as the creation of a coherent image on the basis of autobiographic recollections and the biographic perspective on one's own past. In a general sense, it includes temporal continuity as well as the synchronization of the images of Self and the actions of a narrator in different spheres and periods of life; see Rozhdestvenskaya, "Narrativnaia Identichnost."

13 Rüsen, "Utrachivaia Posledovatelnost Istorii," 12.

14 Rüsen, "Utrachivaia Posledovatelnost Istorii," 13.

15 Rüsen, "Utrachivaia Posledovatelnost Istorii," 13.

16 Here we are not taking into account the category of "outplacedness" (*vnenahodimost'*) of Mikhail Bakhtin as a meaning-bearing construct of exit into beyond, or transcendence, and its religious version in the search of justification of the meaning of life that is also outside of life – namely, in faith. See Frank, "Smysl Zhizni."

17 The Russian language relies far more heavily than English on passive verbal constructions to communicate situations in which external circumstances dictate the action. For example, where the English would say "I have guests," Russians would say "the guests came to me" or "guests are at my place" (editors' note).

18 Nikolai Zaitsev (born 1922), interview by Yelena Rozhdestvenskaya, Pskov *oblast*, Russia, July 2005.

19 Raissa Kriukova (born 1926), interview by Yelena Rozhdestvenskaya, Pskov *oblast*, Russia, July 2005.

20 Liubov Terekhova (born 1921), interview by Yelena Rozhdestvenskaya, Pskov *oblast*, Russia, July 2005.

21 Terekhova, interview.
22 Ekaterina Shipova (born 1924), interview by Yelena Rozhdestvenskaya, Pskov *oblast*, Russia, July 2005.
23 The allusion is unclear. Most likely, he is threatening the women with group rape (editors' note).
24 Ekaterina Aleksandrova (born 1926), interview by Yelena Rozhdestvenskaya, Pskov *oblast*, Russia, July 2005.
25 Kriukova, interview.
26 The Village Council, the main administrative office in a rural community in Soviet times (editors' note).
27 Nina Danilova (born 1932), interview by Yelena Rozhdestvenskaya, Pskov *oblast*, Russia, July 2005.
28 Agamben, *Homo sacer*, 203; Levi, *Kanuvshie i Spasennye*, 179–207.
29 Quoted in Dubin, "Chto Ostaetsia ot Aushvitsa."
30 Aleksandrova, interview.
31 Zaitsev, interview.
32 Kriukova, interview.
33 Rosenthal, *Erlebte und Erzaehlte Geschichte*.
34 Rosenthal, *Erlebte und Erzaehlte Geschichte*, 70.
35 A *piatistenka* house, or house of five walls, has a (fifth) wall dividing it into two separate quarters. In the traditional Russian village, such a house stands as a potent representation of an "established," prosperous, and "fertile" household (translator's note).
36 Danilova, interview.
37 Danilova, interview.
38 This set of key social acts is a result of the encoding of the meaning of the textual procedures that condense the meaning of the narratives. Its reconstruction has been conducted within the tradition of the qualitative analysis of narrative data, following Glaser and Strauss, *The Discovery of Grounded Theory*. Whether this set is complete or the typology is exhaustive is determined by the quality of the sample. We consulted, using the questionnaires, all of the members of the Society of Former Inmates and then selected for interviewing those who represented different fields of experience (recruited as civilians, military personnel, industrial workers, peasants, in the camp, in their households). The emphasis was on the individual's experience in most typical situations. Utterly unique, non-typical lives were analysed as special cases.
39 The so-called disciplinary troupes (*shtrafnoi batalion)* were special military units. In these, diverse offenders against the Soviet regime served their time as military combatants.
40 Regional Office of Infrastructure (translator's note).

41 Kriukova, interview.
42 The tactic applied by the Soviet authorities to those who worked in the occupied territories (editors' note.)
43 Terekhova, interview.
44 Yevgeniia Mikhailova (born 1934), interview by Yelena Rozhdestvenskaya, Pskov *oblast*, Russia, July 2005.
45 Rüsen, "Krizis, Travma i Identichnost."
46 Rüsen, "Krizis, Travma i Identichnost," 60.
47 This took place in the context of important developments within the same timeframe. Applications for financial compensation were considered between 2001 and 2006. The financial compensation program concluded its work in 2006.

5 "We Are Silent about Ourselves": Discussing Career and Daily Life with Female Academics in Russia and Belarus

NATALIA PUSHKAREVA

History and historical narratives can be constructed in many ways. It would not be a novel idea to claim that female perspectives on history – and on the past – are less known and less studied than male perspectives, yet the former can certainly illuminate and balance our understanding of the world and its affairs. What can be learned from a women's perspective on the world? What in our understanding of the past will change if we, for example, attempt to (re)construct a history of society as seen through women's eyes? And how will our understandings of the society and its history change if we focus specifically on the perspective of female academic elite, that is, on the female scientists and researchers who are often on the front lines when it comes to intellectual contributions to the well-being of their respective societies? These questions were the driving force behind our inquiry, whose results we discuss in this chapter. My research into how female scientists and researchers view their own lives and roles in their respective societies asks, among other things, what meanings female researchers – members of various research institutes of the Russian and Byelorussian Academies of Sciences – assign to their own pasts and to the national pasts of their societies. Do these meanings differ from established historical understandings of the past and from the meanings of the past assigned by women's male compatriots? The project *We Are Silent about Ourselves*, which my colleagues and I recently undertook while pursuing the personal life histories of the female intellectual elites in Belarus and Russia, addresses these pivotal questions.[1]

The aforementioned project has been directly informed by our, the project coordinators', recognition of the validity of women's history. We believe in the equal value and equal significance (to men's) of women's social experiences, but we also understand that women's experiences are gender specific owing to the differences between those life experiences – their socialization, societal expectations, spheres of action, and so on. Russian *and* non-Russian historians now recognize that by approaching national histories from a gendered perspective (a relatively new and still not entirely accepted approach to studying the past), we can augment those histories by reclaiming the lost experiences of both renowned and previously unknown women.

Locating women's social experiences of their respective societies, and accessing and recording women's memories of those experiences, requires modes of analysis that for a long time were seen as belonging specifically to sociological research. With the rise and acceptance of multidisciplinary qualitative methodologies across the social sciences, these modes are today contributing to far broader intellectual domains than sociology; they have reached out to encompass history, ethnology, cultural studies, and cultural anthropology. They suggest specific methods for gathering empirical material – in particular, methods that aim to preserve subjectivities engraved on depictions of events.[2] Oral history has been among the most potent methodological tools we have used in our study. In employing the oral historical method in our research, we consulted and followed the example of many well-known scholars of oral history, whose work is available in English.[3] These scholars explored the complexities of oral and written biographical stories of many women and women's subcultures, thus advancing the idea that there is a specifically *gynographical* perspective on the past, one that summarizes and advocates for specifically female experiences of the past. These projects, however, focus on the life stories of ordinary women, whose place and position in society are distinctly different from that of, say, professional women in the same societies. When we began, no project had concerned itself with the oral history of female scholars, scientists, and researchers, whose social position set them apart from most other women in their societies and whose education granted them a distinct sense of reflectivity informed by their experiences in their professions. As we recorded and examined the life stories of these female intellectuals, we realized we were venturing onto new research terrain – our project was the first of its kind.

In this chapter, while examining the narratives that female scholars allowed us to record, I explore how these women understood their own narratives and projected them onto their own life-worlds, life cycles, and lifestyles, as well as how they understood and navigated official restrictions and unofficial codes of behaviour.[4] We were interested in women's perspectives on contemporary life; it was not just the details of the past they described that were significant. Above all, we were interested in accessing the meanings of the past as constructed and held by the female narrators, who offered their own interpretations of those events. The method of oral historical research was most helpful in pursuing such goals, for provided the tools to access various aspects of the personal lives of our informants. With this study focusing on women's reminiscences, we hope to fill in some of the blanks that have been left in traditional historical narratives in contemporary Russia and Belarus – narratives that have long purported to be all-encompassing yet remain incomplete because of the absence of women's voices. Research of this kind can challenge stereotypical constructions of biography and standard conceptions of life experiences.[5]

Our study focuses on everyday life within the life cycle[6] and asks how women reflect on their past experiences. The concept of "life cycle" as it is understood here has been developed by sociologists, cultural studies specialists, and especially psychologists. It is closely associated with age and its accompanying changes in status, social orientation, and aspirations; all of these forces underpin individual transformations.

The individuals who shared their stories with us were educated women of the (intellectual) urban elite. This project was based on a series of in-depth autobiographical interviews conducted between 2004 and 2006 by myself and my colleague Dr Irina Chikalova, a specialist in gender history. The interviews were taped and then transcribed. The questions presented to the respondents did not take the form of a strict questionnaire, and the time allotted to the interviews was not restricted. The respondents who had post-graduate education, and who provided the most complete and detailed answers about their life experiences in the first round of our inquiries, were invited later to recount the stories about themselves for our project. Setting these parameters meant that the possibility of generalizing from the results was more limited; but in our view, the advantages outweighed the disadvantages.

The interviewers prompted respondents only to talk about themselves and their own life experiences; it was up to the respondents to decide what to focus on more in their interviews, whether to prioritize the self or to focus on their life experiences. We encouraged our narrators to follow the progression of events in their lives. We also encouraged them to establish cause-and-effect connections between these events, suggesting that they reflect on how they overcame the obstacles they faced and what emotions they felt with respect to their experiences. A particular group of questions the interviewees were asked concerned their actual life experiences: questions were asked about their family situation, their attitude towards and relationship with their chosen profession, their degree of satisfaction with their profession, and their expectations for the future. Their answers were based on their own memories, impressions, knowledge, and experiences relating to the events in their own lives and those of the people close to them.

After the stories were recorded, we analysed the life conditions the interviewees reconstructed as well as the answers they gave to the above questions. Our goal was to understand our informants' life paths.[7] What personal characteristics and what kinds of social interactions informed women's efforts to construct their successful life strategies? What values and life circumstances, arising from family and culture, had a positive impact on their careers and lives, and what values and life circumstances had a negative impact? What family resources were available to them in their quest for a successful professional life? How were those resources transmitted from grandparents to parents and then to the daughters who went on to pursue a professional career in former Soviet Union? What emotional or psychological price did the generation of daughters pay for their success?

Since we wanted to retain the unique and individually integrated presentations of the cause-and-effect connections in women's life histories, we decided against rearranging the interview transcriptions into categorized interview segments for later exposure to thematic analysis. Had we pursued that route, we would have ended up with many separate accounts, thematically focused but stripped of the overall context in which the accounts had been delivered. The full transcripts of our extensive interviews had a value of their own: they were coherent and fairly complete histories of the lives of our respondents.

All of the respondents and researchers were women. We realized how crucial that gendered symmetry would be for establishing and maintaining good rapport and mutual understanding and how helpful the symmetry of experiences of the interviewer and the interviewed.[8] Respondents and researchers were able to share the conversation as equals, and for both parties, recitations of life experiences and subsequent reflections on them played a significant therapeutic role. An exchange between my colleague Irina and Ms Maria Bespalaia, a historian in Minsk, the capital of Belarus, illustrates this point quite well:

MARIA BESPALAIA: My grandmother knew a lot of poetry, and many different stories about them. She was of great value to the village community – she was tactful and educated. And obviously, she knew a lot.

IRINA CHIKALOVA, HISTORIAN (PROJECT RESEARCHER): You could be talking about my own grandmother – she was just like that. Even without any special education, she knew a lot of poetry. She read Pushkin ... I took that as a given.[9]

Such shared experience helped establish great rapport between the narrator and the researcher, in that both, besides being of the same sex, belonged to the same cohort of Russian intelligentsia women; thus, they had experienced the Russian past in similar terms and had developed similar responses to a variety of cultural and political events that had dominated Russian history over the past forty or so years.[10]

For a number of reasons, we focused on the experiences and life stories of women intellectuals around the age of forty. Cross-analysing stories about their lives, we soon realized that there was much shared content and shared framing in these narratives. The life narratives of many informants were united by a stock of shared vocabulary – by a phraseology that helped them express similar judgments about cause-and-effect relations in their lives. Many of those expressions stemmed from the same books the respondents read in their youth and then again as adults. While cross-analysing their narratives – that is, instead of trying to locate among the narrators a typical representative of this cohort of women or seeking some statistical representation of a large sample (as in quantitative sociology) – I became interested in identifying those life experiences that cross-cut many of the life paths of my narrators, as well as in documenting women's own interpretations of those experiences that resembled one another. My goal has been to reconstruct recent Russian and late Soviet history through the eyes of female representatives of a particular professional and social group; at the same time, I have tried to document the unique perspective these women have to offer on their country's history.

Some historians deem quotidian experience or even traumatic experience to be inconsequential. Also, one might ask what psychological traumas individuals of a privileged social group such as female academics have encountered. Such a question may lead one to imagine that this category of professionals has faced few challenges in life. However, the oral accounts we have gathered reveal that female academics deal with a great many challenges and that these challenges leave a lasting imprint on their understandings of life in difficult circumstances. It is no wonder that many among the academic elite have thought about leaving academe and that some have indeed done so.

Researchers who explore the formation and development of personal memories of daily life do not focus on the course of daily life that is being discussed by the narrator (which is something that ethnologists do, for example). Rather, they turn their attention to specific social experiences of persons who are bound by social connections and conventions over a given period of time. Researchers seek out the logic of actions, recurring models of representation connected to collective phenomena, and the typologies of social behaviour (speech and silence).[11]

Agreement to "talk about oneself" is in itself a response to a challenge to complete a sort of biographical work: an interpretive operation in the construction of the meaning of one's own life against the backdrop of social change. That is why recollection is itself a social practice: both the interviewer and the interviewee "create themselves."

For the seasoned oral historian, most of the autobiographical accounts recorded for this project may seem conventional. The theme of daily life crosses all of the narrators' accounts, although discussions of life challenges – in Russian, *trudnosti zhyzni* ("the trials of life") – were not, as a rule, central to the women's narratives. In other words, the theme of daily life connects various other non-ordinary and non-quotidian facets of their life courses. The details of the ordinary in their accounts are like threads stringing together the beads of important transformative events (graduation from an institution of higher education, enrolment in graduate study, defence of one's first dissertation, the publication of one's first monograph). They provide a narrative base, allowing the listener (the female researcher) to assimilate the events the respondent is reliving and to sense the complicity between the respondent and the person to whom the account is being told.

This sustained profiling of the ordinary evoked in the listener (the researcher) feelings and emotions that allowed her to become the narrator's alter ego and relive (or reject) her own past. This emotional merging in turn fed further exchanges between researcher and narrator. In the end, though, it was we the researchers who identified the project's central topic, as "most of the time, we are silent about ourselves."[12]

The fact that most of our respondents in this chapter wanted to remain anonymous supported our reading of the gathered materials. We followed the wishes of these respondents by assigning them new names. Some repeatedly asked whether their interviews would be published, fearing that their real identities might be discerned from the details the interviews contained. Other respondents were willing to let us use their real name, and we have done so. Thus, some informants are mentioned here only by name, or by name and the name of the academic institute where they work, or by the city where they live, or simply by the state (i.e., Russian Federation or Belarus).

It is not coincidental that many of our respondents compared their own lives and daily experiences with the researcher's or with their parents'. What they had learned from their parents – or, more broadly, from the older generation – demanded confirmation and substantiation. The theoretical work of European psychologists Murray Bowen and Virginia Satir proved especially valuable for understanding the multigenerational process.[13]

A basic hypothesis of this study has been that female academics who rejected physically and emotionally the lifestyles of their parents, and who ignored them, were less successful than those who relied on the symbolic capital of emotional ties with older relatives, learning from them how to overcome difficulties (especially when the relatives were themselves scholars). In other words, links between generations, and to family identity and family values, served as a means to sustain family life even under the stressful conditions in the Soviet Union and post-*perestroika* Russia. This hypothesis is confirmed by the fundamental themes of the life stories. We present here as an example the themes of childhood and the theme of *vybor zhyznennogo puti* (another formulaic Russian expression: "choice of a life path").

Despite their highly varied personal experiences, all of the women who recounted their life histories had achieved, at one point in their lives, success, influence, and social advancement. What internal factors conditioned the respondents' need for personal growth and led to their success and influence? More than one narrator suggested that the key factor contributing to her ambition to succeed was her relationship with her father – her desire to carry out his will and to concretize his vision of his daughter's future. The following narrators referred to impact of their father:

He tried to develop my capabilities, because he had dreamed of having a son, but instead he had a daughter. And so he tried to develop in me male sorts of habits, so that being with me would be interesting to him.[14]

My dad was a scholar. And although there was no attempt to push me to follow the family path, that was how things worked out.[15]

My dad's self-esteem played a role. I think that's what he wanted, that his Marusia would be better than all the others.[16]

Because my dad had a strong inclination towards the humanities – he wrote poetry and created crossword puzzles – he and I agreed that I would study at Moscow University in the Journalism Faculty.[17]

In childhood, I was a humanist, but my dad was a mathematician. Therefore, he drove me forcefully into mathematics school and pushed me to take the entrance examinations with the admonition, "Well, do you really not want to test your own strength?"[18]

When my dad became a physician, he did not go to Moscow to study. Maybe, he said, I could realize his old dream?[19]

Clearly, fathers had a significant influence on the respondents, even though most of the women also had mothers who had achieved professional success and often desired even more than the fathers for their daughters to grow up to be self-sufficient. The striving for independence and self-respect, and the ability to achieve their goals and defend their positions – all of this developed from childhood and from the relationship with fathers *and* mothers. "'Argue with me! Learn to defend yourself!' my mom demanded, and if I felt hurt or cried, she teased me as a cry-baby."[20] Tatiana, an ophthalmologist from Moscow, discusses the same issue:

The regimen in our family was this: "After each failure, you need to have success; otherwise, you won't have any successes." My mom always said this to me, and my father added, "Hang on by your fingernails!" When I was a child, my favourite fairy tale, which was always told to me, was about two frogs who fell into a pitcher of milk – an optimist and a pessimist. You know it, right? The pessimist gave up and drowned. But the optimist kept churning, made butter, and managed to get out. She saved herself. I was raised on that story. Everything is in our hands, and it's most important not to let things fall through.[21]

It was more often fathers, and less often mothers, who played the key role in raising daughters, wanting the best life for them. They explained to their daughters that education was fundamental to social mobility and professional accomplishment. These parents did not talk about possible marriage partners with their daughters; rather, they awakened in them dreams of recognition and designed a life path for them in accordance with those dreams.

The family lifestyle was exceptionally important for daughters. Most often, either they came from an academic family or at least one of their relatives had some connection to the scholarly world. (I might add that this pattern of replicating professional and social status continues in Russian society even at the end of the twentieth century.) It was also important that parents and close relatives believed in these daughters' strength:

> I had an aunt who had a doctoral degree – a biochemist. I watched what she did, and how, and I really liked it. My parents didn't do anything serious about it [my enthusiasm], but they encouraged me.[22]

> My parents treated me as though I was something exceptionally valuable and they talked a lot with me, explained things, and did a lot with me. At home, all sorts of creative … games were common.[23]

Future female scholars who were not raised in an academic family often came from families of the urban or rural intelligentsia, where books and reading – including reading aloud at home – played a large role in family life:

> Tons of books were purchased; there were a lot of books. And all of them were read constantly, in dim light. A whole cupboard of books were read – I remember that exactly.[24]

> There were a lot of fairy tales, and a lot of books. Truly, that developed some sort of youthful imagination in me. In any case, it was clear.[25]

Parents typically perceived their daughters to be like sons. Some openly expressed disappointment that they were not boys. Many of the girls tried to prove they were "no worse":

> Mom told me, ironically, "Learn to iron shirts – it will serve you well in life!" And all my sentient life, it was testimony to the fact that I was not worse than if I had been a boy.[26]

> He tried to develop my abilities, because he dreamed of having a son, but instead a daughter was born, and so he tried to inculcate masculine habits in me.[27]

Other individuals who had an impact on the narrator, most notably teachers, also appeared in autobiographical accounts, although far more rarely than fathers, mothers, and close family members. However, among the respondents who came from rural families (in contrast to urban ones), it was these individuals who were most important in guiding respondents not only in the choice of profession but also in lifestyle:

> For high school, we already went to a neighbouring village. There we had a woman teacher, and I understood that that was my role model. It seems to me that to this very day I imitate her in my dress, in everything.[28]

What most distinguished these girls, "born in place of boys," from typical sons was their exceptional orientation towards results, their conscientiousness, and their understanding of how to overcome difficulties:

> When I complained about something at home, that I couldn't do any more, that nothing was going to turn out for me, Mom asked sternly, "After I can't – what next?"[29]

> Because I was accustomed to studying, and I had a sense of how study was indispensable, I studied and I studied and I studied. I thought everything over, reflected on everything, analysed everything ... There were horrible problems in pharmacology, and I couldn't cram it into my head, but then I learned it all.[30]

All of those women who quickly established successful scholarly careers, defending their doctoral dissertations before the age of forty, were motivated and driven during their high school studies. Literally every one of the respondents recalled that she studied very well:

> Lessons, study ... The first order of business was study. From the very beginning, I was focused on how I had to graduate with the gold medal. And that's what I did![31]

> I was the first person in my school in twenty years who received the medal. My essay was recognized as the best in the district.[32]

It is curious that among the respondents, only one who defended her doctoral dissertation before the age of forty was selected as a member of the Russian Academy of Sciences before the age of fifty. Yet she was the one who pointed out that she did not demonstrate any passion for knowledge or any particular subject from her earliest years, that she had not excelled at school, and who in general did not distinguish herself as a "model student." Even so, it was she who was most professionally advanced at the time we were conducting our research. One wonders whether the orientation towards achieving the highest marks and the strongest participation in scholarly activities somehow undermined the respondents' ability to develop relationships with friends and classmates outside the framework of official activities: communication also takes work, and they did not have time for it.[33]

The Russian female scholars we interviewed, unlike their peers in, for example, Germany,[34] did not emphasize that the choice of professional career was the result of obstacles imposed on them by relatives (brothers or sisters, or parents) or by life circumstances (illness, disability). Feelings of abandonment, of desertion, of loneliness, of a lack of support from the moment the life path was chosen – we did not find these things among Russian women scholars. On the contrary, many respondents were only children. Their parents believed in them and helped them confirm their choices: "In childhood, I won competitions at various levels – district-wide, city-wide. As a result, everyone thought that I would study literature"[35]; "My father inflamed my interest in life. He was, truly, my first teacher; he believed in me!"[36]

But it is important to emphasize that the family member who had the most impact on the narrator was her mother. The respondents often reflected that their own stable lives were very much the result of their being parented effectively by their mothers, who were strict yet supportive and who strongly emphasized the need to learn how to overcome life's challenges. The mothers of our respondents belonged to a different generation of Russian citizens: all were born and raised in Soviet times (the respondents were all born between the 1940s and the 1970s), and the values they passed down to their daughters had been marked by their own times. The evidence of this transmission of values from mother to daughter can be found in some of the biographical accounts:

> You know, I truly reached the goal that my mom did not achieve but very much wanted to. My mother had a different start to life: the early death of her mother and then the departure of her father from the family for

> another woman, leaving her alone from the age of fourteen. Mom left the provincial city, became a Muscovite, defended two dissertations. My life path repeats that of my mother, only without the complications. Mom always demanded from me more and more. Well, if she didn't demand it, then she just expected it.[37]

One way or another, the daughters of these accomplished women, even those who obtained a doctoral degree at a young age, faced their share of difficulties and challenges. Not a single respondent said her life in scholarship was easy or that she always enjoyed the understanding and support of her colleagues and superiors. They were happy to recall this; after all, their accomplishments (such as dissertation defences and scholarly recognition) were all the greater because they had been preceded by difficulties. For most of the narrators, the account of what they had overcome in youth was the basis for their assessment of their career success.

Our narrators rarely pointed out yet another dimension of the challenges and obstacles they faced in their professional lives. I am referring here to the professional challenges that exist in contemporary Russian academe and in other professional contexts. Among these difficulties was the envy of their colleagues:

> In school, I always had problems with classmates ... The class was really confrontational ... and for something like ... half a year ... they bullied me. At first, I became a nervous wreck, but then I learned not to allow offences and to say always what I think, and not care about others' opinions.[38]

> In school, little by little I was badgered ... as the star pupil. In the sixth grade, some sort of negative gossip went on ... It was said, she has all A's, and there's something not right about it.[39]

> I always had the feeling that in life, I am receiving more than I deserve. I never had any desire to enter into a competitive battle. But my husband ... he ... so to speak ... increased this tendency. He always led me to remember where I come from, what my social roots are ... Now I know that he did this because he himself felt extremely insecure. The most amazing thing is that instead of [us] supporting each other, he ... in fact ... tried to distance himself from me.[40]

We can conclude that women who built their careers despite unsupportive circumstances and often traumatic early professional experiences were stimulated rather than impeded by the challenges: "If I didn't succeed at something or I failed in some subject, for example, mathematics, I would reconsider the whole puzzle";[41] "In my third year (of university studies), I had a crisis about the meaning of life … I very distinctly remembered that I chose surgery as my specialization because surgery is the least feminine area of medicine";[42] "Everyone went to enter the university in the closest city – but I went to another country."[43]

We came to realize that the respondents understood success as the ability to pass through all of the stages of professional life until one reached the highest rung of the academic ladder. When the narrators faced delays in getting hired, when their successes were overlooked by their supervisors, these things were noted in the biographical memoirs as unjust. They viewed their responses to these unjust developments as defensive measures forced upon them. Thus, they would attempt to organize their work to their own benefit, they would leave their own scholarly work and position in a research institution in order to teach at a university, or they would take supplemental work because they had not been promoted at their primary job.

The theme of a broken or highly threatened personal life owing to professional engagement repeatedly arose in the biographical narratives. Especially noticeable was the discrepancy between society's expectations of a well-maintained family life and the reality of a family life crippled by circumstances. In open-ended biographical interviews, men could talk about this but do not (as other oral historical interviews show[44]). Yet the women we interviewed routinely returned to the topic of family. Most of them reflected on the impact their success as scholars had on their families. They talked about how their commitment to academic work sometimes led to the destruction of family or other important relationships, and how involvement in academe had a limiting impact on long-term friendships. These were prominent themes.

The general absence of a culture of recognition or a culture of praise in the Russian and Belarusian academic worlds (both direct descendants from Soviet system of scholarship) are still quite characteristic of the academic environment in both countries. Celebrating academic success is not an established practice, yet in many ways it is essential for women, as our interviewees attested. Many female academics work without being regularly and publicly acknowledged for the work they do. One particular story stands out, for it speaks directly about this lack of acknowledgment. Natalia shared it with us:

> My mom, along with several of her friends, created [at her initiative] a "Society of Mutual Adoration." That was how they called their accord – it was arranged that whatever was said about one or another of them about whatever or whenever, they would say only the best things ... Wouldn't that be nice, if my mom or I myself worked not in a "terrarium of the like-minded" – do you know that expression? – but rather in a situation of goodwill ... Really, we need to come to such an agreement and all of us [should] found such a Society.[45]

Our informants were happy to talk about their professional successes but more reluctant to talk about what they perceived to be the failures in their personal lives. They avoided discussing their personal lives, which most of them perceived as under-realized: "[My dear] God! Oh, well, I don't talk about that to anyone. It's not necessary to tell this."[46] Another theme in all of the interviews is worth commenting on here. In the overwhelming majority of life narratives we recorded for this project, especially with women who had achieved success in the scholarly world, men emerged either as rivals or as uninvolved non-supporters. Men came across as either openly envious of the wife's success or as hiding their lack of support under a cloak of indifference.[47] This is not unique to Russia or Belarus; it can be found in the life history interviews with female scholars in other countries as well. For example, a German respondent in an analogous project conducted recently[48] referred to her life story (in which her husband shared her success and helped her) as "completely atypical." Natalia, for her part, recounted a situation not in her own life but in that of a friend and colleague:

> My ex, well, he envied me in everything and always. It seems that this is typical in families where both the husband and the wife are scholars, even in the same field. I myself know of only one exception – they were colleagues of mine from Ukraine, philosophers by training. Here it was, in that family the husband helped the wife organize everything. He let her defend her doctoral dissertation first and become a leader in her field of expertise. How rare that is! I don't know any others like them.[49]

Female scholars displayed strong determination and adaptive capacity in relation to the trials and ordeals they faced in their lives. Their biographies indicate that life crises are not entirely characteristic for them, although the position of women is shakier with regard to success (each of them thinks the confluence of obstacles was not coincidental).[50]

Women representing the intellectual elite rarely admitted to break-ups or crises in their professional lives (such as a "midlife crisis," when basic goals have been achieved and one must set new goals and directions). At the same time, in male biographies about scholarly careers, accounts of the need to fight fractures in consciousness and of development through suffering are typical. One can see this in historian Lev Elnickij's autobiographical texts and in linguist Lev Scherba's analyses of autobiography.[51] We can conclude that biographical accounts contain different characteristics according to sex (or gender?) – a sort of gendered behaviour and self-representation. Male scholars are more active and assertive in the professional domain and recount their lives as a series of victories;[52] women, by contrast, tend to be more emotional and to depend more on relations with a circle of intimates, including family, friends, and work colleagues.

All of the women in our project attempted to give their accounts an air of "gender neutrality," that is, they were reluctant to explicitly discuss sex discrimination against them. This is yet another manifestation of how female scholars, like many other women in Russian and Belarusian society, continue to conform to societal norms and expectations. In many of the narratives we recorded, one can sense the informants' insecurity with regard to their own achievements and their significance. One respondent, an employee of a prestigious academic institute, holder of a doctorate, and professor, Maria (who wanted to remain anonymous) thoughtfully said in response to a request for an interview about her career in scholarship: "Well, what kind of successful woman am I? Surely, I wouldn't do for you."[53] Seemingly unaware of their outstanding success, most of our respondents presented their life stories as steady, gradual, and free of crises or disruptions.[54] In writings about life's battles in general, women are far less likely than men to hear "the call from outside" of those who could compel them to change their perspective on life, including on their profession. In their accounts of adaptation to life circumstances, the women narrators recounted their ability to adapt to changing conditions as a great accomplishment and not in any way as a concession.

But this disguises a more positive reading of the evidence. Women who attained high professional status and position in the academic world rarely complained about the lack of mutual understanding in the family, including in their family relationships, whether the husband left his professionally successful wife or remained in the marriage to preserve the family and support her. When a woman does not defer family leadership to her husband, the price is either a high level of conflict or the dissolution of the marriage, as attested in our interviews. When, by contrast, female scholars do not try to achieve parity in their relationship with the spouse and bear the burden of domestic responsibilities, thinking instead of work outside the home as supplemental to home life, as a means of satisfying personal ambition, they must integrate this double burden into their life objectives.

The respondents differed, of course, in terms of how they organized the details of daily life. But in the final analysis, oral histories and biographies privilege not events themselves but rather assessments or interpretations of them, so it is important to remember how subjective the process of presenting memories is. The "rehabilitation of subjectivity" that has marked the past decade of scholarship in the humanities of many post-socialist societies allows us to place this subjective perception at the centre of historical (or historical-anthropological, or cultural-anthropological) research. This has been the goal of the still unfolding project of history-from-the-margins that has begun to develop in Russia and Belarus.

In support of that goal, of bringing history-from-the-margins into core academic discussions, let us note several key features of analyses of biographies and oral histories. First, when using this method, one must remain aware of the historicity and changeability of biographical material and of the possibility of virtualizing and mythologizing it. Second, the identification of narrators by social status, position, sex, and generation enables scholars to also examine the transmission of memory among participants and witnesses as a sort of "communicative tradition." Third, the women's accounts we recorded for this project expanded beyond the narrations about their own lives. In the interview transcripts, one can see the whole spectre of events and occurrences of the past that affected and defined the narrative strategies.

As George Herbert Mead, a contemporary researcher on oral history and memory, has affirmed, objectivity involves not only critical standards and methods, but also "mortification."[55] It is easy to reminiscence about bygone times because the past is a page that has been turned; the injuries, the sense of principle or loss, have already faded. That is why it seemed important and urgent for us to talk in depth with female scholars about their careers and daily lives; for otherwise, given the current culture of non-celebration of professional achievements in the academic world, they might remain under-recognized and undervalued. We were struck by the fact that many of our informants felt wronged and that many had plenty of their own reasons to complain about the lack of support and the lack of recognition in their professional milieux as well as in their personal (often limited) circles of family and friends. Ultimately, our research did not focus just on this "past overflowing with experience" with all its strategies for suppressing or claiming ownership of history. Rather, our goal was to document and analyse how our women contemporaries experienced and understood the development of their careers in the context of their everyday lives. We wanted to access their memories and perceptions of their own lives so that these memories would become documented and known to the academics themselves. We hope that having received this attention, the history of how female academics achieved their successes will perhaps have greater influence on collective memory of Russian and Belarusian societies about their own histories.

NOTES

1 Chikalova and Pushkareva, *Women-Scientists*. This project has been supported by the Russian Fund for Humanities (RHNF), project no. 11-01-00283.
2 Pushkareva, "Feministskii"; Muravieva, "My Govorim."
3 Fitzpatrick, *Everyday Stalinism*; Engel, *Women in Imperial, Soviet, and Post-Soviet Russia*; Fitzpatrick and Slezkine, *In the Shadow of Revolution*; Clements, Friedman, and Healey, *Russian Masculinities*; Nechemias and Kuehnast, *Post-Soviet Women*; Fitzpatrick and Rasmussen, *Political Tourists*; Krylova, *Soviet Women in Combat*; Fitzpatrick, Kozlov, and Mironenko, *Sedition*; Raleigh, *Soviet Baby Boomers*.
4 Shchepanskaia, "Antropologiia Professii."
5 See this approach: Mülle, Herren, and Meister, "'Ego-Histoire.'"
6 Grabe, "Wo du Stehst."
7 These questions constitute only part of a larger set of questions we concerned ourselves with in this research, which lies beyond the scope of this chapter.
8 See Rosaldo, "The Use and Abuse of Anthropology," 400.
9 Bespalaia (born 1948), interview.
10 Shchepanskaia, "Antropologiia Professii."
11 Wacquant, "For a Socio-Analysis," 4.
12 Kohlt, "'Von uns Selbst Schweigen Wir.'"
13 Regarding these concepts, see Dresse and Langreiter, "Nie Zeit, nie Frei."

14 Olga (born 1958, physicist), interview.
15 Henrietta (born 1957), interview.
16 Marusia (born 1951), interview.
17 Elena (born 1969), interview.
18 Olga Silchenko (born 1958), interview.
19 "Est' Zhenshchiny v Nashei Nauke," 2. Online interviews with Doctors of Chemistry S.B. Artemkina, G.V. Lukovaia, and O.V. Kaliuzhnaia; Zaslavkaia, interview.
20 Natalia (born 1959), interview, 1 June 2005.
21 Tatiana (born 1970), interview.
22 Marina (born 1959), interview.
23 Helene (born 1969, historian), interview.
24 Milena (born 1955), interview.
25 Tatiana, interview.
26 Maria (born 1948, philosopher), interview, 1 February 2005.
27 Tatiana (born 1957, economist), interview, 5 February 2005.
28 Maria (born 1940), interview.
29 Maria (born 1940), interview.
30 Natalia (born 1959, historian), interview.
31 Albina (born 1947), interview.
32 Svetlana (born 1960), interview.
33 See about communication as work that needs sufficient time: Mudrik, *Obshchenie Kak Faktor*.
34 Giegel, "Strukturmerkmale einer Erfolgskarriere"; Hasenjürgen, "Winners and Losers."
35 Silchenko, interview; Maria (born 1940, oncologist), interview.
36 Adelaida (born 1946), interview.
37 Natalia, interview, 1 September 2005.
38 Olga (born 1956, geographer), interview.
39 Helene (born 1949, physicist), interview, 23 December 2004.
40 Silchenko, interview.
41 Silchenko, interview.
42 Helene (born 1949, physicist), interview, 14 January 2005.
43 Milena, interview.
44 Meshcherkina, "Vvedenie."
45 Natalia, interview, 1 September 2005.
46 Elena (born 1969), interview.
47 Tichenor, "Status and Income"; Ely and McCabe, "Gender Differences."
48 Dresse and Langreiter, "Nie Zeit, nie Frei"; Kohlt, "'Von uns Selbst Schweigen Wir.'"

49 Natalia, interview, 1 September 2005. Cf. Bernard, "The Good-Provider Role," 281.

50 Ris, "'Profil Burzhuaznosti,'" 410.

51 Elnickii, *Tri Kruga Vospominanii*; "Three Autobiographies of Lev Scherba."

52 Nurkova and Mosolova, "Kharakteristiki Vospominanii."

53 Maria (born 1957, geographer), interview. Cf. Ortner, *Making Gender*, 9.

54 See, for example, Vasil'eva, "Zhenschiny v Nauke."

55 Mead, "Narrativität."

6 A Commentator or a Character in a Story? The Problem of the Narrator in Oral History

ROZALIA CHEREPANOVA

The recent turning of scholars in the humanities and social sciences in Russia and other post-socialist countries towards questions of memory, memory processes, and resources may have been the result of their satiation with examinations of "discourses of power." In an effort to locate "still warm" sources, born in front of their eyes, many post-socialist researchers embraced oral history, hoping to locate and identify in these freshly produced accounts of the past those perspectives on the world practised by society's less visible, "repressed," "silent" social groups. This tendency, albeit in a different societal context, had been observed by Paul Thompson, who discussed oral history's powerful potential to document and validate "common ordinary people's perspective on the world and its affairs."[1] In today's Russia we find a growing interest in documenting and studying the recent socialist past. Topics such as the cultures of Soviet daily life, the Soviet mindset, and the fate of spiritual life under the Soviet rule compete for the attention of scholars. At the other end of the research spectrum, scholars are becoming more and more interested in reconstructing grassroots understandings of the various political upheavals of the twentieth century, in evaluating various dimensions of social change and examining interethnic relations.[2]

The oral historical method allows scholars to rather quickly access a wealth of narratives describing one or another page of recent Soviet history. The materials gathered during oral history interviews may seem to be "lying on the surface" for easy gathering. Stories recorded by oral historians reveal vectors of social mobility, which unfold both horizontally (i.e., across today's various social milieux) and vertically (i.e., chronologically). These stories illustrate the depth of social change; they also speak about social mores and may contain genuine nuggets of fact. They are laden with details about people's lives, and they offer such a wealth of stories that analysts can claim they have little work left to do – that this rich material can speak for itself. When interviews concern past hardships, scholars perhaps can just add a line here and there to support the claims their respondents are making, thereby providing archival evidence of the "hard times" discussed in the interviews. Another approach to engaging with interview materials in one's analysis is to categorize the "survival strategies" discussed by the informants.

But all of this constitutes the superficial level of engaging with oral historical data. A researcher who works at this level is not venturing beyond surface analysis and surface critique. One reason why researchers often remain at this level of data analysis and interview interpretation relates to ethics. During the interview, the interviewer and the informant develop a certain degree of trust, even a personal relationship. Once that relationship has been established, it verges on sacrilegious to "autopsy" the informant's story. The researcher may not be able to analyse the material as dispassionately as, for example, other types of historians do when they dissect the personal lives of Catherine the Great or Peter the Great. Moreover, "live and present" narrators may resist possibly unflattering interpretations of their biographies, persons, and confessions. This is probably why oral history methodologies have been developing around the interview process itself; the aim is to make the procedure as appropriate and precise as possible and to minimize aberrations. Also, the oral history method has been seeking ways to deepen the analysis of the collected materials without sacrificing ethical distance and respect for the narrator's privacy. In both respects, oral history has been converging with sociology and anthropology, embracing their practices and methods. Yet despite all the efforts to deepen the analytical potential of oral history and broaden its possibilities, its ability to represent genuine historical knowledge has been cast in doubt more and more as time goes by. Thus, from the perspective of those who seek "genuine" or "authentic" memory, situations in which a given narrator has at least two separate representational biographies, with the recorded narratives often resembling textbook formulas and officially approved clichés and opinions, have been a great disappointment.[3] To avoid this sort of "deception" by respondents, it has been proposed to question them through a "trusted intermediary" (or to question that trusted person regarding the respondent), or to corroborate the information presented by respondents using hardcopy sources (both official and personal) such as photographs, diaries, forms, and other documents.[4] When such an approach is used, however, the question "What remains of memory?" remains entirely unanswered. Moreover, oral history itself, as a scholarly direction, loses almost its entire meaning; it becomes a crutch or an appendix to those very written sources, the study of which oral history is supposed to move away from.

Let me turn now to the oral history project "The 20th Century in Evaluations and Memories of the Provincial Intelligentsia,"[5] which I conducted with the help of my research assistants in the city of Cheliabinsk. I took up this project in the hope of uncovering and documenting how today's Russian intelligentsia born and raised under the Soviet political system remember and think about the twentieth century in which they lived. Ever since Emile Durkheim crafted his notion of "collective consciousness," and continuing on to Jan Assmann's work on cultural memory,[6] researchers have become convinced that the mechanisms of human memory are socially determined. Despite this, oral history, based on readings of the "text" of human memory, inevitably leads oral historians to study the inner world of each respondent; this means that when processing their data, they must engage in psychology. Realizing that personal reminiscences are also products of personal psychology, I hoped to access and document the personal, individual dimensions of the collective memory of the twentieth century as lived and experienced by well-educated and reflective people, which members of the intelligentsia usually are. Allow me to elaborate on how my project proceeded and what has come out of this research.

Beginning in 2005, with my colleague Salavat Bayazirov, Professor of History at Chelabinsk Pedagogical University, and our student assistants, we recorded 132 biographic interviews, 97 with women and the other 35 with men. The project's title has prompted many people to think about well-known developments in the history of twentieth-century Russia, and as such, the reader might think that as researchers, we were interested in gathering people's memories about these prominent public events and developments (such as Iurii Gagarin's first space flight, or the deaths of political leaders). However, we were far more interested in accessing memories of private events in our informants' lives in the twentieth century. To elicit these sorts of narratives, we used rather neutrally formulated narrative prompts, asking our informants to tell us about their lives in general, although we suggested they start with their childhood. The mandatory condition during the recording of an interview was the absence of any rigid set of questions. We wanted the respondents to feel free to "construct" their own lives. To protect the privacy of our interviewees, all names were replaced by conditional pseudonyms (in this chapter, we use those pseudonyms). Despite all these measures, which were intended to inspire our informants to "open up," a few of the narratives we gathered were still extremely "closed" – that is, short, limited, and highly generic. However, we consider these interviews to be important to our project and its findings; their "muteness" has its own value.

What did the respondents choose to tell us about themselves? What approaches did they take to telling their own stories? Why were some eloquent and generous in sharing their lives with us? And why did others choose to remain silent about some parts of their personal and public pasts? Were their personal narratives informed by any public discourses of the day? In what ways was their reflectivity affected by public narratives of the past? Which of these various public versions of the past – first the Soviet, then later various post-Soviet narratives – did they recognize and use as their own? As I listened to the interviews and read through their transcripts, I kept thinking that "big" history, the national history-at-large that the narrators seemed to be reminiscing about, in the end turned out to be merely the background for their intimate and treasured personal histories. They worked hard (i.e., performed biographic work) to craft their life narratives so that they emerged as winners or losers, happy people or sad ones, heroes or victims. The respondents who perceived themselves as "winners" (or "hunters," to use the term coined by the renowned Russian psychologist Veronika Nurkova, who examined the psychological dimensions of biographical personal narratives)[7] saw many more positive elements in otherwise challenging situations such as the war or Soviet government repression than those who perceived themselves as "fugitives" or "escapees" (two other of Nurkova's terms) – that is, those who positioned themselves as "unhappy," "unappreciated" or "a victim." The stories told by the latter respondents often shared a certain intonation: the tellers sounded unconfident, complaining, suffering. By contrast, the monologues of the "fighters, gamblers, and winners" were much more energetic. In such situations, it would not be prudent to trust at face value the informants' messages regarding "big" history without taking into account their conceptions of themselves and their lives. At the same time, the observations of Nurkova, who developed the working metaphors of "hunters" and "escapees"/"fugitives," seem to me (a historian) both convincing and useful. For example, she has remarked that "fugitives," who tend to avoid difficulties, are quite verbose in their "free form" narratives, whereas "hunters" (who take an aggressive attitude towards difficulties, who "take on" problems) are much more emotional when describing extraordinary events of their lives. At the same time, "[it is] interesting, that no 'hunter' belongs to the group of those "who accept their past." Furthermore, [the] autobiographic memory itself, pertinent to each of these groups, exists as if in different systems of coordinates that intersect only partially. For the "fugitives," such a system is defined by the *experience of an event* (the meaning-based system of marking), by the feeling along the scale of pleasant–unpleasant. The "hunters" are more interested in the *cognitive aspect of an event* (or in [the] knowledge system). Consequently, the two groups have their "own" dominant mechanisms of achieving the inner comfort. While the "fugitives" are trying to "cover" the whole fields of their lives with [an] uncritical, relatively undifferentiated positive emotional medium, which is independent of the real contents of the events, the "hunters" try to rationally make sense out of the events following their cognitive schemes and scenarios.[8]

This may sound obvious, but it appears that for any individual, the most important topic to reflect on and reminisce about is their own life experiences. Personal past and life experiences may be projected by interviewees onto their interviewers or onto other willing listeners in a variety of ways. The narrators may be producing an optimistic–heroic narrative and thus be effectively embedding their own stories in their country's history, which is seen and understood in the same optimistic–heroic terms. Or the narrators, seeing themselves as victims, may present their life stories as stories of suffering, and in this way the country's history in their reminiscences acquires a corresponding character. The importance of reconstructing and reinterpreting the "role" of the respondent's story's has been pointed out by authorities in biographic studies such as Aleksei Valevskii.[9] Psychologists Ye. S. Kalmykova and E. Mergentaller assert that

> persons, while living their lives, simultaneously construct their stories … Every life event retrospectively receives a certain interpretation, which is determined by the preceding sequence of events. In such a way, a sort of a

> chain is being built ... If the essence of such an interpretation is a positive one, a person perceives the course of their life as a sequence of successful decisions and reached goals, the accidental failures and obstacles notwithstanding. If the fundamental interpretation is negative, then the perception of one's life is coloured negatively independently of person's actual success in their activities.[10]

Nurkova hypothesizes that while "ideally," the autobiographic memory, which plays the most important role in the construction of a personality, balances the traumatic and positive memories, the particular events "filed into memory" are determined by individual inclination.[11]

Everything plays a role in determining life self-perception and the "life scenario": social environment, cultural currents, individual life circumstances, temperament, psychological make-up, relations with parents, childhood lullabies, the first book read in childhood, an illness, and so on ... If we understand all of these aspects or phenomena as texts (which is exactly how they are presented in logocentric postmodern thought), then it makes sense to follow the principle of intertextuality. This principle is understood as the situation where a text is supported by a text and a plot (including the plot of one's own life) is supported by a plot. The term "intertextuality," introduced by Julia Kristeva,[12] has since been reinterpreted by Roland Barthes as the presence in every text of the "texts of the preceding culture and the texts of the surrounding culture," of the "shreds of the cultural codes, formulae, rhythmic structures, fragments of social idioms," "the spatial multilinearity of the signifiers,"[13] and it has since been understood, by Nathalie Piégay-Gros, as the "trace" that is left in the text by culture and ideology,[14] a palimpsest of diverse discourses. Undoubtedly, autobiographic stories are intertextual as well. Moreover, the more "faded" or "erased" seem the traces of other texts in an autobiographic story, the more important those "faded" texts may be for the narrator, for according to the Dutch intellectual historian Frank Ankersmit, "both in psychoanalysis and in history, that which has been repressed, manifests itself only in minor and seemingly irrelevant details."[15] Yet it is exactly by following these "faded traces," "commentaries" (Roland Barthes), "silences" (Frank Ankersmit), "clues" (Carlo Ginsburg), that one can read the person's life scenario the most precisely.

Besides being intertextual and dependent on the psychological profile of the narrator, autobiographic accounts can take on a variety of narrative forms, which we can refer to as genres. In the well-known classification of Hayden White, every presentation of a story (including the story of one's own life) takes on one of these four literary forms: novel, tragedy, comedy, or satire. The "package of events" included in the story as facts depends on the choice of narrative form. A novel is essentially "a drama of self-identification," "a drama of the triumph of good over evil," whereas satire is based on the idea that "the world has grown old – it is a drama of fate that submits to the suspicion that [the] human, in final account, is a prisoner of this world rather than its lord." A comedy achieves the final "peace between humans, with their world and society," because it presents societal conditions as "purer, healthier, and more normal," whereas a tragedy describes the situation of a human facing adverse forces, which are the eternal conditions in which he or she is doomed to live. According to White, tragedy and satire are equally derived from the idea of a certain ever-existing, eternal structure, the "eternal return of the same in the different," whereas the novel and the comedy stress the emergence of new powers and conditions.[16]

In a similar manner and for similar purposes, the plot structures used in the analysis of narratives in psychology either interpret the ideas of Northrop Frye (as did, for example, Kevin Murray)[17] or develop Carl Jung's concept of archetypes in a particular way (as did James Hillman, who distinguished alchemical, heroic, trickster, erotic, Saturnian, animistic, and Dionysian genres of stories).[18] In any case, in our project, autobiographic narratives presented themselves as a combination of individual psychic and social experience, and this "scenario"-based approach allowed us to distinguish these two levels and correctly evaluate their interactions.

Thus, the drama of self-identification and overcoming feelings of guilt towards her mother, who had been repressed by the Soviet authorities in the 1930s, constituted the plot in the life novel of Tatiana T.[19] Tatiana, a retired engineer, born in 1936, was in some ways a typical child of her generation; in other ways, she was not. In the turbulent 1930s, when Stalinist repression reigned throughout the Soviet Union, her parents were exiled to the Gulag, that is, to the state labour internment camps, as enemies of the people. She was too young to remember them, and at the time, her only experience of their absence was not understanding why they were gone. Perhaps that is why, when they returned after eight years' imprisonment, unlike her older sisters and brothers, she continued to harbour resentment towards her mother. As teenager, she lived through the Great Patriotic War and was looked after by her relatives. Only later in life did she come to understand the context of her mother's exile, at which time she began to develop a deep sense of guilt for pushing her mother away all her life. As a result, her life story is informed by her feelings of guilt and by her desire to repay her debt to her mother. Throughout the interview, in which she discussed her life with her family, she repeatedly returned to the topic of her guilt. Throughout her interview, her journey from a broken and fragmented to an integrated self was her main theme:

> Mostly I lived with my aunt who replaced for me my mother, Papa and everyone, who put me on my feet, taught me. Because I was the youngest in the family – from me many things were [concealed], they wouldn't tell me, practically for a very, very long time I did not even know, where my parents were. I did not understand [why they were away]. This was especially hard when I was in the first grade [of elementary school]. It was the year 1942, the war was going on, children, as a rule, were expressing much pride about their fathers – one had a fighter pilot, another – the communications troops member, another one a machine gun shooter. They keep asking: And who is your father? I am silent because I don't know. I would come home and break down crying: where's Papa, why Papa, why everyone has a father and I don't, why I don't know [where he is]? Well, in roundabout ways they tried somehow [to let me know]. In other words, nobody was telling me directly anything. For many long years I did not understand anything, did not know. I did not know where was my Mama, why everyone had one and I didn't. When she came back, she returned in eight years that she spent in Temnikovskie camps, it is in Mordovia, special women's camps, she returned, she experienced a big tragedy [with me], in my opinion – because while the older children still remembered her and communicated with her, I ignored her entirely, to me she did not exist, she was an alien person. And this ice of alienation has melted, I would say, not at once. Many years had passed before I began to thaw towards her.[20]

This woman worked through this childhood trauma for many years. Perhaps as an outcome of this, with the collapse of the Soviet Union, she became the head of the local memorial society,[21] which commemorated the lives of women who had been wrongly persecuted by the Soviet government and sent to its labour camps in Siberia and the Soviet Far East. Working for this society has become for her the meaning of her life. Here we see the obvious (according to White) "novel of redemption," in which the "big history" of the state constitutes the appropriate "stage" in the form of consistent liberalization of the state and the humanization of society.

The story of the oldest respondent in my project, Maria (born 1921), contrasts sharply with the previous one. Maria started her professional path as a village kindergarten teacher but soon transferred to administrative work on her collective farm, where her tasks ranged from building a pharmacy to establishing discipline in the town dormitory. At the time of the interview, she was quite ill, living on a very small pension together with her divorced daughter and granddaughter. Yet her highly organized and even pedantic personality – she was used to ordering her own and other people's lives – still came through in her reflections. Her story reflected her certainty that fools and dishonest people would eternally prevail. She satirically depicted her lifelong struggles against both. She desperately continued this struggle wherever she worked. Poignant human loneliness reverberated throughout her story. It was the loneliness of a strong woman among weak men (her husband, son, and son-in-law) and ungrateful women (her daughter and her subordinates). She perceived the state (independently of any regime, Soviet or post-Soviet), personified by the smart "superiors" who lobbied for her and who valued her honesty and drive, as a rational opposition to the world's chaos and the crowd's destructive instincts:

> I already had left the school. Supervisors were needed [during the war years]. I worked, I checked everything, I kept telling everybody: control, accounting, discipline is everything; if there is no discipline – nothing will be [accomplished] … Before me, [our collective] farm was falling apart. So, the milkmaids would milk – and then they would go home with that milk, they would steal it. They stole all the milk, they did not produce the quota, and it was in the times when we had to [send] everything to the war front.[22] So they put me [in charge]: "Well," I say, "my dears. So you're milking: one comes at five, another comes at seven; this will stop. You'll be coming then, and then begin milking, when I am not here yet." And I came before all milkmaids … I was not afraid of *raikom,*[23] of anybody … Went [once] to the sales outlets, to check. So, I would arrive … and I say: "Why you do not have the new price [tags] on any goods? I am closing the store right now! Immediately put the prices on! You may not sleep this night, but you got to do this – I'll come and check!" … Nobody would complete the plan,[24] but I did.[25]

Once the war ended, Maria continued to rule with the same harshness and rigidity as during the war:

> Oh, how they started hating me! They [called] me a toad – I had a khaki suit, I wore it for a long time; and they shot at me, and threatened to kill me. I would come home at midnight, after I would check everything – [at work] by myself ... I established there such an order – all the city knew [me]. [One day] we were moving into a newly constructed building – everything leaks [in there, the building is unfinished] ... So I refused to sign off the building until they finished everything, I checked the shower stalls myself, so that everything would work. I am a cashier, and an accountant, and a kindergarten teacher. Once I busted one kindergarten teacher – was she ever drunk! And I was saying: "I am a superintendent, I cannot trust you." And so I worked like this for twenty years.[26]

At the apogee of this satire of humanity, she suddenly noticed one day that she had no date of birth in her passport (that she was born "out" of time, before the beginning of time, really):

> I am asking mama: "Mama. When was I born?" My mama was barely literate, and it was famine, I had to get a passport, I was applying to a medical college in Troitsk. I am saying: "Mama, when was I born?" so she sat silently for a while, "It was famine, hunger. It was the Week of Maslianitsa.[27]" But Maslianitsa week is a [whole] week! So you have it. In my passport, I think, there isn't even a date.[28]

However, this shocking statement should not be seen as a manifestation of the senile incoherence of the respondent, not at all. She corrected herself with a smirk: "I think, there isn't even a date." Perhaps these words meant she was sending a new challenge to the world (in this case, represented by the interviewer). In addition, in this case we, without a doubt, are facing the experience of eternally halted, enchanted time. It seems that this halt occurred a very long time ago, probably as a response to her mother's refusal to give her little daughter away to the refugees who were passing through (sometime between 1923 and 1925):

> Already back then our people were fleeing to China, the rich ones, through our Kustanai region. They had gramophones. So [one day] they turned a gramophone on and I started dancing. They were saying: "Oh, give us this child!" Mother said: "How am I going to give you my child?" – I had three brothers and I was the only girl; a princess. She said: "What are you saying! Never!" So well I danced then.[29]

Referring to herself as a "princess," she stressed that she was born for joy and happiness (for "dance"). However, there had been no happiness, joy, or love in her life. At least, they are not found anywhere in the interview – not even in relation to the births of her children. Her life with a husband, whom she did not love, and who was constantly drunk and unfaithful, she interpreted as a failure to fulfil a destiny. The episode with the refugees, which at first seems redundant to her story, thus turns out to be "evidence" (in terms of Carlo Ginzburg) or "commentary" (in terms of Roland Barthes) that reveals its metaphoric, form- and plot-creating meaning and function. In the same way that the offended witch casts a spell on the princess and enchants her, the "offended" and jealous refugees (also a completely metaphoric image) turned the girl, who was born a "princess," into a stern, unfeminine chthonic character.

This calls to mind Hayden White: "Satire paints grey on grey, sensing its own inadequacy as the image of reality. Thus it ... anticipates the return of mythic perception of the world and its processes."[30] The extent to which the satirical perception of life is different from the comic one is demonstrated by the interview with Margarita E. (born 1929), a teacher at Cheliabinsk Teacher College. Margarita was born into the family of a rural school director. She grew up during the difficult war years, graduated from a pedagogical institute, married, and moved with her husband to a new city, where she taught for more than forty years at a teacher's college. At the time of the interview, she was barely subsisting on a tiny state pension but continuing to display a positive attitude towards life. In the most devastating events, she could see positive, life-affirming features. Even her memories of the war were presented in this way:

> Gorki, Nizhnii Novgorod ...[31] They bombed it heavily ... and once when I looked – I could not see the sky, so many airplanes were there, imagine – could not see the sky. It was dark [because of these planes]. This is how many fascist airplanes were there. This is how many of them were on their way to [bomb] Moscow. Oh, how scary it was. The bombs were huge. And one fell without exploding. And so we ran to this bomb, and soldiers chased us away. It was fenced, that bomb, sappers came running, they dug around it for two days, and when they untied all the nuts, took everything from it, they saw that it was full of sand, and there was written in Russian: "Dear Russians! This is a gift from anti-fascists!" Imagine, this means that there were good people. Because if such a bomb exploded in our village, it would blow away everything.[32]

There were no tragic overtones or pessimistic conclusions in her story. Her ability to be amazed by life and enjoy it, and her self-irony, made the listener genuinely respect her. Here is how she described her naive enthusiasm during her youth. In times of bleak poverty and hunger, she actively participated in sports for her college. As an incentive to achieve in sports, her coach promised someday to invite her to eat in a restaurant: "I was an athlete, I took a second place in the institute in long-distance running. So you're running, little fool, and this one, the phys. ed. guy, keeps saying: 'I'll feed you, I'll take you to the restaurant,' was working you up. He always had a chocolate in his pocket, though."[33]

She greatly enjoyed her only trip abroad, to Poland, which she undertook at the age of forty-nine.[34] She described it using youthful, playful vocabulary:

> The girls are telling me: "So, Ritka, we will never be abroad again; we want to see striptease." I am saying: "Lord, who in the world would let us see striptease?" And in Poland, they had striptease in every restaurant. And so, in the restaurant where we had dinner, our group, we had a guide, Janek, I approached him and asked: "You know what, dear: do you have striptease in your restaurant?" – "Yes," – "All girls are asking for striptease," and two boys we had there, too, everyone is asking for striptease. He says, "Ok, girls, I'll arrange for it, but do not stray away after the striptease! [It will take place] right after we have dinner, simply stay in the restaurant." So we had our dinner. And then the lights started blinking, blinking. I have never seen anything like that; first, there was a concert; suddenly, they shout "Striptease!" So a girl comes out, very beautiful. She has this velvet cover, dark blue, or sky blue, a very beautiful colour ... She started dancing in gold sandals, a very beautiful necklace, white hairdo, and I was also a blondie then. So, here she's dancing, first took off her dress, she did not have any shirt, then she begins to take off her bra – and such a beautiful music started playing, we sit silent, and all men started yelling; then she took everything off, even last panties, men started yelling, Americans mostly, young men, forty [years old] or so, there were some Norwegians, some Swedes. She went away, dancing started, and so some Norwegian started clinging to me. And there is such rule: to dance three dances; until you have danced the three dances, you cannot leave. And so, you see, we danced and danced, I finally got bored; and so will you dance the third one? – Well, ok, let's dance. Yes, back then [I was] young, Lord; [we] danced.[35]

Anything that could upset this optimistic view of life (episodes related to her husband, or events of "big history" that did not have upbeat endings) simply was not included in this woman's personal scenario. "He was a ship's bo's'n,"[36] – she said of her husband. "Then he drank himself into being nothing. Let's not talk about him, I don't want, don't want to talk about him."

Tragedy, by contrast, focuses on the negative and dismisses anything that interrupts it. The story of schoolteacher Yulia U. (born 1961) reeks with the tragedy of unfulfilled ambitions, with the conviction that happiness is impossible. Thus, she became a teacher not by own choice but because "fate turned that way." In the beginning, she wanted more:

> In 1978, I entered Cheliabinsk State University, which initially was not a teacher training institution, but in the beginning of the 1980s there was a government decree to make Cheliabinsk State University a teacher-training university. There was no sense of quitting studying, so I had to continue studying.[37]

In the early 1980s, just as *perestroika* was about to take root, there were discussions about closing the institute, but these petered out. In the 1990s, in now post-Soviet Russia, the university was able to significantly raise its ratings. At the same time, though, most university graduates, not just in Cheliabinsk, were ending up as schoolteachers. In other words, there was no sudden and catastrophic change of circumstances with regard to which the narrator presented herself as a passive sufferer. It appears that she simply did not want to articulate (probably even to herself) the real reasons why, after graduating from a university, she was unable to remain in academic scholarship. Indeed, she presented her entire life as one big insult relating to her circumstances and also to her husband, whose frequent business trips only heightened her loneliness. No surprise, then, that she presented the story of her family and of the entire country with the same tragic intonation: everywhere was lies, deceit. Her feelings towards her motherland, the state, reflected the same sense of insult (and she hand-picked the circumstances to fit this):

> My generation grew up in the period of "thaw," after the terrible 1940s and brutal 1950s, and during the period of "stagnation." My childhood was in the 1960s. This is why, probably, I am a lifelong romantic … I strongly feel other people's pain. Probably, it was absorbed in the childhood, from my

> father, whose life was trampled by the 1930s. Then, he lost his father. And the 1940s, the war years – shell-shock, captivity, and later – a lifelong feeling of guilt and oppression. For forty years I have been hearing how father in his sleep was charging in an attack, shouted, protecting me and mama from the fascists, and watching the Soviet movies about war, he sighed bitterly and ground his teeth, seeing the lies on the screen. All doors were closed for him – [Communist] Party membership, a supervisory position, ability to travel abroad. He was not even allowed to go to Kaliningrad[38] to throw a handful of our earth on his brother's grave,[39] where his brother was buried. Then, this all was confusing.[40] And especially [confusing was] a stormy reaction of my father to my refusal, at the end of the 1980s, to join the Party, because this all was artificial, not from the heart – the Party was not with the people. Then, for the first time, I heard revelations, which were unexpected to me.[41]

The male version of the tragedy of unsatisfied ambition and of personal insults, transferred onto the circumstances of the "big history," is represented by the narrator Aleksandr A. (legal consultant, born 1946). Despite being a well-established individual with a stable family, a prestigious job, and financial prosperity, who preferred not to talk about his own successes, Aleksandr positioned himself as a member of the marginal, disenfranchised intelligentsia. He stressed that he played "dissent" jazz and listened to Voice of America and that his poetry and fiction had been rejected by publishers. He readily presented episodes of "oppression." For example, his father, a mining engineer from a wealthy Cossack family, fought by turn for the Reds and the Whites, became a staunch communist and atheist, was arrested in 1937 after his friends reported him to the authorities, and was exiled with all his family. But as Aleksandr's story approached his current successful life, he abruptly ended it. His genuine success in life clashes with his inner scenario of being an outcast, for which he had carefully prepared the stage:

> In high school we were taught by professors and doctors of sciences – all were repressed, from Leningrad. There was even a member of the Academy, but he was prohibited to teach, so he was a maintenance superintendent and he walked around ringing the bell announcing recess … But they treated us very respectfully. Contrary to the teachers of history and geography[42] … The history teacher was the secretary of [a local communist] party organization. She was a lonely, small, but very lively woman with a screechy voice and a sarcastic-arrogant facial expression. Without much

> effort, she humiliated every student, doing this quite artfully and with obvious pleasure, publicly ... The new school principal ... knocked with his hard finger on my forehead while the whole class was watching as I stood stunned, and said: "If we need to, we'll kick out everyone, and not only those who babble about genetics and cybernetics.[43] Enemies' brood! And with your parents they'll talk in a proper place."[44] During the recess, I was given my personal file and sent home. I "babbled" shortly before that with my peers about the future of cybernetics. It is important to mention that two years ago, my friend, the son of a former school principal, being quite drunk, apologized to me for being the one who then "ratted me out," and then went to *Artek* – a Soviet children summer camp for the chosen ones.[45]

It is impossible not to notice the literary sophistication of this text. It is likely that the author had recorded it before, on a different occasion. It is possible that he and some other respondents had "thought through" the approaching interview, rehearsed it, and constructed in their minds the texts about their own lives, together with plot and the meaning, long before the interviews.

I far more commonly encountered stories executed in the genres of the comedy and the novel, rather than tragedy or satire. Probably, this was partly because for those who are getting older and nearing their end, life's results must at least *seem* positive. As they near death, humans need to feel at peace with reality and with themselves. Also, biographic material is better suited to the novel or the comedy. Finally, novels and comedies are studied at schools more than the other two forms, are more often made into feature films, and are more often read, and this creates a "plot template" ready for borrowing.

Sometimes the "originals" – that is, pre-existing stories available in the domain of public discourse – alluded to in autobiographic texts are rather easy to identify. For example, the life story of Liudmila V. (medical doctor, born 1942) can easily be associated with the myth of the Decembrists. The Decembrists were Russian officers who in 1825 launched a coup against the tzar. After it failed, they were either executed or exiled to Siberia. They have long occupied a prominent place in official narratives of Russian (including Soviet) history. The myth that surrounds them has been crystallized in Russian-speaking culture through the poetry of Aleksandr Pushkin ("In the Depths of Siberian Mines"); in the writings of another Russian left-wing intellectual, Aleksandr Herzen ("My Past and Thoughts"); and in literary works by Leo

Tolstoy ("Decembrists"), Nykolai Nekrasov ("Russian Women"), and Marina Tsvetaeva ("To the Generals of 1812"). And in Soviet times, this myth was reinvented in the cult Soviet movie *The Star of Amazing Happiness* (*Zvezda Plenitelnogo Schastia*; 1975).

Liudmila utilized this public story for her own purposes, perhaps because she and her family were also of noble origin and because her father, husband, and son had been the officers, as "the nobles should." She referred to her husband as a "stunning *cavelier-guarde*,"[46] bringing to mind not only a popular song from the aforementioned movie but also the refined image of its main protagonist. Thus, she saw herself as a "Decembrist wife" (after the failed coup, the wives of the noble Decembrists voluntarily followed their exiled husbands to Siberia). The very first sentence with which she began her interview was a quote from Pushkin (who had been part of the Decembrists' circle): "Roots of my family are the affairs of the days long past, the lore of deep antiquity."[47]

Telling about her profession, she stressed its perfect suitability for a "Decembrist's wife": "I chose pediatrics, because my husband was a military man, we moved often … and this profession turned out to be very useful for me … Such was the specialization that I was always in demand and always had a job."[48]

Since "officer's honour" presupposed loyalty to the Motherland, the narrator firmly asserted that the Stalinist repression could never have touched their "loyal" family:

> The repressions were for those who disagreed with that regime that we had. Among us, those who disagreed, my ancestors, they all went abroad. And those who agreed, all were content, and were happy because of construction, because of the development of our state, and everyone was for the Motherland.[49]

The concept of "officer's loyalty" directly contradicted the rebellious love for freedom of the Decembrists, but this narrator did not notice the conflict. Indeed, she conveyed that she would like

> to change what the heroes of the 1825 wanted to change [in the society], and the heroes of the 1812. These heroes are my favourite people on Earth. For me there are no better heroes. I revere them, I know them, I read all about them since my 5th grade, I know them all … I bow to them, and I want now what they wanted and for what they were exiled. But who they were – who? Princes they were. All of them, born as royalty, yet they

wanted people to live well, that there would be no poor, that everyone be rich and happy. I also want the same. I don't know who else wants that though. If somebody wanted that [among the authorities], we would not have been given pensions of three thousand and four thousand [roubles a month], but instead would be getting some fifteen thousand, and would not have to go to welfare offices with the outstretched arm.[50]

The patriotic motif of the "officer's loyalty to Motherland" prompted our narrator to interrupt her critical remarks, addressed to the state powers, and to conclude her interview with an optimistic quote from Pushkin, dedicated to the Decembrists: "I think that everything still will be well, this is simply such time, a little more, just a little bit, everything will be alright. *Our Russia will awaken from slumber, and on the ruins of the despotism they will write our names*!"[51]

Probably, our narrator initially conceived her plot as a "novel," but in its final form it much more resembled a comedy.

The story of Valentina A. (born 1926), a singer and teacher of voice, is a tragic tale of lost paradise. In her account, happiness and a carefree life are symbolized by the dear father's grand piano, which later serves as a table for the cooking stove of evacuated people[52] with whom they must share their apartment. The final parting with the piano signifies the loss of the father as a source of happiness. The narrator's subsequent life is presented as "disenchanted" years on the fallen earth, with the bitterness of the loss remaining forever:

My father [was] a musician, a pianist of a high rank, he played in an orchestra and taught students. I remember my childhood, how musicians gathered in our place, a quartet – a cello, a violin, an alto, and Papa played the piano. Mama sang very well, she was a mezzo-soprano, Mama also played as an amateur, she liked to play. So we had a grand piano in our place, and my child's bed stood in the curved indentation of this piano, this is how we lived, in a private apartment; papa also worked as the editor at music radio ... When the war began ... a very hard life had begun ... When they took papa, our life was, of course, hard. I went to work. I worked there for more than two years, until I got sick ... It was a high hazard factory shop in general ... We were signed to receive some sort of a milk soufflé,[53] but I never, we, minors, never had any. Our supervisors took it all for themselves. Completely. We starved terribly ... Then, the war was over, papa returned ... Life was very difficult. In our apartment, in two rooms out of three, lived the evacuated. In the room where was the grand piano, lived ... mother and son, so they terribly disfigured our piano, they put a cooking stove on it, cooked, and everything would overflow ... When papa returned, he started working again, he had a heart attack and we had to sell the grand piano ... Husband ... was a deep water diver, he worked at Northern Fleet, visited Norway ... When "Kursk"[54] perished, he so deeply grieved, impossibly, he was terribly upset, he had been there literally several days prior, saw all those guys, and so he was saying, that before, when he was in service, we would, he said, lift that "Kursk" easily, and now there isn't the base, you understand, everything they sold. There was no one to lift it, they asked abroad. He was so upset, he really wept, sat in front of a TV and wept ... At first, we lived in a three-room apartment ... We lived so well, supported each other. And after son's death he got sick, and I never left him alone, my daughter moved in, supported me. He had lung cancer, it is not simple, he was choking. His friends visited him, but nobody from the factory helped anymore, everything fell apart there, they changed the management.[55]

The falling apart of paradise signified for Valentina a descent into evil, even though the real facts, which she reported quite unwillingly and by accident, painted her life in much less tragic form. She allowed no place for the positive events of "big history," for they would have clashed with her personal biographic scenario.

The memoir of Yelena L. (singer, voice teacher, born 1928) amounts to a modern Cinderella novel. She was pulled out of misery and boredom by her fairy godmother. In her narrative, the fairy tale is fortified by being doubled through two people: the Moscow singer Basova and Ye.F. Gnesina, a famous pianist and a founder of the music college in Moscow:

During the war ... I worked at a machine plant, machine-building, myself and my sister. Since our family had many children, there were five children, to get personal bread rations, 800 grams, they found us jobs there, at that machine plant. There I worked for a year. To leave the plant – they wouldn't let me go – I had to ask to apply to a mechanics trade school. I did not have to study there, but I spent there half a year ... At fifteen, I had an audition with a certain teacher, she said: "Girl, you have a great voice, but wait until you turn 16 and we'll accept you into our music school." So I wait to turn sixteen, go to that school, study there for five years, if you count the preparation year, because I could not read scores when I was applying; now I perform at concerts, get an honours diploma ... In

> 1949, I find a job singing in the movie theatres, because I needed to make money and help my family. Sing different songs before the feature presentation. But I, of course, was frustrated, I was very traumatized, because there always someone eats ice-cream, they throw stuff … So, they tell me: "You with your voice have to go to study." I only worked there for ten months, so I take my little suitcase, take 30 roubles and go to Moscow … To Gnesina college.[56] So, the first round,[57] I left the hall, this round, the first one, just ended. Gnesina comes out herself, Yelena Fabianovna, takes my arm, like this, she is so imposing, like the Queen of Spades, she came out: "Lenochka, my namesake," she says, "consider yourself already being accepted to Gnesina … Go home, we'll give you a dorm place, you are regarded as our student" … So, my years of studying in Gnesina began to flow. Of course, there was no end to joy. We went to theatres, we were given all kinds of passes, they wanted us to go more … All theatres, the Drama theatre, I've seen all the plays, got to know all the actors … I worked for a month at Vakhtangov theatre, they allowed us to watch all plays, and how they rehearsed. Now, also Comédie-Français came once. And I also got there. We learned one play in French, and we sang in a choir there for three roubles. Then they travel to Leningrad for a month and take us with them, we lived in a hotel, I lived in "Astoria," in a separate suite. For me this was simply a luxury: for such a poor student like myself, to live in a separate suite, telephone, bathtub … everyone thought that we also were French, I was a brunette then. I got to know all the actors.[58]

Identifying oneself within the framework of one or another plot naturally presupposes investing one's life partners with corresponding role functions. Yelena did not love her husband, but since she was Cinderella, she presented him as a prince – he was good-looking, he courted her with style and expensively, and he emphatically did *not* have a name. She did not provide it even when specifically asked:

> He came to the plays, listened. After the performance I would go home, I had a classy apartment, two rooms, theatre assigned it to me, and he walked quietly home, and I didn't know. And then, at the theatre, one day, he came, there was some party. He asked me to dance. So, we started dancing together, introduced ourselves: "May I walk you home?" He was appealing, good-looking, and I already had many years. Since I work in a theatre, achieved what I wanted, and became satisfied with my work, now I wanted to have a family, I wanted a child.[59]

It is telling that Yelena's story, which sounds like the narrative of a heroine being awarded with "happiness" for her goodness and endured sufferings, stops cold the moment her child is born. That her only child was born gravely and incurably ill did not enter the story, for that would have overturned the logic of the plot.

The biographic interview with Vladimir B. (college professor, born 1928) contains a tragic story: an exile lost his homeland and his identity and, like Oedipus, endured a deep conflict with his parents, whom he blamed for his miserable condition. Vladimir was married, had two children, and had taught Russian language and literature at a local college. Neither his mother, who raised him on her own, nor his father, who died in the war, received from the narrator a single word of affection. A few times he even referred to himself as "an orphan." At the very beginning of the interview, he blurted out that he was a Volga German, but thereafter, he thoroughly avoided that aspect of his life. He also said nothing about his children (the interviewer learned by accident, from the respondent's wife, during the post-interview wrap-up, that his daughter had gone to live in Germany). In his story, Vladimir presented Russia, both Soviet and post-Soviet, as a space of "lies," and he contrasted this with his lost but honest homeland, Germany (carefully concealed by the name "Europe"):

> Solzhenitsyn's "to live not by lies" is still applicable [in Russia]: Even today, everyone lies to us, and still we do not believe anything ... Now, for instance, I do not know a single sphere of our Russian life where things would be going well. How normal is this – [to have solid] steel doors [instead of standard apartment doors] and metal bars on the windows – this is the shame of the nation. In Germany – I often visit Germany, Italy, France ... – there, whatever doors they have, they are made of glass. The house keys are [so small] as if they are for a closet, cars there – one would arrive and wouldn't even lock the car, [for many] it is not worth the effort. And no anti-theft alarms [are installed in the cars]! What a shame![60]

To him, everything was equally alien in his "false" Motherland (which predetermined his inclination towards dissent, something that he himself mentioned). The Pyrrhic victory over Fascism he viewed as evil: "Our victory – is when one evil, the Red evil, overcame another evil ... We liberated one evil for the sake of another." He was equally disparaging of the "lies" of Communism and the depravity of "democracy." Everything that the Russian state asserted, even the post-Soviet state, he was ready to call a "lie": "[This is] a lie that there were no children's deaths. Children died of hunger during the war – and 'they' would claim that there was no such thing."[61] And immediately after this programmatic declaration about the deceiving nature of his Motherland, he remembered:

> One girl, want[s] to eat. So she ate a lot of these ripe peas, there, in her stomach, everything swelled up, and by the morning she died. Andriusha Lopatochkin took that grenade, we are children, after all – and blew himself up.[62]

None of this was an attempt to deceive the interviewer. Nor was it a blind reproduction of discourses that had been adopted despite their conflicting nature. These were simply two different semantic layers of "truth."

The realization of such layering becomes the "main research outcome" that a researcher achieves, having analysed the autobiographic text from the perspective of plot analysis. This realization erases the temptation to accuse the narrators of "deceit" and leads to an understanding of why the overall narrative picture was produced the way it was. This in turn allows us to further clarify the narrator's view of "big history."

For example, it is known how tense and at times brutal the battles over the interpretation of the "Soviet past" can be in Russia today. However, the idyllic *and* the grotesque depictions of the Soviet era, resulting from the ongoing "condensation" of recollections and facts, are equally authentic. From this we can conclude, on the basis of contradictory "recollections of the Soviet past," that we can hardly diagnose the scale of the social schism and trauma, and certainly it would be wrong to exaggerate them, when we treat individuals as carriers of collective memory.[63] An individual's unique life drama is built on a complex interweaving of texts, all of which are successively linked.

Recognizing and reading a biographical story as a palimpsest is a difficult task and for a historian an unusual one. Besides possessing erudition, a formidable imagination, and psychological sensitivity, the interpreter must be sufficiently immersed in the narrator's intellectual universe to be able to understand it and at the same time must be sufficiently separated from it to avoid being assimilated or absorbed into it. While working with oral biographic stories, sustaining the latter challenge is especially difficult, because oral narrative has its particular mutating intertextuality (not to mention there is a non-verbal behavioural continuum that forms a separate text layer, which is hard to notice and almost impossible to describe).

But all of these difficulties are worthwhile when they pay off – when the researchers, having an inventory of critical tools at their disposal and maintaining a position of respect and trust, are able to peer into the personalities of respondents. The researcher should never be preoccupied with catching respondents' lies. That would offend the situation, which presupposes mutual sincerity. At the same time, the researcher does not have to pretend that the story is being gullibly taken at face value. It is good to practise methodical doubt as both the respondent and the interpreter join the intertextual exchange, where the "truth of the text" is much easier to discuss than the "truth of life." The researcher may trace the circulation of texts and discourses in a culture, the degree and character of their "interface" with different groups of people, their illustrative capacity, their sequence in terms of arranged "historical facts," and so on.

In this way, the subjectivity of oral history, the "vagueness" and "ambiguity" of its texts, ceases to be a lamentable error of a source and becomes a vital tool for opening the way to deeper and more subtle historical analysis. Even the narrators themselves, "the small people," through this approach stop being mere commentators and finally become characters and actors in their own histories.

NOTES

1 Thompson, *The Voice of the Past*; Thompson, *Golos Proshlogo*, 18.
2 Loskutova, *Ustnaia Istoriia*, 32.
3 Bertaux, Rotkirch, and Thompson, *On Living Through Soviet Russia*, 9.
4 Allen and Montell, *From Memory to History*, 84–6; Hoffman, "Reliability and Validity," 69.
5 "Intelligentsia" is a widely used trope in the Russian and other Slavic languages in the former USSR to designate a unique category of citizens in the society who are educated beyond high school, who are employed in education, culture, research, and science, and who in the former USSR were considered a separate social class (editors' note).
6 Assmann, *Das kulturelle Gedächtnis*.
7 Nurkova, *Svershennoe Prodolzhaetsia*, 156, 162.
8 Nurkova, *Svershennoe Prodolzhaetsia*, 162, 163, 164.
9 Valevskii, *Osnovaniia Biografiki*, 28.
10 Kalmykova and Mergentaller, "Narrativ v Psikhoterapii."

11 Nurkova, *Svershennoe Prodolzhaetsia*, 19, 24.
12 Kristeva, "Bakhtine."
13 See Il'in, "Intertekstual'nost'"; Barthes, *Izbrannie raboty*, 417, 418.
14 Piege-Gro, *Vvedenie v Teoriiu*, 66.
15 Ankersmit, *Istoriia i Tropologiia*, 332.
16 White, *Metaistoriia*, 28–30.
17 Il'in, *Postmodernizm*, 146–7.
18 Hillman, *Arkhetipicheskaia Psikhologiia*; Hillman, *Istseliaiushchii Vymysel*.
19 The names of the respondents in this project have been changed to protect their privacy.
20 Tatiana T. (born 1936), interview.
21 The Memorial Society of Russia creates a historical memory about the crimes committed by the Soviet regime through research and publications, conducts social work for the victims of the Soviet regime and their relatives, and monitors human rights in present-day Russia.
22 One needs to put this presentation in perspective. The mass theft of collective farm produce during the war was a response to the severe deprivation that rural citizens were subjected to by the state, which squeezed all the resources it could from them in order to feed the troops. Stealing milk meant bringing at least something to eat for hungry children at home.
23 Regional Committee of the Communist Party (translator's note).
24 She means a five-year plan, a one-year plan, a quarter-year plan, or any (or all) of many plans (for sales, production, etc.) that existed in the Soviet economy (translator's note).
25 Maria (born 1921), interview.
26 This segment is perhaps confusing, because the respondent tells about her many jobs without any separation between them. I have counted five different jobs but am not sure if that is the correct number (translator's note).
27 The week before the beginning of Lent. *Maslianitsa* is a time of festivities, which are held on the Eve of Lent. In 1921, though, when famine was raging across much of southern Russia, there were no festivities, for the villagers were struck by severe hunger. Even the birth of a child during that time was not a happy event – indeed, it may not have been noteworthy at all, for infants were not expected to survive.
28 Maria, interview.
29 Maria, interview.
30 White, *Metaistoriia*, 30.
31 Nizhny Novgorod was renamed Gorky in 1932, in honour of the Soviet writer Maksim Gorky.
32 Margarita E. (born 1929), interview.

33 Margarita E., interview.

34 For Soviet citizens, trips abroad were rare. Unless the travel was for business, only state-organized tours were permitted. Members of Soviet labour unions working in various Soviet enterprises were allowed to go, but only to neighbouring socialist states (editors' note).

35 Margarita E., interview.

36 "Boatswain" is a close but not precise translation of the Russian/Dutch botsman/bootsmann (translator's note).

37 Yulia U., interview.

38 The Kaliningrad region (former Eastern Prussia) was a semi-restricted area during Soviet times. Any person whose biography was somehow tarnished was not allowed to travel there.

39 "Brotherly grave" is a common trope in Russian culture. It refers to a collective grave of military personnel who died in action. Sometimes this term is applied to the collective graves of civilians (e.g., the cemetery of the victims of the Siege of Leningrad). In this case, it seems that the narrator means the military grave where, at the same time, her father's actual brother was buried (translator's note).

40 This is unclear, but it seems that by "confusing" the respondent means that she did not know about her father's limited civil rights on account of his captivity, about which she also did not know (translator's note).

41 Yulia U. (born 1961), interview. The 1930s were a time of severe repression and persecution in the former USSR; the 1950s were challenging times of post-war reconstruction. The 1960s were known as a period of "thaw," associated also with the rule of Nikita Khrushchev. This was followed by a period of stagnation while Leonid Brezhnev presided over the Communist Party and the USSR.

42 Here, the respondent touches on a subtle issue: a previously repressed and thereby suspect person would never be allowed to teach disciplines that had elements of ideology. Such disciplines could be entrusted only to "ideologically proven and trained" cadres (translator's note).

43 Both genetics and cybernetics were declared "false sciences," and their followers and students were variously persecuted in the USSR until the mid-1960s (translator's note).

44 A thinly veiled threat of the KGB (translator's note).

45 Aleksandr A. (born 1946), interview.

46 This was an officer rank in the first half of the nineteenth century, given only to very "pure-bred" aristocrats (translator's note).

47 The quote from Pushkin is in bold (translator's note).

48 Liudmila V. (born 1942), interview.

49 Liudmila V., interview.
50 Liudmila V., interview. Three thousand Russian roubles equalled 95 or 96 Canadian dollars (editors' note).
51 Liudmila V. The quote from Pushkin is in bold (translator's note).
52 "Evakuirovannye" were people who were moved from territories under threat of being occupied by the enemy, or who escaped from them (translator's note).
53 In the USSR, people who worked in highly hazardous places (with chemical vapours or in the smelters) were entitled to free rations of milk products (translator's note).
54 A nuclear submarine that sank in 2000 (translator's note).
55 Valentina A. (born 1926), interview.
56 It is a "Russian Julliard" (translator's note).
57 Of elimination exams-auditions (translator's note).
58 Yelena L. (born 1928), interview.
59 Yelena L., interview.
60 Vladimir B. (born 1928), interview.
61 Vladimir B., interview.
62 Vladimir B., interview.
63 Narskii, "V 'Imperii' i v 'Natsii,'" 86.

PART THREE

The Past Differentiated: Revisiting the Second World War and Its Aftermath

The most popular topic of oral historical research in Eastern and Central Europe today is the Second World War. Today, many oral historians in that region, both professional and amateur, are bringing to light alternative experiences of the war that never reached public mainstream narratives. At the same time, a great number of oral historians are focusing on questions of memory and how the war and (no less) post-war years in many countries were experienced, understood, and remembered by various constituencies and agents who were actively involved in it, be it as soldiers or civilians. Research into memories of the war in Europe has dominated the social sciences and humanities in Europe for quite some time. In this volume, Alexander von Plato has touched on the importance of this research for European societies. The dominance of war-related topics in this volume is a direct reflection of the state of affairs today in Eastern European oral historical research.

Alessandro Portelli once observed that the war lends itself well to oral historical work, because in researching it, oral historians are able not only to identify and compare competing official narratives and alternative previously silenced memories about the war but also to enhance oral history as both a theory and a method. Portelli's recent book *The Order Has Been Carried Out*[1] is an excellent example of this kind of achievement, in that it shows others how oral history can promote different versions of the past, how it can illuminate alternative memories of the war, and how it might redeem those who were treated as "liabilities" during the grand military actions of various armies.

Inspired by the work of their colleagues elsewhere in Europe, and often supported by EU grants, many Eastern European oral historians have begun exploring alternative memories of the war in their societies. Their research, however, unlike that of oral historians elsewhere in Europe, focuses on the region's post-war history, and much of it is informed by the fact that the post-war ideologies of the Socialist Bloc developed a uniform narrative of the war rooted in communist ideology and shared by all of the states in that bloc. Today's oral historians are seeking the *other* story of the war to share with the public, and the alternative memories they locate, when brought to the surface, at times contradict official, mainstream narratives. This clash between official and alternative narratives of the war has become a hallmark of Eastern European oral historical research into the war.

In this regard, scholars' explorations of alternative memories of the war converge with at least two other important avenues in post-socialist revisionist scholarship. The first involves exposing the crimes the communist states carried out during the war against their civil populations and military personnel.[2] The second highlights the complex history of undergound national movements, which fought against first the expansion and later the dominance of communist rule in Central and Eastern Europe. These oral historians document and explore the memories of those who belonged to undergound national movements (Młynarczyk, in this volume) as well as the experiences of political prisoners in the Gulag system who were persecuted for their "nationalist" activities.[3] None of this work is easy, given the complexity of current political and ideological battles in all post-socialist societies today, for it directly challenges the political establishment of various countries, as has been the case recently with Ukraine and Russia.

Another important direction for oral historians of the Second World War concerns whether and how individual subjects and agents articulate their traumatic wartime experiences in the public domain. This direction has dominated oral historical work on memory since oral history entered the post-socialist European domain. In post-socialist societies, this research has introduced victimhood discourse to the social sciences and humanities. Indeed, that discourse has evolved in scholarly and public discussions on the war as a direct outcome of oral historical work in the region. The victimhood debate in post-socialist oral history about the war reveals that in the Soviet Union during the war, victimization was multi-vectoral. As more oral history research was conducted in the former Soviet Union, it became clear not just that its citizens had suffered at the hands of the Nazi occupiers but that many had been subjected to new rounds of political repression under communism. Similarly, oral historians researching public and personal memory of the war in the region have had to take into account the post-war ideological contexts in which alternative versions of the war there were actively silenced.

A third direction in the oral history of the war is relatively new and in some ways is a response to oral historians' earlier preoccupation with juxtaposing public and private memories of the war and comparing and contrasting the war experiences of different victim groups. This direction is generating a new discourse of reconciliation and shared memorialization aimed at bringing together nations, individuals, and ideological camps who found themselves on opposing sides in the war, whether those sides were real or metaphorical. Here we again see how oral historical work has promoted positive social change in the region, given that the previous political system did not cultivate a culture of shared dialogue and that the absence of such dialogue is still felt strongly in many mainstream Eastern European cultures. The oral historical method, with its focus on the personal, when applied to re-evaluations of war experiences, provides solid ground for such reconciliation work. As Paul Thompson once acknowledged, it is not in the domain of theory but in the domain of real lives of real people that the potential rests for a shared understanding of the past. It is not by explaining or reconstructing historic macro-processes but by reaching into the hearts and listening to the stories of ordinary people who remember the war as the worst experience of their lives that we can build bridges between people.

The articles in this section relate directly to these three dimensions of oral historical work on memory and the war. They examine the relationship between official and private narratives, they reflect on the complexities of narrative reconstructions of traumatic experiences of deportation, and they reconstruct the little-known yet layered phenomenon of women's participation in the underground national resistance to the Soviet occupation.

As we mentioned earlier, much of the oral historical work in Eastern Europe has involved re-evaluating the war's events as experienced by various populations. At the same time, oral historians, while exploring alternative memories of the war, routinely question the very *process* of interpreting the data generated by oral historical interviews. Marta Kurkowska-Budzan, a well-known Polish oral historian, in her chapter about oral accounts of the anti-communist post-war underground in Poland, highlights an important dimension of the debate: the importance of the personal in historical research. She turns to her own interviewing practice in rural areas of Byalystok region, acknowledging that for various reasons, the narratives she recorded often did not fall easily into the analytical categories that have been constructed by scholars working in the tradition of the sociological biographical method. Part of the problem, she asserts, lies in how a historian approaches the respondent's role. Narrators, responding as eyewitnesses to the researchers' interest in some historical event, are often seen as delivering details that will shed more light on the event. Even when the researcher values the personal perspective, ultimately, he or she is not interested in the respondent but rather in the details of his or her account. Kurkowska-Budzan contends that this methodological assumption is not productive, for it prevents us from registering a whole range of important processes – of memory construction, of interpretation, and of tailoring the past to fit today's established imaginings and understandings.

Gelinada Grinchenko, a leading oral historian of Ukraine and the founding President of the Ukrainian Oral History Association, turns to the recollections of former child *Ostarbeiters* of Ukraine who were transported to Nazi Germany. She explores their narrative strategies for coping with their tainted past. Her chapter focuses on two oral history accounts that rely on quite different means of coping. Delving into the narrative organization of these two accounts, she presents two different narrative scenarios of self-positioning. The female narrator's story is organized around the experience of suffering and anxiety; the other respondent, a male narrator, has constructed a combative self-image of instead of positioning himself as a victim of fate and history. Grinchenko's analysis speaks directly to the impact of personal circumstances on the production of meaning and cultural memory. As such, it highlights yet another important dimension of the discussion of what is "personal" and what is "public" in the production of oral historical accounts of the past.

NOTES

1 Portelli, *The Order Has Been Carried Out*.
2 See for example, Geisler, "From the Voice of the Deported"; Uehling, *Beyond Memory*; Hurkina, "Dvi Doli"; Gudziak and Susak, "Becoming a Priest in the Underground."
3 For example, Gheith and Jolluck, *Gulag Voices*.

7 Experience and Narrative: Anti-Communist Armed Underground in Poland, 1944–1957

MARTA KURKOWSKA-BUDZAN

George H. Mead, the famous American philosopher, sociologist, and psychologist, once argued that the past "each time becomes a different past in each of the presents, in which we reconstruct it."[1] I have devoted my research to the issue of "reconstructing the past in the present" and more specifically to how contemporary interpretations of anti-communist resistance in early socialist Poland have endowed this particular past with a range of symbolic meanings pertinent to today's political currents and ideological contestations. Recently, for example, I examined the process of what I call "current symbolization of the past" in the context of the "rewritten" history of the anti-communist underground movement in present-day Poland.[2] The search for answers to the question of how the past is being brought into the present have also informed my most recent research, in which I investigate how we, as members of our communities and followers of our beliefs, reconstruct our personal and collective pasts, and how we, through that reconstruction, assign symbolic meanings to past events and happenings. A reverse question is also worth asking: How do these newly assigned symbolic meanings affect, if at all, individuals and social groups? How do they affect social relations within groups and among individuals? This interaction – between the meanings assigned to the past and those who proffer and adopt those meanings – leads to certain political outcomes. Ultimately, the question is this: What are the political outcomes of this process of symbolization of the past?

These questions have come to the foreground in the context of today's post-socialist re-evaluations of the socialist past, including in today's Poland, especially in the context of recent evaluations of the anti-communist movement after the Second World War. I wanted to uncover how radical political change – such as the collapse of socialism in Poland and the subsequent transformation of the Polish political system since 1989 – had influenced public and private discourse regarding the nationalist Partisans who fought hard against the post-war Soviet expansion into Poland, so I turned my gaze on the nationalist armed underground movement that operated in northeastern Poland between 1944 and 1957. In Polish historical discourse, the term "nationalist armed underground" refers to those armed units that were right-wing or extremely right-wing and that adhered to conservative and nationalist ideology. In post-war Poland, the nationalist armed underground fought relentlessly against the communists, who were swiftly taking over the country with the support of the Soviet Union.

This chapter explores how memories of this past are constructed in the context of oral historical research. I first discuss briefly the historical context in which this movement evolved. The same section sets out current scholarly understandings of the underground in current Polish historical discourse. I then discuss my project and its outcomes, presenting oral narratives about the armed underground in the Łomża district of northeastern Poland, where I conducted my field research. In analysing oral stories of specific events and activities of the underground, I am trying to answer this question: In the contemporary local discourse of memory, what is the meaning of this conflict? To answer, I focus on the language chosen by the narrators, who were either part of the fighting (on both sides) or civilians. I pay particular attention to the moral judgments and values attributed to both parties in the conflict. With reference to Alessandro Portelli's idea of oral history as "dialogic performance,"[3] I also discuss the interview situations in which the narratives were spoken.

What Was the Anti-Communist Underground in Poland?

The end of the Second World War in Europe brought about new political developments in Poland. The most important of these was the expansion of Soviet influence into Poland and the eventual incorporation of that nation into the newly formed Socialist Bloc of Eastern European countries. This was not a smooth process. In what became at the end of the war eastern Poland (in its contemporary borders), Polish communists built new institutions that destroyed the hitherto underground structures of the Polish state.[4] In their efforts, they were supported by

Soviet Red Army forces amounting to several million men (who were already experienced in combating Ukrainian resistance in western Soviet Ukraine, which had recently been added to the Soviet Union), as well as by a special division of the NKVD, the Soviet Union's main security organ.[5]

Around the same time, Poland established its own security police,[6] and all of these forces soon joined the Polish communists in their efforts to build a new, communist Poland. The Polish security police were aided in this effort by the Civic Militia, the armed wing of the Internal Security Corps, and, as necessary, by units of the new Polish Army. In the post-war Polish state, all of these units operated as a "security system" (a term coined by the Soviets).

The Polish Underground State, which had resisted the German and Soviet occupations during the war years, and which many Poles still viewed as the legal state authority and as the fount of Polish nationhood and patriotism, resisted the communist takeover. This resistance evolved over time, beginning in the last year of the war, during which several key events took place. Let us consider some of those events.

On 27 July 1944, the Soviet Red Army captured Białystok, driving the German troops back towards the west. By January 1945, Operation Burza,[7] coordinated by the Polish government-in-exile, had commenced. It was during this operation that the Home Army (in Polish, *Armia Krajowa*), which was loyal to the Polish Underground State, fought its last battle against the Nazi forces. In the same chain of events, the Home Army exposed itself to the Soviet Army. The NKVD responded by arresting tens of thousands of Poles and murdering "hundreds, if not thousands, on the spot."[8]

On 19 January 1945, General Okulicki, the last commander of the Home Army, issued an order dissolving his forces. Not all of the armed units obeyed this order. Meanwhile, among the Polish authorities the belief was growing that armed resistance might destroy the nation. In May of the same year, with the communist terror intensifying throughout Poland, the Council of National Unity, a quasi-parliament of the Polish Underground State, called on the youth who "sought refuge in the forest from the massive persecution and arrests to attempt to return to normal life and productive work anywhere it is possible."[9]

After the Polish Underground Parliament dissolved itself, some units of the Home Army did not give up fighting and created, on 2 September 1945, a civil–political organization called Freedom and Independence (FI), which aimed to remain active until free parliamentary elections could be called in Poland. In eastern Poland, FI retained its military character. Its mandate as defined by its leaders was to support all non-communist parties and organizations whose aim was to establish a free and independent Poland. The same support, however, was not extended to those nationalist military armed organizations – National Armed Forces and National Military Union – which FI criticized for their "totalistic attitude to many issues" and their resort to "the same methods the communists used."[10] In terms of membership, the nationalist armed underground had been since the beginning of the war the second-largest Polish underground army. Linked to the National Party, which was perceived as right-wing because it viewed Soviets and communists, like Germans, as enemies of Poland, the nationalist underground army had fought both the Nazi and the Soviet occupiers as well as other units with roots in various peasant and communist movements.

In February 1945, the National Military Union (NMU) was formed; after October 1945, it went by the official name "National Armed Union" (NAU).[11] The National Party had decided to establish the NMU in the autumn of 1944, but in the Białystok area it was organized only in September 1945.[12] Those members of the Home Army who wanted to continue armed resistance joined the NMU. Meanwhile, the "Lizard Union," a military formation that evolved from the prewar Fascist-leaning National Radical Camp ABC (in Polish: ONR-ABC) retained the name National Armed Forces.

To understand the complexities of the post-war discourse on the armed underground in Poland, especially in the first post-war decade, one must recognize that the Polish underground's activities had a dual nature: there were the NMU and National Armed Forces, and there were those underground forces that had taken a new form with the dissolution of the Home Army and whose ideological agendas varied from unit to unit. The nationalist organizations – the NMU and the National Armed Forces –were hoping above all for a military conflict between the Soviet Union and the West. The nationalist camp and the units that had grown out of the Home Army differed also in their assessments of the political situation in Poland. This led to a number of conflicts, sometimes even armed ones, especially in the Białystok region, the site of my project.[13] Some NMU commanders viewed as traitors those Home Army soldiers who wanted to turn themselves in to the amnesty commissions in 1945 (organized by the communist regime), and those who did so were later sentenced to death. It seems that the focus of this antagonism was the issue of local control.[14]

The anti-communist underground was a national movement, but one that operated through local organizations. The Białystok region was one of the most active sites of anti-communist underground activity from the moment the communists arrived in 1944 until 1957.[15]

The period between the spring of 1945 and June 1946 saw intense underground activity throughout Poland. Armed units temporarily captured towns and created a parallel state. In the Białystok region, in the spring and summer of 1945, the partisans destroyed the offices of the new communist state and disarmed and disabled some 90 per cent of Civic Militia stations.

In 1946, a national plebiscite was held in Poland, in which citizens were invited to vote (in a manner) for or against communism. The results of this vote were falsified by the new communist rulers to conceal the actual results. The disclosure of the honest results would certainly have strengthened the political opposition as well as the will to fight among the members of the armed underground. For instance, in Kraków, where a reliable vote count was conducted, 83.5 per cent of voters rejected the communists. The rigged referendum was the first indication that the communists were on the ascendancy in Poland. The parliamentary elections of January 1947, controlled by the military and the police and manipulated in the same way, became another reason for members of the militant underground to change their views about armed resistance. A month later, encouraged by the amnesty that had been announced on 22 February, the majority of Partisans decided to "leave the forest." It is estimated by the end of April 1947, more than 90 per cent of FI members and around 60 per cent of the members of the nationalist underground had turned themselves in to the authorities.[16] The *Atlas of the Polish Independence Underground* estimates that between 1947 and 1950, in all of Poland, between 1,100 and 1,800 Partisans were active. Their numbers might have been small, but because of their experience and determination, the Security Service found them a hard nut to crack.[17]

Their determination stemmed from the fact that many of those who had turned themselves in returned to the forest after a brief attempt to adjust to normal life, during which they were investigated by the police. One of those individuals still hiding was the last commander of the NMU in the Białystok Province National Military Union, Kazimierz żebrowski – "Bąk" ("Horsefly") – who eventually was killed in an ambush in the Łomża district. By 1950, the number of fighters was already very small. In 1945 there had been an estimated 13,000 to 17,000 Partisans; by 1950, no more than 400.[18] The last "forest soldiers" lost their lives in Białystok province, in the Łomża district, in 1957.[19] In the interim, both Stalin and Stalin's secret police chief Lavrentii Beria had died, Khrushchev had delivered his famous speech about Stalin's cult of personality, and Poland had entered the period that would become known as political "thaw."

Clearly, the history of the anti-communist armed underground in Poland was complex. It was also little explored during Poland's decades under socialism. Memories of this period have been suppressed, albeit for different reasons, both in the public domain and in local areas where the resistance was most active. With the political transformations of the 1980s and 1990s and the collapse of socialism in Europe, the time has come to revisit that history. One thing remains clear: the reconstruction of this history is also a complex process, for a variety of reasons. While during socialism the participants in and witnesses of armed underground activities were silenced (through both social and political means), today they are the principal carriers of the memories of how the underground was seen and understood by local people at the time it was active.

Over the past decade, the anti-communist underground has been the subject of a great deal of advanced historical research. As evidenced by many publications that have appeared in recent years, this subject is gaining more and more interest among the new generation of historians, many of whom are affiliated with the Institute of National Remembrance (INR).[20] The most influential publication, one that summarizes a number of detailed historical studies, has been the above-mentioned *Atlas of the Polish Independence Underground,* issued by the INR in 2007. Research into the anti-communist armed underground has been influenced by the changing political climate in Poland, and vice versa – the growing number of publications supports present-day Polish politics and has made this topic vividly present in public discourse. Its symbolic importance can be seen in the fact that in 2011, the Polish Parliament established a new national day to be celebrated on 1 March – the Doomed Soldiers Memorial Day.

The aim of my research has not been to reveal new historical and political details and facts. Nor has it been my intention to judge the people of the past or to pay tribute to them. I was interested in people's stories and the meanings they are creating today, in the current social and political situation, be it within the prevailing public discourse or in contradiction to it. This approach had not yet been taken by Polish historians exploring the anti-communist resistance.

Seeking Personal Narratives on Anti-Communist Underground

Recognizing the complex history of the underground movement in Poland, especially in the context of the political transition from socialism to post-socialism, and aware of the power of personal narratives, I set out to conduct an oral history project with individuals who had direct experience of that movement – the soldier-veterans on both sides of the domestic front (pro- and anti-communist) *and* the civilians. I started my project, "Nationalist Armed Underground in the Białystok Area: Discourses of Memory," in 2003, but it was not until the spring of 2006 that I was able to launch my research project in full and officially.

Interestingly, the official commencement of this research occurred after parliamentary and presidential elections in Poland, as a result of which conservative parties gained a majority in the Polish Parliament and Lech Kaczyński, the candidate of the Law and Justice Party, became President of the Republic of Poland. I mention this because, in the same way that political context is important to discourses about the past, so it is important for the present – as I was soon to realize. After the elections, a party invoking prewar "national-democratic" (i.e., nationalistic) traditions, the League of Polish Families, entered Parliament. Its chairman at the time, Roman Giertych, became Vice Prime Minister and the Minister of National Education, a position he would hold from March 2006 to August 2007.[21] It was around this time, during my first visit to the Białystok branch of the Association of the National Armed Forces Soldiers (in Polish: Związek żołnierzy Narodowych Sił Zbrojnych; hereafter ANAFS), that I heard these words from the chairman of that organization: "We have been waiting for such a government for eighty years!" (referring to the last time that "national-democratic" politicians had taken part in a Polish government, before 1926).

The Field Research

In my project, I focused on gathering and recording interviews with individuals who remembered the post-war years in the Łomża district of Białystok region. During my visits and longer stays in Łomża and environs in 2003, and then between 2006 and 2008, I conducted in-depth narrative interviews with thirty-two people. My students from Jagiellonian University interviewed eight people as part of their fieldwork practice; I had previously spoken to four of those interlocutors. Most narrations were biographical in nature, except for group interviews, in which it was difficult to maintain the focus on individual biographies. Meetings sometimes lasted more than six hours; some even had to be divided over several days. Also included in this project were three interviews from the town of Jedwabne recorded in 2000, as well as four interviews (from among a dozen) recorded in the town of Goniądz during research performed by the Kraków "Artefacts" Association in August 2008. Audio recordings of the above interviews are preserved in my private archive and in the archives of the "Artefacts" Association. The interviewees were residents of the town of Łomża and the towns and villages of the Łomża, Zambrów, Kolno, Wysokie Mazowieckie, and Mońki districts. Our informants' stories were related to events that took place within the region called by its historical name: "Łomża Province." The interviews did not necessarily take place in the same locations as the events described in them.

I reached my interlocutors through various paths, primarily using the snowball method. This "snowball" originated in the offices of the already mentioned Łomża branch of the ANAFS. I met five veterans who had been active within the nationalist underground as soldiers or members of a conspiratorial network. I also spoke with a retired captain of the Polish Army and with former soldiers of the Home Army. My students interviewed three active members of the Association of Combatants of the Republic of Poland and Former Political Prisoners – wartime members of the Home Army and a soldier of the 1st Kościuszko Division of the Polish Army.[22] The remaining narrators were participants in and/or witnesses to the events that took place in the 1940s and 1950s but were not currently engaged in public activities. All interlocutors were between 73 and 94 years of age (as of 2003 to 2008). In Goniądz, the age was lower – at the time, the youngest person was 60 and the oldest 80. Between 1944 and 1957, they carried out various functions, had many occupations, and represented a variety of social and political perspectives. These people include a former militia officer (a policeman in communist Poland), a soldier for the Security Corps, a secret police officer, a tax enforcer, a teacher, a bank clerk, an accountant, a library worker, a shopkeeper, and a restaurateur, as well as farmers and people who were primary or high school students at the time.

Story-ing the Past – Constructing Interpretations of the Past in Dialogue

The problem that faced me from the very first stage of the research – indeed, from the moment I decided to conduct it – was the relationship between an individual's experience of the past and its transmission in the form of an oral account. This has become the focus of my analysis here.

During my research on the anti-communist armed underground, I spoke mainly with people in the autumn of their lives.[23] They were, of course, people who had survived their experiences as youths in the underground. Yet they were not the same people as they had been sixty years earlier. They did not discuss their pasts through the prism of their youth; rather, they talked about it and interpreted it through the prism of their old age and their experiences. In addition, they were – yet they were not – speaking in the same way with a researcher as they would speak among themselves, within their families, or in their local environment.

An interview is a unique event during which the informant's life story emerges in conversation with the researcher, in front of him or her, perhaps *only* for him or her. This, in turn, is backed by the narrator's experience, which is an integral part of his or her self. Alessandro Portelli refers to this situation as "a dialogic performance" and notes that "the narrative of history is a language in the making, not text."[24] Portelli means by this that during the interview, the narrator creates meanings and thereby creates a language appropriate for his or her non-verbal experiences and that is based on his or her experience. When language becomes an object of interest, Portelli says, we deal with literature.

From this perspective, the historian should be focusing on the content of the oral narrative *and* on the narrator, who is seeking the appropriate form to express and communicate his or her story in the context of the dialogue with the researcher. It is through this exchange that his or her life, experiences, past events, and present reality are all endowed with significance. A person who tells his or her story is not in any way an "informer" or a "witness to history" – he or she is both its main character (in the story) and its narrator and author.

Accessing Stories as Outsiders or Insiders

Oral history is the art of dialogue, notes Portelli.[25] Here he is referring not only to the interlocution itself but also to the meeting of two cultures in the persons of the researcher and the narrator, as well as the exchange between them. An educated middle-aged person who is talking with elderly interlocutors will differ from them in many ways. All attempts to artificially level these differences are not only dishonest but also easily discovered and deplored by interlocutors. While working on this project, I assumed the position of a "native" (insider–outsider) – I come from the surroundings of Łomża. Inhabitants of the areas around Łomża with whom I conversed quickly verified my persona by asking me local insiders' questions, making off-hand remarks, and alluding to local topics while studying my reactions to these. This vetting was the first step towards obtaining all the privileges my status could earn. Such clearance was important, given that the topic of my research turned out to be a borderline taboo.

The activities of the armed post-war underground in Łomża province and other parts of the Białystok area have been widely discussed in the national public discourse, including in electronic and printed media, both regional and national. Yet in the villages where the witnesses and participants of these events still reside, this topic is mentioned only reluctantly. "People have lived here for so many years. It's better to sit quiet, not stir things up" – this is what I was told in one locality when I asked about this history. There are several reasons why local people are so unwilling to talk about this complex and recent history that directly touched their lives. One such reason can be summarized in the words just mentioned: "It's better not to stir things up." Embracing that notion perhaps ensures the continuity of a certain status quo that has evolved over time in the communities affected. Present-day neighbours may have been supporting opposite sides in the conflict sixty years ago, and revisiting those times could mean reawakening old grievances. This current sense of peace may have been achieved at the cost of traumatic silencing of the victims. People "wanted to go on living somehow," so they chose "the blessing of forgetting." In communist times in Poland, silence was also enforced through political control. Certain topics, such the events of the 1950s, were dangerous to raise in public; for doing so, one could be imprisoned, and the memories of such persecutions were still fresh. Today, the silencing, once achieved through political control, is maintained by social control. People are not interested in expressing their opinions on the post-war anti-communist underground because doing so would mean expressing their opinions of their neighbours. Given the change in the public discourse on the armed underground, yesterday's "bandits" have become today's heroes. This means that one must be doubly careful when expressing opinions on past events, if one expresses them at all. Given the radical change in the official message, many people remain cautious in formulating their views and do not want to reveal either their memories or their opinions.

It seems to me (although this is obviously difficult to prove) that people were more willing to open themselves to me because they knew I would understand them because I was familiar with the local idiosyncrasies. Even so, not everything went smoothly. In the village of Łady Borowe in 1947, the Partisan detachment led by Henryk Gawkowski "Rola" ("Soil") murdered several members of one family. I was informed about this only after I had spent some time in the village, by a woman I already knew quite well; I had interviewed her earlier, as well as her cousin. I had tried to arrange a meeting with Mr Zenon Z. from the same village – a friend of the first interviewee – and had called him several times; his wife, however, had always stymied my efforts. Ultimately, Mr Zenon Z. and I met for an interview (although I am certain his wife knew nothing of this) at his friend's house, under the pretext of visiting this mutual acquaintance. Mr Z., just like all the other project participants from Łady Borowe, willingly talked about what he had seen, felt, and thought regarding incidents dating back some sixty years.

Another example of difficulty establishing a relationship with a prospective project participant arose in the little town of Goniądz. There, an old lady living alone in a poor wooden cottage was frightened by the idea of someone wanting to ask about her life and almost begged me to leave her alone. A recommendation, even a written one, did not always lead to the desired result. In another case, a woman who had been a very active member of the anti-communist underground – among other things, she had held positions in the National Armed Forces command – refused to give an interview (stating health reasons) despite a recommendation from a close friend and a previously arranged appointment. Not all of the people permitted me to record the conversation, and I had to respect that.

But by and large, most interviewees trusted me, and some possibly wanted their stories to reach the public through my research and its dissemination. The fact that I was from the region and knew the local history and culture served as important portal to the communities I was studying. At the same time, the informants seemed to especially value that I was an academic, which "elevated me" above the local context.

Although it has its benefits and privileges, being a "native researcher" also brings many limitations. These result from a certain excess of knowledge and experience. There were many issues that seemed obvious to me and to the people I was interviewing, and hence during an exchange with a narrator, some issues were given only superficial attention. Sometimes, I recognize now, I did not develop certain topics that had been touched upon during the conversation, since, as a product of the same culture, it was assumed that I had prior knowledge because of my local roots. This is an obvious disadvantage when conversations are being recorded for later scholarly analysis.

During this research project, I had the pleasure of cooperating for a short time with two students who were studying history and sociology at the Jagiellonian University: Wojciech Chowaniak and Jacek Matuszczak. They were young and inexperienced but extremely willing to embrace the challenges of oral history work. Most crucially, both came from other parts of Poland – from Silesia and Podhale. I decided to invite them to conduct four interviews independently from me. Three of the four narrators whom they were to interview, I had met and spoken to before, and I had already partly recorded their life stories. These individuals were associated with the organization of the veterans of the anti-communist resistance – the Association of Combatants of the Republic of Poland and Former Political Prisoners (in Polish: *Związek Kombatantów Rzeczpospolitej Polskiej i Byłych Więźniów Politycznych*). Because the project participants knew that their interviewers were from elsewhere, and because they were students, the narrators opted not just to share their memories but to some extent to "lecture" our student researchers about their lives and years gone by.

The students conducted the interviews together; in this way, they were able to "control" each other and ask complementary questions. As an outcome of this arrangement, the student researchers sometimes asked questions that to an experienced oral historian would have sounded naive. My informants would not have found this acceptable coming from me; I would have faced their stern gaze and perhaps even have lost their trust. That is why, for example, the interlocutors who met my students in a group of three felt the need to explain what it meant that they were the "nationalists": "Catholics and patriots who hate Communism and are against Jewish domination in politics and economy" (Halina S., Henryk K., Alina K.). Another project participant, an educated man who held a position on the organization's board and thus represented it – when asked about his experiences as a Partisan, gave the students a long, textbook lecture on the history of the Second World War in the territories of northeastern Poland and the campaigns of the Home Army. Fortunately, one of the students turned the conversation towards more personal aspects, asking about the source of the narrator's nickname – "Little Plate." Thanks to this, an exhaustive and sincere answer was gained on the role that a teenage boy played at that time: he lived in a village and supplied food to Partisans in the Biebrza marsh. The local gentleman felt the need to explain this particular experience faced by the Partisans in the Białystok–Łomża area to students who came from a part of the country that had not been occupied by the Soviets during the war.

Another important dimension to how conversations were organized in the field related to the principle of mutuality. Oral historians usually understand interviews to be based on questions posed by the researchers and the answers given to those questions. Actually, an interview is more complex than that. The researcher's involvement in someone's story cannot be limited to this unidirectional way of conversing, especially if the people who have invited us into their homes want a different approach.[26] I am reminded of Daniel James's experience when he came to the apartment of a hero of his then upcoming book, asking her to authorize the text. She responded: "All this time, you have wanted something from me, and yet you have told me nothing about yourself – what you think, what you believe in."[27]

In my previous work in the field, I never avoided sharing my life and my own views. This is not so difficult in most cases, since the researcher and the narrator usually establish a close relationship. Generally, we are guests in someone's house for at least several hours, during which we have crossed the border of his or her privacy; a given person shares his or her sometimes quite intimate experiences, and all of this leads to an atmosphere of trust. With this project, I did face certain difficulties when meeting people whose actions or beliefs (e.g., anti-Semitism) I did not accept. Yet at the same time, these people were extremely hospitable and cordial, and they provided me with truly earnest answers that could not go unappreciated. Unless asked directly, I tried not to disclose my own political views, and I remained stone-faced while listening to utterances that sometimes aroused my strong objections. Unfortunately, I could not afford – perhaps this was a lack of experience, or perhaps my personality – to undertake polemics along the lines of Alessandro Portelli, who precisely in this manner has obtained extremely valuable interviews, provoking people to reveal subsequent layers of their experience.

Private Discourses: Experience, History, and Politics

During the very first meetings with the veterans and villagers who had witnessed the underground's activities, I faced a problem that shattered my expectations of how this research should proceed. Certain aspects of the underground's history that might seem sharply defined for researchers working with archival sources (i.e., territorial divisions, the scope of activity and competencies, commands, branches, and, most of all, the organizational and ideological identification of the Partisans) were not really coming to the surface in conversations. My interlocutors were not bringing up references to or evidence of the above matters; this suggests that individuals who lived through those times were not well versed in and are not now interested in these details of the past. This is not to suggest that human memory fails the historical facts; I am not interested in reconstructions of facts.

Another important observation: the narrators, who were civilian witnesses of past events, when reminiscing about the underground, did not draw clear lines between those who had fought for or against the communists. When discussing the actors in historical events, references would be made to those "carrying guns" as if in opposition to those who were not carrying the guns, and the (front) line would be drawn between the "day men" and the "night men," "the authorities" and the "gangs," the "secret police" and those who "hung around," "democrats" and "national military unionists." In response to my inquiry about daily life at the beginning of 1945 in the town of Jedwabne, Mr Stanisław O. shuddered as he replied: "When the night came, no one visited each other. People just stayed dead put at night. People were afraid to go out. In the daylight, the day men ruled, and at night – the night men."

This divide suggests that it could be difficult to distinguish those on one side from those on the "other." Neither "side" was clearly defined. Back then, everybody was "suspicious" and one could only trust his or her own family. "Don't tell anyone what is going on at home," parents told their children. I heard those words very many times in recollections. Mr Teofil L. told me that while he was returning to his village from a Soviet Gulag in 1946, as he walked down the road in his own village, people discreetly looked from behind their curtains. Because he was wearing an unidentifiable uniform (probably one from an American soldier), people were afraid to open their doors, so no one came out to greet him.

In their conversations about this period, the villagers did not usually differentiate between the nationalist "forest soldiers" and those of the former Home Army. I quickly realized it was pointless to ask the narrators specific questions about the National Armed Forces or to try to discern whether the narrators were referring to nationalists. People seemed distracted by such queries, so I concluded it was neither important for them back then nor relevant now. Given the complicated political landscape in post-war Poland, marked by the armed underground's struggles against communist rule and the competing agendas of political forces, which included the anti-communist Polish government-in-exile and the Provisional (pro-communist) Government of National Unity, the intricacies of political struggles were lost on ordinary people – on the average farmers, housewives, or shopkeepers.[28] The only thing that made a real impact on their lives at the time was that they had found themselves in the midst of those who were armed with guns and other tools of repression. Any decision to join a particular faction had serious consequences.

Furthermore, today's reflections on this past are linked to later life experiences the narrators endured under socialism. The fact that the conflict was settled in favour of the "people's republic" (i.e., the communist government) played a crucial role in what the narrators lived through later and, thus, in how they chose to recount that past now. This political outcome of the post-war civil struggles in Poland affected the narrators' biographies not only in a political sense (i.e., in terms of which suppressive value system they lived in) but also in temporal and symbolic terms, in that it affected people's understandings of their lives as well as their ability to reflect on those lives. The founding and rule of the Polish People's Republic also shaped the public discourse regarding the post-war armed anti-communist underground movement.

Today, this history continues to be discussed and remains ambiguous in both private and public discourses in the districts where the armed underground was most active.

It is natural for witnesses of important events who were not directly involved in them to simplify those events in ways that affect their reminiscences. My narrators seemed to have distilled the past into its primary components as they experienced them; in their accounts, the political dimensions of their acts, encounters, interactions, and singular events were indiscernible. So when speaking of that past in the context of our project, they divided the underground units into what many referred to as the "real thing" or "bandits." This dichotomy does not match scholars' understandings of the conflicting sides. As I stated earlier, villagers were not necessarily familiar with the affiliations of the Partisans whom they willingly or unwillingly hid:

> After the front – this counts in our times – there were Partisans of this and that sort ... There was [real guerrilla fighting] and there were ... hooligans.[29]

> After the war there were lots and lots of Partisans. My father often used to go out in the evenings – he liked to play cards. And this is exactly when Partisans from the surrounding areas used to come by. My mother and me, we were afraid – now I'm not sure if we had reason. Once, I remember, when they came to my father, they said that he was selling shoes at too high a price. One of the Partisans was quite short while my father was a tall man. And this little Partisan jumps and tells my father that he's selling shoes at too high a price. My father managed to explain himself, but we were very afraid then. The other one was a very tall man and pretended to be drunk. I have no idea if they were Home Army, or People's Army, or simply thugs.[30]

> After the war the situation was uneasy here. There were Partisans here, and some people pretended to be Partisans, but quite often they were simply plundering gangs. Even the militia in Goniądz was a militia during the day and a gang at night.[31]

Even among those who had been engaged in underground activities at the time, it was hard to find a narrator who could discuss coherently the various political objectives and tasks of the movement in they were involved. For example, when I asked "Zbych" what he was fighting for, Mr Stanisław K. shrugged and answered with an anecdote:

> Ciupa, a blacksmith who belonged [to the Partisans], was going somewhere [to another village]; he had been offended somewhere else [by other Partisans]. They came to him that same night and they fought – he killed one, injured one, and he was killed. And that was that [Partisans' warfare].[32]

But at the same time, our project participants, although they came across as ordinary people with no more than a school education, had no difficulty offering political comments recalling and comparing facts relating to, for instance, certain figures, Partisan divisions, and entire formations. For example, they referred to the National Armed Forces as the "priestly party": "Here all the rectors belonged to the National Armed Forces."[33] In their accounts of controversial Partisan actions, the "forest fighters" were always linked to members of the National Armed Forces, or the other way around. For instance, Kazimierz żebrowski "Bąk" ("Horsefly") of the NMU enjoyed a favourable reputation among the people and was therefore linked to the Home Army. According to our narrators, the nationalists "[did] not [fight] against the government, but were only doing revenge among the people."[34] Similarly, Stanisław Marchewka "Ryba" ("Fish") belonged to the Home Army, but when the underground movement wound down, his behaviour became predatory. Still, his robberies of shops were not condemned as severely as those by the nationalist Partisans. As it was once broadcast on local radio, this was because "he did not live off the farm, only off the state – they stuck up a bank, raided a shop, and lived on."[35]

A crucial factor in how the Partisans were remembered was whether they stole directly from the narrator. Such incidents do appear in private narratives about those days and were the most serious accusations that were made against Partisans. Committing a theft could destroy a Partisan's reputation. Officer "Ryba" ("Fish") robbed a shop in his own home village, but an eyewitness contrasted his act that that of "the 'beret guys' [who] took a pig, took a calf."[36]

Partisans who confiscated animals and requisitioned food compromised the villagers' subsistence, yet this did not generate physical resistance in the countryside because the villagers feared the armed units on *both* sides (Partisan and "government"). After all these years, the villagers often stated their opinions on Partisans by recounting things that had happened to them or their neighbours, which they remembered in detail. I do not rule out that these details, and certain reconstructions of events, were offered in our conversations somewhat in response to the fact that I was the one who was asking about them. I expect that the presence of a professional historian who, the narrators imagined, wanted to hear these details affected what was said to me and how it was said. These detailed stories focused on the theft of tools, commands to kill a family's only pig in order to prepare a meal for the Partisan unit or to kill a laying hen for chicken soup, and similar. The events the villagers recalled were certainly those that still "stood before their eyes," and the emotions they evoked in the present were the same as those evoked decades earlier. When Stanisław K. told me how "Zbych" ordered the delivery of saddle horses, and ordered the villagers to herd those horses from one village to another, he was reliving his old fear from years ago. This was the only incident in which he took part personally, and it left a strong impression on him of what guerrilla warfare was like.

During all-night foraging expeditions, military units would visit families in villages along the road from Konopki to Podosie and collect food. During a halt in the village of śniadowo, they enjoyed a small feast in a local tavern. When they reached the place, the carters were told to kill the pig taken from Konopki and "cut it into pieces." "Who were the partisans?," I asked Stanisław K. He scoffed that they were "local guys – from Czaplice, Boguszyce, and Zagroby (villages)."

At the time, war had only recently stopped raging through the district. Houses and households had been destroyed and required rebuilding, peasants had no grain to sow nor any animals, and both the state and the underground were increasing their economic hardship. All of this fostered confusion and distrust towards both sides among the villagers:

> You lived between the devil and the deep sea. Here you faced the devil, and there the deep sea pressed you.[37]

> This is how it was: "Did you tend the goats by the ears?" "No." "Well, you should have!" You were in the wrong, no matter what you did.[38]

> If you don't want to join, it's bad. You don't want to go and steal together with them.[39]

> Everyone was afraid of Partisans.[40]

Obviously, these narratives were not using the political terminology of the time. They were not assigning labels such as "informer," "traitor to the state," or "communist." Instead, our narrators spoke of the actors in historical events in terms grounded in their own local understandings of the conflict. When describing someone whom the Partisans viewed as a traitor, the narrator might comment that she or he was "a traitor when the Russians were here" (i.e., she or he might have been employed in the cooperative or served in the militia during the Soviet occupation of 1939–41), or that "he brought things from the UNRRA" (which could have meant the Partisans – in other words, she or he got on well with the post-war local communist authorities who distributed UNRRA parcels).[41] However, the vast majority did not cite this kind of rationale, and the witnesses even tended to emphasize that they did not know why people encountered repression from the underground:

> And they slaughtered many of these people at night ... How many of these people simply did not return?[42]

> People died at night. People were afraid to go out. He left home, for example, to the outhouse, and was gone. Gone like the wind.[43]

Working in the field with the narrators who were not engaged in the conflict between the communists and the underground but who witnessed it, I registered the whole set of characteristics the narrators assigned to the Partisans in their conversations: aggression, arrogance, vengefulness, hooliganism, false piety, ingratitude, disloyalty, cruelty, cowardice (shooting helpless people), intimidating people, forcing services, and theft. The vindictiveness of the Partisans and tales about how they robbed and murdered villagers were the main themes in private conversations and local discourses. "Sałaninowcy" – "Pork-fat" (in local dialect, *sałanina*): "AK – and give us hens, and give us ducks,"[44] "give us your sheepskin, give us your swine," "Take the last cent from the poorest" – these are terms still used in this district today. According to the narrators, the Partisans liked partying and drinking:

> As soon as there was a wedding party, lots of Partisans would come around, well ... and along with them came the Secret Police.[45] They came to us, to our village ... They also had parties. And "Zbych" came once to my parents and told us – my cousin and me – to go to such a party. And we, kids, we were only fifteen years old. But my mummy allowed us and we went ... but we were afraid. Somehow we were able to flee this party.[46]

A Partisan "walked around" (the combatants themselves used this word), or "ravaged" the area in a "gang" or "band." "'Mad Stasiek' ['Wiarus'] on a white horse, with a whip in his hand invading the villages" – this was the mythical vision shaped in the environs of Jedwabne.

Yet other characteristics were assigned to them as well: honour, frugality, honesty, faith, wit, and creativity (in hiding oneself). These traits were assigned to the underground officers Kazimierz żebrowski "Bąk" and Stanisław Marchewka "Ryba." According to inhabitants of the village from which "Ryba" came, "Bruzda," his commander, and he swore that the militia would not take them alive; they vowed to kill each other first.[47]

Similarly, interviews with former militia officers and underground combatants tended to present the actors in the conflict in a number of ways. In their accounts, former militia officers and underground combatants tended to rely on the parlance of their own professional milieu. From time to time, terms informed by official writing practices, such as "entered into a marriage," "was drafted into service," and so on, entered the narratives of former militia men or post-war security officers. This contrasted with the overall speech patterns, steeped in local dialect, in which these narrators communicated with the researchers and among themselves. But apart from these linguistic preferences, neither group of narrators demonstrated attitudes that might have been expected of them, given their professional or vocational affiliation. In other words, in their narratives of guerrilla warfare, these narrators said nothing that distinguished them as former officials of the early communist government. Moreover, their perceptions of the anti-communist underground were extraordinarily moderate. They spoke of Partisans without any particular emotions, they did not use epithets, they did not demonize the underground, and they did not raise political issues from the past or present. For them, that past was over and they no longer wanted to rehash it.

Former underground combatants who perform duties on the boards of their various associations, or who used to do so, participate in public life of their communities, even if only by attending celebrations of national holidays. These individuals in their conversations with us tended to utilize stock phrases used commonly in public ceremonies. But this reliance on public ceremonial language and phraseology normally occurred only at the beginning of the interviews, before the ice was broken and the narrators still felt somewhat restrained in what they could say and how they could say it. Early in their narrations, out of shyness or nerves, they would assume the position of a public speaker rather than a private witness. But the desire to share their stories, to express a historical message to a wider audience, soon overcame this. Once they began recounting their thoughts and personal experiences, they would return to "private" language, which in this case was the language of local culture and personal life experiences. The selection of a language register was also a consequence of the specific circumstances of the interview, which was usually conducted in the narrator's house, in familiar surroundings, quite often with the family's active or passive participation, and with coffee and refreshments. Many times I was invited to a home-cooked meal, introduced to other members of the family, and given a tour of the home and farm. As noted earlier, crucial to establishing trust was that I was from the district where the research was being conducted; this ensured a warm and cozy atmosphere. Hence, the language of the conversations and stories was the natural, "home" language.

Commonly, while sharing their own experiences of underground movement, the former combatants chose to frame their stories in a form close to that of any other biographical narration. These segments of Partisan veterans' accounts revolved around descriptions of intimate matters, as well as pragmatic evaluations of events and actions, which took the same language and form as the accounts of other narrators. Once the narrators moved on to discuss the events and matters that concerned their organizations and official activities, their language also shifted, from personal and familial to more official and ideological.

Accounts by veterans of both fighting camps displayed the same tendency towards differential use of linguistic strategies when discussing their personal lives and experiences and organizational ones. Regarding the latter, they expressed their ideas in generalized political or military parlance. The narratives of former "government" representatives whose life paths unfolded in the public domain of the socialist state were strongly marked by their subsequent experiences and the current political context. Some spoke in a manner suggesting that the divide between the communists and the underground was not a serious one and that the communists had not really battled the underground with the commitment once ascribed to them by the public discourse of socialist Poland.

The narratives recorded with civilian witnesses often revolved around the unique personalities of specific Partisans – the most controversial ones. In these descriptions, the interviewees tended to rely on vernacular language as they recalled details, material objects, and family relations; in this way, they conveyed both the ordinariness and the extraordinariness of the reality that once was theirs. Lacking fluency in the political intricacies of the day, and not fully comprehending the ideological battles or the reasons for the armed conflict in post-war Poland, the narrators discussed the Partisans in the terms that they knew and understood, highlighting at the same time the local roots and "down-to-earthness" of these conflicts. They did so because they perceived – and still do – the world in terms of their own cultural categories. As they recollected the underground movement that had once held power over their lives, and the physical violence of those conflicts, they referred not to those who had struck fear in them, but to actors like "Józek – lame duck," "Mad Stasiek," or simply "our guys."

The narratives of the former underground combatants have begun to enter the public discourse only recently. Those combatants have an insatiable desire to talk and explain, to break through their own barriers and convince others of their beliefs from that era. These discussions and debates have grown into a unique discourse of "rehabilitation" – a discourse that is currently being shaped in the dialogue with other public discourses in Poland, both political and scholarly. Narratives of the veterans that have been shared with me and in other local contexts have been informed by the ongoing political, ideological, and public debates in Poland concerning, among other things, the history of the armed underground. Thus the meanings and interpretations that are being assigned and reassigned to the history of the armed anti-communist resistance in the post-war years (by the narrators and others) are also informed by dynamic exchanges in the public, political, and scholarly discourses in Poland. This symbolization of the armed underground, this re-evaluation of the past so as to endow that past with new, fixed symbolic meanings, continues to unfold in Polish society. The current public discourse around the anti-communist armed underground is moving towards a mythologizing of the movement. Scholarly discourse is being pushed into the shadows, or it is adjusting to the dominant narrative by paying tribute to "doomed soldiers" and by avoiding critical reflection.

Historians often describe the life and the world of the "common person" by applying categories they acquired during their training in the discipline of history. The same categories might seem ontologically strange, irrelevant, and out of place by those whose histories these scholars aspire to examine and write about. To avoid such unnecessary contradiction of perspectives, we should explore how people whose pasts we are interested in themselves describe their past reality. We can do so by engaging the individuals in the research and by working with them in the field (and as I have done in my own practice), bringing into this work the oral history method. This requires acceptance of the assumption that history is embedded in experiences composed of "everything" – most of all, the present time in which the narrator is living.

The general question in my project was how the past lives amidst us and how we make it "history" by assigning certain meanings to it. As a historian working with oral narratives performed in specific personal contexts, through the narrators' experiences, I learned very little. As an anthropologist, I learned so much.

NOTES

1 Mead, *The Philosophy of the Act*, 22–3.
2 Kurkowska-Budzan, *Antykomunistyczne Podziemie*.
3 Portelli, *The Battle*; Portelli, *L'ordine*.
4 The Polish Underground State (*Polskie Państwo Podziemne*) was a collective term for the underground Resistance organizations in Poland during the Second World War, both military and civilian; they were loyal to the government of the Republic of Poland, then in exile in London. The Underground State, a legal continuation of the prewar Republic of Poland and its institutions, waged armed struggle against the occupying powers, Nazi Germany and the Soviet Union.
5 The NKVD (*Narodnyi Komissariat Vnutrennikh Del*) was a law enforcement agency of the Soviet Union and had an extensive network of agents in the Soviet satellite states of Central Europe after the Second World War. It collaborated with other secret police agencies and was involved in political persecutions in the Soviet Union and other socialist countries.
6 31 December 1944, Ministry of Public Security.
7 Operation *Burza* (Tempest) aimed to seize control of German-occupied cities and towns while the Soviet Red Army was preparing its offensive. The Polish Underground hoped to take power before the Soviets arrived.
8 Paczkowski, *Pół Wieku Dziejów Polski*, 128.
9 Quoted in Paczkowski, "Aparat Bezpieczeństwa," 15.
10 Wnuk, "Polityczne i ideowe," 17.
11 Kulińska, *Narodowcy*, 63.
12 Kułak and Sychowicz, *Podziemie Niepodległościowe*, 7.
13 Poleszak, *Podziemie Antykomunistyczne*, 333–56; Poleszak and Wnuk, "Zarys Dziejów," xxvi; Jerzy Kułak, *Rozstrzelany Oddział*, 126–8.
14 Łabuszewski and Krajewski, *Od "Łupaszki" do "Młota"*, 84–6.
15 Poleszak and Wnuk, "Zarys Dziejów," xxix.
16 Poleszak and Wnuk, "Zarys Dziejów," xxxii.
17 Poleszak and Wnuk, "Zarys Dziejów," xxxiii.
18 Poleszak and Wnuk, "Zarys Dziejów," xxxiii.

19 In 1954, Major Jan Tabortowski, "Bruzda" (Furrow), a former inspector of the Łomża 'F&I'; in 1957, his subordinate, 2nd Lieutenant Stanisław Marchewka, "Ryba" (Fish).
20 The Institute of National Remembrance was established by the Polish Parliament in 1998. It has four functions: archival, investigative, research, and educational. The institute's authorities are appointed by Parliament and the President of the Republic.
21 Roman Giertych is a son of Maciej and grandson of Jędrzej Giertych, a prewar activist of the political movement Camp of Great Poland and the National Party. In 1989, he founded the All-Polish Youth, invoking the tradition of the prewar Academic Union of All-Polish Youth.
22 The Home Army (*Armia Krajowa*) was the official army of the Polish underground state; the 1st Kościuszko Division of the Polish Army was formed under Soviet supervision and on Soviet territory.
23 Kurkowska-Budzan, *Antykomunistyczne Podziemie Zbrojne.*
24 Portelli, presentation.
25 Portelli, *The Battle.*
26 Portelli, personal communication with author, quoted in Drobik et al., *Historia mówiona,* 21.
27 James, *Dona Maria's Story*, 130.
28 In the January election of 1947, in blatant disregard of the Yalta and Potsdam agreements, the communist-led Democratic Bloc gained power. The voting was widely viewed as "irregular." Stanisław Mikołajczyk, leader of the opposition *Polskie Stronnictwo Ludowe* (Peasant Movement) was condemned as a foreign agent and was forced to flee for his life from Poland (October 1947).
29 Stanisław O., interview.
30 Teresa C., interview.
31 Jerzy W., interview.
32 Stanisław K., interview.
33 Jan K., interview.
34 Zenon Z., interview. "Revenge" here means "fight" or "violence."
35 "Fish," interview.
36 "Fish," interview.
37 "Fish," interview.
38 Zenon Z., interview.
39 Mirosława Z., interview.
40 Władysława K., interview.
41 UNRRA, the UN Relief and Rehabilitation Administration, was an international relief agency, especially active in 1945 and 1946. Its purpose was

to "plan, co-ordinate, administer or arrange for the administration of measures for the relief of victims of war in any area under the control of any of the United Nations through the provision of food, fuel, clothing, shelter and other basic necessities, medical and other essential services." Visit Ibiblio.

42 Mirosława Z., interview

43 Lucjan Z., interview.

44 This is a play on words linked to Armia Krajowa: "AK, A kury, a kaczki."

45 Natalia G., interview.

46 Zofia K., interview.

47 "Fish," interview.

8 Forced Labour in Nazi Germany in the Interviews of the Former Child *Ostarbeiters*

GELINADA GRINCHENKO

Nazi Germany's vast forced-labour program has been a key topic in Second World War history for the past twenty-five years. There are several reasons for this, including the launching of negotiations over compensation for this category of victims fifty years after the end of the war and the broad social and political discussion this has produced. Hundreds of books and articles have been written about the Nazis' use of forced labour, and these allow for a multidisciplinary analysis of how these labourers were "recruited," be it as prisoners of war or civilians of all occupied countries, including the Soviet Union. These same sources analyse how forced labour was used throughout the Nazi economy and how these workers were treated. Many of those workers – *Ostarbeiters* – were children from Ukraine, Russia, and Poland.[1]

In this chapter, I analyse two stories about childhood years spent in Germany.[2] We recorded these stories while working for "Memory, Responsibility, and the Future," a project launched by a German foundation that is dedicated to collecting the oral testimonies of people who were forced labourers or slaves on the territory of the Third Reich.[3] This project involved research teams from twenty-seven countries, including the United States, South Africa, and Israel. Ukraine was represented in this project by two organizations, the Centre for Educational Initiative (Lviv) and the Kowalsky Eastern Ukrainian Institute (Kharkiv), in cooperation with the National Academy of Sciences of Ukraine. Our team conducted interviews in central, eastern, and southern Ukraine (although not Crimea). We recorded half the interviews in large and small cities and the other half in rural townships and villages. Of the 40 interviews we recorded, 23 were with women and 17 with men. The mean age of informants was between 82 and 84. Most of the informants were born in the years 1924 to 1926 and thus represented the largest cohort of forced labourers. We also recorded one interview with a female *Ostarbeiter* who was born in 1914, and three with people who were younger than twelve at the time of their forced deportation (born in 1933, 1936, and 1937). For the presentation and analysis in this article, I have chosen two interviews: one with Aleksandra Georgievna Goreva, born in 1936, and the other with Yevgenii Nikolaevich Rudnev, born in 1937. Both informants are native Russian speakers currently residing in Kyiv.[4]

My approach to these oral histories is based on the following. First, on Alessandro Portelli's understanding of the unique features of the oral historical narrative as a particular genre with a particular type of plot.[5] Second, on the sequential and reconstructive approach to the thematic field of the interview as developed by Gabriele Rosenthal.[6] Third, on the understanding that an oral interview is a conversational narrative, as set out in the works of Ronald Grele.[7] Integrating these three approaches is the principal that only narrative can give meaning to human actions and that this narrative is achieved by organizing the individual's elements of existence into a whole. I also see oral autobiographic narrative as a result of the verbalization of autobiographic recollections, the analysis of which must take into account contemporary approaches dedicated to researching personal autobiographic memory.[8]

In this chapter, I focus on several things. First, I attempt to identify thematic priorities within the narratives; then I analyse the main plot lines, the motifs of the stories, and the "narrator's place," which may be located *in* the story or *outside* it, within the character or not. Another goal of this chapter is to ascertain what place the memories of being in Germany occupy in the autobiographic narratives, as well as what meanings our respondents invested in the events they described and what influence those memories and meanings have had on their subsequent lives. With this in mind, I concentrate on the narrative efforts of informants to create images of events *and* of themselves as participants. I also focus on the general model of self-presentation and the thematic interview field. Finally, I identify and discuss the particularities of the articulation of specifically childhood memories that were related to participation in forced labour in Nazi Germany during the Second World War.

Historic Note

During the Second World War, Ukraine was the largest Soviet republic to be fully occupied by the Germans, and it was held longer than the areas of Russia under German control. In the course of the conflict, 6.8

million people were killed; 1.4 million of them were military personnel who perished either at the front or as prisoners of war.[9] Estimates made in the Soviet Union between 1945 and 1948 indicate that from the territory of today's Ukraine, 2.4 million people were transported to Germany as forced labourers.[10] Thus they constituted the largest group of forced labourers and those with the fewest rights among all foreign labourers who worked in the Reich.

In the Reich territory, Ukrainian forced labourers worked in all spheres where forced civilian labour was used: in plants and factories, on railways and construction sites, in agriculture and in households. According to the Imperial Ministry of Internal Affairs, presented in the works of Gisela Schwarze, on 20 July 1944, the Third Reich also employed 75,000 child *Ostarbeiters* – 58,000 Polish children and 8,300 other children.[11] However, Russian researcher Pavel Polian suggests that if we take into account non-registered children under twelve years old, the real number must be at least two times larger.[12] Most often, children ended up in Germany with their parents, and when they worked, it was as part of the forced labour force at the same location as their older family members. This might include menial work such as cleaning the labour camp that was attached to a factory or a plant, or hard labour in agricultural sector, where children were expected to work alongside the adults. From the end of 1943 on, children were often sent to clear away rubble and to take down buildings that had been destroyed during air raids. Regarding the age of employed children, until the end of 1943, only children older than fourteen were employed. Their work day was limited to four hours.[13] After 29 November 1943, according to a Gestapo directive, it was permitted to employ children older than ten, and another directive (6 January 1944) prescribed for them the same food rations as adults. A directive of the Labour-Use Deputy General of 2 May 1944 prescribed the use of Soviet and Polish child labourers for more than four hours a day.[14]

Interview with Aleksandra Georgievna Gorina

Biographic information. Aleksandra Goreva (maiden name Dvornichenko) was born on 1 April 1935 in Kyiv, to the family of Georgii Ivanovich Dvornichenko and Yelena Teodorovna Gertz. The family had three children: daughters Lidia (b. 1931), Aleksandra (b. 1935), and Liudmila (b. 1937). After being drafted into the army, in the summer of 1941,

Aleksandra's father went missing in action. (It was learned only in 1990 that he died in 1942 in the Kremenchug POW camp.) She was transported to Germany with her mother and sisters in October 1943. Until March 1944, she and her mother and sisters were in the Soldau labour camp,[15] where her mother and older sister worked on the railway. From the spring of 1944 until the spring of 1945, the family stayed in the city of Luckenwalde in the *Land* of Brandenburg, where lived a maternal relative. Throughout her time in Germany, Aleksandra did no forced labour. After the war, the family returned to Kyiv. In 1957, she married Vladimir Gorev. Their daughters (Liudmila and Svetlana) were born in 1958 and 1960 respectively. Between 1952 and 1990, she worked at the "Arsenal" plant as an engineer-dispatcher at a optical-mechanical college affiliated with the plant. Her husband, Vladimir Gorev, died in 2000. Today, she is retired and living on her own.

In general, her interview is a chronologically consistent story built around a single plot line: the story of her family. She devotes the main narrative – that is, the part of the interview that was not interrupted by questions – to her childhood years and the experiences of being in Germany as part of a forced labour group. She presents her post-war life quite briefly and with little detail. This is characteristic of all the interviews we recorded for the project: past knowledge of the topic oriented our narrators towards a thematic rather than autobiographic presentation. While preparing for the analysis, I divided the text into narrative episodes. The criterion for defining their boundaries was the transition from one theme to another. This part of the interview, then, has been presented as a sum of the following thematic modules: prewar childhood, the war's beginning and life in occupied Kyiv, the stay in Germany, resettling in Kyiv after the war, and the autobiographic summary.

The house "at Kozlovka,"[16] where five generations of Aleksandra's family were born and lived, served as the main organizing or compositional element of the interview's first part. At the beginning of the interview, she related that the house does not exist anymore. This drew the temporal boundaries of the main narrative as well as its main thematic component:

> But, unfortunately, it doesn't exist anymore. At this place ... ours ... exactly in the place of our little house, so beautiful, so wonderful. Because

> everyone was admiring, they visited us. We had this little front yard [sighs], there. [short pause]. Now, this [short pause], precisely on the land where were our little houses, they built two or three monsters [with indignation]. The architect, probably, is not Ukrainian, because he spoiled the landscape of our beautiful wonderful Mariinsky park.[17] Because these monsters, they have detrimental effect on everyone, not only on me. When I saw, I thought I would have a heart attack. Well, this ... God be their judge![18]

During the interview, Aleksandra several times digressed towards continuing to tell the story of her house. Her family on her mother's side twice returned to live in that house after leaving it. The first time, before the war, they left to stay temporarily in a small town in Kyiv *oblast*. The second time, they were in Germany as forced labourers. This motif of return carries the main structuring and plot-forming functions in the first part of the interview, which, as noted earlier, our narrator limited to the story of her childhood years, war, Germany, and the return home.

Before the war, Aleksandra's father had been dispatched to the town of Zdolbuniv. He was soon followed by his wife and daughters. Aleksandra says very little about life in that town. This, however, was the sole theme of her spontaneous narrative in the first part of the interview, during which she recounted an episode related to her childhood memories of her father. This episode was about meeting her father after work when she was four years old and had wandered out to the street. This caused panic among her family and delight and amazement among her neighbours: "Wow, look here, what an adventurous girl! On her own, she went to meet her father!" This episode contrasts with one that follows, about a final parting with her father: "We then left, said our goodbyes to father quickly, at the train station, here. That was it. After that, we never saw him again."

In Kyiv, besides the family on her father's side, before the war Aleksandra had a maternal grandmother and great-grandmother. These were the people whom she, her sisters, and her mother were going to visit when they parted with her father at the train station in the previous episode. They were going to visit them during the summer school vacation, on 18 June 1941. Structurally, the subsequent story about the occupation of Kyiv is organized around the family's return "to Kozlovka" and their life there until they were transported to Germany.

She confines her childhood memories about the German Army's entry into Kyiv to a single comment – "as they marched along the Khreshchatyk."[19] Her first emotionally charged memory of the occupation is related to the escape from the destroyed city centre to her grandparents' house:

> After a while ... after some time ... well ... Khreshchatyk began to explode ... And so mama, well, she's packing some stuff so that ... one takes one bag, another one, another. Milochka, the youngest one, grabbed her Jonik, we had a doll, Jonik [short pause], a negro. Here. Lidochka grabbed a pack, me, too – another pack, and so we went running down, running, because everything is exploding, all Khreshchatyk is exploding.[20] [Sighs]. Mama also ... some wrapped pack ... because she knew that everything would perish. Yes [sighs] ... So we run out. We are running out, and, here we also have this house, the one where we lived, number 38, it had an arch and the iron gate. And, you see, Germans closed this gate at once. People are pleading, let us go, Khreshchatyk is exploding, and they are not letting. Panic! People are wailing! Children are crying! We, too ... Mother is holding us three, like this. "Stay by me! Stay by me!" So we all stay, stand there. All this in such a terrible state, I cannot even express. But, later, well, these gates open. So, they opened the gate and, well ... and people [short pause] were throwing those packs, were dropping everything only to get out, to escape. Because what if all this explodes. [sighs] Our mama, too ... running, running, along Khreshchatyk, towards the square [short pause] Stalin's square ... So we make it, running, to grandma Katya. Grandma Katya is home, grandpa Vanya [too]. Well. So we came running, that is, all of us, and poor grandma Tanya also limped along ... limping ... because ... she's old. But everyone was running, and so we arrived to Kozlovka. And, of course, grandma Katya took us all in. Well, this is a private house, she has there three or four rooms, that's why she took us all in. So we began to live [there], and Germans were blowing up Khreshchatyk and we were at Kozlovka. All of us started living at Kozlovka. [pause] Well. And then, of course, such horrible times began, that it is impossible to convey, so horrible![21]

Aleksandra assembles the story of her subsequent life in occupied Kyiv from much less developed and detailed episodes. She tells about the "traditional" survival practices of urban dwellers in the occupied cities, such as forays to the countryside to barter, the difficulties and dangers involved in these forays, the hunger, illnesses, and deaths of her relatives and friends. She barely mentions her participation in these episodes. This part of her narrative focuses on her mother's experiences. It seems that these, which her mother told her about, rather than her own experiences, formed the foundation of this part of the story. It was her mother who went to the countryside to trade things for food, who saved children from dying of hunger, and who eventually buried Goreva's grandmothers, who died during the occupation. This feature of the story – that it is told through her mother's experiences rather than her own, continues in the thematic module of the narrative that focuses on forced labour in Germany. In terms of analysis, her choice of narrative strategy is noteworthy: she tells the story in the first person and allows herself to be its main character.

The thematic module about German forced labour camps begins with three short episodes: the failed attempt to escape from Kyiv, the raid during which she, her mother, and her sisters were caught, and their transportation to Germany. This last is followed by a description of the Soldau camp, which is offered very briefly and schematically: barracks, guard towers, barbed wire, a distant railway, and big piles of sand, which in her initial explanation were there for protection from fires. A few episodes later, she adds that children played on those sand piles: "We had no toys so we were making something there, some sort of houses."[22]

An emotionally charged episode in her account of the labour camp is about the illness of Aleksandra's younger sister. Like the story of the occupation, this is presented through her mother's emotions:

> There were cases when children would fall ill, but they did not return to the barracks. That's all, nobody knows. Maybe Germans liquidated them, maybe because [short pause] nobody treated them and they died. But there were [such] cases. And mama was very afraid that she would lose Milochka. But God gave us, He did what he did – … all three children survived.[23]

In this thematic module, the motif of the mother's anxiety (as opposed to a particular act, as was the case with the subtheme of occupation) serves as the narrative's main plot-forming component. Aleksandra continues this strategy as she builds five short episodes that describe the camp in terms of her mother's feelings and anxieties, even though she also participates in them. In terms of the narrative structure, the first episode of these five carries the central meaning and is the most symbolically and emotionally charged. This episode and its "sequel" conclude the chronologically ordered sequence of the narrative segments of the interview. Each of those segments possesses its own complete plot, with nine-year-old Aleksandra as the main character:

> But children[24] still bullied us. Children, I remember, one boy ... [short pause], there was this one [sternly], perhaps he was SS, no, not "perhaps," he was in the SS for sure. So he shouted all the time, like this [threateningly]: "Russische Schweine! Russische Schweine!" – like this, with such contempt. And I ... Well, our Lidochka, she was in general a very tender girl, she was afraid of everything. The oldest daughter. Oh, "daughter" – my sister! She was afraid because mama would say: "Don't touch anybody, don't tell anybody anything! Nobody, nothing ..." And I was so boisterous, was a very boisterous chick. I was afraid of nothing. I thought: "If ours come, I'll do you in!" [angrily] Like that I felt, you understand. Like that.[25]

In that passage, having marked herself as part of this episode, she stresses her mother's instructions and her own emotions, which she "lets out" in the final part of this episode. She returns to this episode later in the interview:

> And so I met him once on the street. He was a big boy though. He was ... Well, if I was nine – ten years old. No, I wasn't yet ten, not yet in 1945, when we had already returned to Kyiv, then [I turned] ten. Or was I eight then ... So, well ... I looked at him like this and said ... "Deutschland, Deutschland uber alles ... *Dralis, dralis*"[26] [laughs] ... And, I said this word[27] entirely, you understand? And then he – at me ... he went all white. And he looked at me like that ... He would have killed me right then and there [loudly]. But I told him all I wanted [calmly]. And I felt so at ease. At ease, because, [it was] as if I had my revenge, for his bullying [weeps]. Oh [sighs], well, these are children – this is just natural. Like that.[28]

This two-part story, which is central in the narrative about forced labour in Nazi Germany, carries symbolic weight in several ways. First, it carries symbolic meaning, invested by the narrator in the episode and in her experience of being in Germany in general. For the climax of her story, she chose a succinct and punchy term that children aren't supposed to know or use (the author was too shy to complete the term during the interview). With that term, she summarized her experience not just of forced labour but of the entire war. The "constructed" anti-hero's image also carries a lot of significance. On the one hand, he is a "big boy" (i.e., also a child), whose bullying is somewhat absolved by Aleksandra in her final utterance in this episode: "Well, these are children – this is just natural."[29] On the other hand, the description that "he was in the SS for sure" and "would have killed me right then and there" alludes more to the constructed image of the Nazi enemy than to a particular teenage bully who, given his age, might have been be a member of Hitlerjugend but could not have been SS.[30]

The story's significance is found in its functional peculiarities. A structure-forming meaning is carried by the motif, a theme of justice restored. Its cathartic manifestation completes the thematic module of Goreva's story that is dedicated to the war and its place in the autobiographic narrative. The utterance that brings the feeling of ease compensates for the bitterness of the child's hurt and serves as symbolic amends for all her trials of wartime.

Finally, this story is typical from the perspective of the general strategy of self-presentation – namely, the author's compensatory attempt to present herself as a brave, "boisterous" child who could disobey her mother (although this disobedience may have been based on some sort of assurance that she would be able to get away with it, since the episode ends with the arrival of "ours").[31] Most psychologically significant for the narrator is the justification of her own childhood bravery (let us recall the episode of meeting her father after work, presented earlier, which also took place in the context of transgressing her mother's proscription, but in Aleksandra's narrative resulted in everyone's amazement). Within the framework of the presented narrative, this is the only episode in which the narrator implicitly seeks the audience's approval (one can clearly see and hear in the recording the narrator's expectation of the audience's reaction and the approving laughter of those present). This confirms the episode's emotional and psychological significance.

As was the case with other participants in the project, Aleksandra's preliminary knowledge of the research topic (the experience of forced labour in Germany) led her to conclude her story with the episode of returning home. Although the researchers tried to explain that we wanted to hear about their *entire* lives, the overwhelming majority of our interviewees saw their German experience as our main interest.

This, we think, makes all the more interesting the presence or the absence of evaluations the narrators make of this period of their lives. In Aleksandra's case, these evaluations were entirely absent. She did not characterize her stay in the camp in any way except "very terrible." Conspicuously absent from her main story is any talk of how her time in Germany affected her subsequent life. The difficulties related to settling back in Kyiv after the war she "assigns" to her mother than herself. Only in response to a direct question did she tell a story that indicated her own attitude towards this part of her autobiography. This story that is rich with meanings. In concentrated form, it contains not only a personal but also a societal evaluation of her wartime years in Germany. We will present this story in its entirety.

INTERVIEWER: Had you any incidents? That you were in Germany, sort of ... in your childhood, with *Komsomol*,[32] for example ...

ALEKSANDRA: I had. I had. I had lots of incidents. I was kicked out of *Komsomol* [pause] one day.

I: Well, please tell this story.

A: One day, I was kicked out of *Komsomol*. Why was I kicked out? Well, in our house lived this ... [short pause] woman. I know her name, Natalia Ivanovna Kush. [short pause] She was this total *parteika*[33] [with contempt]. She was a *parteika*, you understand, there were different party [short pause] members of the party. There were communists, there were party people, there were workers, there were ... [short pause] there were different people. And she was from those. She came from the evacuation[34] and said: "I'll make order here." [pause] She herself was not a Kyevan, she never saw in her life Kyiv or ... [short pause] Ukraine, did not know what it was. [short pause] Such a *katsapura*[35] [angrily] ... from those faraway [short pause] places, you understand. But she decided to create her order here. And so [pause]. Well ... this was something like that [short pause]. She had a son. And I, with her son, I told you, that I have a little explosive character. You understand, like that [short pause]. And when I was a girl, and when I was a child, I always wanted to see more and something, and I always paid attention to conversations. If something was not just, I would argue with people – like that I was. Not to get into conflict, but to defend somehow – I am like that. And so this young man, he was several years older than me. And, I think, there was something, that I and he [short pause] we had a fight. There was a physical fight: he and I. Well, naturally, he was two or three years older, and naturally, he punched me in the face real good. But I also gave him a few.

And so they filed a complaint [short pause]. That I, so and so, came from Germany and also started a fight ... And, you know [with the sense of hurt] – they called me up for a trial.[36]

I: Tried at school?

A: Tried and said that this was petty hooliganism [short pause]. And, really, she has to be punished for such petty hooliganism. [short pause] But he was a man. Well, he was a boy, but he was a future man, and I was a girl, a future woman. Could I have yielded or not, something like that ... No. I was punished. But I, of course, I was in such ... in such a terrible state ... *Komsomol* – it was, it was something [short pause]. My Lord! It was [short pause] a miracle when we were joining *Komsomol* [emotionally]. We were such happy people ... that I was a *Komsomol* member! I was very proud of it [emotionally]. But [sighs] [now] I was in such a state that once I thought: "I'll jump off the bridge!" And then I thought: "My Lord! My mama, who survived Gestapo, Germans, what has she not survived! Hunger, cold, deaths – and she did nothing like this. And I, only because they kicked me out ... Well, it means that I have to prove [short pause] that you are not that person! Indeed, I have to prove that I am a real *Komsomol* member!" And so I started going to the offices. They took interest. That's what I am saying – the world has some good people. One woman took interest. She was also a party member, obviously, because it went further, not to the District Committee, but to the City Committee.[37] She called up everyone. And, right when I was present, I remember, she said the following: "When you chop wood, splinters fly.[38] What are you doing, why are you torturing the child!" [short pause] Well, I already was a teenager then.

I: How old were you, fourteen?

A: Yes. Maybe even fifteen. [short pause] And so my membership was restored. [short pause] I still have, still keep this party card, this *Komsomol* card. As a memento. I proved that I was still a normal person. Obviously, normal people interceded for me. Because the not normal ones, abnormal ones, they [short pause] well ... kicked me out, you know. Kicked me out. "Well, you are not worthy of being a *Komsomol* member, because you are like this and like that." That's how it was [short pause]. So, all kinds of things happened.[39]

What draws attention in this story is that Aleksandra chose a similar narrative logic for her stories about her German experience and its influence on her later life. The main motif of the story of her expulsion from *Komsomol* and restoration of her membership, presented above, is the restoration of justice. This links the story to the episode in which our character told the German boy "all she wanted." In both cases, the narrator began by describing the hurt or injustice inflicted on her and concluded with the satisfactory (for her) resolution of the situation.

Both stories reflect the "typical mood" of their time: the "common unofficial" attitude towards the defeat of Germany, and the "solemn-official" attitude towards *Komsomol*. It is known that an individual's significant autobiographic memories carry the social stereotypes that dominated a given society at the time the event was imprinted in memory. Later, though, people may slightly "correct" their evaluations of their past.[40] Aleksandra did not re-evaluate either of the described events. But at the personal emotional level, both events were still very important to her. She included in her discourse her own words and thoughts "from that time" in the same form as she uttered them right when the events were taking place, thus stressing their profound psychological importance. Given the features of these recollections, we might regard them as flashbulb memories,[41] or, using the terminology proposed by Veronika Nurkova, as "bright moments of life" that maintain a special "space metric" that corresponds to the age of the person at the moment of the event and to the circumstances of the perception of the situation, in which the "world of experiences" taking place during the event's "imprinting" is actualized.[42]

Both events are also important as elements of the narrator's constructed self-image. Aleksandra describes the features of her character that are important for her self-representation as something that had been formed in her childhood: "boisterous character," "a little explosive." These features manifest themselves in situations related to her desire to restore justice: "If something was not just, I would argue with people – like that I was. Not to get into conflict, but to defend somehow – I am like that."[43] At the same time, in the story about the expulsion from *Komsomol*, the motif of "restoration of justice," serving as the imperative that actualizes her feelings and actions, is manifested by the narrative of the happy ending, that is, her restoration in *Komsomol*. From our perspective, the same imperative determines her unethical utterance regarding the nationality of the mother of the boy with whom she got into a fight. She stresses her ignorance of Kyiv and Ukraine – in other words, her incorrect and unjust treatment of her motherland – and thereby allows herself to use the politically incorrect term *katsapura* (remember here the evaluation of the architect at the beginning of the interview, who is "not our Ukrainian, because he spoiled the landscape of our beautiful wonderful Mariinsky park").

Both analysed episodes also refer to the narrator's mother, another typical feature of Aleksandra's story. In the story about her expulsion from *Komsomol*, it is quite noticeable how her own experiences in overcoming difficulties track those of her mother. The yearning to be worthy of her mother, who survived the war as well, prompted Aleksandra to start "going to the offices" to prove she was "still a normal person."

In most of the situations related to her life's difficulties, Aleksandra acknowledged the people who helped her resolve them. Regarding her expulsion from *Komsomol*, this help was provided by a woman who "took interest" in her case. However, her importance to the story is not simply that she helped. The narrator invested her benefactor's statement – "When you chop wood, splinters fly. What are you doing, why are you torturing the child!" – with her own attitude towards the German experience as well as with the desired view of the Party institutions on that experience. Thus, her benefactor came to represent this ideal. Like all of our interviewees, she absolutely did not see her time in Germany as a crime or as something that might bring accusations of the type, "So and so came from Germany and also started a fight." In her view, all "normal" people who interceded for her must have seen her stay in Germany just like she did – as something for which a person should not be blamed. It seems that this episode played a decisive role in determining her subsequent behaviour regarding "the fact that she had been on German territory during the war."[44] She mentioned it in the forms and questionnaires, yet she had thoroughly concealed it from her acquaintances, limiting the "circle of the initiates" to her husband and children:

> From my husband I did not conceal. We concealed this from all our acquaintances ... Well, you would tell this to some person, and he would understand this wrong. Other people were saying: "But you went voluntarily. Nobody took you away. You were going, in these, SV, or, what's they are called, coupes."[45] Try to prove to them that you did not go in a coupe! ... That's why, of course, even my acquaintances, with whom I later was friends, from the "Arsenal" plant – nobody knew that we were in Germany. Only the forms and questionnaires knew that.[46]

Summarizing our observations and discussion about the Aleksandra's autobiographic narrative, we note the following. The main thematic horizon, against which background evolved her autobiographic narrative, was her family, constructed around her family home and the city of her birth. Her self-representation was oriented towards images of a daughter, wife, and mother; her work or career biography was much less informative. Our narrator assigned to these latter a secondary place in her life's priorities. Throughout the autobiographic material, we can trace her powerful emotional attachment to her mother. Many of her childhood as well as "adult" memories were connected to her mother; indeed, she also represented her mother's point of view on the events she described. This particular feature determined the construction of her story about forced labour in Germany: her personal experience was "mediated" by her mother's anxieties and other feelings.

All of this found concentrated expression in the story about the "big" German bully: both the perception of the event and the overcoming of the hurt appeared in the form of child's "space" so as to actualize "the world of experience" of a child and to demonstrate the logic not of an adult but of a little person. In the main part of the interview, she did not interpret or evaluate her German experiences in terms of their impact on her subsequent life. In a sense, this experience remained "locked" in childhood until the moment she specifically proposed to "work it through." We suggest that this avoidance of any discussion of the consequences of her German experience can be explained by the conflict between this experience and the "family" model of the narrator's self-presentation. Her adult life, in which the actualization of her family roles had been a priority, was not influenced by her stay in Germany. In other words, this experience did not result in any rejection among the narrator's family and her other closest and most significant people. But at the same time, in her interactions with the people beyond her family circle, until recently she had concealed this fact of her biography quite successfully, revealing it only to "forms and questionnaires." This inclusion of traumatic experience in one's shared family story, where such experience is not judged but on the contrary finds compassion, acceptance, and support, represents one way to construct the story of being involved in forced labour in Nazi Germany.

A different strategy of coping with a "German" past and a different form of narrative about it will be examined in the next interview.

Interview with Yevgenii Nikolaevich Rudnev

Biographic information. Yevgenii Nikolaevich Rudnev (Kreizburg) was born in 1937 in the town of Mironovka in the Kyiv region into the family of a professional officer, Nikolai Fiodorovich, and a housewife,

Polina Aleksandrovna Kreizburg. He had an older sister, Liudmila, born in 1930. In 1937, Nikolai was stripped of his rank, but later he was rehabilitated and continued serving in the medical corps. Before the war, the family was living in Kyiv. After a raid on 3 November 1943, Yevgenii, together with his mother and sister, was transported to Germany. A year previous to this, his father had been taken prisoner and shipped to Germany as a POW. In the transit camp in Frankfurt (Oder), the mother was separated from Yevgenii and Liudmila and sent to work at a chemical plant. Her children were sent to a labour camp in Köpenick, then later to Kölnische Heide (both near Berlin).

During their time in Germany, Liudmila worked as manual labourer at the post office and on the railway. Yevgenii cleaned the camp grounds and train station and helped clean away rubble after air raids. After the Soviet Army liberated them, Yevgenii and his sister walked to the city of Landsberg,[47] where they found their mother again in the filtration camp there. The family returned to Ukraine in September 1945 but were barred from Kyiv and were deported to Mironovka. In 1947, on his parents' advice, Yevgenii changed his last name, Kreizburg, to his mother's maiden name, Rudnev. After graduating from school in 1955, he entered Kyiv Geological Surveyors' trade school. Later, he graduated from the Department of Geology of Kyiv University as an hydro-geologist. He worked in geological surveying expeditions and wrote several works of fiction about his professional experiences. These books brought him public acclaim. Since 1982 he has been a member of the Writers' Union of the USSR. He has been the recipient of several prestigious awards. Since the mid-1990s, he has been a member of the Writers' Union of Ukraine. He defended his Candidate (PhD) Dissertation in 1982 and his DSc Dissertation in 2002, both in hydro-geology. Currently, he works in a research institute of the Ukrainian Academy of Sciences. He is married and has a son. Since 2000, he has been publishing memoirs about his experiences in Germany in various Ukrainian periodicals.[48]

Like Aleksandra, Yevgenii dedicated the first, free part of the interview mainly to his childhood and to the experience of forced labour in Germany. He began with the story about the "little town of Mironovka in the south of Kyiv region," where he was born and spent the first years of his life. In the mid-1930s, the Kreizburg family ended up in Mironovka as a result of "notorious Army purges," during which the narrator's father was kicked out of the army. According to Yevgenii, his father's discharge happened not in the least because of his German last name. But in 1939, the elder Kreizburg was reinstated in the army:

> He was reinstated … Reinstated, but! But! Reinstated, alas! Alas, alas – as a private. Here, in 1939, there is a photo, father in military uniform – he has three triangles,[49] this is senior sergeant. He did not get his rank back! Only when he returned from the Finnish [campaign], mother told, only then he had one triangle. He was sort of starting from scratch. What is most important, he was not allowed to serve in the troops that were connected with military equipment, there. Do you understand? Well, in that form, let's say, is written that he defended Kyiv as a part of the nurse battalion, and he was in charge, mama told, of the company that was responsible for supplies. They were supplying machines and equipment and so on. Yes, and, for example, with the artillery or tanks or motorized infantry, for example, he still was not allowed to deal. Obviously, again, because of his last name. There. Well, now, father … obviously, he had some connections, yes … He, that is, again began serving in the Army.[50]

This episode is very important in the following story, which Yevgenii tells about himself. His father, who "was sort of starting from scratch," and the reason for his repression – a German last name – serve as the foundations for structural and symbolic parallels of the narrator's self-presentation. In this respect, the logic of self-presentation of our two interviewees is similar. Both establish implicit or open parallels with their parents' experiences, which structure their stories about themselves and serve as thematic backdrops for articulating their childhood memories. This is especially so in Aleksandra's interview: the "anchoring" in her mother's experience not only determines the entire autobiographic narrative but also serves as the underlying theme of the post-war stories, which she spent with her mother. Five-year-old Yevgenii parted with his father at the very beginning of the war. In his story about the war years, in two thematic episodes, he attempts to transmit his father's experience while keeping to his own story's chronological order. The first episode he presents from his own experience; the second is based on his mother's words. Only one memory of his father has remained from the beginning of the war:

> Remember, that father visited us then in July, several times. Linden trees were blooming already. Yes. Over there … yes. And he would come in the black *emochka*.[51] That I also remember, yes. And that is what he then

said: "Here, build a special cellar dugout to hide from shrapnel, because Germans may bomb." And so in the yard[s] of these military houses we together dug – well, other families gathered there, yes, and we had dug them, the cellars like that, we had lots of firewood and could saw it, adults did everything and we also helped some. So we made some sort of dugouts, or something, I don't know … There … I remember how we sat in them sometimes, and above us, over our heads, the airplanes would fly, they were humming, humming, yes, and they were with crosses, yes … Yes, this was imprinted, this most likely was, by the smell of blooming linden, which I remember, this most likely was July or beginning of August. After that we never saw our father. Yes. We never saw him. Here, at this stage. There …[52]

This way of verbalizing his own recollections constitutes a peculiar feature of Yevgenii's autobiographic narrative. The unification of the narrative and the description are typical. The description – the story about the remembered image, about the bright episode from the past – is the dominant component of all episodes. In Yevgenii's stories, the images are not only visual but also auditory, kinaesthetic, and olfactory, and this lends the picture volume and substance. This approach is exemplified by an episode from the thematic module centred on his time in Germany:

And so, later, that is, when we were liberated, and this was on April twenty-sixth, yes, of 1945. I remember, well, smoke is crawling all over the camp. And our soldiers are running, yes, pulling a machine gun. One is pulling, and more running behind and shouting: "Hide, children, hide!" Yes. And we are not hiding, we are looking at them. And ahead, well, ahead the bridges over the Spree are visible. Well, something like … from a point of view of a today's geologist I can say, that that was about five, maybe six kilometres away. Yes. It had to be, because I was seeing these outlines. Visually, we can determine the distances. We were taught as geologists how to do this. So … And also everything … smoke was coming … This I remembered, yes … And … Well, when, they, this wave has gone, here comes another wave of our soldiers, more than before, yes. And then we rushed towards them, started kissing them, kissing their boots. Yes, exactly, these boots smelled with clay, tar and something unusual, unpleasant, something German. Yes, this I remember, is, like, imprinted. This third smell has imprinted. This smell I have never sensed again. It is a very peculiar, sharp, unpleasant smell. And not only one soldier's [boots], but the other one's, and the third one's. Where were they, I don't know. But this smell – yes, it stays in memory. There ...[53]

The second peculiar feature of Rudnev's childhood recollections is their thorough "space organization": he places every episode-snapshot into a precisely drafted space of geographic and material objects/markers such as streets, houses, forests, rivers, buildings of all kinds. In determining the location of different objects as he remembers them, he draws from his present-day professional knowledge and skills:

From a point of view of a today's geologist I can say, that that was about five, maybe six kilometres away. Well, generally, as I see it now, as I flew, as a geologist, all over the Soviet Union, that was not that far. But then, we perceived it as being very far, the Frankfurt (Oder) ... And we had to make it through the east of Germany, from Berlin it was, I looked on the map, already now, it was something like a hundred and twenty – a hundred and sixty kilometres from Berlin to Landsberg.[54]

He tries to provide both the past and the current names of buildings and streets where the described events took place:

Well, and ... this is how I remembered September. Especially that arrival of Germans in Kyiv ... Yes, this was September 19. So we stood with my sister ... then went to Khreshchatyk and so ... here, at Kalinin Square,[55] where now is the Nezalezhnost' Square, I think this is how it is called now, there then was the Ginzburg house,[56] the tallest house ... and there gathered ... I think, now there is a fountain ... gathered a huge crowd of people. There. A huge crowd of people gathered there. And I recall, that the Germans were moving in from here, from the Philharmony,[57] on motorcycles. On motorcycles, and all the asphalt was covered with flower bouquets. Flowers, flowers, flowers – they were covered with flowers. I remember priests in black robes and also, for some reason, women, also in black robes. Why, I don't know. Such a thing [laughs] got carved into my memory. I remember this. And flowers, the sea of flowers ... Yes, these motorcyclists rode, and people threw flowers at them. All their motorcycle sidecars, they were covered with flowers, it was like some blooming field. Yes, this ... I recall how Germans were greeted. Yes. But let's say "Babii Yar"[58] in Kuznetsov's novel – it is different about that [chuckles] ... But still, this I remember clearly, my sister also remembered ... yes.[59]

Besides localizing the event in a particular space, the presented episode has other organizational features of a "snapshot story" – features of the sort that are also present in other episodes and stories in the interview. For example, there is the narrator's reference to an "authoritative source" (a well-known book by Anatolii Kuznetsov,[60] and, later in the interview, to the popular in Soviet times *Memories and Thoughts* by Georgii Zhukov[61]), and also to the similar or corroborating recollections of other people (in the presented episode, to his sister's memories; in other episodes, to those of his mother). These references support the narrator's own recollections with those of other people who witnessed the events in question (besides bringing these people into a story as characters); they also expand the meaning-forming aspect of the event by including "official" and "expert" testimonies and evaluations, which help legitimize the narrative. In general, Yevgenii's narrative draws a clear line between his own memories and those of other participants in the events. He often inserts utterances that specify the "authorship" of a given passage: "this I did remember," "this is what I remember," "this got imprinted into my memory," "from mama's words," "mother has told me," "this was told by my sister," and so on.

The memories of other *Ostarbeiters* occupy a special place in his narrative. Quite often, these people's stories refer to the stories of other forced labourers whom they knew, for the purpose of corroborating and "factually" supporting their own narrative. Such references are especially typical of introductions to a story or corrections of details such as daily schedules, working conditions, daily life, and so on. This indicates his desire to integrate his personal experience with the experiences of others and thereby turn individual experiences into collective ones. And these references to others' memories play yet another role. To show what that is, in the concluding episode of the interview, Yevgenii borrows the "other's" memory in order to facilitate the construction of his own narrative and articulate his own experience:

YEVGENII: She tried never to touch these topics, nothing, to no one ...

INTERVIEWER: Even to you she never told how she worked at this plant?

Y: Only, like, in passing. Yes. It was hard ... only general phrases, air raids, humiliation, rapes ...

I: Even such things happened? By the German guards?

Y: Yes. Yes.

I: Or by our own?

Y: Well, she said that there were rapes. Yes. So, she says, God forbid to live through something like that. But she did not like the details, would start crying right away, would start shaking just like Liudmila.
I: Liudmila seems to be holding up pretty well.[62]
Y: Well, because she is not telling everything. I can feel that she would cry, for sure. This is like … this one should not tell about, especially a woman, for her it is really hard, any woman suffers from it, this is an offence to her feminine dignity. Because Germans, Germans, I know it well, that's what they were doing to girls. They were turning them into animals. They were stripping them naked, it is not even comfortable to talk about this, I remember that.
I: This was when they have medical exams …
Y: What medical exams! This is a joke! What medical exams, it's a camp …
I: So, the guards?
Y: Yes. They had a separate room. They would take them there and harass them, they did to them anything they wanted. Then, they [women] would hang themselves. So you wake tomorrow morning, and two are already hanging. Hanged themselves. Well, of course. Because not every person, not every girl can survive such tortures … yes. This I remember clearly. It happened many times …[63]

In this episode, Yevgenii focuses not so much on the events as on the lives of the former women-*Ostarbeiters,* on his knowledge of harassment and rapes in the camp. He possesses this knowledge, but it is very hard for him to articulate. On the one hand, this is the "other's" knowledge, because he himself did not go through this torture personally. On the other, as indicated by the story, remarks about rape are present in the recollections of his mother, who is a deeply private person for Yevgenii. To help construct the narrative about this experience, he has invoked a third "event carrier," a woman he knows who also participated in forced labour in Germany as a child.

Returning to Yevgenii's story about the beginning of war, note that as a plot, this part of the narrative is organized around stories related to finding food for the family. As in Aleksandra's story (and those of the overwhelming majority of our interviewees), descriptions of barter (*menka*), during which household items, cloth, matches, and so on were traded by the city dwellers for food in the countryside, are prominent.

A notable feature of Yevgenii's story is his desire to examine the war from different angles without concealing the experiences of those who were close to him. For example, he could have omitted mentioning that his uncle, his mother's brother, went to Germany voluntarily:

> Well, naturally, we did not want to go to Germany … But Nikolai, mom's brother, the Khvorostenko one, born in 1924, he and Shurka Khamaza, there was a third one, I forgot his last name, these three guys. They decided to go. To go voluntarily, yes. Well, this can be explained simply. First of all, there was very strong propaganda, that it was Western Europe, that this is "class," that this is German order, German culture and so on, and so forth … And all the time they showed films where they showed how well, ostensibly, those Soviet guys and girls who went, lived there. There. And this played its role, I remember that clearly … Nikolai died in '69, when he was forty-five, and he told me that … well … "We went there voluntarily!" There. Voluntarily, well. So, there were [people] like that. Yes, so he, well, went.[64]

With this example of voluntary departure to Germany, which he contrasts with a description of his own forced deportation, Yevgenii begins the second part of his narrative, which focuses on his stay in Germany. In the organization of this module, the short and succinct "snapshot" episodes that are typical of an interview's beginning occupy a much less important place. Yevgenii builds this part of his story in a different way, alternating detailed descriptions of living conditions (the camp's organization, food, clothing, and so on) with elaborate and "complete" stories.

In the organization of these "complete" stories about his time in Germany, the role the narrator allots for himself as a participant draws our attention. Most often, this role is passive. He conveys his own participation in the context of the described events either as determined by external circumstances or as a non-autonomous element within the framework of a collective initiative – together with his sister or with other forced labourers. Against this backdrop, the following story, in which the narrator presents himself as active, acquires a special significance:

> There were about six of our soldiers walking in a file and I was the last and, so, we came into this, into this greenhouse, or how should I call it, a flower one or something. So we are walking looking at things, yes. Here, soldiers are talking something among themselves … and so over there by these vases with flowers, yes … Everything was so beautiful, aromas everywhere,

sun shines through the glass … Standing the photos of German soldiers, German officers in these beautiful frames, not just in places, everywhere. Well, I don't know, maybe women worked here and these were husbands, sons, but, still, our troops had gone through here before then, they liberated this [place]. Even Zhukov writes how they stormed Landsberg, his troops … yes, in his memoirs. But, nonetheless, everything remained. For some reason, somewhere, all this was still standing. Maybe because there was a lot of these flowers, or something. Well, nonetheless. And when I saw these photographs, yes … I began to crush all this. Crush, yes. Well, Germans, German photos, German officers …

I: And you, a child, then hated …

Y: Yes! Terrible hatred, big hatred I had. Yes.

I: It remained from back in Kyiv …

Y: And in Kyiv, I forgot to tell about this kitchen. But I will.

I: Yes, please, later.

Y: Yes, remind me about this kitchen that [is?] by the Zoo. This is where the hatred comes from, this kitchen and when we were coming back, how a Gestapo car ran over, over here, by the Kerosinnaia, a boy. This I forgot to tell, this I will tell later. Yes. And I started to crush it all. And there, some soldier says: "Kid, stop it! Stop crushing good stuff!" And another says: "Let him let his feelings loose, let him! At least here he'll get even with fritzes!"[65]

The peculiarity of this story consists in the specific way the narrator conveys his own experience, which has deep emotional importance. In articulating this experience, he uses the "help" of other participants in the event, whom he includes in his narrative: the line, which explains his action as well as his feelings, is expressed not from his own narrative perspective, but through the words of the soldier who observes the event. Yevgenii quite often uses the present tense. This allows both him and the audience to "live through" the narrative, to feel as if it is happening again. But in this case, the direct speech carries another meaning: the narrator conveys his point of view as one that is shared by other people. Also in this episode, we can see clearly the help provided by the interviewer: the words about enormous hatred are a response to the interviewer's prompts. The same with the reference to a later part of the story about the cause of this hatred, the cold-blooded murder of a boy, about which Yevgenii would go into more detail later. This appeal for the interviewer's help, the construction of the story in the form of answers to questions, was noted earlier during the analysis of the story of the cases of rape. As before, this reflects the narrator's difficulty in articulating these memories.

The beginning of the episode, where Yevgenii says that "everything was so beautiful, aromas everywhere, sun shines through the glass,"[66] is presented as symbolically important. Here, we are not trying to evaluate Yevgenii's act. For us, the importance lies in how the narrator uses language to articulate his memories. By describing his own hatred towards Germans and how he "let his feelings loose," he is attempting to convey his attitude towards the war in general. To that end, he contrasts the "beauty" with the subsequent destruction. This resort to contrast carries an important compensatory function: the narrator-character symbolically acts the same way that the ones he hates acted, that is, the ones who destroyed the "beauty" of a peaceful life.

Yevgenii's narrative of the post-war years, like Aleksandra's, was largely directed by the interviewer's specific questions. Those questions, in line with the main research topic, returned the narrator to his recollections of wartime Germany. In this part of the interview, in response to a specific question, Yevgenii for the first time talked about his own participation in forced labour, in the context of compensation payments:

> Sister worked, yes, and she has received her first [money] transfer, she got it, because she worked, something like a thousand four hundred euros, she told me. She still has to get something in the order of nine or eight hundred euros. But she … the second one her sons have gotten, in my understanding, because she has died already. So … I got something like four hundred ninety-nine, and the second one, with addition, something like four hundred and twenty, something like that, yes. She worked, well, as I have told already, at the railway station, she sorted parcels for Germans, German soldiers. There … In Berlin … Later, she worked at some sort of factory in Berlin. Yes. But she did not work there for long, she stole something there and this situation was somehow remedied, but she was kicked out. There. And, also, usual work, the clearing of ruins and rubble after the air raids, everybody was forced to do. Everyone, small and old.
>
> I: You, as well?
>
> Y: Yes. Everyone. Absolutely everyone. What they say – that according to German laws of the Third Reich, children younger than twelve did not work. Possibly there was such law! But children worked. Worked. Yes. At the cleaning of the camp, and harvesting turnips, carried those turnips, [they] always gave assignment. There. Turned the piles [of turnip] so that it wouldn't rot. Well, and in taking apart the ruins, of course, children

> there … there … they did this lightest work. Swept there, if … there was cleaned, there they swept. Well … and so on. And adults? Adults [did] harder work: took apart those blocks, carried on stretchers … There.[67]

As noted earlier, in most cases Yevgenii did not personalize his own experience in Germany. His narrative about himself oriented mainly towards generalizations, that is, towards collective rather than individual experience. In this, and in many other episodes, he showed his interest in modern perspectives on the events in question. He tried to introduce details and corrections to these interpretations; it seems that this is why, in his approach, he followed the logic of generalization rather than personalization. The episode in his narrative that immediately follows the one above, is quite representative:

> Well, and about whether or not *Ostarbeiters*, these prisoners, struggled against Nazis? Yes. It took place. This Liudmila told, and I also remember a little myself. Because, say, they put sand in railway carriages' brakes, and they would start to smoke, and, basically, the carriages would break. This has been known for a long time. And this happened, I know, I saw guys doing that. There …
>
> Let's say, these parcels, as Lyuda told, there they switched. So she worked sorting the parcels that went to the East. To the Eastern Front. Yes. These parcels were switched very often. [They were] asked to switch. Through a chain [of orders]. Where did this come from, from what organization? About this, naturally, nobody asked, but anyway, who would answer there this question? But still, yes this clearly [coughs]. Then, information would come that there and then a carriage blew up. Yes. And generally, [we] calculated, that the cart, in which there was this parcel, blew up. Yes. Naturally, nobody asked what was inside of this parcel. If it needs to be switched, so be it, everyone did it. There … Well, it is certain, that the majority of these, those who in one way or another were complicit in these acts of sabotage, Germans either would execute right away, or would hand to the Gestapo. Well, this, of course, was also a sure death [short pause]. But this is what everybody took for granted, because everyone knew that the Red Army would be in Berlin any day. There. And it was impossible to live differently, to act differently. Only like that.[68]

This episode contains the peculiarities of Yevgenii's story-building style that were discussed earlier – namely, his intention to provide further, more up-to-date details and to give clear information about the "author of the recollection," with corroborating reference to other participants in the event ("This Liudmila told, and I also remember a little myself"). Another noteworthy aspect of this episode is the material that constitutes not so much its factual but rather its "narrative truth,"[69] which presupposes additional ways to understand the lived event and its importance in Yevgenii's life. In this episode, the narrative truth, as the episode's organizing principle, determines the appearance of "*Ostarbeiters'* struggle against Nazis." Yevgenii here means to demonstrate the courage of the Soviet forced labourers and to imply that an "organization" existed that directed their "struggle." It also shows the general mood among the *Ostarbeiters*: they knew they would soon be liberated by their own Red Army, and meanwhile, "it was impossible to live differently, to act differently."[70]

In this, as in other episodes of the interview, Yevgenii proceeded from the contemporary discourse about forced labourers in Nazi Germany, a discourse that revolved semantically around two key images: the fighter and the victim.[71] This episode was one of the narrative's focal points: in conditions of extreme danger, *Ostarbeiters* struggled against the enemy by all means available. The fighter obviously takes priority in his story, and this is the main difference between his story that of Aleksandra, which is organized mainly around the experience of privation, suffering, and fear, notwithstanding the "fighting spirit" that seems to dominate in her narrative. Another distinctive feature of Yevgenii's narrative is that he invests his episodes with highly generalized meanings. He strives to present the totality of experience of all *Ostarbeiters*, not just that of himself and his family (as was the case with Aleksandra). Comparing these two autobiographic narratives, we can talk about two distinct strategies of coping with the "German" past, which simultaneously determine the form and the content of the interview. Aleksandra integrated this past into her family history; Yevgenii, into the experience of *all* forced labourers.

In this chapter we have tried to demonstrate how an attentive listener, by analysing the form and structure of the texts of oral historical interviews, can access subsurface networks of thoughts, feelings, and self-presentations of the narrators. Drawing on just two autobiographic narratives, we can discern two distinct strategies of coping with a "German" past. Aleksandra wove her experience fully into the family history; Yevgenii projected his experience as shared by *all* forced labourers.

This might suggest distinct female and male self-representational styles; however, these two styles do not exhaust all of the approaches that former forced labourers took to discussing their lives. Our observations and speculations here also do not claim to provide an all-encompassing interpretation of the meanings to be found in oral histories. By focusing in depth on the stories of two individuals who experienced forced labour first-hand, we hope we have provided English speakers with an opportunity to follow the experiences of Ukraine's former *Ostarbeiters*, to step into the world of their memories and to witness their skills at reconstructing their personal past.

NOTES

1 For a large, detailed, and systematized bibliography on forced labour, see Kühnel and Sydow, "Bibliographie." For oral history about forced labour, see the articles in von Plato, Leh, and Thonfeld, *Hitlers Sklaven* (translated into English as *Hitler's Slaves*). For oral histories of Ukrainian *Ostarbeiter*, see also: Grinchenko, "Ostarbeiters"; Grinchenko, "The Shaping of Remembrance"; Grinchenko, "Zwangsarbeit."

2 This essay is the revised version of earlier analyses that appeared in Ukrainian and Russian in 2009 and 2010. See Grinchenko, "Prymusova pratsia" and "Prinuditelnyi trud."

3 For more on this initiative, see von Plato, Leh, and Thonfeld, "Einleitung."

4 The interview with Goreva was video recorded on 22 December 2005. The interview with Rudnev was audio recorded on 22 April 2005. Copies of these materials are in the archive of the Kowalsky Eastern Ukrainian Institute, entry codes FL005 (Goreva) and FL027 (Rudnev). Both interviews were conducted and transcribed by Tetiana Pastushenko. The Goreva interview is 2 hours 30 minutes long, the Rudnev interview, 3 hours 10 minutes.

5 Portelli, "Oral History as Genre."

6 Rosenthal, "Biographical Research"; Rosenthal, "Reconstruction of Life Stories."

7 Grele, "Oral History as Evidence"; Grele, "Movement without Aim."

8 For example, see Hoerl, "Episodic Memory"; Curci and Lanciano, "Features of Autobiographical Memory"; Nurkova, "Avtobiograficheskaia Pamiat."

9 Krawchenko, "Soviet Ukraine," 15.

10 Nazarenko, *Ukrainskaia SSR*, 153.

11 Schwarze, *Kinder*, 125.

12 Polian, "Ne-pe-re-no-si-mo!," 8.

13 Polian, "Ne-pe-re-no-si-mo!," 8.

14 Schwarze, *Kinder*, 127.

15 The modern city of Działdowo in north-central Poland. In the winter of 1939–40, in Soldau, a *Durchgangslager* for POWs was organized. It was turned into a civilian *Arbeitserziehungslager* in the summer of 1941.
16 Name of a street in the Pecherskii district of Kyiv.
17 Kyiv's Mariinsky Park, on the Dnieper, is a popular spot for both tourists and residents. It is named after the wife of Emperor Alexander II, Empress Maria Aleksandrovna.
18 Goreva (born 1935), interview.
19 Khreshchatyk is the main street of downtown Kyiv, as well as the city's oldest street.
20 The girls were running "down," because the street goes downhill (translator's note).
21 Goreva, interview.
22 Goreva, interview.
23 Goreva, interview.
24 Goreva is referring to local German children, probably members of the Hitler Youth (translator's note).
25 Goreva, interview.
26 The first part of the quote is, of course, the first line of the Nazi anthem ("Germany, Germany above all"). In the second part, "*dralis, dralis,*" which rhymes with "*alles,*" means "they brawled, they brawled." This is part of a children's "teasing song" about Nazis. A drunken bully who gets beaten up has been the most popular representation of the enemy both in Soviet "official" satire and in folklore (translator's note).
27 This word in Russian is *obosralis* – in English, "shit their pants." The Russian *obosralis* also rhymes with *alles*.
28 Goreva, interview.
29 Goreva, interview.
30 *Schutzstaffel*: the SS, a powerful military organization under Hitler's Nazi Party.
31 For example, the Soviet Army.
32 The youth branch of the Communist Party (Communist Youth Union), of which everyone had to be a member.
33 A career Communist, "apparatchik."
34 Deep in the homefront.
35 This is a peculiar reference. In Ukraine, "katsap" is a pejorative word for a Russian. Thus, this term, the way she uses it, refers not so much to the ethnicity, but to a complex socio-political status (as if Manitobans or New Brunswickers were to call other Canadians "feds") (translator's note).

36 Not a court trial. *Komsomol* had its own system of "comrade trials," which had no direct (i.e., legal) repercussions but could result in indirect ones, such as expulsion from school, loss of career, and so on (translator's note).
37 Either of the Communist party or of the *Komsomol*.
38 This proverb has the same sense as "you can't make an omelette without breaking eggs." Here, besides genuine Nazi collaborators, Goreva was referring to innocent people who had been punished after the war.
39 Goreva, interview.
40 Wallace, "Reconsidering the Life Review," 120.
41 For more on "flashbulb memories," see Brown and Kulik, "Flashbulb Memories."
42 Nurkova, *Avtobiograficheskaia Pamiat'*, 88–90.
43 Goreva, interview.
44 This phrase has been placed in quotation marks because it conveys an irony that only (former) Soviet citizens can understand: it is the formula from a much feared mandatory document/questionnaire that all Soviet citizens had to fill out several times in their lives (translator's note).
45 *SV* and *coupe* are relatively expensive and luxurious sleeping accommodations on a train (translator's note).
46 Goreva, interview.
47 Present-day Gorzów Wielkopolski in Poland, one of two municipal centres of Województwo Lubuskie.
48 See, for example, Rudnev, "Plenennoe Detstvo."
49 Until 1942, rank marks were worn on the lapel (translator's note).
50 Rudnev (born 1937), interview.
51 *Emochka*, or *Emka*, was the nickname for the Soviet pre-war "people's car," the MK-1. At the time most Soviet citizens had never ridden in a car. Thus, any car trip was an event – exciting, or foreboding (translator's note).
52 Rudnev, interview.
53 Rudnev, interview.
54 Rudnev, interview.
55 The main square in Kyiv – now Independence Square (*Maidan Nezalezhnosti*) – in different periods had different names: *Kreshatitskaia*, *Dumskaia*, *Sovetskaia*, and, from 1935 to 1977, Kalinin Square. Before it was renamed Independence Square, it was October Revolution Square.
56 Ginzburg House was the first twelve-storey building in Kyiv. It was built in 1912 near Khreshchatyk Street and was named after its owner. In the autumn of 1941, during the retreat of the Soviet Army, it was blown up, along with almost all of Khreshchatyk.

57 The building formerly known as the Traders' Club, which was home to the Kyiv State Philharmonic Orchestra before the Second World War. It was one of few buildings in Khreshchatyk that remained standing.
58 A mass grave, a place of mass executions of civilians during the Nazi occupation of Kyiv.
59 Rudnev, interview.
60 Kuznetsov, *Babii Yar*.
61 Zhukov, *Vospominaniia i Razmyshleniia*.
62 Liudmila Nikolaevna Tarasenko-Zalevskaia, an acquaintance of Rudnev's, who helped collect oral testimonies about forced and slave labour in Nazi Germany.
63 Rudnev, interview.
64 Rudnev, interview.
65 Rudnev, interview. Slang for "Germans" that emerged during the war and is still sometimes heard.
66 Rudnev, interview.
67 Rudnev, interview.
68 Rudnev, interview.
69 On "narrative truth," see Benezer, *The Ethiopian Jewish Exodus*, 44–5.
70 Rudnev, interview.
71 For discussion of specific features in the construction of the image of forced labor in Ukrainian Soviet and post-Soviet commemorative culture, see Grinchenko, "The Ostarbeiter."

PART FOUR

Locating Other Memories of Late Socialism

Besides researching traumatic aspects of the Second World War and the socialist past, oral historians examine less distressing aspects of life under socialism.

As noted in our introduction, oral history has been an effective means to reclaim alternative histories of socialism. By emphasizing individual and personal experiences, oral historians have been constructing and resurrecting socialist history's alternative agents, who for decades found themselves silenced in public discourses and national historiographies because of their political beliefs, experiences of repression, particular ethnicity, sexual orientation, or simply gender.

In this section, we focus on the uses of oral history for re-evaluating late socialism. It is not our task to define clearly what social experiences constituted late socialism – something that other scholars have accomplished.[1] For the purposes of this volume, "late socialism" refers to the era during which at least one generation of citizens grew up without facing political cataclysms, mass repression, or social experiments. Personal experiences and memories were being shaped during a relatively stable time in which individuals knew *one* kind of life, that of socialism. While the historical and political context varies from country to country, it is safe to say that most of the political battles that socialism fought in Central and Eastern Europe had been won by the end of the 1960s (in the aftermath of the Hungarian Revolution of 1956 and the Prague Spring of 1968). The Soviet Union and its European satellites had entered a period of relative stability during which the communists were able to assert that a more advanced stage of socialism had been reached: "mature socialism."[2]

Late socialism in Eastern Europe has been studied by both Eastern and Western academics and policy analysts. In the East, with post-war reconstruction over and new economic initiatives taking root, socialist ways of life and, later, "mature" socialism were examined by the political establishment and, subordinate to it, the social sciences and humanities. Research on socialist economies, cultures, and ways of life was directly informed by the socialist states' need to propagandize at home and abroad about socialism's achievements. For example, the disciplines of folklore and ethnography – precursors of oral historical work in the region – devoted their attention to socialist folk life.

Meanwhile, after the Second World War, the West studied and monitored Europe's socialist regimes. This research, too, was driven by the political agendas of the day. This led to the emergence of Sovietology and, later, Eastern European Studies. The first centres for the study of the Soviet Union and Eastern Europe were founded in the 1950s, staffed by former military intelligence officers and political émigrés, who injected academe with a Cold War mentality and Old World national antagonisms.[3]

These academic camps were not especially focused – nor could they have been – on what it was like to live under socialism. Ultimately, reflections on socialist experience were limited mainly to the arts and literature. Heavily affected by the Cold War mentality, Western studies of socialism generated an image of the Communist world as a monolithic social entity – the Socialist Bloc. There was little investigation of real people because the differences between peoples in the Socialist Bloc were thought to have been eliminated by socialism.

Western interest in the experiences and meanings of late socialism was reignited by the political transformations of the late 1980s. With the collapse of the socialist system, this interest extended itself to the experiences of the post-socialist transition. Meanwhile, as noted earlier, Eastern European researchers in the humanities and social sciences began to engage in expository and revisionist scholarship, which opened new windows onto their national pasts and enabled them to develop new perspectives on socialism as experienced by those groups in their societies that had been marginalized, repressed, or exiled. For a while, academics showed little interest in socialism as a way of life. With revisionist and expository research having now taken hold, and with a post-socialist generation having grown up since socialism, both Eastern and Western scholars have turned their attention to socialism proper and what it was like to live under it for ordinary citizens. Much of this work is being done today by a new cohort of post-socialist anthropologists.[4]

Scholars like Katherine Verdery with her seminal book *What Was Socialism and What Comes Next*, and Alexei Yurchak with *Everything Was*

Forever, Until It Was No More: The Last Soviet Generation have reflected on how socialism framed people's lives and dictated their life choices in times of late socialism and later. Oral historians based in the West tend to pay more attention to the experiences of late socialism than the region's own scholars, who continue to participate in broader intellectual debates about the wrongdoings of socialism.[5] But even these scholars have begun to pay attention to late socialism, although their work does not yet dominate the field of oral history.[6] The contributors to this section can be viewed as pioneers of this kind of oral historical research. As time goes by and new generations are born, and the distance grows between the socialist past and post-socialist present, the topic of late socialism will continue to gain weight among the region's oral historians.

The chapters in this section illustrate the uses and accomplishments of oral histories of late socialism from the perspective of today's informants. The contributors explore specific aspects of the recent socialist past while focusing on narratives as vehicles of memory, relying on their own prolonged exposure to the culture and the people whose experiences and memories they explore.

David Curp is an American historian and a specialist in Polish history. In his chapter about the powerful presence of Catholic culture in socialist Poland, he attempts to account for the processes of political desecularization and sacralization of Polish society in times of late socialism, using both archival and oral historical sources. The interviews in his chapter demonstrate the fertility and diversity of the sacral–cultural–democratizing synthesis that had been developing in Poland for decades prior to the political transformations of the 1980s. These personal accounts indicate how the sacralizing elements of the political transformations of Polish society throughout the 1980s continue to resonate in ways as uniquely personal and public as were the political changes themselves.

Natalia Khanenko-Friesen, an anthropologist and oral historian, examines memories of post-war socialism in Ukraine. Her chapter concerns the memories of life under socialism as they evolved among the former collective farmers who in the 1990s confronted rapid and painful decollectivization of socialist collective farms. Her project focuses on memories of decollectivization itself; her conversations with former members of collective farms reveal a particular kind of memorialization of collective farming before the post-socialist transformation. From Khanenko-Friesen's interviews emerges a particular narrative stance characteristic of that generation of collective farmers whose adult life unfolded during a time of relatively stable post-war socialism. She explores the shared identity of Ukrainian collective farmers who were decollectivized, and like other contributors to this volume, she questions the hidden and open intersections of the private and the public in the villagers' reminiscences.

Irina Romanova and Irina Makhovskaya offer a rare glimpse into the memorialization of *perestroika* times in post-Soviet Belarus. Seeking a personal perspective on the collective trauma of the transition to post-socialism, they found that the dominant theme in *perestroika* narratives focused not on the positive achievements of that period leading to personal freedoms and the collapse of socialism, but on the day-to-day challenges of the material world, characterized at the time by severe shortages of basic needs and by particular economic practices in which Belarusians had to engage. Examining individual experiences of *perestroika* allowed the researchers to register the shift from the euphoria of early *perestroika* times to the ensuing economic deprivations. Romanova and Makhovskaya conclude that the post-*perestroika* Belarusian political establishment, by promoting nostalgia for the Soviet past, has strongly affected the memories of *perestroika* times as expressed in personal life stories.

All in all, as the contributors to this volume demonstrate, oral history in and of post-socialist Europe has been gaining a new and powerful position in the region's scholarly discourses. At the same time, it has served various political and cultural agendas. While exploring the alternative experiences of socialism, detailing the variety of local perspectives on socio-cultural change in the region, and critically evaluating the applicability of Western methodological approaches to doing oral history, oral historians in Belarus, Poland, Russia, and Ukraine have contributed directly and effectively to epistemological transformations that have been taking place in the humanities and social sciences in post-socialist Europe over the past three decades. They have helped shift the focus to the role and place of the individual and the personal in the advancement of history and sociocultural change.

NOTES

1 See, for example, Verdery, *What Was Socialism, and What Comes Next?*

2 In the USSR, such pronouncements were made as early as 1967, on the occasion of the fiftieth anniversary of the so-called October Revolution of 1917.

3 Verdery, *What Was Socialism*, 4–5.

4 The Eastern European Anthropologists Group, a working group of the American Association of Anthropologists, began publishing its *Anthropology of Eastern Europe Review* in 1983. In the late 1980s a new research group, SOYUZ, was set up by post-Soviet anthropologists (as they referred to themselves). This gave rise to productive dialogue among scholars working in various post-socialist counties.

5 Messana, *Soviet Communal Living*; Bertaux, Thompson, and Rotkirch, *On Living through Soviet Russia*.

6 On life in a socialist village, see, for example, chapter 5 in Shcheglova, "1950-1970-e Gody." Women's oral history is another direction that touches on the period of late socialism without directly focusing on social life. See, for example, Peto, *Zhenskaia Ustnaia Istoriia*; Shinkareva, *Zhenskaia Ustnaia Istoriia*.

9 "Renew the Face of the Land, of This Land!" Catholic Culture and the Crises of Sacralization in People's Poland

DAVID CURP

Michnik turns attention above all to the dialogue at the level of power, and so the basis [of it] is: the episcopacy – the government – the bishop – the premier, the Church – the Party apparatus ... [Yet r]eal dialogue and values are tied to the choices of the nation. It is the nation, the so called simple people, filling the churches and the places of pilgrimage who have defended against the process of socialization. The voice of the bishop was most often only teaching that which was going on in the soul of the people.[1]

Fr Tischner, review of the secular dissident
Adam Michnik's *The Church and the Left*

For many Poles, the course and the success of their struggle for national liberation in the 1980s appeared miraculous. So did its success.[2] Prior to 1989, at a time when Poles and others in Central and Eastern Europe were striving to bring about fundamental political change, Poland's communist party-state elite were far from willing to surrender to the democratic aspirations of their countrymen. A desire for ongoing political power and privilege, fear of their personal complicity in state socialist crimes and corruption, and the seductions of a totalizing nationalist/socialist ideology continued to inform the resistance of Poland's old party-state functionaries to their countrymen's struggle for liberation until the transformation wrought by the 1989 elections and the fall of the Berlin Wall. Behind Poland's rulers loomed what appeared at the time the world's second superpower, the Soviet Union, whose highest leadership saw General Wojciech Jaruzelski and People's Poland as a strategic ally, and who right to the end believed that protecting the state-socialist system in Poland was a key Soviet task.[3] Many in Poland were aware of the complex of ideologies and interests (in both the East and the West) that had built an international order whose stability rested partly upon their unfreedom.[4] But faced with the formidable forces ranged against them, the Polish people drew upon and hybridized a variety of religious and secular cultural resources to mobilize themselves politically and to extricate their country from the Soviet Union's collapsing empire.

Catholicism, through its institutions, and most importantly of all, through millions of religiously conscious and engaged believers, from the beginning played a key role in Poland's successful struggle for national liberation.[5] Before they began directly confronting the authorities in 1976, many Poles had deepened their understanding and practice of their faith. They did so by continuing older religious practices and by maintaining traditional institutions as well as by developing innovative new religious movements, such as the Light-Life Movement (*Ruch Swiatło-Zycie*) and the charismatic renewal movement of the 1970s.[6] In their struggle to free Poland before and after martial law, millions of Poles appropriated religious symbols and values. They also used a variety of institutions affiliated with the Church, from parishes and student pastoral centres to the Clubs of Catholic Intelligentsia (*Klub Inteligentsii Katolickiej*, KIK) and the Catholic press, to educate themselves on a range of sacred and secular subjects outside of boundaries of official culture.[7] Most importantly, they built communities of solidarity within which collective experiences, such as the Papal pilgrimages and other religious commemorations, merged all but seamlessly with a variety of old and new Catholic practices to promote a language of human dignity that would play a key role in their forceful but nonviolent struggle for national liberation.[8] Yet despite the central importance of popular tradition and the development of an innovative, religiously grounded counterculture, the historiography of Polish religious life remains overly focused on narrow circles such as "the episcopacy – the government – the bishop – the premier, the Church – the Party apparatus." I hope to recentre our attention on people as agents of these processes in order to better understand the capacity of Catholic religious power to bring about a sacralized revolution.

For many if not most Poles, the struggle with state-sponsored *laïcité* was based on a Catholicism that in the post-war years drew upon and accepted "być Polakiem, być Katolickiem" (to be a Pole is to be a Catholic) and the tremendous moral credit that the institutional Church in

Poland had earned in the crucible of war and in resistance to Polish Stalinism.[9] Their traditional God-and-country vision saw conflict with their Moscow-backed, laicizing regime in black-and-white, at times even apocalyptic, religious and national terms.[10] From a secular perspective, such visions at best lacked nuance; at worst, they threatened to politically empower a fundamentalist version of religion. Yet these more "fundamentalist" views also expressed deep convictions among a broad sweep of the population and were founded on the experience of decades of anti-religious repression by the authorities – repression that elements of the secular left had often viewed with indifference or even silent approbation.[11]

A significant minority of believers, by contrast, developed a new, hybrid political language and culture that integrated what they regarded as their faith's strictures and wisdom with a concern for human rights and political freedom, even as they struggled for a more secular and inclusive politics. These Catholics were well positioned to build coalitions with their more traditionalist co-religionists while collaborating with non-believing or religiously indifferent political activists, who themselves were becoming more open to religiously grounded arguments for human rights and political reforms. The hierarchical Church, its hand immensely strengthened (but also complicated) after 1978 by the election of a Polish Pope, also played a role in harmonizing cooperation among these disparate voices. In itself, though, the institutional Church created neither the discontent nor the popular desire to channel much of this cooperation through religious terms, institutions, and symbols. That was the choice of Polish society, which employed the language and signs of faith and turned to the Church as a symbolic resource of wide-ranging social power and influence even in the midst of the regime's repression.

Yet as Fr Tischner noted in the quote cited above, post-war Polish history presents us with a complex interplay of the approaches many Poles took, individually and collectively, to harnessing religious power to the task of political desecularization and sacralization.[12] The varieties of *popular* religious power in Poland have informed – and perhaps even deformed – the experience of solidarity, reconciliation, and memory, especially those counter-memories that do not fit into either the construction of state socialism or a tolerant, Western-style secular liberal democracy. The desecularization and sacralization of Polish politics that accelerated in the late 1970s shows little sign of abating more than twenty years after the fall of state socialism in Poland.[13] This alone should reconfigure our understanding of religious power and its relation to personal and popular religious engagement. The stubborn resistance of many Poles to both totalitarian Communist and liberal-democratic efforts to develop a secularized public life has deep roots that need to be uncovered and studied and that cannot be understood solely by reference to the institutional Church.

Oral history is a crucial source for understanding the primary agents of the sacralization of politics and public life in Poland – the Catholic laity – as well as the manner in which they ensured that religious life flourished in the time between the twilight of state socialism in the 1970s and the birth of a democratic Polish society in the 1980s. It is an especially useful, and unique, tool for understanding the experience, quality, and character of religious life of lay people in a would-be laicizing dictatorship, where the institutional Church often loomed overly large as the primary locus of scholarly inquiry on religion.[14] Both archival records and religious literature in the last decades of state socialism highlight the prescriptive, normative programs of secularists and religious leaders, thinkers and activists, for ordinary Poles. In the regime's archives, official documents are triply burdened by the authorities' inflexible anti-religiosity, by their constant, intrusive monitoring of the lives of these religious others, and by the incomplete and deceptive nature of the security services' anti-religious tasks and their accounting of them.[15] Personal testimonies, by contrast, allow researchers immediate access into how Poles remember negotiating the shifting and at times porous boundaries between public and personal aspects of religion and culture in times both of seeming stability and of crisis and radical change. Oral historic evidence thus serves as a crucial corrective to the state and ecclesial record, which closely tracked the comings and goings of the faithful for the purpose of nurturing or hindering faith, but which sheds little light on the subjectivity of those who were monitored. Finally, and most importantly, none of the official records account for how either the regime's or the religious leadership's policies and initiatives affected believers in the immediate or long term. Oral history is a means to bridge the distance between state socialist and clerical propositions on the one hand and popular dispositions on the other.

Furthermore, oral history methodology can help uncover not only the complex role that religion played in cultural, social, and political developments before and during the collapse of the Communist regime in Poland, but also how the memories and habits acquired at this time remain a force in the ongoing sacralization of Polish public life. Oral history illustrates just how dialectical sacralization and laicization efforts were at a personal level. "Secularization" was not a unidirectional phenomenon; in this regard, personal testimonies of religious enchantment and disenchantment provide a unique demonstration of what Charles Taylor spoke of as a peculiarly modern problem: the collapse of the dominant paradigm of secularist triumphalism that has seen modernity as the rational remnant of reality after disenchantment with religion takes hold.[16] Oral history interviews can reveal the changing quality of religious life and practice as well as popular reactions to coercive secular environments.[17] Religiously, the Poles I interviewed demonstrated remarkable creativity in bending and blending a variety of matters – their memories of past injustices, their concerns about human rights and artistic freedom, and even their student activism. Clearly, both personal and public engagement remain part of the broad "socio-cultural Catholicism" that continues to play a role in the sacralizing of Polish public life and politics. Oral history creates the possibility of exploring, in a qualitative way, continuities in how Poles have blended (and continue to blend or seek now to un-blend) their personal *and* public memories and actions in the past *and* in the present; it also reveals the plasticity and expansiveness of religious life during and after Polish state socialism.[18]

This chapter focuses on the grassroots aspects of religious life in Communist Poland and represents initial findings in a long-term study of the shifting roles, influence, and memory of religious culture in Poland over the past forty years: the last two decades of Communist rule and the first two decades of freedom. In addition to conducting archival research at the Archives of New Records (*Archiwum Akt Nowych*) and the Institute of National Remembrance (*Instytut Pamięc Narodowej*), which houses the documents of the Security Services (*Służba Bezpieczeństwa*), my research assistants and I interviewed more than thirty individuals for this project. The interviewees were identified with the help of the History Meeting House, *Dom Spotkań z Historią*, in Warsaw and the Lublin Historical Society "Brama Grodzka – Teatr NN" (both of which have important oral history collections), as well as through my own personal contacts, which I developed through my participation in events offered by the Institute of Religion and Public Life's *Centissimus Annos* Seminar as well as through acquaintances I made during my sabbatical year affiliated with the Stefan Wyszyński University in Warsaw. All of my interviewees were in some way significantly involved in religious milieux during the 1970s and 1980s, as high school or university students or as young adults. Most but not all were affiliated with the intelligentsia in Warsaw or Gdańsk. Their experiences of religious life before and during the revolutionary transformations of Polish society and the Polish state demonstrate the fertility and diversity of the sacralizing–democratizing synthesis that had been developing in Poland in the decades prior to the rise of the Solidarity movement. Their accounts also show how the sacralizing elements of this revolution continue to resonate in Poland in ways as uniquely personal and public as was the original revolution itself.

Przydź Krolestwo Twoje ... / Thy Kingdom Come

> In our relations with the Church we can conduct in different periods sharper or milder policies, at times using the force of logic and at other times acting with the logic of force. One thing must however stay consistent: the policy of strengthening a group of loyal clergy in the Church.[19]
>
> Stanisław Kania, in memo to the Interior Ministry

In December 1970, when a botched but bloody repression of a workers' uprising on the Baltic coast led to a change in regime leadership, Poland gave little appearance of a society on the verge of a successful, non-violent popular revolution.[20] The party-state authorities enjoyed real, if shallow, social support in the early 1970s during a brief period of outward social peace and economic development as they trumpeted with increasing confidence a "propaganda of success" of state-socialist economics. In retrospect, this "propaganda of success" sounds ironic, but at the time, it had popular resonance. Dr Piotr Broda-Wysocki (born in 1970) has childhood memories of this period. As he noted in his interview, his father, a factory worker, already owned a car (the ubiquitous Polski Fiat) and in 1977 was able to buy his entire family new skis and provide a two-week vacation to the mountains – purchases well out of reach of most contemporary academics.[21] Yet among the party-state's citizen-subjects, the comforts created by loan-fuelled prosperity produced neither solidarity nor even gratitude towards the regime. Dr Broda-Wysocki notes that even during these "happy" times in the 1970s, the (violent and violently repressed) 1976 strikes in Ursus and Radom near Warsaw involved looting and destructive behaviour by workers. He adds that a visit to

West Germany introduced him to an intensely colourful world full of capitalist mysteries. One such mystery, for him, was how purchasing more than one item could lower the price one paid – how could buying 10 bottles of juice be cheaper than buying them one at a time? Like many young Poles at this time, Dr Broda-Wysocki emerged with a strong sense of critical distance both from his own changing working-class milieu and the official truths of People's Poland "propaganda of success" – a distance that only increased over time under the strains of Martial Law.

Rampant alcoholism was another sign of deep alienation even at the height of Polish prosperity in the 1970s, and it only increased during the 1980s. Alcoholism was both a social plague and a fixture of social life throughout this time – even during "sacred" functions and in spite of the clergy's at times draconian efforts to police it.[22] Karen Kovacik, an American of Polish descent, resident in Poland in 1982–83 and 1986–87 as a scholar (eventually a Fulbright Scholar), tells how she was deeply indignant that during the First Communion of a friend's son in 1987, the priest instructed the children to inform on their parents if alcohol was served at their celebratory party – an admonition that, she admitted, seemed to bother no one present. During the party, the family made an effort to conceal vodka by mixing it with orange soda; they were discovered when the first communicant took a sip from one of the spiked bottles and burst into tears. (Dr Kovacik later noted that the father of the First Communicant was – and remains – an alcoholic.) [23] Given the reputation of the Polish state-socialist regime during this time as technocratic and non-ideologically pragmatist, on the surface it is striking how tense Church–state relations remained under a facade of cooperation, which both ecclesial and political authorities attempted to maintain during the 1970s.[24] In terms of religion, the 1970s were a study in contrasts and contradictions. Officially, the party-state authorities at the highest levels grew increasingly willing to accept traditional religious practices, which in their view reflected a stubborn but non-threatening core of folk culture that they could undermine through benign neglect and strategic subversion of the Catholic clergy. However, the security services never abandoned their conflict with the Church, and meanwhile, the attitude of the party-state reflected a variety of local interests and concerns that sometimes softened and other times intensified Church–state conflict.[25] Even more strikingly, considering later events, many Church figures felt themselves to be on the defensive in the 1970s even as their influence over Polish society's elite strengthened.[26] The 1970s saw a flowering among Poland's elite of a range of religious initiatives from above and below, the way for which had been paved by the sustained religious activism of the Polish clergy and much of the laity throughout the post-war years. Before the 1960s, the Church had invested enormous effort in sustaining staples of ecclesial life such as religious education, traditional religious celebrations (which grew increasingly elaborate), and the refurbishing of infrastructure; the late 1960s saw the beginning of experimentation. Many educated Poles found in the Catholic Church's various pastoral initiatives (especially the Light-Life Movement, discussed below), and those of independent Catholic organizations such as the Clubs of Catholic Intelligentsia (*Klub Inteligentsii Katolickiej*, KIK), highly congenial and even compelling environments in which to develop a range of interests and contacts.[27] The ground on which new ecclesial and popular religious initiatives would flower had been well prepared by traditional popular religious culture and institutions. Katarzyna Boruń-Jagodzińska's life experiences demonstrate just how wide-ranging and eclectic even traditional religious life among the Warsaw intelligentsia could be. The daughter of a journalist and a teacher/social activist, both of whom were Home Army and Warsaw Uprising veterans (and religiously engaged but critical, almost anticlerical, non-practising Catholics), she was born in 1956 and grew up in the żołiborz neighbourhood, where she infrequently attended the Catholic parish of the Child Jesus, known as a haven for the intelligentsia. Childhood illnesses led to her spending a good deal of time with relatives in Polish mountain villages, where she was exposed to a rural religiosity whose folk artistic sensibility and *a cappella* singing left a deep impression on her. Her participation in high and low Polish religious experiences paved the way for her own eventual return not only to personal religious practice but also to cultural/religious activism in the 1980s.[28] Krzystof Górski, who in the 1970s was a student of classical philology and later a teacher in Warsaw, recounts the wide range of religious activities – from ongoing theological and philosophical education/discussions to cultural events and aesthetically satisfying liturgies – that churches and other religious organizations such as KIK and Oasis (*Oaza*, a program of retreats and religious formation offered by the Light-Life Movement to bring about the renewal of Catholicism[29]) offered during this period. Krzystof had been religiously engaged before 1978, but the election of Karol Wojtyła as Pope deepened that engagement (to the point that he now describes some of his attitudes at that time as "fundamentalist"). The late 1970s he described as "his best years" – a time of real intellectual development and creativity. Warsaw provided opportunities for him to engage in a wide variety of Church-sponsored gatherings, including theological and philosophical discussions of the works of the Christian mystics Simone Weil and Thomas Merton (which enabled him to link his Catholic faith to his growing interest in Eastern religions), presentations by such Catholic intellectuals as Tadeusz Mazowiecki, and opportunities for religious worship as varied as the aesthetically pleasing worship at St Martin's parish and the more emotionally and personally engaging meetings of Oasis communities. Tomasz Wiścicki, like Górski and Boruń-Jagodzińska a member of the Warsaw intelligentsia, experienced a similarly varied religious life through his involvement with the Catholic student ministry as a university student in Poznań in the 1980s. His religious activities as a student were rarely if ever overtly political, but they were enough to earn him and other religiously engaged students the attention of the security services (*Służby Bezpieczeństwa*, or SB, whose functionaries were often referred to as *Esbeks*). These officials intermittently harassed him in spite of the ostensible guarantees of freedom of conscience in Communist Poland's constitution. Wiścicki and his official tormenters both understood that the religious counterculture that played such a key role in Poland's universities, while it might be formally legal, was deeply alien to the official vision of Poland's rulers.[30] Górski adds that for him, the eventual opposition of the clergy (and many believing laity, such as himself) to the regime was something "natural," "a matter of course." Wiścicki observed that a complete rejection of the regime's propaganda ("of course official history was a lie and General Jaruzelski was a criminal") went without saying and was entirely unnecessary to dwell upon in this milieu.[31] This level of freedom from ideological entanglements with the party-state made an integral, religiously grounded opposition to the authorities not just possible but all too easy.

Jako Mi Się Odpuszczamy Naszym Winowajcom / As We Forgive Our Debtors

> We ask for freedom from revenge and hatred, for that freedom which is the fruit of love.[32]
>
> From a prayer that ended a homily
> of the martyred Solidarity priest,
> Fr Jerzy Popiełuszko, in September 1982

The year 1989 signalled a sharp turn in the history of Poland and of other countries in the region. The collapse of socialist regimes in Europe led to major transitions in the intellectual domain of Polish society, requiring a new approach towards its recent socialist past. The politics of the thick line, which had to be drawn between the socialist past and democratic present, were actively advocated by the new democratic government of Poland. In 1989, many of those who were involved in creating a democratic Poland regarded drawing "a thick line" between past and present – that is, not prosecuting state-socialist functionaries for crimes they had committed before or during Martial Law – as key to their reconciliation efforts. Yet this approach proved to be politically – and, for many, personally – costly and unsustainable. Experiences of deprivation (even in the "best of times"), a sense of being marked by this time of unfreedom (and at times feeling keenly aware of how different their own experiences were from those of their children[33]), and inherited social pathologies such as alcoholism and intractable political conflicts rooted in the past, produced different degrees of frustration, anger, and bitterness on the part of many of my interviewees.[34] For many of my interviewees, their sense of shame at their helplessness in the face of the party-state's repression was compounded by other injuries, including the blurring of boundaries between religion and politics that both non-believers and (perhaps especially) many believers who desired a more secular polity found disconcerting. After decades of official efforts to decouple *polskość*, or Polishness, from Catholicism and society from religious life, all of my interviewees agreed that the national/religious synthesis remained strong and that anti-religious repression rarely touched ordinary people. Broda-Wysocki and Anna Bielak observed that for (non-Communist Party members of) the working class, the authorities made no effort to disrupt ordinary religious life and celebrations, although they did monitor religious activities. Both Wiścicki and Boruń-Jagodzińska noted that in their families and among the Warsaw intelligentsia, religion was simply an accepted part of life whose ordinary, low-key rhythms were undisturbed by official propagations of secularism and dialectical materialism (and, at least until the 1970s, by the various pastoral initiatives and elaborate liturgical celebrations of the Church). Wiścicki had stopped attending religious education as a teenager, but he ascribed this to his own personal searching and not to the impact of a militantly secularized educational environment.[35]

Fr Wiesław Dawidowski and Tomasz Wiścicki had somewhat different experiences of anti-religious repression when they participated in religiously innovative activities.[36] Here, they were running up against the ambivalence of the regime itself. On the one hand, the authorities hoped for, and worked to bring about, Polish society's secularization; meanwhile, they constantly proclaimed that they did not discriminate against believers as such, and in the 1970s they made some important albeit reluctant concessions to believers.[37] On the other hand, the authorities – often at the prompting of the more militantly anti-religious SB – remained convinced that Catholicism in general was an "anti-socialist" force and that religiously innovative activities were particularly suspect. Such activities were targets of monitoring and repression.[38]

As teenagers in the 1970s and early 1980s, Wiesław Dawidowski and Jacek Bielak both attended Oasis retreats sponsored by the Light-Life Movement.[39] Tomasz Wiścicki was drawn back to a deeper engagement in his faith during his studies at Adam Mickiewicz University in Poznań, a place where the authorities acknowledged a total failure of efforts to preserve even the pretence of *laïcité*.[40] There he was also involved in independent student government activities, which in the 1980s were dominated by practising Catholics. The SB regarded both Oasis in the 1970s and Catholic involvement with student government in the 1980s with deep hostility as violating the unwritten (and unconstitutional) rules of state-mandated secularism. This official hostility was not hidden. Fr Dawidowski recounted how some families' parents wanted their children to "take vacations with God," that is, participate in summer Oasis retreats for religious development (even if more worldly reasons – such as parents wanting to have time for themselves – intruded). Those parents encouraged this even though they knew that they or their children might be harassed or discriminated against by the authorities. This was seen as an opportunity for their children to suffer for their faith – far from being a deterrent, such harassment was viewed as a badge of (religious) honour and personal integrity. This illustrates the asymmetrical nature and high costs of the state's undeclared conflict with popular religious practice. Polish parents were willing to introduce their children directly to the contradictions of state-sponsored *laïcité* – to allow the state to perform a kind of religious instruction on the meaning of secular "tolerance." As the *Esbeks* broke up Oasis camps and interrogated and discriminated against young people, this reinforced among religiously engaged Catholics the perception that the authorities, for all their official protestations, were "fighting against God." Finally, and perhaps most importantly, by making young people's identification with religious values and activities a threat to their future prospects, the regime invited even young Catholics to engage in deeper reflection on the personal and political dimensions and importance of their faith. That many hundreds of thousands of young people elected, like Bielak and Dawidowski, to continue to participate in movements like Oasis throughout the 1970s and early 1980s was a sign of a fundamental realignment of their values and attitudes and of their willingness to live with a question mark over their future in Poland. This led to a deeper questioning not only of their future in such a state, but of the future of the state-socialist regime itself.[41] Of course, religious life often did contain anti-regime content, but this was not always initiated by the clergy.[42] Broda-Wysocki is now critical of the (what he describes as few) occasions when clergy spoke to contemporary political issues, but he acknowledges that during Martial Law, participants at Sunday Mass often were impatient with sermons that focused primarily on religious themes. Working-class congregations wanted (and valued) the clergy's commentary on current events – which he remembers was often offered with humour. On pilgrimage as a high school student, Bielak encountered for the first time a survivor of the Warsaw Uprising, who openly and convincingly contradicted the official narrative of Soviet helplessness – much to the chagrin of the priest leading the retreat, who encouraged her "not to mix a religious pilgrimage with politics" (especially given that a particularly silent member of the group was regarded by other pilgrims as an SB informer).[43] Thus, for my interviewees, official hostility to religion and the popular (even if at times clerically frowned upon) mixing of religion and politics were acknowledged facts of life – at times personally costly and terrifying, but limited and ultimately ineffective. If anything, what Broda-Wysocki described as the grotesque aspects of the authorities' presence in religious milieux – which often led priests to begin sermons by greeting not only their parishioners but also members of the security services whom they knew were present to record sermons – accentuated the distinct public place of religious venues as politicized sanctuaries, privileged even by the authorities themselves.

I Nie Wódz Nas Na Pokuszenie / And Lead Us Not into Temptation

> Thou shalt not bear false witness against thy neighbour.
>
> Exodus 20:16

Oral history has required me to rethink key problems in current Polish history and religiosity. Before conducting interviews, my research and a review of the current literature on Church–state relations indicated that for all its efforts to create a more secularist environment, the Polish Communist regime became enmeshed in the Church as an institution and in Polish society through a variety of political and cultural processes that had sacralized Polish politics, not always intentionally. The regime's (mostly) low-level religious persecution and discrimination against believers throughout Communist times and its efforts to advance a "socialist world view" in education and culture gave the lie to its claim to respect freedom of conscience – and effectively politicized much of religious life. The Church sought directly to maintain a role in public life – especially in Polish culture and intellectual life – but its approach to politics was much more ambivalent: while some clergy engaged in anti- and pro-regime politics, they often found themselves being called in by the authorities to calm protests and violence elicited by the regime's own economic and political failures.

While the unintended consequences of the regime's largely ineffectual religious persecution can be discerned in the literature of Church–state relations in Poland, oral history has allowed me to identify new problems as well. As I asked my informants to consider the relationship between their personal religious values and public life in the state-socialist past, it became clear that most of them back then welcomed their own and other lay religious – and even clerical – interventions into "secular issues" in their state-socialist past, interventions they find troubling today. Since, as an interviewer, I was collaborating with my interview subjects to create a new historical source, I have found it necessary to engage in an ongoing critical evaluation of my role in the production of the final text of an interview. This is doubly difficult. First, there is the presumption of my own cultural imperatives, which demand that democracy be secular, and the interviewees' experiences of the central role that sacred forms of popular mobilization played in bringing about Poland's democratization. Second, my interview subjects and I faced the challenge of distinguishing between their "simpler" past, during which they participated in a sacralized political mobilization integral to their country's democratization, and their attitudes towards religion and politics today.

In addition, there are two other problems I anticipate are likely to keep growing over the course of this project. The first is the difficulty of judiciously assessing the past and present importance and varieties of Poland's national/religious synthesis: the ideal that "to be a Pole is to be a Catholic." This ideal is rejected both by those non-Catholic Poles whose minority religious – and irreligious – experiences would read them out of such a definition of Polishness, as well as by many Polish Catholics who do not admire the *bogoojczyźniany*/"*dewotki*"/"God-and-fatherland"/"overly pious" faith of many Polish Catholics in a democratic Poland.[44] This seems to be the case even among Poles who once participated in such a *bogoojczyźniany* culture and politics, such as when Górski spoke of having gone through a "fundamentalist phase" of belief.

Second, when I present my research to generally highly secular academic audiences, I take it as a given that I have to make a case both for faith's relevance and for its intellectual/cultural and spiritual complexity and creativity – that religion not only matters but also has as thoroughly a modern (or postmodern) contemporary historical reality as any other factor in social, cultural, or political life. In particular, I understand that for secular, usually liberal, audiences, any union of nationalism and religion – such as by those now labelled *bogoojczyźniany*[45] (who in the struggles of the late 1970s the regime's spokesmen referred to as "Polish ayatollahs") – is understood as an unholy alliance.[46] If faith is to have a positive social role, it cannot be in the identification of a people as such with religious values, since that is regarded as somehow (for reasons themselves grounded in faith in a secular order) more exclusive and intolerant than other forms of social and ideological cohesion. Yet in Poland, transgressing boundaries between Poland's religious and secular spheres – by secularists as well as by believers – was, and to a large extent remains, normal.[47] Even more striking is that while most of my interviewees agreed that the current transgressions of the boundaries between religion and politics by believers advocating a more sacralized politics are not a sign of social or religious health, they acknowledge and praise the public role of Catholicism (and their own religiously informed rejection of the party-state's laicizing politics) during the Solidarity era. Indeed, Małgorzata Strękowska-Zaremba, who returned to the practice of Catholicism during Martial Law, echoed and amplified Broda's observation on the important role that religion and sacred spaces played for oppositional political life by claiming that "the Church was the only place one could get the truth [about current events in Poland]."[48] The foundations of Poland's socio-cultural Catholicism were dug and solidified by a Polish people for many of whom the experience of religious-national political unity remains both a powerful symbol and a symbol of power. The relatively uncontroversial role of

Catholicism then as a popular resource in the struggle for national liberation thus tends to distort current discussions (as well as memories) of the place of Catholicism in public life. It also makes it more difficult to critically analyse the relationship between memories of religiously informed national unity and other experiences of social and political division.

Conclusion: Zbawiony od Złego? / Delivered from Evil?

> The wind blows wherever it pleases. You hear its sound,
> but you cannot tell where it comes from or where it is going. So it is with everyone born of the Spirit.
>
> John 3:8

Throughout the post-war era, Catholic, non-Catholic, and secular Poles resorted to ecclesial institutions and Catholicism to accomplish a bewildering variety of political and social tasks. In spite of their consistent anti-religious animus, the authorities, and eventually members of the anti-regime secular intelligentsia, turned to religious leaders for political assistance in what these actors thought of as primarily a secular struggle to maintain, or disrupt, social and political peace.[49] Even for many non-believers, it was natural and even necessary for religion and the institutions of the Catholic Church to play a pivotal political role in helping Poles navigate the collapse of state-socialism. This need to turn to religion as a key source in bringing Poles together into one nation suggests that both institutional and cultural realities generated by state-socialism in Poland had become thoroughly totalitarian under late socialism. Only communities of belief, be they those of the party-state or of popularly supported institutional religion, were able to wield public power in the cultural and political desert created by state-socialism. Both the state-socialist authorities and Catholic religious communities relied on popular national and religious sensibilities to draw many Poles towards one another. Furthermore, for most Poles, their state and the Catholic Church – whatever their differences – posited an essential political and personal unity of the Polish *naród i lud* (nation and people) based upon shared beliefs. These experiences, in which the political power of belief played a key role in creating a solidarity (and a Solidarność), ultimately helped liberate their country from socialism. It has also produced a widely shared political theology (or, perhaps, a religious sensibility) that can delegitimize the rough and tumble of free political life and that continues to encumber religiosity with public obligations that many believers and non-believers regard as harmful. Such a past is often fondly remembered as heroic and valuable and as a time of deep unity (even if that unity was founded on the negation of the old regime). This makes the construction of secular spaces all the more difficult. Many of the interviewees were aware that much of the unity they experienced was mythical; even so, it was at that time both a fruitful and a constraining myth. Its force was sufficient to drive the party-state's ruling class from power, and it has continued to shape many of the cultural and political responses of believers and non-believers towards religion in Poland's public life. Exploring the memories and personal experiences of how this occurred and what it means, and the witness of those who were touched by and who helped build this mythology, are essential to understanding Poland's past, present, and future.

NOTES

1 Quoted in Nowak, "Kościół jako Azyl," 352.

2 Kosiński, *Nastolatki '81*, 303–5.

3 According to Gorbachev's long-time adviser, Anatoly Chernyaev, "he [Gorbachev] thought that Jaruzelski was a man who was capable of gradually leading Poland out of a crisis and to normalcy, to preserve it as an ally, as a friendly state." Quoted in Savranskaya, Blantion, and Zubok, *Masterpieces of History*, 123.

4 For example, the Federal Republic of Germany continued to cooperate with the Jaruzelski regime even after the declaration of martial law, in spite of criticism from the Reagan administration and real popular opposition from many Poles involved in Solidarity. See Malinowski, *Polityka Republiki Federalnej*, 42, as well as "Polacy."

5 Bird and Maneli, "The New Turn," 29–30.

6 Pawlicka, *Polityka Władz*, 151–6. Also in A. Zieliński, "Nowe Ruchy Religijne," 231–51; and Załęcki "Between Spontaneity."

7 Arkuszewski et al., "Oaza na Freta" (on one important milieu in which several of my interviewees were engaged in the 1970s). Barbara Strassberg notes in general the weakness of analysing Poland in terms of a secularization thesis that does "not fit the Polish case very well." Instead, she discusses the range of activities noted above and asserts that Poland

underwent a process of religious change that created a "broad socio-cultural Catholicism" in Poland. Strassberg, "Changes in Religious Culture," 342.

8 Firouzbakhch goes so far as to speak of the "decisive role" that the mutual collaboration of the clergy and workers in helping to organize the first papal pilgrimage played in creating the conditions for later working-class protests. Firouzbakhch, "Rewolucja Islamska w Iranie," 302–3.

9 Robert Brier and Jan Kubik both discuss the crucial role of Catholicism in informing working-class protest during and after the Solidarity era. Brier, "The Roots of the 'Fourth Republic,'" 74–5; Kubik, *The Power of Symbols*. See also Zieliński, *Kościół w Polsce*, 20–1, on the moral credit the Church accumulated among wide sections of Polish society between 1939 and 1956 (and beyond) in their struggle with the invading Nazis and Soviets and in resisting the worst excesses of Polish Stalinism.

10 The authorities claimed that the Church in general, and particular priests like Jerzy Popieluszko, were engaged in an anti-regime activism that threatened to "sacralize" public, secular life. See Krawczak, "Władze PRL"; also in Zaryn and Majchrzak, "Ofensywna Antykościelna." Choma-Jusińska, *środowiska Opozycyjne*, in her discussion of opposition attitudes among students in Lublin (47–8), notes how many of them understood themselves as carrying on the same struggle for independence as had been waged by Polish anti-Communist partisans since 1944.

11 Michnik, *The Church and The Left*, 88.

12 In all fairness to Michnik, it seems that Cardinal Wyszyński's views of the Church's ties to political power were not that different from his own. In a note to the new authorities in March 1971, Wyszyński ended by claiming that "the nation is our common good. The State-Government, Church-Episcopate in their own proper ways serve this same people." See Friszke, *PRL wobec Kościoła*, 15. Yet whatever the cardinal's understanding (or representation) of his role, the Catholic hierarchy's power ultimately derived from Poles' willingness to invest their time, talents, and resources.

13 Szostkiewicz, "Linia Michalika," 10–12.

14 Oral testimony has played a central role in post-war Polish historiography. This is clear from the interviews conducted by the Solidarity journalist Teresa Torańska with former Stalinist functionaries, published in Toranska, *Them: Stalin's Polish Puppets*, a key source of information about Poland's Stalinist rulers. As Portelli observed, "orality is woven into the texture of many key official documents," sometimes in ways that strengthen state power. In the Polish case, such documents included many that reported

on (usually) private conversations between security agents and informers. See Portelli, *The Death of Luigi Trastulli*, 5. The challenge of making the leap from understanding the role of religion to analysing *how* and *why* Catholicism played its role is addressed by Osa, "Creating Solidarity," who addresses how social and political power was sacralized by ecclesiastical leaders, especially Wyszyński. She does not address, though, why Poles supported clerics' mobilization initiatives.

15 In the summer of 1973, Colonel Straszewski, head of the Internal Affairs Ministry's Church–State Division (the Fourth Department), outlined a plan of action for his unit. That plan emphasized that his department's goals were to combat the Catholic Church's "open and actually hostile and injurious political-ideological activities," to neutralize the Church hierarchy and clergy and to compel them to support the socio-political system of the PRL. All of this would weaken the Church's influence on society, but success would require "employing specific means and methods that would not be ... appropriate" in other situations, as well as expanding his department's operations to include "offensive" ones. See Dziurok, *Metody Pracy Operacyjnej Aparatu*, 70–4.

16 Taylor, *A Secular Age*, 573.

17 Peter Berger makes an important point about the resurgence of more integralist and fundamentalist religion: religions that are less willing to "adapt" to modern values often flourish; yet at the same time, many "traditional" religious movements are surprisingly adept at addressing modern (and postmodern) concerns in original and creative ways. Berger, "Introduction," 4.

18 Thomson, "Four Paradigm Transformations," 53–8.

19 Woloszyn, *Chronić i Kontrolować*, 2.

20 Choma-Jusińska notes that even committed anti-regime activists did not expect to significantly change Polish politics in their lifetime. *środowiska Opozycyjne*, 32. Tomasz Wiścicki, in an interview, observed that one of the few ways the party-state's propaganda succeeded was in convincing even those thoroughly alienated from it that the party-state was a permanent fixture of Polish life. See Pawlicka, *Polityka Władz*, 95.

21 Broda-Wysocki, interview.

22 Kovacik, interview.

23 Kosiński, *Historia*, 237. In 1960, Poles over sixteen drank on average 8 litres of vodka, 1.3 litres of wine or *miod pitny*, and 20 litres of beer a year. By 1987, the figures were 16, 11, and 41 litres respectively (a decline from the 1980 high of 20, 13, and 41 litres respectively).

24 Marek, *Kler to Nasz Wróg*.

25 Maniewska, *Kościół katolicki w Bydgoszczy*, xxf.; Cecylia Kuta, *"Działacze" i "Pismaki,"* xx–xxi.

26 Słodkowska, *Społeczeństwo Obywatelskie*, 95. The Church's concern over its place in Polish culture was prompted by chronic structural weaknesses, including the lack of Church buildings in major population centres and what many clergy regarded as the relentless secularization of schools. This was compounded by education laws passed in 1973 that prompted the episcopate to contemplate a "declaration of war" against state efforts to secularize Polish youth. See Instytut Pamięci Narodowej (hereafter IPN) WR 053/2185, 31. The security services reported in January 1973 (i.e., even before the education reforms) that religious leaders saw state efforts secularize the schools as a threat to the Polish Church's very existence. IPN DR 08/250, no. 5, 97.

27 Zieliński, *Kościół w Polsce*, 171–83.

28 Boruń-Jagodzińska, interview.

29 Zieliński, *Kościół w Polsce*, 180–1.

30 See IPN Kr 08/250, no. 1, 27–9, regarding complaints about the expansion of KIK activities among young people in Kraków.

31 Górski, interview.

32 *Bóg i Ojczyzna*, ix.

33 Dr Broda and Ms Strękowska-Zaremba remarked on this, Dr Broda on several occasions.

34 Such feelings at times coexisted with a sense of the importance of these experiences in forming their character. Many Poles took deep pride in their personal and family actions of overt resistance. For example, Anna Bielak greatly admired her father's activities as a worker-activist in Gdańsk. See Bielak, interview.

35 Wysocki, interview.

36 IPN KR 08/250, no. 2, 142–3. While interrogating a participant in pastoral activities who objected to being interviewed about her private religious activities, the security officers explained that religious activities were only private "to the degree to which they were done in a traditional way and in a space approved for such activities." Pastoral work, when it was carried out in student centres or private apartments, or when it took innovative and non-traditional forms, was fair game, in the view of the security services.

37 Zielinski, *Kościół w Polsce*, 183–91. Zieliński argues, however, that these concessions did little to repair the fault lines in Church-State relations.

38 IPN Ka 010/5, no. 2, 1. In the 1970s, Interior Ministry documents often emphasized conflicts with the Church and called for sterner measures to combat the rising tide of religiosity among youth, especially in universities. IPN 0639/155, 142.

39 "Oases" were religious retreats organized by Father Franciszek Blachnicki as part of his movement for religious renewal. That movement was known

variously as *Kościół Domowy* (The House Church) and *Ruch światło-życie* (The Light-Life Movement). This was a "cadre" movement aimed at forming a religious elite. Over the course of the 1970s, more than 1.5 million took part in its events; by early 1980, it had 42,000 members in 1,500 small communities throughout the country. Zieliński, *Kościół w Polsce*, 181. See also Dziurok, *Metody Pracy*, 549.

40 IPN Po 282: 14.

41 Dr Bielak was the first interviewee to discuss how his refusal to participate in violent protests in the late 1980s was motivated both by his religious belief in non-violence and by his conviction that he needed to prepare for a legal career in the free Poland that he anticipated. As a young man – seventeen at the time – he had been able to break with the regime's insistence that Poland's state-socialist order was permanent; see Bielak, interview.

42 IPN 0713/258, 442. In Kraków and Wrocław, the clergy (including Cardinal Wojtyła) expressed concern over dissidents' efforts to carry out political work in pastoral settings, especially among students.

43 Bielak, interview.

44 Ash, *History of the Present*, 105.

45 *Bogoojczyźniany*, adj, "of God and Homeland" (editors' note).

46 In Poland, secular liberals' critiques of religious politics can be fierce. In Filipowicz's 1993 interview with the Polish feminist and writer/critic Anna Bojarska, Ms Bojarska opines that a "coup d'état" could improve what she describes as a silent seizure of power by the Polish Catholic Church. Filipowicz and Bojarska, "From Communism to Khomeinism," 9. See also Eberts, "The Roman Catholic Church."

47 This was most apparent in the discussions surrounding Poland's accession to the EU. An SLD-led government openly collaborated with the episcopacy to win religious support for (or at least acquiescence to) Polish membership in that body. Zieliński, *Kościół w Polsce*, 357.

48 Strękowska-Zaremba, interview. Krzysztof Bolin, who admitted that during the 1980s he had a highly instrumentalist approach to religion (he viewed the work of Fr Popieluszko as primarily that of political activism and not of priestly service, and he regarded the pontificate of John Paul II as significant mainly to the degree to which a Polish pope could pressure the Soviet state) still argued that religion must play an ongoing role in current public life, since "religion also is morality, and we have to have moral foundations" – hence, "religion in public life is not a problem." Bolin, interview.

49 Friszke, *PRL wobec Kościoła*, 51.

10 In Search of History's Other Agents: Oral History of Decollectivization in Ukraine in the 1990s

NATALIA KHANENKO-FRIESEN

In 2007–9, an oral history project called "Decollectivization in Ukraine in the 1990s: Rural Perspectives and Experiences" was conducted in Ukraine, during which 117 autobiographical interviews were recorded with former collective farmers in ten of that country's regions. The goals of this study were many. It would document the personal reflections of former collective farmers regarding their experiences of post-socialist reforms in the Ukrainian countryside in the 1990s. It would also identify a shared subjectivity regarding the transition to post-socialism and the formation of new collective memories of late socialism among the rural population. The project also hoped to give these Ukrainian villagers an opportunity to present their own views on the profound socio-economic changes they had lived through in the 1990s to audiences beyond Ukraine. In this chapter, I focus on the approaches these Ukrainian villagers took to telling their life stories. After discussing agricultural reform in Ukraine in the 1990s and defining the term "decollectivization," I outline some methodological considerations regarding how the project was conceived and why a particular cohort of villagers with long experience in Soviet collective farming was selected for the study. After that, I turn to the villagers' narrative construction of their identities and some of the characteristics their narrative presentations shared. Together, the narrators present a unique profile of decollectivized Ukrainian villagers. Their interviews make clear that decollectivized farmers have long occupied a unique position in Ukrainian history as both its agents and subjects.

Decollectivization

After Ukraine achieved independence from the Soviet Union in 1991, a series of post-independence governments subjected Ukrainian rural communities to a dramatic and poorly coordinated reorganization of Soviet collective farms. These reforms, which started six months before Ukraine's independence, lasted for ten years, and which to a great degree remain unfinished, involved denationalizing agricultural lands and redistributing collective farms' productive resources to individual members of those enterprises. The first phase of reforms focused on redistributing land while it continued to be held by the state. Thus, in early 1990s, the collective and state farms were swiftly reorganized into so-called collective agricultural enterprises (CAEs), based on principles of cooperative governance and self-sustainability. The CAEs were meant to assume greater control over their land and thereby inject a measure of pluralism into resource management.[1] In the first round of farm reorganization and land privatization, the former collective farmers, who for generations had been deprived of the right to own land, were reassigned the rights to land use. "Paper" land shares – that is, certificates stating the individual's right to a share of the collective farmlands and assets – were distributed to the villagers. In this way, former collective and state farms were transformed into corporations and former collective farmers into shareholders. However, this new relationship between the former collective farmers and the former collective farm resources remained poorly defined.

It was not until 1999, when a second round of land reforms began, that the government drastically changed this relationship: now, instead of holding paper shares that provided the right to hold land, these one-time collective farmers would acquire their own fully titled plots of land. The villagers who had received paper land shares during the first round of reforms now had to exchange those shares for land title certificates. Having done so, the holders of these title certificates did not become landowners in the fullest sense of the word, for certain prohibitions were still in place regarding the sale and purchase of agricultural land. The certificates could only be used to establish private farms or to enlarge existing household plots. Also, individual certificate holders could lease their land to corporate farms.[2] The villagers were not permitted to buy or sell their land; they were, however, allowed to transfer the rights to it to other holders in limited ways as set out by the legal system of the day.

Land reform has been a long and difficult process in Ukraine, as many analysts have noted. The first round of farm reforms, in 1992–3, saw a sweeping transformation of some 12,000 collective and state farms into CAEs, which later underwent share-based privatization. Thus, land and asset shares were distributed to farm employees, who – at least theoretically – could exercise the right of exit. The second round of reforms, which began in 1999, saw further rapid changes: collective agricultural enterprises were turned into corporate farms (limited liability companies, joint stock companies, partnerships, cooperatives, etc.). It is worth mentioning that the 1999 presidential decree on the reorganization of farm enterprises[3] – referred to by some analysts as the "Big Bang"[4] – stipulated that all collective agricultural enterprises were to distribute fully titled land plots to their shareholders within four months from the date those shares were issued (December 1999). This decree reflected the Ukrainian government's momentous decision to complete land privatization by converting paper land shares into surveyed and titled physical plots.[5]

On paper, these and other changes constituted badly needed efforts to transform Ukraine's agricultural sector, and in that sense they were progressive. But that effort was marred by bureaucratic hurdles and government inefficiency, with the result that key players – including the former collective farmers – were often unaware of the reforms' goals, meanings, and outcomes. Regarding the first nine years of reforms, World Bank experts wrote that they "have failed to radically change the traditional collective organization of Ukrainian farms ... Break-up and internal restructuring of large farms has been very limited. Hence it should not be a surprise that the transition process is not delivering in terms of increased profitability and efficiency."[6]

While the reforms were being carried out, Ukrainian sociologists studied the rural population's opinions of the changes the reforms were bringing about. Iryna Prybytkova, a well-known sociologist and rural researcher, pointed to a 1994 study that found that farmers – be they managers, specialists, or labourers – did not sufficiently understand the goals of reorganizing collective farms into corporations. Most of the workers who had been assigned rights to their collective farm's land and property had neither the legal nor the economic opportunity to exercise those rights, so they did not see the value of the reforms. According to the survey respondents, continues Prybytkova, these reforms were conducted "on paper" and did not introduce any mechanisms that would have allowed the villagers to create new kinds of agricultural enterprises outside of the only two available to them: form small family farms, or stay with the large collective enterprise. Importantly, many respondents had no understanding of the reforms whatsoever. Still others did not even realize that reforms were being carried out.[7]

Analysts have concluded that the first decade of agrarian reforms in Ukraine failed in terms of socio-economic outcomes. Economic output in that sector of the Ukrainian economy fell dramatically. Livestock suffered the most: about one-third of all the Ukrainian livestock once held by collective farms were lost in the course of the decade. The collective farms had once been centrally coordinated and financially supported by the Soviet state; now, the CAEs had to rely on their own resources to continue, and in transitional times the result was often deteriorating property and equipment. Also, the distribution of productive resources to individual shareholders, however positive this sounded on paper, often led to the dismantling of collective farm property so that farmers could at least take construction materials home as their share.

The reforms hit the people themselves especially hard. The initial reorganization of collective farms in the early 1990s, followed by the dismantling of the CAEs in 2000, severely disenfranchised former collective farm workers. A sociological survey conducted in Ukraine in 2004 found that 57 per cent of rural Ukrainians stated they were unemployed. Every third villager (32.9 per cent) self-identified as a hired worker; only 5.2 per cent saw themselves as self-employed. In addition, 11.4 per cent of all rural families had one or more members working abroad, and 6.1 per cent of all respondents intended to seek work abroad.[8] Media commentators routinely cited failed agricultural reforms as the principal reason for the high outmigration of Ukrainians to other countries – a trend that would result in the Ukrainian population falling by 5 to 6 per cent in two decades.[9]

As a result of the government's half-measures to reorganize Ukraine's agricultural sector, villagers faced profound changes to their way of life in terms of social and economic stability. They had once been a powerful productive force in the Soviet economy as well as being one-third of Ukraine's population.[10] No longer. Agricultural reforms affected people's lives in so many ways that we must not limit our examination to economic matters. The demolition of a particular mode of economic production left Ukrainian collective farmers disenfranchised and disempowered. The reforms strongly affected the rural social fabric, triggering a collapse of the social relations and cultural and economic practices that socialism had established. The reforms affected modes of production *and* village culture. The only way of life that many people had known – collective farming – had vanished.

In many respects, the agricultural reforms of the 1990s affected the Ukrainian countryside as profoundly as collectivization had in the 1930s.[11] It is in this regard that I propose to refer to the profound changes that took place in the Ukrainian countryside throughout the 1990s as the decollectivization of rural Ukraine.[12]

Oral History of Decollectivization

We launched our oral history project in 2007; most of the interviews were conducted in 2007–9.[13] Our fieldwork aimed to document the personal perspectives of Ukrainian villagers who had been both subjects and agents of socio-economic change during the 1990s, with regard to their lives during and after the socialism. After the fieldwork was concluded, we entered the analytical phrase of the project, which involved identifying within the collected oral narratives a particular reflective mode, a kind of shared subjectivity that both underscored and governed the ongoing memorialization of the post-socialist transition and the formation of new collective memories of late socialism.

As happens in times of major social transformation, or "historical rupture," the breakdown of familiar life-world structures generates a need for people to come to terms with their disappearing world. The growing distance between people's present-day lives and the traditional structures of their life-world, with its unquestioned meanings, transforms them into observers of their own lives. Stephan Cornell suggests that the risk of losing sight of this disappearing life spurs them to write about it. In times of rupture, narrating is an important way of positioning oneself in the past, the present, and the future, against a background of change. According to the psychologist Nico Frijda, people narrate because they desire to locate themselves in time (which is constantly on the move) and space (which is also constantly changing).[14] Recent observations from post-Soviet countries, including Ukraine, confirm all of this. In these countries, cultural deconstruction of the previous regime has been accompanied by an active *re*construction – through narration – of the recent as well as the pre-Soviet past. In today's Ukraine, we continue to witness a surge of autobiographic and memoir writing. At the same time, narratives about the past are not found solely in the domain of print – many stories never reach paper (or an Web page) but remain in oral circulation, and some have yet to be formulated and spelled out. Oral history as a method of historical research contributes to the narrative memorialization of the past. Through its method of open-ended interviewing, it allows those who may never write down their life stories to formulate and share their testimonies about the years gone by.

Our project has aimed to capture the flow of memories and narratives of transitional times that are being shaped in rural Ukraine. The focus, though, is not on the facts of the past but rather on its narrative representations. Oral narratives are a rich source of historical data, especially if one wants to study changes in personal reflectivity and identity from a historical viewpoint. Oral narratives of the type we recorded with the villagers are not rehearsed and are not assembled in a manner characteristic of a written text, a memoir, or an autobiography. "What is spoken in a typical oral history interview has usually never been told in 'that form' before,"[15] Portelli writes. They are perhaps richer than written personal testimonies (which are being discovered today in rural Ukraine as well), for their narrative organization stems from an implicit interplay of public (ideological) and vernacular discourses of the day, whereas written personal accounts (memoirs, diaries) are more thought out and tend to contain less vernacular spontaneity. In addition, personal memoirs tend to be written by the rural intelligentsia[16] – a reflective, proactive, and better-educated group.

Searching for Agents of Memory

To locate a metanarrative of decollectivization emerging from the totality of all our project interviews and to register a particular collective stance in them that would speak of some shared memory of recent historic times, we had to address the question of whose memory we were seeking. A shared perspective on the past presented in respondents' interviews is not necessarily representative of a given social class – in our case, peasants. Since interviews are the products of individual minds and are based on individual lives unfolding in particular historic times, shared understandings of past experiences are more likely to be recorded in the same generational cohort of villagers.[17]

Which generation were we to consider in our efforts to understand how collective memories of decollectivization are formed? After some deliberation, we decided to collect life stories based on autobiographical interviews with individuals who were entering the workforce in the

1950s.[18] There were several reasons for this decision. First, the post-war generation of villagers – those who were born just before the war, during the war years, or just a few years later – were a little-known and poorly understood generation of Soviet Ukrainians, for their life trajectories were not cut across by the most dramatic events of the twentieth century. They were *not* collectivized in the 1930s. In the 1940s, they did *not* fight the war on either side of the front line, and they were *not* transported to Germany as *Ostarbeiters*. Also, they were psychologically perhaps less affected than their parents by post-war economic chaos, political purges, and collectivization in western Ukraine. These transformative events preceded their formative years of adolescence. Any exposure they had to these dramatic events would have been second-hand, through family stories rather than direct participation.

In short, their generation had been spared the cataclysms of Soviet history as well as prolonged academic scrutiny. Not counting the disruptive war years, their generation was entering a social world that had been established for their parents at least a decade prior to the war and thus pre-existed their coming of age.[19] Throughout the 1950s and 1960s, their life trajectories were predictably confluent with the flow of Soviet history that eventually and seemingly uneventfully brought them into a period known as the stagnation of the 1970s (*period zastoia*).

Their coming of age between times of profound "ruptures" in the social order (the war, the collapse of the Soviet Union) was another reason to explore this generation's take on decollectivization. Their formative years – from the teens to the early twenties – did not coincide with the war and post-war years; rather, they came of age and joined the workforce during a time of relative political "stability" and relative economic growth, in the mid-1950s and later. So we can presume that their memories did not revolve as strongly around dramatic "outside" events as would have been the case with the preceding generation.

Third, their generation worked most of their productive lives within the collective farm system. That is, they had known – as a generation – no other life than life under socialist rule. By the time they entered the workforce, collective farming as an economic mode of production was contributing to the formation of a particular way of life in the Ukrainian countryside (to a lesser degree in western Ukraine). This shaped new social relations and new values, which together came to define the social order of late socialism (1970s and on). They had been socialized into the world of collective rather than collectivized farming. Thus, their memories of decollectivization were profoundly shaped by life under socialism. Fourth, in today's Ukraine their generation occupies an important place in Ukraine's rural demographic, in that they represent more than one-third of the rural population (those 60 years or older). And finally, we expected these individuals to be more introspective than others, given their age and accumulated life experiences.

In terms of methodology, the project resorted largely to open-ended life-story interviews as developed within the framework of the academic discipline of oral history. Interviewing was organized into two phases: the autobiographic or life story interview proper, followed by questionnaire-oriented interviewing. The focus of the interviews wasn't the specific facts of the collapse of a given collective farm. Rather, we were seeking each person's perspective on their life in general as well as on that part of their life that had been unfolding since 1991. The open-ended interview with follow-up questions on various topics provided an opportunity for our informants to relate their personal stories with a great deal of narrative and conceptual flexibility.[20]

Reading through the Villagers' Narratives

The villagers' narratives indicate that those who came of age after the Great Patriotic War were a unique generation of Soviet citizens whose experiences in their totality would never be replicated.[21] Whether they were from western Ukraine or some other part of the country, they shared the experience of being raised in a close-knit community. Many grew up without a father, who had perished in the war (or who had been internally exiled after it); others were surrounded by neighbours and relatives whose households were headed by women. When prompted to reflect on their own lives, they often projected their experiences as inseparable from the lives of others in their community. Personal recollections of their early years often highlighted how similar their lives had been to those of their village neighbours. They routinely mentioned that in their youth they had lived in simple conditions if not in poverty, like many others in their village. Many spoke of working on the collective farm as children, some as early as ten, or working for their sick mother's *trudoden'*. Others joined the *kolhosp* officially at the age of sixteen.

How articulate and reflective were these rural narrators? There is an important relationship between (a) personal articulation and reflectivity as observed in these testimonies, and (b) the narrative structures of public discourses in the society where the narrator lives. For example, in the oral history project on socio-cultural change among Ukrainian Canadians on the prairies, which I conducted about five years ago in Saskatchewan,[22] many informants were able to easily move between their personal life circumstances and the circumstances of Ukrainian Canadian community life. Stories we recorded with Ukrainian Canadians in 2003 often used metaphors and tropes from the Ukrainian Canadian foundational narrative of origin (to borrow Anthony Smith's take on popular histories of ethnic communities) when retelling personal developments in their own lives.[23] One example would be the use of the term "generation." I have discussed elsewhere the importance of this trope in Ukrainian Canadian consciousness and how it is used to structure public narratives of community origins, progress, and so on.[24] Interestingly enough, my Canadian informants made similar use of this trope in their stories of growing up in their communities on the prairies. The generation metaphor provided them with a sense of collective (cohort) identity; it also helped them locate themselves on the trajectory of Ukrainian Canadian history (public history) and on the genealogical trees of their own families (personal history). The ease with which my informants operated with this public trope speaks to the conventions of the Canadian Ukrainian discourse and how established this community's ideology is. Thus, personal oral narratives, life stories, can tell us much about the historical context beyond their local lives and local histories.

When we look at oral testimonies recorded for the project at hand, we find that they present the researcher with a different kind of narrative reflectivity than narratives by Canadian Ukrainians. Ukrainian villagers seemed to produce shorter initial autobiographical statements than Ukrainian Canadians. Their introductory autobiographical narratives often lacked elaboration and at times came across as disjointed. An impression one may have from listening to the recorded interviews is that the speakers, although interested in the conversation, were not orienting their stories towards the interviewer (the interlocutor). Instead, they shared parts of their past without elaborating and connecting those parts.

The listener (interviewer, reader) may perceive the stories as nonlinear, as confusing events and people, as evasive and lacking specifics (names, dates, geographic locations, and so on, are often missing). The chronological order of life presentation is often not observed, topics may "jump." Part of this has to do with the performative aspect of oral history. It is possible to assume that the interviewer may not have been inclined to open up completely, even though the project was set up in such a way as to provide for good rapport between the interviewer and the informant. Let us turn to Nina Kazimirova from the village of Zhovten', Odesa *oblast*:

> I was born in Frunze district of Odesa *oblast*. To Zhovten I came in 1968. Finished technological college in Kryvyi Rih and was assigned to go to Dnipropetrovsk. But my mother was ill and I asked to be closer and I came to Shyriaevo and I was appointed to be a second director of public eating. There I worked for a month perhaps and they then say that in Zhovten they need a director for a tea house. And then there were 23 eateries along the Kyiv highway, Lastochka, Zirka, as canteens and I met my husband there, since he came here as agronomist. And he was in Kazakhstan for 6 years as chief agronomist, since then it was like that – if you don't go into the Army service then you had to go to Kazakhstan, and he was from Kirovohrad *oblast*. Here in Tea House there was the wedding, we got married and then the child was born. And then I am coming to a conclusion that I will change my profession, the work is very difficult, since we had a military station and often had generals coming, Marshal Chuikov was here. And here came the head of the village council, he came and says "Do you want to take over the House of Culture?" It was located near the church, and earlier they were prohibiting it, and there was a building but no domes. So I went to work here and now it is 35 years that I work here. We already build a new House of Culture. Thus I worked with the youth, with people. And my husband was both an agronomist and the head of the collective farm, but not in this collective farm.[25]

Although Mrs Kazimirova represents the rural intelligentsia, her initial life story, compressed into a short paragraph, is characteristic of many other narratives from people who are less educated than she is.

Often, interviewees do not present their life stories as coherent and well-structured. It is not uncommon for a narrator to compress her memories and recollections into a series of short statements, creating a certain "cumulative," brew-like effect. The metaphor that comes to mind here is bread making. Many ingredients go into the bowl to be mixed together, but only after they are left to sit for a while does the proper batter develop. The batter will soon be bread, but for now, it is not particularly edible or digestible. In a similar way, the autobiographic narrative that surfaces first during the interview often comes across as "raw." "Baking" is left up to an interpreter. The interview with Hanna Holovyn serves as an example of this:

HANNA: I don't even know where to start [tears in her eyes].

INTERVIEWER: Start where you want. What you think you should start with. Think about it … As you want ...

H: Here my life is so that I am confused, that I cannot … So I live from day to day. I don't know how to tell it to you. What to tell.

I: Well, for example, when were you born.

H: Well, I was born in 1947. In 1947. Finished 4 years in Ozirtsi. It was a primary school. Then I began to attend [school] in Poliske until the eighth grade. Using my feet. No one was driving us then, no one. We would get up early and so would go to school. Winter or no winter. Then there were such snowbanks. Blizzards. So we would go. Studied, I studied well. And I would go to that school – a workcoat, *kufaika*, and rubberized, *kirzovi*, boots. Once upon a time there were such boots. So you see, those who would go elsewhere [to work] for a season, made some money. And our family – there were six of us with our father. Father worked in the *kolhosp*. Mother was ill, worked little. So we had to work for the mother, they made us, so we had to do mother's work [in the *kolhosp*]. Well I studied. I studied well, but could not go to study further [in the college]. Finished eight grades. Did not have even one *triika* [a grade of 3, on a scale of 5]. Went for a while to work on the beets, for some three years, two years. And got married into Poliske. Here finished an evening school because I already worked in the *kolhosp*, I was a brigade leader, *lankova*. I was the youngest in the brigade. I was in … in the whole *kolhosp* the youngest. Since no one wanted to go into that *kolhosp*. But I went. Here there were no parents. He [husband] was an orphan. So he was in *argitechnika*, *sil'hosptekhnika*, and I went to the *kolhosp*. We needed land, *soty*, we needed to live somehow. And I finished all those eleven grades. And such I worked all my life in the *kolhosp*. Linen. I was *lankova*. That's it. What is else? What do I know? I worked until my pension. Whatever life was it had to be lived. The worst is the pain, it is killing me now. As I buried two sons … As it was, they worked and laboured. And I buried the two sons, and so my life ended. That is my life, and I did my best, in that *kolhosp*. I did not know that the life would end the way it did. I thought there will be joy, there will be happiness – but there is none [cries].[26]

Mrs Holovyn was not the only person who preferred to speak in this manner about her life. This extreme compressing of past experiences into selected, short comments/statements is one characteristic of rural narratives of this generation. But it was not only abstract implicit rules of condensation that governed the formulation of Mrs Holovyn's story.[27] She herself was not interested in elaboration, for many years of her life were consumed by the same activities and chores over and over again, to the point that the chronological order of representation of her life felt unnecessary to her.

Another important observation about narrative representations of the past concerns the intersection of private and public horizons in informants' autobiographical narratives. Oral historians have long observed that when an individual's life unfolds against the background of important historic events (Stalin's death in 1953, Gagarin's flight into space in 1961, etc.), narrators often use those events as important markers for situating their own life stories in the flow of time. In rural autobiographies, the narrators tend to make little use of external public events.

These aspects of rural narrative reflectivity (lack of cohesion or elaboration, extreme compressing, minimal presence of the public horizon in private stories) are not an indication of failed communication or bad memory or uninteresting informants. On the contrary, they are very telling. Richard Cándida-Smith suggests that contradictory, confusing, and vague elements in a narrative do a great service to historical analysis by highlighting areas of concern that communities have not been able to resolve narratively.[28] This relates both to individuals who are trying to make sense of the changing social world and to communities that are trying to redefine their own past in light of those changes. Ukraine's recent past is contested terrain, and public debates continue to produce different understandings of that past. Hence, narrative presentations remain unfinished, "undone." The past may have been narrated, but it has not been *narrativized.*

How do the narrators project themselves in their narratives? What identities are being created in their stories, in the context of autobiographical interviewing? In his analysis of Greek novels, Mikhail Bakhtin addressed the question of how the protagonists' identity and moral qualities are constructed.[29] According to him, if the hero is depicted as someone who has matured from one state of consciousness to another – as someone who, as a result of his ordeal, has changed into a better (or at least different) person – then such a depiction is attempting to present the real human being who, moving through life, acquires new qualities, develops his own character, and forms new values. Such depictions more realistically reflect the changes in a person, whose personality and identity indeed change over the course of his life. If, on the other hand, the hero is depicted so that the "hammer of events shatters nothing and forges nothing," and merely tests the durability of the hero's already established character and identity, then, Bakhtin notes, the reader is dealing with a depiction that attempts to present not a real human being but a folkloric man, one whose qualities are known from the beginning of the story and will remain the same until the end.[30]

Luisa Passerini, an oral historian, in her book *Fascism and Popular Memory*, points out that her informants often re-create themselves in their oral autobiographies in a manner similar to how "folkloric man" was created out of the protagonists of ancient Greek novels. Passerini, independently of Bakhtin, concludes that the narrative identities of her informants tend to have folkloric, static characteristics and that this feature of oral autobiographies needs to be accounted for.

What identities are being projected in the rural narratives on decollectivization that we have recorded for our project? Do the narrators re-create themselves in their stories as unbending, as maintaining the same ethics and values throughout their lives? Or do they present the interviewers with stories of growth and personal development?

First and above all, the narrative identities as projected by the narrators revolve around work on collective farms. This was the case with Nina Kazimirova and Hanna Holovyn. Their two cases reflect two particular ways in which work identity was self-stated. Regarding Mrs Kazimirova, throughout her initial life story she defined herself in terms of her profession, as a student and then as the director of a culture club. Mrs Holovyn presented herself in her initial autobiographical statement as someone who worked all her life: she had been a seasonal worker (*sezony*), she had worked for her mother's crew (*za matir*), she had worked in the beet fields (*poiikhala na buriaky*), and she had *khodyla v kolhosp* (kept working on the collective farm). She stated her other identities – that of a mother, for example – against the backdrop of this overarching lifelong identity of worker/labourer. "And so it was – [we all] laboured, worked. But as my two sons died, so my life ended." Interestingly, in comparison, in the Canadian project, both men and women presented more versatile projections of themselves. In their stories, they emphasized their genealogical rootedness in their families (genealogical identities). Many spoke of their lives as Ukrainian

Canadians (ethnic identities), and only after that did they speak of themselves as teachers, nurses, farmers (professional identities), mothers, wives, and so on.

Our informants often projected their identities as unchanging (just as in Passerini's project). The life story of Vira Oleksashenko, from Poltava *oblast*, provides an example of this unchanged narrative identity. Note how the subject of "labour" erupts into her other stories:

> INTERVIEWER: When you were in school, did you work in the *kolhosp*? Did you help?
>
> VIRA: Oh my! We were so joyous, as for these combines, the youth … It goes, the hay is released. And we, the youth, they would let us come there. We would weed, we would harvest cucumbers. They would take us to [work in the] *kolhosp*. And later, they would accept us [to work] on combines … We milked the cows, even in the evenings. We would go to do the hay, we stack it, we were so happy to do this. Well, for some reasons, we were interested [in working], we were not into wasting our time, such as, they have opened up everything these days, those bars and the like. Then we did not have it. It was different. There was so much harmony. If there would be a wedding, in one corner of the village or another, there would be so much joy. Now you cannot go like that to the wedding, they will ask you why did you come? And in those days, if there would be a wedding, the youth would gather, would dance. But now … So then, we were happy to work. [An] old man would gather us, I guess he was assigned to us, that old man, with the cart. We would climb up into the cart, I remember we are sitting in it, and he would tell us stories. So we went like this to weed the beets, to weed other fields. It was all interesting. Of course, if one loved to work. I was still in school, when – "she will not turn out an educated person, she will be – she loves working – she will be working hard all her life" – so said the school director [laughs]. So it turned out this way – I just work, work away all life. So it is.[31]

To some degree, these and other narratives present the interviewer (and reader) with strong identity continuity. Early in her story, Vira said that all her life she loved to work, that she was "no good for anything else but work." The story about her life revolved around labour, and she wanted the listener to know that "love for labour" (*vona trud liubyt'*) constituted the very core of who she had been all her life.

Rural narratives also allow the careful reader to register a particular "collectivistic" stance in people's reminiscences about their lives.

In many narratives, the collective pronoun "we" comes forward as an important source of personal identity. In some cases, "we" stands for the immediate family, in others, for a wife–husband partnership (this seems to be more the case with female narrators). Often, the "we" represents a particular age group, as was the case with Vira Lukashenko. In the narratives of more reflective or more educated individuals, "we" stood for all members of their community or collective farm. Although the sources of collectivized personal identity were different, the routinization of this narrative technique – moving away from "me" and adopting "we" when telling of one's personal past – revealed something important about this generation of then-Soviet villagers.

Yet another observation. Many of the interviewees projected themselves as jointly participating in the economic growth of their collective farms throughout their long careers. Many, therefore, considered themselves, in their narratives, as the creators of their own lives and of their own well-being, even if in relative terms this well-being is questionable now.[32] Thus Yurii Bedziura, a former chief engineer of a collective farm in Lviv *oblast,* kept returning to the question of the relationship between fate (*dolia*) and personal agency, as if asserting to himself that the human life is indeed guided by the person rather than by circumstances or fate.[33]

Narrative attestations to what I would call "short genealogical memory" were another common feature of villagers' reminiscences. Short genealogical memory among Soviet citizens has long been a recognized phenomenon; even so, it is striking that the second generation of collectivized villagers (outside of western Ukraine) was in many ways severely deprived of their family history and memory. It is worth noting that this abrupt severance of memory occurred in settings where oral culture had at one time been the driver for social continuity.[34]

In eastern and central Ukraine, many did not know where their family land used to be, and many of the interviewees had very little knowledge of their ancestors:

INTERVIEWER: Tell me, did your family have any land before collectivization?
HA: No they did not.
I: They did not?
HA: No.
I: Where did you parents work?
HA: My father was a blacksmith, and as for my mother, no one was talking about that, and now there is no one to ask. In the summer, when my

> brother would come, he knows more. I will ask. Somehow, he knows more ... I know my father was a blacksmith, because people used to say that one had to look hard for a better blacksmith than Andrukh.[35]

Even in western Ukraine, there were respondents whose genealogical memory had been severely shortened by the circumstances of their lives under Soviet rule. For example, the children of the Lemkos, who had been resettled in Ternopil *oblast* from Poland, could provide little information about their parents and their original homeland in southeastern Poland.[36]

All in all, the Great Patriotic War generation of Ukrainian villagers came across as unique and as having a broad spectrum of shared experiences. There were, however, important differences in how the western Ukrainian villagers projected themselves relative to those elsewhere in Ukraine, differences that fall outside the scope of this chapter. Note, however, that this generation of villagers was directly involved in the rebuilding of the Soviet economy and collective farming in their villages, both of which were carried out during the times they came of age. Most villagers, then, developed in their advanced years an understanding of themselves as active agents in the building of their country as well as of their own lives and fates. But when narratives moved to the topic of decollectivization, this sense of agency changed.

Decollectivization Narratives

I mentioned earlier that we had chosen this generation to interview because their life itineraries had *not* cut across pivotal historical events that profoundly changed social life in their communities. That said, the collapse of the Soviet Union and the collective farming system was a life-altering experience that the respondents remembered well. I expected that the respondents' memories of decollectivization would be detailed and elaborate, since they were relatively recent. Given the haphazard approach the government had taken to collapsing the collective farms, especially after the 1999 land reform,[37] I also expected their commentary on decollectivization to be emotionally charged, especially given that deconstruction of *kolhosp* properties had been undertaken less than a decade earlier. In other words, I thought that because decollectivization had been so recent and so earth-shaking, the villagers would be eager to talk about it at length.

They were not. Instead, when telling their life stories, they rarely discussed this period at length on their own initiative. The matter had to be left for the second, topic-oriented, phase of the interviews. The questionnaire included a number of questions that addressed the topic of decollectivization, and some of these were usually asked in the second part of the interview. The answers we received were often emotional (as expected) and revealed an unresolved ambivalence regarding the relationship between the villagers and the collective farms, between collective property and the land itself. When the issue of the breaking up of collective or state farms arose, the conversation focused on two aspects: the land redistribution, and the redistribution (read "ruination") of collective farm property.[38]

Usually, the narrator's position vis-à-vis these processes was passive and accepting. The villagers projected themselves as observers rather than agents of change. Yustyna Stebliuk from Lviv *oblast* recalled:

INTERVIEWER: Do you remember how the *kolhosp* was pulled apart? What was happening?

IUSTYNA: Listen, whoever could, whoever was cunning, had access to a vehicle ... and those who were none of it, what would they take? We did not take. Our folks in our village did not take [anything away], they could not. To take something, you had to have something to take it with, a car, a truck.

I: How did they divide land in your village? Did they give you a *pai* [paper share]?

IU: There was one who measured it, a *mirnyk* [surveyor]. He would measure it and would give it out. Some took more, others, less. Whatever he gave me, it was good enough. So he gave me some 10 *soty*, then [they] gave me again, near the church.[39]

Mykola Rud of Dnipropetrovsk *oblast*, once a tractor driver, spoke of the redistribution of land and property in similar terms:

INTERVIEWER: And with parcelling, what did you think, how much [land] would you get?

MYKOLA: Oh, we did not think anything. Whatever came to us, came to us ... But as far as *kolhosp* property [*maino*] is concerned, they screwed us ... Imagine, if all of us here – who are working in the *kolhosp* – going to go to the pig farm or livestock shelter. One would pull it from one side, the other from the other side. So it was ...

I: Pig farms and livestock shelters – when they were torn down?

M: Well, it is ... how to say, it has been three or four years since when they disappeared. Little by little. As one said, "the fish rots from the head." First, the administration started helping themselves a bit. But people saw everything and [they] went themselves, especially because they were not paid salaries. They did it as they could. Some were given land, others were assigned *kolhosp* property [*maino*]. So he [the head of KSP] announced – grain elevator goes towards *kolhosp* property [to be redistributed, i.e., demolished – NKF], brigade building – went towards the property, pig farm – was divided as property, people demolished and took everything away [as part of their property shares – NKF].[40]

Even former *kolhosp* leaders, and chief economists, and engineers, and farm directors, who often were rumoured to have benefited from the breaking up of the collective property more than others, spoke of decollectivization as an unwelcome imposition on their lives. Hanna Hlushchuk, former director of a milk farm in Rivne *oblast*, commented:

Oh yes, they have divided that land, they divided it. One and a half hectares – and what do I need it for? I cannot do fifty *soty*. All fifty? Ten [*soty*] of potatoes and ten of beets – I cannot do that! Fifteen *soty*, that would do. And I don't need that parcel, *pai*, let them have it. They did it cunningly – stuck money away and you take just a *pai*. And what is in that *pai* for me? And for my children? When was it that the peasant[s] succeeded on the land? Have become rich from land?[41]

Such passivity and lack of agency in narrative identities was not what I expected. After all, many interviewees when speaking of socialist times wanted to come across as having some control over their lives. Three factors may help explain this tendency. First, decollectivization was still a recent event at the time of the interviews, which meant that the speakers had not had time to crystallize their reflections on it so as to offer dignified representations of their experience of it. Second, decollectivization was such an overwhelming and life-altering process that changes resulting from it had not yet been fully comprehended. Third, decollectivization had resulted in new economic relations and new relations of power in the countryside, and most of the collective farmers of that generation were not prepared to adapt. When, in the first interview sessions, respondents shared their life stories, they often tried to come across as ethical agents of history, as responsible for their own actions. Even when a narrator recognized the role of fate in his or her life (a strong vernacular concept well represented in Ukrainian rural discourses), he or she attempted to come across as someone who knew how to respond to fate's challenges. This confidence tended to disappear in conversations about decollectivization: the narrator was often transformed into a passive object of someone else's actions.

Constructing Another Agent of Ukrainian History

New cultural and ideological demands of the two decades since Ukrainian independence have encouraged Ukrainian historians to fully engage in the rewriting of the twentieth-century history of the country and its people. The past 120 years of Ukrainian history have witnessed a multitude of political tragedies that cost the lives of some 17 million people, so it is only logical that in post-Soviet times, scholarly and public attention has been directed mainly at the most traumatic events of that past, such as the Holodomor of 1933, the Soviet repression of the 1930s and 1940s, the Great Patriotic War, the post-war fate of the *Ostarbeiters*, the eradication of the Ukrainian Insurgent Army in western Ukraine, the political persecutions of the 1970s, the Gulag penal system, and so on. While re-evaluating these events, contemporary scholars have offered us a new vision of Ukraine as a nation with many pasts and many contested memories. In this rewriting of Ukrainian history, we can observe the emergence of various agents of this history, corporate or unincorporated, representing the whole spectre of ideological tides and currents as well as historic experiences that developed under the various pressures of Soviet rule. Some of these groups, such as the collectivized Ukrainian peasants of the 1930s and the political prisoners of the 1970s, began receiving media attention as early as the *perestroika* years. Others, such as members of OUN-UPA or former *Ostarbeiters*, have entered the public debate relatively recently.

As the last century drew to an end, another traumatic rupture took place in (rural) Ukraine, albeit in the context of an independent rather than Soviet Ukraine. The breaking up of the collective farming system in the 1990s, coupled with unfinished land reform and the collapse of the Soviet savings system, quickly resulted in the total dismantling of long-established and "sufficiently" functioning social worlds in rural communities across the country. The decollectivization of the 1990s in Ukraine, as attested by the rural narratives recorded by this project, became yet another trial for Ukrainians and especially for Ukrainian villagers. The decollectivized villagers have been living a personal history that requires careful recording, analysis, and representation. Scholars in a variety of disciplines, both Ukrainian and foreign, have been researching and analysing the processes of decollectivization;[42] but the subjective processes of re-evaluating and memorializing these recent historical events have yet to be fully addressed. Our oral history project, described in this chapter, has set out to (a) record subjective perspectives on decollectivization formulated by those directly affected by them and (b) represent the villagers' own views and understandings of that process to other audiences. In effect, we have tried to construct yet another subject of Ukrainian history – decollectivized Ukrainian villagers.

Will their perspective be further used in the subsequent process of collective memory formation about the post-Soviet transition in rural Ukraine? Time will tell, and meanwhile, the process of constructing a shared collective memory of the recent past – of the post-Soviet transition – continues.

APPENDIX ONE. PROJECT STATISTICS

General Information

Total number of respondents	117
Female	65
Male	53
Transcribed interviews	78

Interviews per *oblast*

Oblast	Total number of interviews
Dnipropetrovsk	13
Crimea	10
Kharkiv	10
Kyiv	12
Lviv	10
Odesa and south	21
Poltava	16
Ternopil	10
Rivne	15

Respondents' Birth Year

1921	1
1922	0
1923	0
1924	0
1925	1
1926	1
1927	1
1928	0
1929	1
1930	1
1931	0
1932	1
1933	2
1934	1
1935	8
1936	7
1937	9
1938	4
1939	9
1940	6
1941	9
1942	4
1943	6
1944	2
1945	3
1946	2
1947	4
1948	2
1949	5
1950	4
1951	7
1952	1
1953	2
1954	1
1955	1
1961	1
1963	1
Unknown	9
Outside of margins	16

Informant's Occupation (self-identified)

Holova / Head of the collective or state farm	5
Traktoryst / Tractor driver	15
Mekhanik / Mechanic	4
Vodii / Driver	8
Doiarka / Milkmaid	15
Ptashnytsia / Worker at the poultry farm	1
Teliatnytsia / Worker at the cattle farm	3
Skotar / Cattle Farmer	1
Zootekhnik / Veterinary technician	5
Veterynar / Veterinary doctor	1
Uchytel / Teacher	1
Ekonomist / Economist	1
Laborant / Lab assistant	1
Zaviduiuchyi Poshtoiu / Post office manager	1
Zaviduiuchyi Fermoiu / Farm manager	7
Povar u shkoli / Cook at school	3
Bryhadyr po ovochakh / Vegetable brigadier	1
Lankova / Head of primary work unit (lanka)	3
Vynohradar / Grapeyard worker	2
Na poli / Field farmer	2
Riznorobocha/y / Worker	14

NOTES

1 Kobzev, "Land Reform in Ukraine."
2 Lerman et al., *Rethinking Agricultural Reform,* 15.
3 Presidential Decree No. 1529/99, "On immediate measures to accelerate the reforms in the agricultural sector" (December 1999).
4 Lerman et al., *Rethinking Agricultural Reform,* i.
5 Lerman et al., *Rethinking Agricultural Reform,* i.
6 Csaki, Lerman, and Sotnikov, *Farm Debt in the CIS.*
7 Prybytkova, "Metamorfozy." Soon after the cited survey was conducted, two more presidential decrees were issued: "Pro nevidkladni zakhody shchodo pryskorennia zemel'noii reformy u sferi sil's'kohospodars'koho vyrobnytstva" (10 November 1994) and "Pro poriadok paiuvannia zemel', peredanykh u kolektyvnu vlasnist' sil's'kohospodars'kym pidpryiemstvam ta orhanizatsiam" (8 August 1995). These documents further

addressed the mechanisms for privatizing land. Only members of collective agricultural enterprises and those already retired were assigned landholding rights (but not the right of land ownership). Only land currently held in the CAE was subject to this redistribution of rights.

8 Prybytkova, "Metamorfozy."

9 Ukraine's population at the time of the collapse of the Soviet Union was around 51 million; twenty years later, it was around 46 million. Popular media, human rights activists, and various politicians routinely point out that between 2 and 3 million Ukrainians are foreign migrant workers, 1 million of these in Russia (Malynovska, "International Migration," 14). This migration started prior to the Soviet collapse and then accelerated in the mid-1990s, affecting especially rural areas of the country.

10 In 2005, 32.3 per cent of Ukraine's population (about 15.3 million people) lived in rural areas. See Lytvyn, *Istoriia*, 546.

11 In the 1930s, collectivization in Soviet Ukraine and the total destruction of private farms resulted in huge population losses through famine, which claimed between 3 and 7 million lives in two years (1932–3). That was about 20 per cent of Ukraine's population at the time.

12 Chris Hann and the Property Relations Group provide a thorough anthropological analysis of various dimensions of decollectivization in Eastern Europe. On deeper meanings of decollectivization, see Hann, "Introduction."

13 The field phase of the project (2008–9) has been financially supported through my Sabbatical Research Grant by St Thomas More College, University of Saskatchewan. I conducted my research in association with the Ukrainian Association of Oral History and selected academic research centres where oral historical work is actively pursued: the Department of History of Ukraine, Poltava State Pedagogical University (Dr Yuri Voloshyn); the Department of Ukrainian Studies, Kharkiv National University (Dr Gelinada Grinchenko); the Oral History Centre, Pereiaslav-Khmelnytskyj State Pedagogical University (Mr Taras Nahajko); the Department of History, National University Kyiv-Mohyla Academy (Dr Natalia Shlikhta); the Department of History and Theory of Sociology, Lviv National University (Dr Tetiana Lapan); the Department of Archeology and Ethnology, Odesa National University (Dr Oleksandr Prigarin); and the Institute of History of Ukraine, Ukrainian National Academy of Sciences (Dr Tetiana Pastushenko, project local coordinator in Ukraine). Data organization and interview transcription were financially supported by the Oral History Program at the Prairie Centre for the Study of Ukrainian Heritage at St Thomas More College.

14 Frijda, "Commemorating."
15 Portelli, *The Battle*, 4.
16 See recent publications by the Zaporizhzhia Offices of the Institute of Ukrainian Archaeography and Primary Sources (National Academy of Science of Ukraine) and the Kovalsky Eastern Institute of Ukrainian Studies. *Dzherela z Istorii Pivdennoi Ukrainy* published two volumes of rural memoirs and diaries recently located by various field expeditions in rural southern Ukraine. See Boyko and Plokhii, *Dzherela z Istorii*.
17 The generational approach to the study of history has not been privileged in the post-Soviet historiography, or in history in general. Theodor Shanin, a British sociologist now working in Russia, has argued that this approach needs to be brought back into analyses of Russian and Soviet history and social change. Shanin, "Istoriia Pokolenii." Oral history as a discipline, because of its double interest in organizing and transmitting social memory, long ago adopted the generational approach into its analytical framework.
18 The interviewers were to locate men and women born between 1936 and 1951 who had at least twenty-five years' experience working in rural enterprises. These could be collective farms (*kolhosps*), state farms (*radhosps*), engine-tractor stations (MTS), forest enterprises (*lishosps*), or rural schools, hospitals, and services. Ideally, the informants were to be still employed at the time of the collapse of the Soviet Union in the 1990s.
19 Except in western Ukraine, where collectivization took place after the Second World War. By 1951 almost all 1.5 million peasant households were on collective farms. See Subtelny, *Ukraine*, 491.
20 In turn, this enabled us to pursue the project's initial goal, which was to identify the particular mode of reflectivity in the ongoing formulations of the collective memory of decollectivization. How do villagers formulate their own autobiographies? And what do they choose to include and exclude from their personal life stories? What aspects of the past, recent or not so recent, are important to former collective farmers? How much reminiscence relies on *(re)presenting the past* and how much on *interpreting the past*? Is there some collective stance in villagers' narratives?
21 Special consideration is to be given to the life trajectories of the project respondents in western Ukraine, for their families were brought under Soviet rule only in 1939, two decades later than in most of Ukraine.
22 *Oral History of Sociocultural Change in the Second Half of the 20th Century: Ukrainian Canadians on the Prairies*. Oral History Project of the Prairie Centre for the Study of Ukrainian Heritage, St Thomas More College,

University of Saskatchewan (2003–5). Project coordinators Theresa Zolner and Natalia Khanenko-Friesen (Shostak).

23 Smith, "Chosen Peoples."

24 Shostak, "Local Ukrainianness"; Khanenko-Friesen, *Inshyi Svit*, 144–9.

25 Nina Kazimirova (born 1947), interview.

26 Holovyn (born 1947), interview.

27 For more on rules of condensation, read Zhuravlev, "Narrativnoie Interv'iu"; Schütze, "Biographieforschung."

28 Cándida-Smith, "Analytical Strategies for Oral History Interviews," 725.

29 Bakhtin, "Forms of Time."

30 Bakhtin, "Forms of Time," 105–7.

31 Vira Oleksashenko (born 1943), interview.

32 Many commented on significant savings they accumulated by the end of their careers, amounting to four or more thousand roubles. With the collapse of the Soviet banking system, their savings were quickly devalued.

33 Yuri Bedziura (born 1943), interview.

34 William Noll, among others, has written about the severe disruption of traditional culture that collectivization in the 1930s brought about. The Second World War further contributed to the "shortening" of genealogical memory among the second generation of collective farmers. Noll, *Transformation of Civil Society*.

35 Halyna Andruch (born 1937), interview.

36 As attested by several respondents in the village of Pidhorodnie, Ternopil district, Ternopil *oblast*.

37 Presidential Decree No. 1529/99, December 1999, "On immediate measures to accelerate the reforms in the agricultural sector."

38 The decree resulted in a rushed reorganization of collective enterprises into private ones. The parcelling of land and redistributions of collective and state farm properties were conducted within a year, without establishing consultative procedures. This resulted in much physical destruction of collective farms' productive resources and property.

39 Iustyna Stebliuk (born 1935), interview.

40 Mykola Rud (born 1948), interview.

41 Hanna Hlushchuk (born 1949), interview.

42 Among others, see Alina-Pisano, *The Post-Soviet Potemkin Village*.

11 "Where Has Everything Gone?" Remembering *Perestroika* in Belarusian Provinces

IRINA MAKHOVSKAYA AND IRINA ROMANOVA

When we look back to the dramatic political changes that occurred between 1989 and 1991 in Central and Eastern Europe, we rightly assume that the events of those three years, beginning with the dismantling of the Berlin Wall and ending with the collapse of the Soviet Union, were what triggered the global political transformation that saw the end of socialism in Europe. Those years are understood by many as the beginning point of decades of profound cultural change that would shred the fabric of social life in the former Socialist Bloc. Yet in some countries, and certainly in the countries of the former Soviet Union, the 1980s were no less dramatic in terms of the transformations inspired by *perestroika,* a new form of politics launched by Michael Gorbachev.

In many ways, because they preceded the actual collapse of communist rule in the Soviet Union and elsewhere, the transformation of the political and social order in the Soviet Union in the era of *perestroika* was felt and experienced by people who lived through those times as the most dramatic change they had faced in their post-war lives. How did ordinary people experience those transformations? How did they view and understand the political changes? How did they perceive the collapse of the Soviet Union and emergence of a new geopolitical entity – the Republic of Belarus?

The Project

To address the above questions and to document the process of identity transformation in Belarusian society, in 2009 we carried out an oral history project, "European versus Soviet Identity: Political Discourse and Individual Social Practices in the Age of *Perestroika* as Reflected in Biographical Narratives."[1] Our goal was to analyse how the new political discourse during the period of drastic reforms collided with individual social practices rooted in the Soviet experience.

In this chapter, we revisit this project and examine the Belarusians' memories of the sweeping reforms of the late 1980s and early 1990s. We focus on the experiences of the "breakdown" that required people to abandon their old patterns of behaviour and find ways to adapt and to a rapidly changing society. Our research targeted people born in the 1940s, 1950s, and 1960s. We chose this group for several reasons. First, in the 1970s and 1980s, it was this generation that played the most active role in Soviet society; as Alexei Yurchak has pointed out, it was they who reproduced the existing authoritative discourse, in form if not in substance.[2] Second, this generation did not have first-hand experience of the Great Patriotic War or of post-war economic and social struggles; thus, their judgment of living standards was not based on the trauma the war had brought. Finally, it was this age group (people aged thirty to fifty in the late 1980s, when the most radical reforms were introduced) that was most adversely affected by the social reorganization brought about by *perestroika*. They were well established in society and had acquired social and material "capital"; it was they, then, who would have to respond most strongly to the changes in order to gain a place for themselves in the new order of things. Unlike the generation that would follow them, they had a great deal to lose; at the same time, it was too early in their lives for them to retire and "rest on their oars." More simply, they had no choice but to respond, but they were old enough to do so.

We conducted our research in all six *oblasts* of Belarus. It involved interviewing 80 residents (25 men and 55 women) of small and medium-sized provincial towns and villages between May and October 2009. Thirty of the interviewees had a higher education, 40 had a secondary education or vocational training, and 10 had received only basic schooling. These were "average" people: none was a "star" although many saw themselves as very successful. Most had been born in rural areas and had left home to get an education that would allow them to lead a life that was different from what their parents knew.

Our research covered only the small provincial towns and villages of Belarus, on the premise that residents of large cities would have had better access to resources for adapting to a new society. That said, living conditions in small towns, townships, and villages were quite comparable to those of cities.

In accordance with our respondents' wishes, we omitted their last names. Even though we were asking them about "days gone by," many of them firmly refused to give their names; others agreed to do so only after we promised them complete anonymity. The reason for this was, quite simply, fear. The current political situation in Belarus is not unlike it was in Soviet times, when Belarus was part of the Soviet Union: people still fear the authorities and are afraid to voice their opinions not only about the present government but also about their past leaders.

Remembering "Big Politics"

A crucial event, one that marked the beginning of change, was the rise to power of Michael Gorbachev, who in March 1985 became the General Secretary of the Central Committee of the Communist Party of the Soviet Union. Gorbachev openly admitted the existence of economic and social problems in the Soviet Union and acknowledged that the country was approaching a crisis. He began saying what people had long wanted to hear: that change was necessary. And though they had heard the word "change" before, in the relentless Soviet propaganda, people believed him. It seemed to them that from now on everything really would be different. A host of new terms rapidly gained popularity in society: "acceleration," "new mindset," "democratization of social life," "socialism with a human face," and, finally, the word that would encapsulate the era, "perestroika," which first meant "radical" and later meant "revolutionary" reforms to the entire system.

In our respondents' narratives about the early days of *perestroika*, Gorbachev's image set the emotional tone. His public speeches, which were broadcast on TV, enchanted the entire country: he could speak without notes, he felt at ease in a crowd, and his mixing with the common people caused a sensation. This was a radically new mode of public conduct for Soviet leaders. Nina V., 66, retired seller of glasses (Pruzhany, Brest *oblast*): "Oh, how I loved that guy, Gorbachev! After all those Brezhnevs and Chernenkos[3] he appeared to be speaking so brilliantly! I liked so much his way of approaching people and speaking to them!"[4] Liudmila S., 65, retired teacher of foreign languages (Pruzhany): "Somehow everybody liked him. His appeal was in everything, the way he ... well ... first he himself was such a handsome, attractive man, he spoke so nicely, we were fascinated by his speeches, which had something new and fresh in them."[5]

Our respondents often expressed their attitude towards Gorbachev and his reforms with strong admiration and enthusiasm: "It was a breath of fresh air"; "His speeches injected a new life in us"; "[We were] hanging on his lips"; "[We were] lured by his speeches"; "Gosh, how I loved that straight away!"; "[Everyone] just went into raptures!"

From the respondents' point of view, Gorbachev completely met the Western standards of a leader. They were not embarrassed by him or his behaviour (in contrast to his predecessors). Galina V., 61, retired engineer (Pruzhany):

> We kind of accepted him with some sort of pride. Because a Western president was always shown with his wife, and always so articulate, while ours used to read from notes ... And this one – no trouble with speaking in public, no notes, and the wife beside him, and handsome as he is, and his wife is beautiful ... We thought that there was progress at last, we were going to have the kind of president we wouldn't feel embarrassed about.[6]

An important underlying theme in our respondents' earliest memories of *perestroika* was "anticipation of change." Liudmila P., 55, rural teacher (Gritsovichi, Minsk *oblast*): "We had a feeling that *perestroika* would be very fast, hugely successful, and everything would work out just fine. Everyone believed that socialism had a future, it was just that some minor problems had piled up that needed to be taken care of."[7] The announcement of reforms was welcomed with great enthusiasm. Yet most of our respondents could express their expectations of *perestroika* only in very general terms: "There was an impression that we were in for something new"; "We had a feeling of imminent changes"; "We started hoping for the best"; "It seemed everything was going to be better from now on"; "We expected something huge"; "Something was bound to improve."

Other members of society – and this certainly included former members of the Communist Party, whose communication skills had been shaped by the authoritative discourse – used their own distinct narrative means to express their opinions of *perestroika*. Because of how they were placed in the party and in the society, they were well acquainted with and perhaps had been overexposed to party speeches, resolutions, and government decrees. As they recalled *perestroika*, while expressing their ideas of what should have been changed in the Soviet society (and how), the one-time members of the CPSU reproduced the authoritative discourse of *perestroika* times. Their style of speaking, which abounded in clichés, was reminiscent of that discourse: they relied on stock phrases such as "increasing labour capacity," "fighting discipline violations and misappropriations of state property," "accumulation of capital and investing it in manufacturing enterprises," "fighting bureaucracy and law bending," "ensuring healthy competition in all spheres of life," and, of course, "the human factor." In other words, the ex-communists articulated the version of "socialism with a human face" that had been dictated by the official discourse. Their historical distance from that discourse ensured almost complete convergence between official views about how to reform socialism and their personal positions. What was originally imposed from above was now presented as one's own opinion.

A breakthrough on the road to freedom and real political competition in the Soviet Union was the election of delegates to the First Convention of People's Deputies, held in Moscow in March 1989. This was the first competitive election ever held in the post-war Soviet Union. For the first time in their lives, the people could witness, if not actually take part in, real discussion of the candidates' election programs. This was an astonishing departure from the token elections that had long prevailed in the Soviet Union: people could actually choose their representatives. The entire population watched and listened to the broadcast of the convention's sessions (25 May–9 June 1989). In past conventions, everything had been prearranged to smallest detail; this time, in defiance of that established practice, the events were unfolding without a scenario. The people's deputies raised actual burning issues: the war in Afghanistan, the ethnic conflict in Nagornyi Karabach, the Molotov–Ribbentrop pact. Valentina L., 57, rural paramedic (Luban, Minsk *oblast*): "The hall of the regional hospital's surgical department, where the TV was, was packed with people"[8] watching the convention debates on TV. And after the TV program, people would have long and heated discussions about what they had seen and heard.

The ensuing economic crisis ended the euphoria generated by *perestroika*. Speeches and calls for change had not led to prosperity. Failed hopes and the disruption of the established lives were blamed on Gorbachev.

Liudmila P., 55, rural teacher (Gritsovichi, Minsk *oblast*): "But we didn't realize what sort of scuffle we got into. And then suddenly there was an awful disappointment, regret."[9] Igor M., 61, soldier (Pruzhany, Brest *oblast*): "Gorbachev was right that the economy was ill. It should have been cured but in a different way, not by giving freedom, which led to the dissolution of the Union."[10] Evgeny V., 47, worker (Mir, Grodno *oblast*): "Gorbachev declared the right ideas and programs, but acted otherwise. He destroyed the Union. All these democracy games are very dangerous."[11] Alla K., 57, nurse (Pruzhany, Brest *oblast*): "Perestroika turned out to be a destruction, not a rebuilding. A great country was taken apart. It is the most frightening and the most important thing. Gorbachev was wrong."[12]

The Soviet state was "destroyed" on 8 December 1991. On that day, at a meeting in Belovezskaya Pushcha, the leaders of Russia (Boris Yeltsin), Ukraine (Leonid Kravchuk), and Belarus (Stanislav Shushkevich) announced that "the USSR ceases its existence as a subject of international law and geopolitical reality." A key way of coping with this traumatic experience, as the interviews suggest, was by disparaging the events. The leaders' decision was depicted as ill-conceived, outrageous, disgraceful – metaphorically, it was compared to a common drinking binge. Nikolai K., 49, builder (Mariina Gorka, Minsk *oblast*): "Independence came as a result of a booze-up in Belovezskaia Pushcha."[13] Anatolii L., 57, retired head of a collective farm (Rechen, Minsk *oblast*): "Independent – is it about this thing at Viskuli?[14] Oh, yes, there were the four of them, guzzling down *gorelka* (vodka) there."[15]

During the interviews, we registered many shifts in chronology, "errors" in dating the events of *perestroika*. In many cases (far too many to disregard), *perestroika* was dated back to the beginning of the 1990s. The historical milestones in the biographical narratives were facts of the narrators' personal lives, which served as reference points for dating political events.

Tatiana G., 52, engineer (Pruzhany, Brest *oblast*): "At that time life was still not bad. The maternity leave was a year and a half, and in 1988 I got back to work … And then *perestroika* began, oh, what a mess it was!"[16] Valentina M., 57, cleaner (Slutsk, Minsk *oblast*): "When *perestroika* began, our workshop at the plant got closed [in 1990], because nobody needed any more what we produced. I'd been working there for twenty years. *Perestroika* began and that was the end of it."[17] Faina M., 47, paramedic (Mariina Gorka, Minsk *oblast*): "It was in 1990 that *perestroika* began.

That was when my husband died too. Yes, that's when it all started – both in the country and in my family."[18]

As we see, there is not only an error in dating, but also a semantic discrepancy that is contrary to the authoritative discourse. In the narratives, the term *perestroika* is inherently tied to the economic crisis (unpaid salaries, closure of a plant workshop, loss of a job). Here we are dealing with the phenomenon discussed by Portelli in *The Death of Luigi Trastulli*, in which several significant events merge into one narrative in a people's memory. The reason for this collective error lies not in the event itself but in the meaning attributed to it and its relation to the later events.[19] Some twenty-five years later, *perestroika* had come to be associated not with democratic freedoms but with transformations of comparable magnitude, events that affected people's of behaviour and lifestyle and that brought considerable changes to the world outlook of the "Soviet individual."

Another important observation: the events that played a key role in the contemporary history of Belarus – the Declaration of Independence on 27 July 1990 and the founding of a republic on 25 August 1991 – got lost in this long and traumatic experience. Most of our respondents could not remember exactly when these events took place. Against the background of strikingly vivid emotions relating to the collapse of the Soviet Union, this "memory block" is highly revealing. With regard to the collapse of the Soviet Union, the reminiscences demonstrate involvement in the issue; yet when they speak of Belarusian independence, the respondents focus largely on the reasons for their non-involvement instead of expressing their position on this important matter. Nina K., 57, worker (Mariina Gorka, Minsk *oblast*): "I don't remember. I don't know much about political matters. I am living just the same way I used to."[20] Nina T., 59, collective farm worker (Zakalnoe, Minsk *oblast*): "We were working so hard, we didn't see anything. Until I retired, I didn't hear anything at all about this."[21] Larisa A., 58, mathematics teacher (Chervonoe, Gomel *oblast*): "No, I don't remember. Nothing. What's over is over. We, common people, somehow didn't care."[22] Clearly, the memory of the Soviet collapse constantly surfaces in people's minds, whereas the memory of the logical consequence of that dissolution – the formation of a new state – remains latent and is viewed as non-essential in the present day.

In post-Soviet Belarusian history, the topic of state independence has become the ideological focus for the forces opposing the government, whose position in the Belarusian provinces is rather marginal.

Meanwhile, the official ideology of today's Belarusian government, which since the Soviet collapse has chosen to retain Soviet-style rule, conspicuously ignores the issue of Belarusian independence and has imposed on people a nostalgic view of the Soviet era. As early as 1995, new national symbols were introduced that were stylistically identical to the Soviet ones: the red-and-green flag and the national emblem, nicknamed the "cabbage" owing to its shape and colour. Besides relying on visual symbols of the Soviet past, the Belarusian authorities continue resorting to traditional Soviet propaganda clichés, such as "the unity of fraternal nations" and "the state's paternal care of its people." In general, they promote a return to the Soviet values.

Surviving Perestroika

Ordinary Belarusians' memories of *perestroika* centre largely on personal privations and stunted lives. Contrast this with the discourse of the Belarusian authorities, whose rhetoric regarding the *perestroika* era focuses on political reforms.

Our respondents were utterly indifferent to the political reforms in their country. They were much more concerned about how they were going to survive the economic depression those reforms caused. Disappointment, irritation, anxiety, and despair prevailed in their recollections of this time.

Their political disorientation and moral confusion were compounded by the hardships of physical existence: life had become a constant struggle for survival. Galina S., 43, teacher (Orsha, Vitebsk *oblast*): "It was terrifying. We didn't know what was to come next. We were not sure if we would be able get out of all this at all."[23] Alina K., 57, teacher (Gritsovichi, Vitebsk *oblast*): "Well, it was when the country fell apart. We couldn't make head or tail of where we were going and who was to lead us ... We didn't get our salaries for a long time.[24] We were scared, it was real fear. There was no proper government, we had nothing."[25] Galina K., 52, technician (Pruzhany, Brest *oblast*): "Like I used to say, just as some people lived through the revolution of 1917, so we had to survive all that ... You know, it was awful. We had no peace when all this happened."[26]

Dealing with Shortages

In our respondents' personal narratives about *perestroika* and its consequences, political changes lost their primacy, giving way to memories of day-to-day survival. The centrality of these experiences in people's lives and later in their memories was a direct outcome of the collapse of the Soviet centralized economy. By the mid-1990s, that collapse had led to severe and unprecedented shortages of foods and other goods. Absolutely everything vanished from the stores: toothpaste, soap, washing powder, sugar, copybooks, oil, bedclothes, and so on. And these shortages were long-lasting. Liudmila S.: "The shops were empty as if an army had marched through the place. Only bored sales-assistants in the shops."[27] Valentina L., 57, paramedic (Luban, Minsk *oblast*): "The counters were empty. One would come into a store and see only three-litre jars of juice and rye bread. Empty shelves! Total absence of any groceries."[28]

To deal with chronic shortages of food and other necessities, many enterprises started their own distribution systems for their employees. However, the amounts provided in this way were never enough to meet demand. The privations were so severe for many that it is not surprising that our respondents spoke about them at great length. Tamara Sh., 56, supply manager (Baranovichi): "We would not work at work, but queue on the plant's premises for sausage or tinned meat, with which they would sometimes give us[29] something like bay leaf and coffee beans as a tie-in."[30] All the organizations, on their own accord and almost simultaneously, started the same method of distribution – drawing lots – which in theory guaranteed equal rights to everyone. Tamara D., 65, dairy maid (Minsk *oblast*):

> They would deliver us, say, three units of something. Who was going to get it? We just drew lots. Say we received blanket covers, boots, or something else. We just rolled up some pieces of paper and put them into a hat. Then we drew them out. The items were numbered: a blanket – 21, boots – 22, and so on. So you took home what you drew. You drew the boots – you take the boots no matter whether it's your size or not. Lucky you, if you got a blanket, because blankets are one size.[31]

Aleksandr M., 47, warrant officer (Pruhzany, Brest *oblast*):

> Our military base received a kind of humanitarian aid: "Maliutka" mini-washing machines. They were handed over straight to the colonels. Then there were also children's shoes and boots of certain sizes. A package of baby food, baby linen, and a massage brush. So we got this list. So we started thinking who's got small kids. "You have a boy. What size is he?" – "The hell I know!" – "Anyway, he will grow into this size, sooner or later.

> OK, signing you up for this." At other times we did a kind of lottery – scraps of paper in a hat. Say the unit's been allocated a pair of boots – one pair for about twenty servicemen, both general soldiers and warrant officers. We took turns to draw lots, and finally it was my turn. I looked at the piece of paper in my hand and saw "boots" on it. I was like on cloud nine! Paid for the boots and brought them home. Who cared whether you needed them or not, 'cause something is anyways better than nothing.[32]

Inflation, product shortages, and feverish demand revived the "crisis" consumer practices of Soviet times (described by E. Osokina as typical for the 1930s).[33] Queues became part of everyday life. People used to gather in front of the shops long before opening time, not knowing what would be available because the goods haven't been delivered to the outlet yet. Often they stayed in the queue all night after the shop closed. They drew up lists of people queuing and checked now and then who was present, "throwing out" the absentees. Sometimes people fought (quite literally) for their place in a queue and a potential purchase. Tamara D.:

> We thought the end of days had come. It was like this. Say, we are milking cows. Those who live close to the shop arrive and ask: "Did you join the queue?" Others are already queuing there since 4 or 5 [a.m.]. Something is to be put on sale, but what – who the hell knows. When you're done with milking, you rush there and stand in a line no matter whether you are hungry or not … It was like total doom and gloom … Sometimes you were lucky to buy something, but more often you were not. You didn't even think about whether you needed this thing, you just got what you could. I remember once two women in a queue started pulling each other by the hair! Then it turned into a kind of an all-in brawl – a lot of people crowding, screaming, jostling each other, pushing on the counters, nearly breaking them … Really felt like the end of days was near.[34]

This deprivation legitimated behavioural patterns that were unthinkable in normal circumstances. Svetlana K., 45, teacher (Pinsk, Brest *oblast*):

> There were such long queues in stores, and products like sausage were sold in limited quantities, say, no more than 1 kilo per person. Once I was shopping, actually queuing for sausage carrying a baby in my arms. Suddenly the child bent over the counter, grabbed a slice of sausage and took a bite at it. This slice actually was sold to us afterwards, even though the

woman before us in the queue was willing to buy it even after my baby chewed on it.[35]

Shoppers who were unable to buy what they needed were often forced to settle for things they had not intended to buy, or to buy things they didn't need at the time.[36] Galina V.:

We snapped up just anything. I still have a useless blue-and-white nylon jacket tucked somewhere in the attic; no one ever once wore it. And I still have a brand new calico outfit lying somewhere safely.[37]

Tatiana G.:

They said the shop would put up some curtain lace for sale and I needed it, because my brother had moved into a new flat and needed new curtains. And the shops were always out of stock. All our family spent a whole night queuing in the department store. A whole night! With roll-calls. That curtain lace was never delivered to the shop, so all that queuing was in vain. So I thought, well, just what do they have in stock? It turned out they had blankets for sale. So we got ourselves a blanket. Well, I thought that if I have a small daughter, then a blanket anyways would come in handy. So that we hadn't queued for nothing.[38]

The government's attempts to regulate public access to goods by introducing rationing led to the resurrection of past "work-around" methods: if the queue was long enough, people joined it again after making the purchase and repeated the trick as many times as the length of the queue allowed. Liudmila S.:

The sugar ration was one kilogram per person, so I always went shopping for groceries with my daughter in order to get as much sugar as we needed. And even so we had to queue two or three times. We needed sugar for everything: jam and other stuff, and in general sugar was always in very high demand.[39]

A domestic chore as commonplace as procuring goods for the home turned into panic and impulse buying.[40] Tamara D.:

As for shopping ... You felt like something was eating you, like "I need to get more salt," "I need more pasta" and so on ... You just didn't think about what on earth you needed the stuff for. Like my friend, she went, "I

> already have ten kilos of flour." And it's two kilos per person at the grocer's. So you go and take two kilos here, two kilos there. I've no idea what it would have come to, if it went on like that a little longer. We'd have got completely down and out.[41]

Consumers were deprived of choice and forced to buy what was on sale at the moment, when it was their turn in the queue. In those circumstances, retailing turned into a machine for the mechanical distribution of rations. Galina E., 54, kindergarten teacher (Pukhovichi, Minsk *oblast*):

> We purchased any sizes. If it was a pair of child's boots, you would take it, even if the child was yet to grow into this size. If it does not fit at all, then you come out of the store and exchange it for another size with other buyers ... I remember how we were standing in a queue and they [the sales assistants] were almost throwing at us heaps of all kinds of clothes – and we were grabbing them each and all. I was standing in the centre and the whole pile of clothes fell on me. So I snatched something not knowing what it was. Then I saw – it was two raincoats ... The others were wrestling them from my hands, so I clutched at them and dashed to the check-out to pay.[42]

Those who lived in small towns went on "shopping tours" around the neighbouring villages. Rural people went to towns to do their shopping, and all of them went to the capital (Minsk) to buy what they couldn't buy at their place of residence. There was a kind of stock joke at that time: "What is long and green and smells like sausage?" "A train from Minsk."[43] Vladimir Sh., 44, builder (Mariina Gorka, Minsk *oblast*): "People used to go to the capital just to buy food."[44] Galina E.: "Minsk was better in those times, though, of course, the situation there was tough as well, but we would go there anyway and buy at least something if not at this store then at another."[45]

Having *blat* (a personal connection)[46] in a store – better still, in a grocery or consumer goods warehouse – remained the best (albeit not available to all) way of getting hold of needed items. Buying became almost a dramatic event. As American anthropologist Nancy Riese has noted: "In response to a sudden disappearance of goods there was born (or reborn) one of the most vibrant genres of oral communication – 'a saga of heroic shopping.'"[47]

In 1991, consumer coupon books were introduced in Belarus. After a purchase, a corresponding coupon for that product was cut from the book. In January 1992, these were replaced by a new kind of coupon:

sheets of checked paper with different monetary units filled in each square: 1 ruble, 3 rubles, 10 rubles, and so on. Every purchase was to be "paid for" not just in cash but also in coupons. Usually, the coupons were given out along with the salary and for exactly the same amount of money (obviously, very soon the coupons could be illegally bought and sold).

According to the Belarusian government, all of these measures were being taken to protect the domestic market from the massive uncontrolled export of goods. However, the respondents note that the rations, along with the cards and coupons (which they blended in their spoken narratives into a broad term "coupons") did not guarantee problem-free purchase of even a minimum monthly basket of consumer goods. Maria G., 64, zootechnician (Mir, Grodno *oblast*): "It was the time when we did a good deal of walking. The store counters were empty, even pasta was absent from the shops. There was hardly anything, really, and you needed coupons even for that. It was a harsh time, just like after the war."[48] Galina E.:

> I took a leave from work to find some clothes for my children. It was around 1992 or 1993. Every day I got up and went shopping [in a department store or a children's store] to be there at 9 a.m., and I spent the whole day waiting until something was put out for sale. It was much like full-time work. The queues were so long, everybody was jostling, pushing each other. You were lucky if you ended up buying anything.[49]

Meanwhile, a new trend that would be quite inconceivable in normal circumstances was developing: goods were purchased not because people needed them or might need them in the future, but because they had coupons that had to be used. Aleksandr M.:

> And then it all started ... coupons, I mean. Looking back, it was Gorbachev's biggest mistake. Because people were forced into buying things they had no use for. Alcohol and cigarettes. If you didn't buy what you had coupons for you felt like you were losing something.[50]

Liudmila S.:

> Everything was sold for coupons. So we were rushing around buying things. Stockings, even the stuff you didn't need at all. It was a pity if even a single coupon went to waste. You just bought things, no matter whether

> you needed it or not ... By the way, I still have stuff in my wardrobe that was bought in that frenzy. I have no use for them.[51]

Decades of chronic shortages had nurtured in many Soviet citizens a passive, acquiescent attitude to queues that was not subjected to much reflection.[52] Aleksandr M.: "Queues were the way of life. We got used to queues and didn't mind them. They were like something that always existed and was there to stay."[53] Prior to *perestroika,* commodity deficiencies in the Soviet Union had been rather moderate. It was difficult to purchase some kinds of merchandise, such as household appliances and imported goods. But in the early 1990s, as noted earlier, stores became quite literally empty. Everyone was puzzled: Where had everything gone?! Not so long before, things had been in good supply, and suddenly nothing was. Liudmila Z., 69, retired physical education teacher (Pruzhany, Brest *oblast*): "I remember huge rolls of calico lying on the counter in a store, and then – everything vanished. Well that was a crazy time? Now it's hard to believe we went through all this."[54] Alina K.:

> It was dreadful, naturally. You know what we used to think about? Not about our plight or what the country was doing to us. No, it was basically, "Where has everything gone?" Shops used to have everything and in copious amounts, how come it was all gone? See? Those were really tough times.[55]

Anti-Alcohol Campaign in Reminiscences

On 16 May 1985, the Decree "On Further Intensification of Anti-Alcohol Measures" was issued by the Presidium of the Supreme Council of the Soviet Union. This decree launched Gorbachev's now notorious prohibition campaign along with a wide range of administrative and propagandist measures to advance the cause. The number of shops selling spirits was greatly reduced, and the sale of liquor was restricted to certain hours of the day. All of this led to longer queues and increased profiteering. The initiative (popularly known as "the Dry Law") provoked strong discontent throughout the country.

The decree and the subsequent policy regarding the sale of alcohol drove nearly everyone to reactive and adaptive practices. Attempts to restrict the sale of liquor led to a feverish demand for it. Nikolai Zh., 47, mechanic on a collective farm (Zakalnoe, Luban distric, Minsk oblast):

> Actually, it was just another example of a state waging a war on its people. It used to be like this: a working man finishes a hard day's work and on the way home drops in at a liquor shop, has his half-glass of vodka and a snack and goes home quietly. Not exactly sober anymore, but definitely not drunk either. But when they brought in that "dry law," people started to really hit the booze. It's like "I must get plastered today, because tomorrow I might not have anything to drink." ... We bought it wherever we could lay our hands on it. One could call his friends in another town to find out if there is wine on sale, and if yes they would get a car and do 50 kilometres to get drunk. It's like five men could each take a crate of wine. And then they'd guzzle down those five crates until there's nothing left. You call that abstinence? It was more like a struggle between the people and the government![56]

The long-established and greatly cherished tradition of friend and family hosting demanded that liquor be in plentiful supply at any more or less festive occasion. It was a disgrace not to provide your guests with a wide selection of tipple. And at events such as weddings or funerals, a shortage of alcoholic drinks would have been perceived as outrageous. Being unable to buy liquor when needed and in sufficient amounts, people were compelled to develop ample "reserves." Tamara Sh.: "People would keep crates of wine and vodka at home. They would buy any liquor the moment they saw it in store just in case."[57]

There was another important factor: for people in the provinces, vodka or moonshine (*samogon*) was the equivalent of money. Any service rendered by any civil servant beyond (or sometimes within) the scope of their official capacity had to be paid for in alcohol. The value of this currency increased sharply under the new law. Tamara Sh.: "Say you ask someone to give you a hand with something or repair something at home – no one needs money, everybody wants 'a bottle.'"[58] Aleksandr M.:

> You show them a bottle – your granny's patch of land is weeded in no time. Everything was done "for a bottle." It was even called "the liquid dollar." Real money was not held in high esteem much. Give me a bottle – I'll do the job. As for money – what the hell do you need it for if you can't buy anything?[59]

In the early 1990s, spirits as well as other goods were rationed: one bottle of vodka and two bottles of wine per month per person. This innovation further aggravated matters. In response to another attempt to impose abstinence on them, people began mass-producing moonshine. In the 1990s in Belarus, almost every family was making moonshine for its own needs. Our respondents mentioned a great number of ingenious recipes, and new ones were constantly being created due to lack of the usual ingredients. As it turned out, moonshine could be made out of almost anything that was in stock at a grocery store at any given moment – caramel, tomato paste, and even washing powder. Vladimir Sh.: "Everyone had their own original recipe. All the time people came up with something new. Someone wanted it to be cheap, someone wanted a better quality."[60] Vladimir T., 61, retired rural cultural manager (Rechen, Minsk *oblast*): "There was an old woman living nearby – she knew some age-old recipes."[61]

The producers of moonshine traditionally have been and still are condemned because they are "only seeking profits" and "forcing people into hard drinking to cash in on their weakness." However, significant allowances were made for times of crisis. The matter of this activity being illegal almost never surfaced in people's memories. A moral position on this issue was articulated only in one instance, by Gennagy S., 53, fireman (Mariina Gorka, Minsk *oblast*): "A neighbour of mine comes from Starye Dorogi [village], so we used to go there and made home brew right in the forest. It was a kind of illegal, but one had to survive somehow. Everyone did what they could to survive."[62]

Notions of honour and honesty were linked to the quality of the *samogon*, not to abstaining from making it. Vladimir T.: "If, God forbid, people in the village found out that you made such [low-quality] *gorelka*, they would slander your name all over the place! Everyone would know. Don't you understand?"[63] This situation was quite indicative of the interdependence of deprivational conditions and moral attitudes.

All attempts to combat drinking and alcoholism failed. Indeed, substance abuse soared. The consumption of surrogates often led to lethal outcomes. According to the respondents, the consequences of the ill-conceived anti-alcohol campaign were being felt to this day. Nikolai Zh.:

> That was when people started to drink harder. I believe that anti-alcohol legislation was fundamentally wrong. If this issue hadn't been brought up and that policy hadn't been enforced, then today people wouldn't be drinking so heavily. It was all going in a natural way and so it would have remained, people wouldn't be so bent on drinking.[64]

Gorbachev's anti-alcohol effort lasted only a few years, from 1985 to 1988. But as with the confusion about the chronology of *perestroika*, in the narratives this campaign merged with "the spirits crisis" that occurred much later, in the early 1990s, and that affected many aspects of daily life. But whatever the dates, in people's memories Gorbachev remains the chief culprit of all the "problems with alcohol." Gennagy S.: "It was the state that taught us to make moonshine. People learned how to make their own distillers. We used to make this stuff from sugar, bread, or whatever else, depending on the kind of device each had. Gorbachev taught us all this."[65]

Losing the Savings

In 1991, shock monetary reforms were implemented in Belarus. Today the reforms are known as the *pavlovskie,* after the name of their architect, the Soviet prime minister. In January 1991, the President of the Soviet Union issued a decree that withdrew 50 and 100 rouble banknotes from circulation. The people had only three days to exchange those old notes for new ones. Also, bank deposit withdrawals were limited to 500 rubles. Panic spread throughout the country, with the banks literally besieged by huge crowds. In April 1991, prices were raised three times in a row – inflation was taking on colossal proportions. Large amounts of money could not be retrieved from the banks and rapidly lost all their value.

The social ideal of a Soviet person included an aspiration to create a solid economic foundation for one's future. A healthy savings account was an indication of success. A respectable family ought to have saved enough to own their own home, provide for decent weddings for their children, and help them with a head start in life. People would save up "for a rainy day," "to buy a car," or "just in case." In the Soviet welfare system, education and health care were free and the state pension provided for basic retirement needs such as groceries and utlitity payments; savings were viewed as important means augment these. Having long suffered privations for the sake of "a better tomorrow," our respondents worked extra hours, cut their expenses, and denied themselves simple pleasures for the sake of depositing a little more money in the bank. Anatolii T., 46, farmer (Pruzhany, Brestskaya *oblast*):

> I wouldn't say my parents were in a terrible plight, but the system forced people to be thrifty. They had money in the savings account, but were averse to spending it on some extras for themselves, even on clothing … At that time, well, everybody was like that. When it all [monetary reforms] started, some families lost as much as 50,000 roubles blocked in their savings accounts. They all loathed spending money. They could be wearing

> rags, but had 50,000 rubles in the bank. It gave them some kind of comfort and security … Saving up all their lives … not even knowing what for … Well, that's what the system was like … Such were the people … All Soviets were like that. Everyone had a lot of money but was unwilling to spend it.[66]

Vladimir T.:

> Village people kept pigs, cows. When they sold a calf or something, all the money went straight to the savings account. People were really frugal with money. Did their "shares" at the collective farm[67] … and put all the money into the savings account.[68]

There were rumours that deposits would be lost, but it was so unimaginable that no one believed it. The propaganda of Soviet power diligently cultivated people's belief in the state's "paternal care." This regime could not betray them – that was the prevailing feeling. Galina D., 67, teacher (Orsha, Vitebsk *oblast*): "I didn't think the state could betray us – this much I trusted it."[69] Maria R., 51, retired seller (Pruzhany, Brest *oblast*):

> His [husband's] parents had 35,000 in their savings account. His father trusted the authorities so much that he believed this money could never be lost. He was a collective farmer … and to earn some extra he kept poultry and sheep … had about a hundred sheep and as many geese.[70]

But even those who realized it was time to rescue their deposits had no means to do so. In total, the thirty-five families of our respondents lost more than 700,000 rubles in deposits during the monetary reforms of the 1990s. To compare, the dream of many Soviet people, their symbol of prosperity – the Zhiguli car – cost between 6,000 and 7,000 rubles. And one couldn't buy such a car even if one had the money; the waiting list was so long it took about five to ten years simply to get the chance to buy the car.

The respondents described their deep frustration as they contemplated their suddenly vanished opportunities. Olga K., 43, manager (Orsha, Vitebsk *oblast*): "Tonia, my sister-in-law, told me that she could have given me the money for the cooperative[71] or bought Sasha a car. But when she took out the money from the bank, all it was worth was a bag of groceries."[72] Valentina K., 62, worker (Soligorsk, Minsk *oblast*):

> After this [husband's] money was lost, the only thing he was able to buy was two dolls for our granddaughters with those 12,000. And it even wasn't enough, he had to add another thousand. Two Barbies. That was it. How do you like that. It was somewhere in 1998.[73]

Galina V.: "We bought a pair of plain summer shoes, a sack of sugar and a crate of vodka. And it cost 4,000."[74]

Returning to the Land, Post-Independence Style

When analysing how people tried to adapt to a new environment, one should take into account the limited possibilities available for them in provincial towns and villages compared to the big cities. For the former, there were far fewer opportunities for occupational mobility, continued education or retraining, secondary employment, and so on. On the other hand, in the country there were more opportunities to adapt to hardship – for example, by growing food on one's own patch of land. Remember that rural people – and indeed, many urban dwellers – had never completely abandoned household production. During the crisis of the 1990s, that production grew steadily. Valentina L.:

> Why didn't we starve to death in the country? Because we had our gardens. It was a great help. Potatoes, vegetable patches ... We made our own butter and cheese. We had a cow ... And we had flour, a sack of it. We baked bread – well, a kind of pie, nothing fancy.

Galina V.:

> God knows how many jars of pickled vegetables we preserved – cucumbers, tomatoes, all sorts of antipastos! We made a lot of jam from all kinds of berries.

Liudmila Z.:

> People started buying plots of land and building cabins, with whatever building material they could find or take from state enterprises. Because land gives you food. What else was there to do? Looking back on it now – it was a horrible nightmare. But we survived.[75]

In other words, economic life in the provinces was taking on the characteristics of a subsistence economy. Many people also cut expenses in various ways. Nikolai Zh.:

> We didn't buy wheat bread, as it was expensive. Maybe once a month, on pay day. We would bring the loaf home and our kids would leap with joy and yell: "Hurray!" Then they'd sit down and scarf it all up. Not a crumb left for us.[76]

Valentina L.:

> White [bread]? We could hardly afford even brown bread. My friend used to say: "I'm allergic to white bread." I didn't get it at first and believed her. Then she went on: "I'll probably soon develop an allergy to brown bread, too." She had two children, two students to provide for. "If it goes like this the only thing I'm not allergic to will be potatoes," she said. Then I got it. Allergic to food![77]

Sharing, Hoarding, and Taking from the State

With the total collapse of the economy, the practice of commodity exchange was revived: Maria R.:

> We would share with each other what we had. Clothes, too. It was impossible to buy a white shirt to wear to school! So the kids shared one shirt for the line-up on the first day of school. Say, in one school it was scheduled for 10 a.m., and at ours for 8:30, so we could do with one shirt. Like it was some fancy dress for the New Year party.[78]

People exchanged not only second-hand clothes but also new ones that were unnecessary or the wrong size. These were purchases with a view to exchanging them later. Linore Goralik cites a typical commentary: "In 1990 people tried to be put on the list[79] for any product just because it was a product, and you could later exchange for another one, more suitable."[80]

The late Soviet economy was characterized by deficient supply. This encouraged people to create reserves of anything that could be stored, because no one knew what product would be in short supply next. This habit proved especially useful in the early 1990s. Liudmila T.,

66, businesswoman (Luban, Minsk *oblast*): "In those times you didn't feel good if you didn't have five blanket slips in your closet and so on. That's how we survived the crisis. Thanks to what we had set aside."[81] Valentina L.: "I always had an ample stock of everything – sacks of sugar and flour, stuff like that. I kept a good reserve. We all liked to have something in a reserve."[82] People also started to make their own clothes and became experts at mending old ones. Valentina L.: "We were sewing, patching up, even remodelling clothes. Knitting became a favourite pastime."[83] Villagers also reported that it was around this time that pilfering soared at the collective farms. Households had more cattle than before, and these would be fed by whatever could be taken from collective farm storehouse or at night in the field. Valentina L.:

> Apart from sweating our guts out at work so hard, we were forced to steal – beetroots or potatoes from collective farm fields or whatever else … You just go there, dig the stuff out, drag those two sacks home, have a little rest and then think, "OK maybe I should do the thing one more time now?" And those mosquitoes, getting in your face and under the clothes! And you make another trip, and a third one. And then suddenly the day is breaking. You just change your clothes and go to work. We didn't have enough potatoes of our own. I kept five pigs to sell later and fed them on potatoes. Lena was still a student, I had to give her education … Yeah, we did the farm fields alright! Everybody did.[84]

Urban dwellers were no different. Everyone grabbed what they could lay their hands on and afterwards exchanged it for something else with others who had done the same. Nikolai K.:

> Workers at the winery were smuggling wine home by the barrel. There's no secret in that. We stole all kinds of stuff from our crisps plant: oil, crisps, potatoes. We had to keep food on the table for our children. … Oil was smuggled in plastic soda bottles. We hid those in bags, tied to the waist, stuffed in the trousers, or under the jacket. Everybody in their own way. If it was a small bottle, about half a litre, we slid it down the jacket sleeve.[85]

Trading

But it would be wrong to assume that people in the provinces relied on internal resources only when it came to making their living. They took other opportunities to navigate the shortage of supplies and earnings. In the late 1980s, commercial expeditions to Poland and Russia became widespread.[86] This was incredibly hard work, and mainly women engaged in it. With so many goods in short supply, you first had to find a way to buy something you could later sell. Galina V.:

> You had to have *blat* in the store to purchase the goods in bulk. And sales assistants had their own vested interest in it. I would come up to her, we'd make a deal, she'd get a fiver for the favour. Then the goods had to be carried literally on one's back to the point of sale, which could be rather far.

Maria R.:

> It was so hard carrying those bulky and unwieldy bags. You could hardly lift them. And each of us had two or three. In your hands, on your back, and in a wheelbarrow tied to your waist. It was a life of toil. And all that for peanuts. The shoulders were all bruised from the backpacks.[87]

At the time, railway stations and marketplaces were crime-ridden and the "shuttle business" was outright dangerous. Nina V.:

> Almost all the time I travelled by myself, and if had I gone missing, I wouldn't stand a chance of being found. Gosh! I spent nights at the railway stations, and in other places! And in what sort of apartments did I stay! Oh! No words can ever express that![88]

Nadezhda R., 54, engineer (Pruzhany, Brest *oblast*):

> 120 jackets, each worth 1,500 roubles. Can you imagine what a load of money I was carrying on me? In a shoulder bag! And somehow manage not to get robbed! It's not like now with all those plastic cards! ... The marketplace in Warsaw, there was some racketeering! Really scary. People were robbed of their money right inside the exchange offices. It was horrible. I wasn't as much frightened anywhere else. They would cheat you and leave with a roll of fake bills, or simply take away your money.[89]

Maria R.:

> People like us were always the first to be deceived. They could do anything to us. They didn't have any shame![90]

In just a few days, this business could yield a return several times larger than one's monthly salary. But few people dared to quit their day jobs, and they often spent several years combining the two.

The deeply entrenched Soviet way of thinking and its established practices became interwoven with new practices and modes of thought. In the Soviet mode of thought, private trading was viewed as humiliating. This reflected an understandable (considering the traditional Soviet values) unwillingness to lose status. As it happened, it was often the intelligentsia (teachers, professionals, researchers, academics), who had enjoyed high social status in Soviet times, who now became shuttle traders. The old model of social stratification was now competing with a new model in which money was taking the place of cultural prestige.[91] Even so, however quickly our respondents adapted their behaviour to the changing times, their old social attitudes and values[92] held sway over them long afterwards, so that entrepreneurs often found themselves being looked down on by the community.

Lost "Fraternal" Ties

In the post-Soviet era, the official discourse of the political establishment in Belarus vigorously exploited the theme of "separated fraternal nations" and "broken ties," building on images such as the "heart-broken old mother who cannot visit her daughter in Moscow" to communicate a message of nostalgia for the "great power destroyed by evil forces." This message resonated strongly with our respondents, many of whom, regretting the Soviet Union's collapse, focused eagerly on the theme of former unity and solidarity. During our interviews, the following exchange was typical: "There were no borders, no customs. You could go wherever you wanted." – "Can't you go now where you want to?" – "Yes, but it costs such a lot of money! It's so expensive!"[93]

Here, again, we see an obvious discrepancy between the communicated nostalgic message and real practices. When asked about "big politics," our respondents typically switched topics to the matter of everyday consumption.

This nostalgia for the supposed "absence of borders" and ability to travel anywhere is especially significant in that most our respondents who had relatives in Poland were able to start visiting them regularly only *after* the Soviet collapse. And if they did not themselves, then their children started going abroad on vacations regularly. Remarkably, some of our respondents neither found it necessary to go abroad then nor were willing to do so now.

Also, the geographical terminology our respondents used to express their nostalgia was noteworthy. In the phrase "could go everywhere you wanted," "everywhere" meant only the territory of the former Soviet Union. This reflected the prevailing Soviet world view. The collective term "the South"[94] was no less significant. Liudmila S.: "You could go wherever you wanted to. Could go to the South for example, it was not a problem. You could just go, if you wanted."[95] Nina V.: "Our people used to travel to Latvia, Lithuania and to the South. I didn't go anywhere because my husband didn't let me."[96] In people's narratives, the term "South" still referred to "the southern regions of the Soviet Union." But when the interviewees talked about their children spending holidays abroad now, they used more specific geographical names: Bulgaria, Turkey, and so on.

It is also interesting that although these discrepancies were obvious, the respondents did not seem to see them as a problem. This was probably because these facts represented totally different planes of experience. Nostalgia for the Soviet Union was a product of collective representations; it was a mythological reality subject to laws totally different from the laws of objective reality, and as such, it was something taken for granted, without reflection.

In Conclusion: Remembering *Perestroika*

In our research, we attempted to take a broad look at the process of *perestroika* and to evaluate its consequences from the perspective of the present. That meant considering the historical experience of the past two decades.

We approached the theme of *perestroika* in our interviews after the discussion of everyday life in the 1970 and 1980s (in which prevailed the themes of short supply, *blat*, and the like). The respondents summarized it thus: "We are grateful to *perestroika*, at least the stores are not empty like before"; "At least we are driving cars nowadays." However, when looking at that period from a different perspective – that is, evaluating it against the backdrop of the traumas of the early 1990s – the interviewees articulated a different attitude, one in which the Brezhnev era was a kind of "Golden Age" characterized by stability and national well-being.

Contrary to the authoritative discourse, in people's personal narratives the term *perestroika* was inherently linked to economic crisis. They combined multiple significant events in their memory into a single narrative. The reason for this collective "error" lay not in the events themselves but in the meanings attributed to them.[97]

The interviewees perceived *perestroika* as a pivotal event (setting aside whether it was positive or negative). In their commemoration practices, and from the experiential distance of two decades, they linked it to sweeping social transformations. It demanded that they change their established patterns of behaviour and even of thought. It also demanded that they reorganize their lives, and thus, it came to embody all subsequent experience. It became linked not to political freedoms, *glasnost* (freedom of speech), and competitive elections, but to how they were being forced to adjust to fundamental changes in their lives.

When analysing people's recollections of the *perestroika* period, remember that personal recollections of those times were affected by the post-*perestroika* experience. Their relative deprivation, followed by their frustrations in the early 1990s, when they could barely meet their basic material needs, often determined their current representations. Today's *perestroika* narratives can be somewhat conventionally defined as "memories of shattered hopes." And it is noteworthy that while the expectations for *perestroika* were articulated in a general and vague manner, the grievances were very specific. In narrativizations of *perestroika*'s consequences, the issue of political change boiled down how consumer habits had been transformed.

At the time of the interviews, Belarusian authorities were actively promoting nostalgia for the Soviet era, before the Soviet collapse and the economic crisis, and were calling for the return of Soviet ways and values. The Soviet "breakdown" was interpreted as traumatic; the notion of independence was imbued with negative connotations associated with people who had "destroyed the great country." This rhetoric had become accepted and was being blended into mass communications, albeit (as the interviews show) on the declarative level. This clash of symbolic connotations expressed itself as a transfer of assessments of political processes into the realm of consumer experience. The mythological character of the nostalgic discourse manifested itself in multiple obvious discrepancies with actual practices.

The spiritual legacy of the Soviet era continues to have an enormous influence on present-day Belarusian values and behaviour models. At the same time, adaptation to the new mode of existence brought to life new behavioural and thinking patterns that have enabled Belarusians to exploit new opportunities and resources for the purpose of improving their quality of life. For all the nostalgia about Soviet times, the interviews exposed people's general unwillingness to return to the Soviet system.

NOTES

1 The research project was funded by a grant issued by the European Humanities University with sponsorship support provided by the European Parliament President, Mr Jerzy Buzek.
2 Iurchak, "Pozdnii Sotsializm i Poslednee Sovetskoe Pokolenie," 97.
3 Leonid Brezhnev was the General Secretary of the Central Committee of the Communist Party of the Soviet Union (CPSU), presiding over the country from 1964 until his death in 1982. Konstantin Chernenko was the Fifth General Secretary of the CPSU. He led the Soviet Union from 13 February 1984 until his death thirteen months later, on 10 March 1985. Chernenko was also Chairman of the Presidium of the Supreme Soviet from 11 April 1984 until his death.
4 Nina V. (born 1943), interview.
5 Liudmila S. (born 1944), interview.
6 Galina V. (born 1948), interview.
7 Liudmila P. (born 1954), interview.
8 Valentina L. (born 1952), interview.
9 Liudmila P., interview.
10 Igor M. (born 1948), interview.
11 Evgeny V. (born 1962), interview.
12 Alla K. (born 1952), interview.
13 Nikolai K. (born 1960), interview.
14 *Viskuli* is a government residence in Belovezskaia Pushcha, where the declaration of the dissolution of the Soviet Union was signed by the heads of three republics: Russia, Ukraine, and Belarus.
15 Anatolii L. (born 1952), interview.
16 Tatiana G. (born 1957), interview.
17 Valentina M. (born 1952), interview.
18 Faina M. (born 1951), interview.
19 Portelli, "Smert' Luidzhi Trastulli," 216–18.

20 Nina K. (born 1952), interview.
21 Nina T. (born 1950), interview.
22 Larisa A. (born 1951), interview.
23 Galina S. (born 1966), interview.
24 In addition to shortages of foods and consumer goods, people were faced with "salary shortages." Most continued working in their enterprises (all being in the government sector) but without receiving payments for several months (editors' note).
25 Alina K. (born 1952), interview.
26 Galina K. (born 1957), interview.
27 Liudmila S., interview.
28 Valentina L., interview.
29 The Soviet distribution system gave birth to a variety of euphemisms related to the sale and purchase of goods. Instead of "sell," people used words such as "[they are] giving [something at the store]" (although it is obvious that the goods were not given away, but sold; the new idiom emphasized that even having money didn't guarantee people the ability to purchase goods); and "[they have] thrown in [some goods at the store]" (this phrase quite accurately reflected the irregular availability of hard-to-get goods as well as the speed at which they disappeared from the stores). The successful acquisition of the treasured products was described as "getting hold of [them]."
30 Tamara Sh. (born 1953), interview.
31 Tamara D. (born 1944), interview.
32 Aleksandr M. (born 1962), interview.
33 Osokina, "Proshchalnaia Oda Sovetskoi Ocheredi."
34 Tamara D., interview.
35 Svetlana K. (born 1964), interview.
36 Kornai, *Defitsit*, 474.
37 Galina V., interview.
38 Tatiana G., interview.
39 Liudmila S., interview.
40 Riese, *Russkie Razgovory*, 102.
41 Tamara D., interview.
42 Galina E. (born 1955), interview.
43 There was a similar riddle about trains from Moscow.
44 Vladimir Sh. (born 1955), interview.
45 Galina E., interview.
46 *Blat* is a term for the reciprocal practice of using a network of friends and acquaintances for gaining access to goods and services in short supply, bypassing the established rules.

47 Riese, *Russkie Razgovory*, 106.
48 Maria G. (born 1945), interview.
49 Galina E., interview.
50 Aleksandr M., interview.
51 Liudmila S., interview.
52 The Soviet queues as a social, cultural, and economic phenomenon has been a subject of extensive scientific research. It has been labelled the "inevitable attribute of the Soviet existence" (Osokina, "Proshchalnaia Oda Sovetskoi Ocheredi") and "the focal point of the Soviet culture"; see Nikolaev, "Sovetskaia Ochered."
53 Aleksandr M., interview.
54 Liudmila Z. (born 1940), interview.
55 Alina K., interview.
56 Nikolai Zh. (born 1962), interview.
57 Tamara Sh., interview.
58 Ibid.
59 Aleksandr M., interview.
60 Vladimir Sh., interview.
61 Vladimir T., interview.
62 Gennagy S., interview.
63 Vladimir T., interview.
64 Nikolai Zh., interview.
65 Gennagy S., interview.
66 Anatolii T., interview.
67 A "share" at the collective farm was a strip of a crop field allocated to individuals for cultivation and harvesting in addition to the mandatory amount of work done at the farm. The work was rewarded based on the volume of crop harvested.
68 Vladimir T., interview.
69 Galina D., interview.
70 Maria R. (born 1958), interview.
71 The "cooperative" here means a cooperative apartment. In the Soviet Union, people could either receive an apartment from the state free of charge or build one with their own money through a cooperative. The first kind was free but involved waiting for ten to fifteen years; the second kind meant joining a cooperative building society to acquire accommodation in an apartment building at the construction stage.
72 Olga K., interview.
73 Valentina K., interview.
74 Galina V., interview.
75 Valentina L., interview.

76 Nikolai Zh., interview.
77 Valentina L., interview.
78 Maria R., interview.
79 Most durable consumer goods could not be bought freely but were distributed by means of waiting lists created before the goods were delivered in the retail outlets.
80 Goralik, "Antresoli Pamiati."
81 Liudmila T. (born 1953), interview.
82 Valentina L., interview.
83 Valentina L., interview.
84 Valentina L., interview.
85 Nikolai K., interview.
86 This new kind of entrepreneurship involved travelling abroad to procure goods in short supply and then selling them at a good profit. Because this meant going on frequent trips, these entrepreneurs were called "shuttle-traders" by analogy with the part of a weaver's loom that constantly moved back and forth.
87 Galina V., interview.
88 Nina V., interview.
89 Nadezhda R., interview.
90 Maria R., interview.
91 Tsvetaeva, "Praktiki i Tsennosti v Epokhu Peremen."
92 Gotlib, Zaporozhets, and Khasaev, "Sotsialno-Ekonomicheskaia Adaptatsiia."
93 Quotations here represent characteristic expressions of the day and were present in practically all interviews.
94 The expression "go to the south" was used to refer to going to the seaside resort for a holiday.
95 Liudmila S., interview.
96 Nina V., interview.
97 Portelli, "Smert' Luidzhi Trastulli," 216–18.

Bibliography

Adelaida. Interview by Irina Chikalova. Minsk, Belarus. 18 April 2005.

Adler, Nanci. *Victims of Soviet Terror: The Story of the Memorial Movement*. Westport and London: Greenwood Publishing, 1993.

Agamben, Giorgio. *Homo sacer. Chto Ostaetsia Posle Osventsima: Arkhiv i Svidetel* (*Homo Sacer. Quel che resta di Auschwitz: L'archivio e il testimone*), trans. Olga Dubitskaia, Izabella Levina, and Pavel Sokolov. Moscow: Evropa, 2012.

Agapova, Raisa. Interview by Iulia Ivanchuk. *Finskaia Okkupatsiia Karelii*, ed. Alexey Golubev and Alexandr Osipov. *Ustnaia Istoriia v Karelii*, vol. 3: *Sbornik Nauchnykh Statei i Istochnikov*, 155–9. Petrozavodsk: Petrozavodsk State University Press, 2007.

Aleksandr A. Interview by Andrei Voitiuk. Cheliabinsk, Russia. 13 December 2008.

Aleksandr M. Interview by Irina Makhovskaya. Pruzhany, Brest *oblast*, Belarus. 15 August 2009.

Aleksandrova, Ekaterina. Interview by Yelena Rozhdestvenskaya. Pskov *oblast*. July 2005.

Alina K. Interview by Janina Lavrenko. Gritsovichi, Nesvizh district, Minsk *oblast*, Belarus. 2 August 2009.

Alina-Pisano, Jessica. *The Post-Soviet Potemkin Village: Politics and Property Rights in the Black Earth*. Cambridge: Cambridge University Press, 2008.

Alla K. Interview by Irina Makhovskaya. Pruzhany, Brest *oblast*, Belarus. 12 July 2009.

Allen, Barbara, and William Lynwood Montell. *From Memory to History: Using Oral Sources in Local Historical Research*. Nashville: American Association for State and Local History, 1981.

Alperin, Emil, D. Zhuravlev, and V. Ivashchenko, eds. *My Pobedili Smert: Vospominaniia Kharkovchan-Byvshikh Uznikov Fashistkikh Kontslagerei*. Lviv: Kalvaria, 2005.

"An Oral History of Ukrainian Independence." *Ukrainian Weekly*, 18 August 1996. Accessed 19 June 2011 at http://www.ukrweekly.com/old/archive/1996/339615.shtml.

Anatolii L. Interview by Irina Romanova. Rechen, Luban district, Minsk *oblast*, Belarus. 2 August 2009.

Anatolii T. Interview by Irina Makhovskaya. Pruzhany, Brest *oblast*, Belarus. 22 August 2009.

Andruch, Halyna. Interview by Albert Venger. Village of Zhovtneve, Dnipropetrovsk *oblast*, Ukraine. 23 February 2008.

Ankersmit, Franklin. *Istoriia i Tropologiia. Vzlet i Padenie Metafory*. Trans. M.Kukartseva, E. Kolomoets, and V. Kashaev. Moscow: Progress-Traditsiia, 2003.

Appadurai, Arjun. "Global Ethnoscapes: Notes and Queries for a Transnational Anthropology." In *Recapturing Anthropology: Working in the Present*, ed. Richard Fox, 191–216. Santa Fe: School of American Research Press, 1991.

Aretxaga, Begona. *States of Terror: Begona Aretxaga's Essays*. Reno: Centre for Basque Studies, 2005.

Arkuszewski, Wojciech, Jan Tomasz Lipski, Wojciech Ostrowski, and Andrzej Wielowieyski. "Oaza na Freta: Sekcja Kultury Warszawskiego KIK w Latach Siedemdziesiątych." *Więź* 69 (2006): 69–80.

Ash, Timothy Garton. *History of the Present: Essays, Sketches, and Dispatches from Europe in the 1990s*. New York: Vintage Press, 1999.

Assmann, Jan. *Das kulturelle Gedächtnis. Schrift, Erinnerung und politische Identität in frühen Hochkulturen*. Munich: C.H. Beck, 1992.

Bäckman, Johan. "Fashistskaia Okkupatsiia Sovetskoi Karelii v 1941–1944 gg. v Finskoi Literature 1970–2000 gg." *Sever* 7–8 (2005): 112–19.

Bakhtin, Mikhail. "Forms of Time and of the Chronotope in the Novel." In *The Dialogic Imagination: Four Essays by Mikhail Bakhtin*, ed. Michael Holquist, trans. Caryl Emerson and Michael Holquist, 84–259. Austin: University of Texas Press, 1981.

Baron, Nick. *Soviet Karelia: Politics, Planning, and Terror in Stalin's Russia, 1920–1939*. New York and London: Routledge, 2007.

Barthes, Roland. *Izbrannye raboty. Semiotika: Poetika*. Trans. Georgii Kosikov. Moscow: Progress, 1989.

Baryshnikov, Nikolai. *Mannerheim without the Mask, 1940–1944*. Helsinki: Johan Beckman Institute, 2005.

Bedziura, Yuri. Interview by Oksana Khymovych. Village of Rozvadiv, Mykolaiv district, Lviv *oblast*, Ukraine. 20 July 2008.

Benezer, Gadi. *The Ethiopian Jewish Exodus: Narratives of the Migration Journey to Israel 1977–1985*. London and New York: Routledge, 2002.

Berger, Peter. "Introduction." In *The Desecularization of the World: Resurgent Religion and World Politics*, ed. Peter Berger, 1–18. Grand Rapids: W.B. Eerdmans, 1999.

Bernard, Jessie. "The Good-Provider Role: Its Rise and Fall." In *Men's Lives*, ed. Michael Kimmel and Michael Messner, 611. Boston: Allyn & Bacon, 1989.

Bernecker, Walther, and Sören Brinkmann. *Kampf der Erinnerungen. Der Spanische Bürgerkrieg in Politik und Gesellschaft 1936–2006*. Heidelberg: Graswurzelrevolution, 2006.

Bertaux, Daniel, Anna Rotkirch, and Paul Thompson, eds. *On Living through Soviet Russia*. London: Routledge, 2004.

Bespalaia, Maria. Interview by Irina Chikalova. Minsk, Belarus. 21 January 2005.

Bielak, Jacek. Interview by David Curp. Gdańsk, Poland. 21 June 2010.

Bird, Thomas, and Mieczyslaw Maneli. "The New Turn in Church–State Relations in Poland." *Journal of Church and State* 30 (1982): 29–51.

Bloch, Ernst. *Erbschaft dieser Zeit*. Frankfurt am Main: Suhrkamp, 1962.

Bóg i Ojczyzna (Publikacja dla duchowieństwa). Warsaw, 1984, ix.

Bolin, Krzysztof. Interview by David Curp. Gdańsk, Poland. 16 October 2010.

Bories-Sawala, Helga. *Franzosen im "Reichseinsatz": Deportation, Zwangsarbeit, Alltag – Erfahrungen und Erinnerungen von Kriegsgefangenen und Zivilarbeitern*. Frankfurt am Main: Lang, 1996.

Borisova, Aleksandra, K. Kozak, and H. Stuchinskaia. *Lager Smerti Osventsim: Zhivye Svidetelstva Belarusi*. 2nd ed. Minsk: I.P. Logvinov, 2010.

Borneman, John. *Settling Accounts: Violence, Justice, and Accountability in Postsocialist Europe*. Princeton: Princeton University Press, 1997.

Boruń-Jagodzińska, Katarzyna. Interview by David Curp. Warsaw, Poland. 20 April 2010.

Borysenko, Valentyna. *A Candle in Remembrance: An Oral History of the Ukrainian Genocide of 1932–1933*. New York: Ukrainian National Women's League of America, 2010.

Boyko, Anatolii, and Serhii Plokhii, eds. *Dzherela z Istorii Pivdennoi Ukrainy*, vol. 5, bks. 1 and 2: *Memories and Diaries*. Zaporizhzhia: RU Tandem-U, 2005.

Brier, Robert. "The Roots of the 'Fourth Republic': Solidarity's Cultural Legacy to Polish Politics." *East European Politics and Societies* 23, no. 1 (2009): 63–85.

Broda-Wysocki, Piotr. Interview by David Curp. Warsaw, Poland. 10 April 2010.

Broszat, Martin, Elke Fröhlich, and Anton Grossmann. *Bayern in der NS-Zeit: Soziale Lage und politisches Verhalten der Bevölkerung im Spiegel vertraulicher Berichtem*, 6 volumes. Munich/Vienna, 1977–1983.

Brown, Roger, and James Kulik. "Flashbulb Memories." *Cognition* 5 (1977): 73–99.

Bruner, Jerome. *Acts of Meaning*. Cambridge: Harvard University Press, 1990.

– "The Narrative Construction of Reality." *Critical Inquiry* 18, no. 1 (1991): 1–21.

Brzostek, Błażej, and Joanna Wawrzyniak. "Wiklina: Z Historii Pewnej Warszawskiej Kawiarni Lat Małej Stabilizacji." In *Metamorfozy Społeczne. Badania Nad dziejami Społecznymi XIX i XX Wieku*, vol. 2, ed. Janusz żarnowski, 233–57. Warsaw: Wydawnictwo Neriton, Instytut Historii PAN, 1998.

Budeancă, Cosmin. *Prison Experiences in Communist Romania*, vol. 2. Bucharest: Polirom, 2008.

Butvilo, Andrei. "Formirovaniie Territorii Karelskoi Trudovoi Kommuny kak Politicheskaia Problema." *Rossiiskaia Istoriia* 3 (2009): 169–76.

Cándida-Smith, Richard. "Analytic Strategies for Oral History Interviews." In *Handbook of Interview Research*, ed. Jaber F. Gubrium and James A. Holstein, 711–32. Beverly Hills: Sage Publications, 2001.

Chikalova, Irina, and Natalia Pushkareva. *Women-Scientists in Belarus and Russia in Post-Soviet Period: Comparative Study of Social Identity, 1991–2001*. Moscow and Minsk: Russian Foundation for Humanities, 2004–5, 2006.

Choma-Jusińska, Małgorzata. *środowiska Opozycyjne na Lubelszczyźnie 1975–1980*. Warsaw: IPN, 2009.

Clements, Barbara Evans, Rebecca Friedman, and Dan Healey, eds. *Russian Masculinities in History and Culture*. Houndmills and New York: Palgrave, 2002.

Cornell, Stephan. "That's the Story of Our Life." In *We Are a People: Narrative and Multiplicity in Constructing Ethnic Identity*, ed. Paul Spickard and W.J. Burroughs, 41–53. Philadelphia: Temple University Press, 2000.

Coronil, Fernando, and Julie Skurski. "Introduction: States of Violence and the Violence of States." In *States of Violence*, ed. Fernando Coronil and Julie Skurski, 1–31. Ann Arbor: University of Michigan Press, 2006.

Cruikshank, Julie. *The Social Life of Stories: Narrative and Knowledge in the Yukon Territory*. Lincoln: University of Nebraska Press, 2000.

Csaki, Csaba, Zvi Lerman, and Sergey Sotnikov. *Farm Debt in the CIS: A Multi-Country Study of the Major Causes and Proposed Solutions*. Washington: World Bank, 2001.

Curci, Antonietta, and Tiziana Lanciano. "Features of Autobiographical Memory: Theoretical and Empirical Issues in the Measurement of Flashbulb Memory." *Journal of General Psychology* 136, no. 2 (2009): 129–50.

Dalhouski, Alexander. "Belarusian Forced Labourers: Types and Recruitment." In von Plato, Leh, and Thonfeld, *Hitler's Slaves*, 211–25.

Danilova, Nina. Interview by Yelena Rozhdestvenskaya. Pskov *oblast*, Russia. July 2005.

Dawidowski, Wiesław. Interview by David Curp. Warsaw, Poland. 20 January 2010.

Demoskop Weekly. "Vserossiiskaia perepis naseleniia 2010 g. Naseleniie po natsionalnosti, polu i subiektam Rossiiskoi Federatsii." Accessed 9 January 2012 at http://demoscope.ru/weekly/ssp/rus_etn_10.php?reg=20.

– "Vsesoiuznaia perepis naseleniia 1926 goda. Natsionalnyi sostav naseleniia po regionam RSFSR." Accessed 9 January 2012 at http://demoscope.ru/weekly/ssp/rus_nac_26.php?reg=53.

Denisevich, Nikolai. *V Finskom Kontslagere. Vospominaniia i Razmyshleniia*. Minsk: Istoricheskaia masterskaia v Minske, 2007.

Dobrochna, Kałwa. "*Historia Mówiona w Krajach Postkomunistycznych. Rekonesans*." *Kultura i Historia* 18 (2010). Accessed 21 June 2011 at http://www.kulturaihistoria.umcs.lublin.pl/archives/1887.

Dresse, Gert, and Nikola Langreiter. "Nie Zeit, nie Frei: Arbeit und Freizeit von Wissenschaftlerinnen." *Bewegte Zeiten. Arbeit und Freizeit nach der Moderne*, ed. Sabine Gruber, Klara Löffler, and Klaus Thien, 121–38. Munich: Ed. Sigma, 2002.

Dubin, Boris. "Chto Ostaetsia ot Aushvitsa. Arkhiv i Svidetelstvo." *Polit.ru*. http://www.polit.ru/article/2009/03/26/agamben/.

Dziurok, Adam, ed. *Metody Pracy Operacyjnej Aparatu Bezpieczeństwa Wobec Kościołów i Związków Wyznaniowych 1945–1989*. Warsaw: Instytut Pamięci Narodowej, 2004.

Eberts, Mirella. "The Roman Catholic Church and Democracy in Poland." *Europe-Asia Studies* 50, no. 5 (1998): 817–42.

Elena (social anthropologist). Interview by Natalia Pushkareva, Moscow, Russia. 12 September 2004.

Elnickij, Lev. *Tri Kruga Vospominanii*, vol. 3: *Na Paperti Khrama Nauki*. Moscow: AGRAF, 2013.

Ely, Richard, and Allyssa McCabe. "Gender Differences in Memories for Speech." In *Gender and Memory*, ed. Selma Leyesdorf, Luisa Passerini, and Paul Thompson, 17–31. Oxford: Oxford University Press, 1996.

Engel, Babara Alpern. *Women in Imperial, Soviet, and Post-Soviet Russia*. Washington: American Historical Association, 1999.

"Est Zhenshchiny v Nashei Nauke … Interviu Natalii Deminoi s Pobeditelnitsami Konkursa Zhenshchin-Uchenykh L'Oreal-UNESCO" (There are

Women in Our Science ... Interview by Natalia Demina with the winners of the competition of women-scientists L'Oreal-UNESCO). *Troitskiii Variant*, 17 March 2009.

Evgeny V. Interview by Elena Balyko. Mir, Grodno *oblast*, Belarus. 2 July 2009.

Faina M. Interview by Inna Simonova. Mariina Gorka, Minsk *oblast*, Belarus. 10 August 2009.

Felsen, Doris, and Viviana Frenkel. "The Deportation of the Italians, 1943–1945." In von Plato, Leh, and Thonfeld, *Hitler's Slaves*, 310–23.

Filipowicz, Halina, and Anna Bojarska. "From Communism to Khomeinism: Halina Filipowicz Interviews Anna Bojarska." *Women's Review of Books* 10, nos. 10–11 (1993): 9–10.

Filipkowski, Piotr. "Daz Zentrum KARTA." Presentation at the colloquium "Zwangsarbeit und Oral History," Osteuropa-Institut, Berlin, 7 January 2009.

Firouzbakhch, Homa. "Rewolucja Islamska w Iranie a Rewolucja Solidarności w Polsce." *Studia Socjologiczne* 3, no. 198 (2010): 301–25.

"Fish," anonymous interviewee. Radio reportage by Adam Dąbrowski. Polskie Radio Białystok. 22 January 2007.

Fitzpatrick, Sheila. *Everyday Stalinism: Ordinary Life in Extraordinary Times: Soviet Russia in the 1930s*. New York: Oxford University Press, 1999.

Fitzpatrick, Sheila, Vladimir Kozlov, and Sergei Mironenko, eds. *Sedition: Everyday Resistance in the Soviet Union under Khrushchev and Brezhnev*. New Haven: Yale University Press, 2011.

Fitzpatrick, Sheila, and Carolyn Rasmussen, eds. *Political Tourists: Travelers from Australia to the Soviet Union in the 1920s–1940s*. Carlton: Melbourne University Press, 2008.

Fitzpatrick, Sheila, and Yuri Slezkine, eds. *In the Shadow of Revolution: Life Stories of Russian Women from 1917 to the Second World War*. Princeton: Princeton University Press, 2000.

Foucault, Michel. *Society Must Be Defended: Lectures at the Collège de France, 1975–1976*. New York: St Martin's, 1997.

Frank, Semen. "Smysl Zhizni." In *Smysl Zhizni. Antologiia*, ed. Nikolai Gavriushin, 489–583. Moscow: Izd. Gruppa "Progress-Kultura," 1994.

Frei, Norbert. *Vergangenheitspolitik. Die Anfänge der Bundesrepublik und die NS-Vergangenheit*. Munich: Deutscher Taschenbuch Verlag, 1996.

Frijda, Nico. "Commemorating." In *Collective Memory of Political Events: Social Psychological Perspectives*, ed. James Pennebaker, Dario Paez, and Berhard Rimé, 103–27. Mahwah, NJ: Lawrence Erlbaum, 1997.

Friszke, Andrzej. *PRL wobec Kościoła: Akta 1970–1978*. Warsaw: Instytut Studiów Politycznych PAN, 2010.

– *PRL wobec Kościoła: Akta Urzędu do Spraw Wyznań 1970–1978*. Warsaw: Biblioteka "Więzi," 2010.

Galina D. Interview by Sergei Sakuma. Orsha, Vitebsk *oblast*, Belarus. 12 September 2009.

Galina E. Interview by Inna Simonova. Pukhovichi, Minsk *oblast*, Belarus. 5 July 2009.

Galina K. Interview by Irina Makhovskaya. Pruzhany, Brest *oblast*, Belarus. 15 August 2009.

Galina V. Interview by Irina Makhovskaya. Pruzhany, Brest *oblast*, Belarus. 15 July 2009.

Galina S. Interview by Serhey Sakuma. Orsha, Vitebsk *oblast*, Belarus. 2 July 2009.

Geisler, Irene Elksnis. "From the Voice of the Deported: The Mass Latvian Deportation of June 14, 1941." *Oral History Forum* (D'histoire Orale) 29 (2009): 3–15. Accessed 21 June 2011 at http://www.oralhistoryforum.ca/index.php/ohf/article/view/47/73.

Gennagy S. Interview by Inna Simonova. Mariina Gorka, Minsk *oblast*, Belarus. 18 August 2009.

Gerlach, Christian. *Kalkulierte Morde*. Hamburg: Hamburger Editions, 1999.

Gheith, Jehanne, and Katherine Jolluck. *Gulag Voices: Oral Histories of Soviet Incarceration and Exile*. New York: Palgrave Macmillan, 2011.

Giddens, Anthony. *Modernity and Self-Identity: Self and Society in the Late Modern Age*. Palo Alto: Stanford University Press, 1991.

Giegel, Hans-Joachim. "Strukturmerkmale einer Erfolgskarriere." In *Biographien in Deutschland. Soziologische Rekonstruktionen Gelebter Gesellschaftsgeschichte*, ed. Wolfram Fischer-Rosenthal, Peter Albeit, and Erika Hoerning, 213–31. Opladen: Westdeutscher Verlag, 1995.

Glaser, Barney, and Anselm Strauss. *The Discovery of Grounded Theory: Strategies for Qualitative Research*. Chicago: Aldine, 1967.

Goffman, Erving. *The Presentation of the Self in Everyday Life*. Edinburgh: University of Edinburgh Social Sciences Research Centre, 1958.

– *Forms of Talk*. Philadelphia: University of Pennsylvania Press, 1981.

Golubev, Alexey, and Alexandr Osipov, eds. *Ustnaia Istoriia v Karelii. Sbornik Nauchnykh Statei i Istochnikov*, vol. 4: *Kareliia i Belarus: Povsednevnaia Zhizn i Kulturnye Praktiki Naseleniia v 1930–1950-e gg*. Petrozavodsk: Petrozavodsk State University Press, 2007.

Goralik, Linor. "Antresoli Pamiati: Vospominania o Kostiume 1990 Goda." *NLO* 84 (2007). Accessed 1 December 2009 at http://magazines.russ.ru/nlo/2007/84/go23.html.

Goreva, Alexandra. Interview by Tetiana Pastushenko, Kyiv, Ukraine. 22 December 2005.

Górski, Krzystof. Interview by David Curp. Warsaw, Poland. 16 November 2009.

Gotlib, Anna, Oksana Zaporozhets, and Gabibulla Khasaev. "Sotsialno-Ekonomicheskaia Adaptatsiia v Postsovetskoi Rossii: Publichnye i Privatnye Praktiki." Federalnyi Obozrevatelnyi Portal JeSM. Accessed 17 October 2011 at http://www.ecsocman.edu.ru/data/900/848/1231/006.GOTLIB.pdf.

Grabe, Lindquist. "Wo du Stehst." *Geschichte von Unten. Fragestellungen, Methoden und Projekte Einer Geschichte des Alltags*, ed. Hubert Ch. Ehalt, 295–305. Vienna: H. Böhlau, 1984.

Granet-Abisset, Anne-Marie. "Témoins et Témoignages en Situation Limite." In *La Shoah, Témoignages, Savoirs, Oeuvres*, ed. Anette Wievioka and Claude Mouchard, 189–202. Vincennes: Presses universitaires de Vincennes, 1999.

– "The French Experience: STO, a Memory to Collect, a History to Write." In von Plato, Leh, and Thonfeld, *Hitler's Slaves*, 113–23.

Grele, Ronald. "Movement without Aim: Methodological and Theoretical Problems in Oral History." In *Envelopes of Sound: The Art of Oral History*, by Ronald Grele, Studs Terkel, Jan Vansina, Dennis Tedlock, Saul Benison, and Alice Kessler Harris, 126–55. New York: Praeger, 1991.

– "Oral History as Evidence." In *Handbook of Oral History*, ed. Thomas Charlton, Lois Myers, and Rebecca Sharpless, 43–104. Walnut Creek, CA: AltaMira Press, 2006.

Grinchenko, Gelinada. *Nevyhadane: Usni Istorii Ostarbaiteriv*. Kharkiv: Vydavnychyi dim "Raider," 2004.

– "The Ostarbeiter of Nazi Germany in Soviet and Post-Soviet Ukrainian Historical Memory." *Canadian Slavonic Papers* 54, nos. 3–4 (2012): 401–26.

– "Ostarbeiters del Tercer Reich: Recordar y Olvidar Como Estrategias de Supervivencia." *Historia, Antropología, y Fuentes Orales* 35 (2006): 123–37.

– "The Shaping of Remembrance: Individual, Group, and Collective Patterns of Memory of former Ukrainian Ostarbeiters." In *Beyond Camps and Forced Labour: Current International Research on Survivors of Nazi Persecution*, ed. Johannes-Dieter Steinert and Inge Weber Newth, 496–504. Osnabrück: Secolo Verlag, 2008.

– "Zwangsarbeit im nationalsozialistischen Deutschland im Kontext des lebensgeschichtlichen Interviews einer ehemaligen ukrainischen Ostarbeiterin." In *Erinnerungen nach der Wende: Oral History und (post)sozialistische Gesellschaften*, ed. Julia Obertreis and Anke Stephan, 133–50. Essen: Klartext Verlag, 2009.

– "Prymusova Pratsia u Natsystskii Nimechchyni v Usnykh Istoriiakh Kolyshnikh Ditei-Ostarbaiteriv." In *Visnyk Kharkivs'koho Natsionalnoho Universytetu, Series Istoriia Ukraïny. Ukraiinoznavstvo: Istorychni ta Filosofski Nauky* 12 (2009): 52–74.

– "Prinuditelnyi Trud v Natsistskoi Germanii v Ustnykh Istoriiakh Byvshykh Detei-Ostarbaiterov." In *Vtoraia Mirovaia Voina v Detskikh*

"Ramkakh Pamiati": Sbornik Statei, ed. A. Iu. Rozhkov, 103–46. Krasnodar: Traditsiia, 2010.

– ed. *"Proshu Vas Mene Ne Zabuvaty": Usni Istorii Ukraiinskykh Ostarbaiteriv.* Kharkiv: Pravo, 2009.

Gruner, Petra. "'Nun Dachte ich, Jetzt Fängt's Neu an, Nun Soll's Sozial Werden …' Zur Kritik des Neulehrermythos." *Zeitschrift für Pädagogik* 41, no. 6 (1995): 943–57.

Gubrium, Jaber, and James Holstein. "Narrative Practice and the Coherence of Personal Stories." *Sociological Quarterly* 39, no. 1 (1998): 163–87.

Gudziak, Borys, and Victor Susak. "Becoming a Priest in the Underground: The Clandestine Life of the Ukrainian Greco-Catholic Church." *Journal of Oral History Society* 24, no. 2 (1996): 42–8.

Gusarov, Dmitrii. *Za Chertoi Miloserdiia*. Petrozavodsk: Karelia, 1977.

Halbwachs, Maurice. *On Collective Memory*, ed. and trans. Lewis Coser. Chicago: University of Chicago Press, [1941]1992.

Hammermann, Gabriele. *Gli Internati Military Italiani in Germania 1943–1945.* Bologna: Il Molino, 2004.

Hann, Chris. "Introduction: De-Collectivization and the Moral Economy." In *The Post-Socialist Agrarian Question: Property Relations and the Rural Condition*, ed. Chris Hann, 1–47. Muenster: LIT Verlag, 2003.

Harvey, David. *The Condition of Postmodernity: An Enquiry into the Origins of Cultural Change.* Chichester: Wiley-Blackwell, 1990.

Hasenjürgen, Brigitte. "Winners and Losers. Sozialwissenschaftler Innen an der Hochschule." In *Kategorie. Geschlecht? Empirische Analysen und feministische Theorien (Geschlecht und Gesellschaft)*, ed. Ute Luise Fischer, Mathilde Schmitt, Marita Kampshoff, and Susanne Keil, 41–55. Opladen: VS Verlag für Sozialwissenschaften, 1996.

Helene (historian). Interview by Natalia Pushkareva. Moscow, Russia. 23 December 2004.

Helene (physicist). Interview by Irina Chikalova. Minsk, Belarus. 23 December 2004.

Helene (physicist). Interview by Natalia Pushkareva. Moscow, Russia. 14 January 2005.

Henrietta (physicist). Interview by Irina Chikalova. Minsk, Belarus. 1 April 2005.

Herbert, Ulrich. *Fremdarbeiter. Politik und Praxis des "Ausländer-Einsatzes" in der Kriegswirtschaft des Dritten Reiches.* Berlin-Bonn: Dietz, 1985.

Hillman, James. *Arkhetipicheskaia Psikhologiia.* Trans. Iuri Donets, Valerii Zelenskii, and M. Pazina. Saint Petersburg: BSK, 1996.

– *Istseliaiushchii Vymysel.* Trans. Yuri Donets. Saint Petersburg: BSK, 1997.

Hirsch, Marianne, and Leo Spitzer. "Testimonial Objects: Memory, Gender, and Transmission." *Poetics Today* 27, no. 2 (2006): 353–83.

Hlushchuk, Hanna. Interview by Maria Melenchuk. Village of Bystrychi, Berezne District, Rivne *oblast*, Ukraine. 5 January 2008.

Hoerl, Christoph. "Episodic Memory, Autobiographical Memory, Narrative: On Three Key Notions in Current Approaches to Memory Development." *Philosophical Psychology* 20, no. 5 (2007): 621–40.

Hoffman, Alice. "Reliability and Validity in Oral History." In *Oral History: An Interdisciplinary Anthology*, ed. David Dunaway and Willa Baum, 67–86. Walnut Creek, CA: AltaMira Press, 1984.

Holovyn, Hanna. Interview by Maria Melenchuk. Village of Bystrychi, Berezne district, Rivne *oblast*, Ukraine. 5 January 2008.

Hurkina, Svitlana. "Dvi Doli: Hreko-Katolytske Dukhovenstvo i Radianska Vlada." *Skhid – Zakhid: Istoryko-Kulturolohichnyi Zbirnyk* 11–12 (2008): 265–82.

Ibiblio. Public's Library and Digital Archive. "Agreement for United Nations Relief and Rehabilitation Administration, 9 November 1943." http://www.ibiblio.org/pha/policy/1943/431109a.html.

Igor M. Interview by Irina Makhovskaya. Pruzhany, Brest *oblast*, Belarus. 13 July 2009.

Il'in, Il'ja. "Intertekstualnost.'" In *Sovremennoe Zarubezhnnoe Literaturovedenie (Stran Zapadnoi Evropi I SShA). Kontseptsii, Shkoly, Terminy. Entsiklopedicheskii spravochnik*, ed. Ilia Ilin and Elena Curganova, 320. Moscow: Intrada, 1999.

– *Postmodernizm. Slovar Terminov*. Moscow: Intrada, 2001.

Institute of National Remembrance. "The Act on the Institute of National Remembrance – Commission for the Prosecution of Crimes against the Polish Nation dated 18 December 1998." http://ipn.gov.pl/en/about-the-institute/documents/institute-documents/the-act-on-the-institute-of-national-remembrance.

Institute of National Remembrance. "Act of 18 October 2006 on the Disclosure of Information on Documents of State Security Agencies from the period between the years 1944–1990 and the Content of such Documents." http://ipn.gov.pl/en/about-the-institute/documents/institute-documents/act-on-the-disclosure-of-information.

The Intellectuals and the Communist Regime: The Stories of a Relationship. Bucharest: Polirom, 2009.

Iurchak, Aleksei. "Pozdnii Sotsializm i Poslednee Sovetskoe Pokolenie." *Neprikosnovennyi Zapas* 52, no. 2 (2007): 81–97.

Iusupova, Liudmila. "Voiennoe Detstvo v Pamiati Pokoleniia, Perezhivshego Okkupatsiiu Karelii." In *Voienno-Istoricheskaia Antropologiia. Ezhegodnik 2003/2004*, 345–51. Moscow: ROSSPEN, 2005.

Jakshova, Viola. "Slovak Republic (1939–1945)." In von Plato, Leh, and Thonfeld, *Hitler's Slaves*, 59–70.

James, Daniel. *Dona Maria's Story: Life History, Memory, and Political Identity*. Durham: Duke University Press, 2000.

Jan K. Interview by Marta Kurkowska-Budzan. Kolno, Poland. 28 October 2005.

Jarská, Sarka. "Czechs as Forced and Slave Labourers during the Second World War." In von Plato, Leh, and Thonfeld, *Hitler's Slaves*, 47–58.

Jerzy W. Interview by Jacek Matuszczak and Wojciech Chowaniak. Łomża, Poland. 10 May 2007.

Kalmykova, Yekaterina, and Jerhard Mergentaller. "Narrativ v Psikhoterapii: Rasskazy Patsientov o Lichnoi Zhizni (Chast 2, Teoreticheskaia)." *Psikhologicheskii Zhurnal* 5 (1998): 97–8.

Kangaspuro, Markku. *Neuvosto-Karjalan Taistelu Itsehallinnosta: Nationalismi ja Suomalaiset Punaiset Neuvostoliiton vallankäytössä Vuosina 1920–1939*. Helsinki: SKS, 2000.

Kanyo, Tamás. "Zur Geschichte Deer Oral History in Ungarn." In *Bios. Zeitschrift für Biographieforschung und Oral History* 1 (2004). Cited in Kałwa *Dobrochna, "Historia Mówiona w Krajach Postkomunistycznych. Rekonesans." Kultura i Historia* 18 (2010). Accessed 21 June 2011 at http://www.kulturai-historia.umcs.lublin.pl/archives/1887.

Karelskii Soiuz Byvshikh Maloletnikh Uznikov Fashistskikh Kontslagerei. "Pisma KS BMU Vlastiam i Nekotorye Otvety." Accessed 25 May 2010 at http://www.autistici.org/deti-uzniki/pisma.html.

– "Rezoliutsiia VI Otchetno-Vybornoi Konferentsii Obshchestvennoi Organizatsii "Karelskii Soiuz Byvshikh Maloletnikh Uznikov Fashistskikh Kontslagerei." Accessed 25 May 2010 at http://www.autistici.org/deti-uzniki/konferencia6.html.

– "Sozdanie KSBMU." Accessed 25 May 2010 at http://www.autistici.org/deti-uzniki.

Karner, Stefan, Peter Ruggenthaler, and Barbara Stelzl-Marx, eds. *NS-Zwangsarbeit in der Rüstungsindustrie: Die Lapp-Finze AG in Kalsdorf bei Graz 1939–1945*. Graz: Verein zur Förderung der Forschung von Folgen nach Konflikten und Kriegen, 2004.

Kazimirova, Nina. Interview by Olena Petrova. Village of Zhovten, Shyriaiiv District, Odesa *oblast*. 2 February 2008.

Kemliakova, Valentina. Interview by Alexey Golubev. *Finskaia Okkupatsiia Karelii*, ed. Alexey Golubev and Alexandr Osipov. *Ustnaia Istoriia v Karelii*, vol. 3: *Sbornik Nauchnykh Statei i Istochnikov*, 49–59. Petrozavodsk: Petrozavodsk State University Press, 2007.

Kenney, Padraic. *A Carnival of Revolution: Central Europe 1989*. Princeton: Princeton University Press, 2002.

Khanenko-Friesen, Natalia. *Inshyi Svit abo Etnichnist u Dii: Kanadska Ukrainskist Kintsia 20 Stolittia*. Kyiv: Smoloskyp, 2011.

Kharitonova, Elena. "Perevod Russkoi Lagernoi Leksiki na Angliiskii Iazyk: Semantiko-Stilisticheskie i Lingvokulturologicheskie Aspekty." Moskovskii Gosudarstvennyi Oblastnoi Universitet, Avtoreferaty. http://www.avtoref.mgou.ru/ar/ar139.pdf.

Kobzev, Alexander. "Land Reform in Ukraine: Achievements and Tasks for the Future." Policy Documentation Center. 2004. 3pp. Accessed 14 November 2011, at http://pdc.ceu.hu/archive/00002107.

Kocevar, Monika. "'Mother, Are the Apples at Home Ripe Yet?' Slovenian Forced and Slave Labourers during the Second World War." In von Plato, Leh, and Thonfeld, *Hitler's Slaves*, 138–50.

Kochanova, Antonina. Interview by Irina Osipova. *Finskaia Okkupatsiia Karelii*, ed. Alexey Golubev and Alexandr Osipov. *Ustnaia Istoriia v Karelii*, vol. 3: *Sbornik Nauchnykh Statei i Istochnikov*, 129–33. Petrozavodsk: Petrozavodsk State University Press, 2007.

Kohlt, Martin. "'Von uns Selbst Schweigen Wir.' Wissenschaftsgeschichte aus Lebensgeschichte." In *Geschichte und Soziologie. Studien zur Kognitiven, Sozialen und Historischen Identität einer Disziplin*, ed. Wolf Lepenies, 428–65. Frankfurt: A.M., 1981.

Korablev, Nikolai, et al., eds. *Istoriia Karelii s Drevneishikh Vremen do Nashikh Dnei*. Petrozavodsk: Periodika, 2001.

Kornai, Janosh. *Defitsit*. Moscow: Nauka, 1990.

Kőrösi, Zsuzsanna, and Adrienne Molnár. *"Carrying a Secret in My Heart …": Children of the Victims of the Reprisal after the Hungarian Revolution in 1956. An Oral History*. Budapest and New York: Central European University Press, 2003.

Koshkarova, Tamara. Interview by Alexey Golubev. *Finskaia Okkupatsiia Karelii*, ed. Alexey Golubev and Alexandr Osipov. *Ustnaia Istoriia v Karelii*, vol. 3: *Sbornik Nauchnykh Statei i Istochnikov*, 176–9. Petrozavodsk: Petrozavodsk State University Press, 2007.

Kosiński, Krzysztof. *Nastolatki '81: świadomość Młodzieży w Epoce "Solidarności."* Warsaw: Wydawnictwo Trio, 2002.

– *Historia Pijaństwa w Czasach PRL. Polityka, Obyczaje, Szara Strefa, Patologie*. Warsaw: Wydawn, Neriton, 2008.

Kostin, Ivan, ed. *Sudba. Sbornik Vospominanii Byvshikh Maloletnikh Uznikov Fashistskikh Lagerei*. Petrozavodsk: Karelia, 1999.

Kostin, Ivan, and Klavdiia Niuppieva. "Nas Zharili v Bane i Travili Izvestiu." *Kurier Karelii*, 12 February 2005.

– eds. *Plenennoe Detstvo: Sbornik Vospominanii Byvshikh Maloletnikh Uznikov*. Petrozavodsk: Karelia, 2005.

Kovacik, Karen. Interview by David Curp. Warsaw, Poland. 21 October 2009.

Kowal, Paweł. "Dlaczego Doszło do Okrągłego Stołu? Przyczyny Zmian Politycznych w Polsce w Latach 1989–1990 w Opiniach Polityków, Aktywnych Uczestników Wydarzeń Tego Okresu." In *Komunizm. Ideologia, System, Ludzie*, ed. Tomasz Szarota, 156–73. Warsaw: Wydawnictwo Neriton, Instytut Historii PAN, 2001.

Kozak, K., and V. Balakireva, eds. *Pravedniki Narodov Mira: Zhivye Svidetelstva Belarusi*. Minsk: I.P. Logvinov, 2009.

Krawchenko, Bohdan. "Soviet Ukraine under Nazi Occupation, 1941–1944." In *Ukraine during World War II: History and Its Aftermath*, ed. Yury Boshuk, 15–38. Edmonton: Canadian Institute of Ukrainian Studies, 1986.

Krawczak, Tadeusz. "Władze PRL wobec Kościoła Rzymskokatolickiego w Stanie Wojennym." In *Kościół i Społeczeństwo wobec Stanu Wojennego* Wiesław, ed. Jan Wysocki, 71–96. Warsaw: Oficyna Wydawnicza RYTM, 2004.

Kristeva, Julia. "Bakhtine, le Mot, le dialogue et le roman." *Critique* 239 (1967): 438–65.

Kriukova, Raissa. Interview by Yelena Rozhdestvenskaya. Pskov *oblast*, Russia. July 2005.

Krylova, Anna. *Soviet Women in Combat: A History of Violence on the Eastern Front*. Cambridge: Cambridge University Press, 2010.

Kubik, Jan. *The Power of Symbols against the Symbols of Power: The Rise of Solidarity and the Fall of State Socialism in Poland*. University Park: Pennsylvania State University Press, 1994.

Kuhn, Annette. *Family Secrets: Acts of Memory and Imagination*. London and New York: Verso, 1995.

Kühnel, Karsten, and Karsten Sydow, eds. "Bibliographie zur Zwangsarbeit im NS-Staat." Das Bundesarchiv, http://www.bundesarchiv.de/zwangsarbeit/literatur/Bibliographie_Zwangsarbeit/index.htm.

Kułak, Jerzy. *Rozstrzelany Oddział. Monografia 3 Wileńskiej Brygady NZW – Białostocczyzna 1945–1946*. Białystok: Jerzy Kułak, 2007.

Kułak, Jerzy, and Krzysztof Sychowicz. *Podziemie Niepodległościowe w Województwie Białostockim w Latach 1944–1956*. Białystok: Instytut Pamięci Narodowej, 2001.

Kulińska, Lucyna. *Narodowcy. Z Dziejów Obozu Narodowego w Polsce w Latach 1944–1947*. Warsaw/Kraków: Wydawnictwo Naukowe PWN, 1999.

Kurkowska-Budzan, Marta. *Antykomunistyczne Podziemie Zbrojne na Białostocczyźnie. Analiza Współczesnej Symbolizacji Przeszłości*. Kraków: Historia Iagiellonica, 2009.

Kurkowska-Budzan, Marta, and Krzysztof Zamorski, eds. *Oral History: The Challenges of the Dialogue*. Amsterdam and Filadelphia: John Benjamins, 2009.

Kuta, Cecylia. *"Działacze" i "Pismaki:" Aparat Bezpieczeństwa wobec Katolików świeckich w Krakowie w Latach 1957–1989*. Kraków: Instytut Pamięci Narodowej, 2009.

Kuznetsov, Anatolii. *Babii Yar: Roman-Dokument*. Moscow: Molodaia Gvardiia, 1967.

Kuznetsov, Sergei. "Uzniki Biurokratisma." *Argumenty i Fakty Karelia*, 25 October 2006.

Łabuszewski, Tomasz, and Kazimierz Krajewski. *Od "Łupaszki" do "Młota" 1944–1949. Materiały źródłowe do Dziejów V i VI Brygady Wileńskiej*. Warsaw: Oficyna Wydawnicza "Volumen," 1994.

Laine, Antti. *Suur-Suomen Kahdet Kasvot. Itä-Karjalan Siviiliväestön Asema Suomalaisessa Miehityshallinnossa 1941–1944*. Helsinki: Otava, 1982.

Langer, Lawrence. "Hearing the Holocaust." *Poetics Today* 27, no. 2 (2006): 297–309.

Larisa A. Interview by Irina Romanova. Chervonoe, Zhitkovichi district, Gomel *oblast*, Belarus. 8 August 2009.

Lass, Andrew. "From Memory to History: The Events of November 17 Dismembered." In *Memory, History, and Opposition*, ed. Rubie Watson, 87–104. Santa Fe: School of American Research Press, 1994.

Lerman, Zvi, David Sedik, Nikolai Pugachov, and Aleksandr Goncharuk. *Rethinking Agricultural Reform in Ukraine*. Halle (Saale): IAMO, 2007.

Levi, Primo. *Kanuvshie i Spasennye (I sommersi e i salvati)*, trans. Elena Dmitrieva. Moscow: Novoe izdatelstvo, 2010.

Leviatin, David. "Listening to the New World: Voices from the Velvet Revolution." *Oral History Review* 1 (1993): 9–22.

Liulkina, Ekaterina. *Voina i Ukradennye Gody: Zhivye Svidetelstva Ostarbaiterov Belarusi*. 2nd ed. Minsk: I.P. Logvinov, 2010.

Long, Michael. *Making History: Czech Voices of Dissent and the Revolution of 1989*. Lanham: Rowman and Littlefield, 2005.

Loskutova, Marina, ed. *Pamiat o Blokade: Svidetelstva Ochevidtsev i Istoricheskoe Soznanie Obshchestva*. Moscow: Novoe izdatelstvo, 2006.

– *Ustnaia Istoriia. Metodicheskie Rekomendatsii po Provedeniiu Issledovaniia*. Saint Petersburg: Evropeiskii dom, 2002.

Lucjan Z. Interview by Marta Kurkowska-Budzan. Zanklewo, Poland. 23 September 2000.

Liudmila P. Interview by Janina Lavrenko. Gritsovichi, Nesvizh district, Minsk *oblast*, Belarus. 26 September 2009.

Liudmila S. Interview by Irina Makhovskaya. Pruzhany, Brest *oblast*, Belarus. 2 August 2009.

Liudmila T. Interview by Irina Romanova. Luban, Minsk *oblast*, Belarus. 28 August 2009.

Liudmila V. Interview by Elena Pastukhova. Cheliabinsk, Russia. 25 October 2008.

Liudmila Z. Interview by Irina Makhovskaya. Pruzhany, Brest *oblast*, Belarus. 9 September 2009.

Lukianov, Vasilii. *Tragicheskoie Zaonezhie*. Petrozavodsk: Karelia, 2004.

Luleva, Ana. "Forced Labour in Bulgaria, 1941–1944: Tracing the Memories." In von Plato, Leh, and Thonfeld, *Hitler's Slaves*, 188–98.

Lytvyn, Volodymyr, ed. *Istoriia Ukraiinskoho Selianstva. Narysy v 2-kh Tomakh*. Kyiv: Naukova Dumka, 2006.

Lyman, Ihor, and Viktoriia Konstantinova, comp. *Usna Istoriia Holodomoru 1932–1933 Rokiv u Pivnichnomu Pryazovii: Berdianskii Vymir*. Zaporizhzhia: A.A. Tandem, 2009.

Mace, James, and Leonid Heretz, eds. *Oral History Project of the Commission on the Ukraine Famine*. Washington: Superintendant of of Documents, US GPO, 1990.

Maksimova, Taisiia. Interview by Alexey Golubev. *Finskaia Okkupatsiia Karelii*, ed. Alexey Golubev and Alexandr Osipov. *Ustnaia Istoriia v Karelii*, vol. 3: *Sbornik Nauchnykh Statei i Istochnikov*, 75–82. Petrozavodsk: Petrozavodsk State University Press, 2007.

Makurov, Vasilii. *Voiennaia Letopis Karelii 1941–1945*. Petrozavodsk: Rossiiskaia Akademiia Nauk, Karelskii Nauchnyi Tsentr, Institut Iazyka, Literatury i Istorii. 1999.

Malinowski, Krzysztof. *Polityka Republiki Federalnej Niemiec wobec Polski w Latach 1982–1992*. Poznań: Instytut Zachodni, 1997.

Malynovska, Olena. "International Migration in Contemporary Ukraine: Trends and Policy." *Global Migration Perspectives* 4 (2004): 28.

Malysheva, Maria, and Daniel Bertaux. "The Socialist Experiences of a Country Woman in Russia." In *Gender and Memory*, ed. Selma Leydesdorff, Luisa Passerini, and Paul Thompson, 31–42. Oxford: Oxford University Press, 1996.

Maniewska, Katasrzyna. *Kościół katolicki w Bydgoszczy. Wobec Prób Laicyzacji i Dezintegracji Społeczeństwa w Okresie Rządów Edwarda Gierka*. Warsaw: Instytut Historii PAN, 2007.

Marek, Łucja. *Kler to Nasz Wróg. Polityka Władz Państwowych wobec Kościoła Katolickiego na Terenie Województwa Katowickiego w Latach 1956–1970*. Katowice: IPN, 2009.

Margarita E. Interview by Salavat Bayazirov. Cheliabinsk, Russia. 14 April 2005.

Maria (geographer). Interview by Natalia Pushkareva. Moscow, Russia. 22 September 2010.

Maria (oncologist). Interview by Natalia Pushkareva. Moscow, Russia. 28 February 2005.

Maria (philosopher). Interview by Natalia Pushkareva. Moscow, Russia. 28 February 2005.

Maria. Interview by Salavat Bayazitov. Cheliabinsk, Russia. 25 April 2005.

Maria G. Interview by Inna Simonova. Mir, Grodno *oblast*, Belarus. 6 August 2009.

Maria R. Interview by Irina Makhovskaya. Pruzhany, Brest *oblast*, Belarus. 1 July 2009.

Marina (physical anthropologist). Interview by Natalia Pushkareva. Moscow. 28 November 2004.

Marusia (astronomer). Interview by Irina Chikalova. Minsk, Belarus. 6 June 2006.

Mashezerskii, Viktor, ed. *Ocherki Istorii Karelii*, vol. 2. Petrozavodsk: Karel. kn. izd., 1964.

Mashin, Vladimir. "Tiazhelyi Plen Vospominanii." *Severnyi Kurier*, 27 January 2005.

Matyjaszek, Leszek and Roman Kaniowski. Personal communication with Anna Witeska-Młynarczyk. Roztok, Marianowice district, Poland. 11 May 2007.

Mead, Christian. "Narrativität. Geschichte und die Sorgen des Historikers." In *Geschichte – Ereignis und Erzählung*, ed. Reinhart Koselleck and Wolf-Dieter Stempel, 571–85. Munich: Poetik und Hermeneutik, 1973.

Mead, George. *The Philosophy of the Act*. Chicago: University of Chicago Press, 1972.

Meshcherkina, Elena. "Struktura Zhenskoi Biografii v Otlichie ot Muzhskoi." In *Ustnaia Istoria, Biografiia i Zhenskii Vzgliad*, ed. Elena Meshcherkina, 221–53. Moscow: Nevskii Prostor, 2004.

– "Vvedenie v Ontologiiu Muzhskoi Zhizni." *Sudby Liudei. Rossiia XX Vek. Biografii Semei kak Obekt Sociologicheskogo Issledovaniia. Sociologiia, Kulturologiia, Istoriia Byta*, ed. V. Semenova and K. Foteeva, 298–325. Moscow: Institute of Sociology RAS, 1996.

Messana, Paola. *Soviet Communal Living: An Oral History of the Kommunalka*. New York: Palgrave Macmillan, 2011.

Michnik, Adam. *The Church and the Left*. Trans. David Ost. Chicago: University of Chicago Press, 1993.

Mikhailova, Yevgeniia. Interview by Yelena Rozhdestvenskaya. Pskov *oblast*, Russia. July 2005.

Milena (born 1955, oncologist). Interview by Irina Chikalova. Minsk, Belarus. 28 February 2005.

Mirosława Z. Interview by Marta Kurkowska-Budzan. Zanklewo, Poland. 10 September 2005.

Möding, Nori, and Alexander von Plato. "Nachkriegspublizisten. Eine erfahrungsgeschichtliche Untersuchung." In *Biographisches Wissen. Beiträge zu*

Einer Theorie Lebensgeschichtlicher Erfahrung, ed. Peter Alheit and Erika Hoerning, 38–69. Frankfurt: Campus, 1989.

Morozov, Konstantin. *Kareliia v Gody Velikoi Otechestvennoi Voiny (1941–1945)*. Petrozavodsk: Karelia, 1983.

Morris, Pam, ed. *The Bakhtin Reader: Selected Writings of Bakhtin, Medvedev, Voloshinov*. London: Arnold, 1994.

Mudrik, Anatolii. *Obshchenie Kak Faktor Vospitaniia Shkolnikov*. Moscow: Prosveshchenie, 1984.

Mülle, Albert. "Alte Herren, and Alte Meister: 'Ego-Histoire' der Österreichischen Geschichtswissenschaft. Eine Quellenkunde." *Österreichische Zeitschrift für Geschichtswissenschaften* 4 (1993): 120–33.

Muravieva, Marianna. "My Govorim 'Gendernye Issledovaniia,' Podrazumevaem ..." *Gendernye Issledovaniia* 13 (2005): 260.

Mytsyk, Yurii, comp. *Ukraiinskyi Kholokost 1932–1933: Svidchennia Tykh, Khto Vyzhyv*, vols. 1–7. Kyiv: Publishing House "Kyievo-Mohylianska Akademiia," 2003–10.

Nadezhda R. Interview by Irina Makhovskaya. Pruzhany, Brest *oblast*, Belarus. 29 August 2009.

Nahaiko, Taras, comp. *Dzherela Pamiati: Istoryko-Kraieznavchyi Almanakh*, vol. 1: *Narodzhennia Dlia Vyprobuvan*. Ternopil: Aston, 2007.

– comp. *Dzherela Pamiati: Istoryko-Kraieznavchyi Almanakh*, vol. 2: *Ostarbaitery: Zhyva Pamiat—Zhyvyi Bil*. Pereiaslav-Khmelnytskyi: Aston, 2007.

Narskii, Igor. "V 'Imperii' i v 'Natsii' Pomnit Chelovek: Pamiat kak Sotsialnyi Fenomen." *Ab Imperio* 1 (2004): 85–8.

Natalia (historian). Interview by Natalia Pushkareva. Moscow. 1 June 2005.

Natalia (historian). Interview by Natalia Pushkareva. Moscow. 1 September 2005.

Natalia G. Interview by Marta Kurkowska-Budzan. Łomża, Poland. 20–2 September 2000.

Nazarenko, Ivan, ed. *Ukrainskaia SSR v Velikoi Otechestvennoi Voine Sovetskogo Soiuza 1941–1945 godov*, vol. 3: *Sovetskaia Ukraina v Zavershaiushchii Period Otechestvennoi Voiny (1944–1945gg)*. Kiev: Politicheskaia Literatura, 1975.

Nechemias, Carol, and Kathleen Kuehnast, eds. *Post-Soviet Women Encountering Transition: Nation Building, Economic Survival, and Civic Activism*. Washington and Baltimore: Woodrow Wilson Center Press and Johns Hopkins University Press, 2004.

Neumann, Thomas. "Die DDR: Ein Land Tausender Guter Lehrer? Erfahrungen von Pädagogen im Schulsystem der DDR." In *Erfahrungsgeschichte der DDR*, ed. Alexander von Plato and Almut Leh, 117–34. Studienbrief der Fernuniversität Hagen, 2005.

Niethammer, Lutz. Die Jahre Weiß Man Nicht, Wo Man die Heute Hinsetzen Soll. Faschismus-Erfahrungen im Ruhrgebiet. Berlin: Dietz, 1983.

– "Von der Zwangsarbeit im Dritten Reich zur Stiftung 'Erinnerung, Verantwortung und Zukunft.'" In *"Gemeinsame Verantwortung und moralische Pflicht": Abschlussbericht zu den Auszahlungsprogrammen der Stiftung "Erinnerung, Verantwortung und Zukunft"*, ed. Michael Jansen and Günter Saathoff, 13–84. Göttingen: Wallstein, 2007.

Niethammer, Lutz, and Alexander von Plato, *Lebensgeschichte und Sozialkultur im Ruhrgebiet: 1930–1960.* Bonn: Dietz, J. H. W., 1983–1985.

Niinistö, Jussi. *Heimosotien Historia 1918–1922.* Helsinki: SKS, 2005.

Nikolaev, Vladimir. "Sovetskaia Ochered: Proshloe kak Nastoiashchee." *Neprikosnovennyi Zapas* 43, no. 5 (2005). Accessed 7 December 2009 at http://magazines.russ.ru/nz/2005/43/oso10-pr.html.

Nikolai K. Interview by Inna Simonova. Mariina Gorka, Minsk *oblast*, Belarus. 25 September 2009.

Nikolai Zh. Interview by Irina Romanova. Zakalnoe, Luban district, Minsk *oblast*, Belarus. 12 July 2009.

Nina K. Interview by Inna Simonova. Mariina Gorka, Minsk *oblast*, Belarus. 9 August 2009.

Nina T. Interview by Irina Romanova. Zakalnoe, Luban district, Minsk *oblast*, Belarus. 10 August 2009.

Nina V. Interview by Irina Makhovskaya. Pruzhany, Brest *oblast*, Belarus. 2 July 2009.

Noll, William. *Transformation of Civil Society: An Oral History of Ukrainian Peasant Culture of the 1920–1930.* Kyiv: Rodovid, 1999.

Nora, Pierre. "Between Memory and History: Les Lieux de Mémoire." *Representations* 26 (1989): 7–25.

Nowak, Jerzy Robert. "Kościół jako Azyl dla Lewicy Laickiej." In *Kościół i Społeczeństwo Wobec Stanu Wojennego*, ed. Wiesław Jan Wysock, 526. Warsaw: Rytm, 2004.

Nurkova, Veronika. "Avtobiograficheskaia Pamiat (Struktura, Funktsii, Mekhanizmy)." PhD diss., University of Moscow, 1998.

– *Svershennoe Prodolzhaetsia: Psikhologiia Avtobiograficheskoi Pamiati Lichnosti.* Moscow: Izd-vo URAO, 2000.

Nurkova, Veronika, and Galina Mosolova. "Kharakteristiki Vospominanii o Detstve i Psikhologicheskii Oblik Vzroslogo." *Psikhologicheskaia Nauka I Obrazovanie* 4 (2009): 1–16. *PSEYDO.ru.* http://psyedu.ru.

Obertreis, Julia, and Anke Stephan, eds. *Erinnerungen nach der Wende: Oral History und (Post)Sozialistische Gesellschaften / Remembering after the Fall of Communism: Oral History and (Post-)Socialist Societies.* Essen: Klartext, 2009.

Oleksashenko, Vira. Interview by Natalia Sherstiuk. Town of Semenivka, Semenivskyi District, Poltava *oblast*. 12 January 2008.

Olga (geographer). Interview by Natalia Pushkareva. Moscow. 8 January 2005.

Olga (physicist). Interview by Natalia Pushkareva, Moscow. 14 January 2005.

Olga K. Interview by Sergej Sakuma. Orsha, Vitebskaya *oblast*, Belarus. 13 September 2009.

Ortner, Sherry. *Making Gender: The Politics and Erotics of Culture*. Boston: Beacon Press, 1996.

Osa, Maryjane. "Creating Solidarity: The Religious Foundations of the Polish Social Movement." *East European Politics and Societies* 11, no. 2 (Spring 1997): 339–65.

Osipova, Klavdiia. Interview by Irina Osipova. *Finskaia Okkupatsiia Karelii*, ed. Alexey Golubev and Aleksandr Osipov. *Ustnaia Istoriia v Karelii*, vol. 3: *Sbornik Nauchnykh Statei i Istochnikov*, 137–149. Petrozavodsk: Petrozavodsk State University Press, 2007.

Osokina, Yelena. "Proshchalnaia Oda Sovetskoi Ocheredi." *Neprikosnovennyi Zapas* 43, no. 5 (2005). Accessed 7 December 2009 at http://magazines.russ.ru/nz/2005/43/oso10-pr.html.

Ostarbeiter: Weißrussische Zwangsarbeiter in Österreich. Graz: Ludwig-Boltzmann-Inst. für Kriegsfolgen-Forschung, 2003.

Osterloh, Jörg. "Die Lebensbedingungen und der Arbeitseinsatz von Kriegsgefangenen im 'Dritten Reich' und in der Sowjetunion." In *Zwangsarbeit im Europa des 20. Jahrhunderts. Bewältigung und Vergleichende Aspekte*, ed. Hans-Christoph Seidel and Klaus Tenfelde, 155–86. Essen: Klartext Verlag, 2007.

Paczkowski, Andrzej. "Aparat Bezpieczeństwa w Walce z Podziemiem w Polsce w Latach 1944–1956. Struktury Organizacyjne i Kierunki Działań." In *Aparat Represji a Opór Społeczeństwa wobec Systemu Komunistycznego w Polsce i na Litwie w Latach 1944–1956*, ed. Piotra Niwiński, 69–76. Warsaw: Instytut Pamięci Narodowej, 2005.

– *Pół Wieku Dziejów Polski, 1939–1989*. Warsaw: Wydawnictwo Naukowe PWN, 1996.

Pawlicka, Katarzyna. *Polityka Władz Wobec Kościoła Katolickiego (Grudzień 1970–Październik 1978)*. Warsaw: Wydawnictwo Trio, 2004.

Penter, Tanja. "*Zwangsarbeit im Donbass unter stalinistischer und nationalsozialistischer Herrschaft, 1929–1953*." In *Zwangsarbeit im Europa des 20. Jahrhunderts. Bewältigung und vergleichende Aspekte*, ed. Hans-Christoph Seidel and Klaus Tenfelde, 227–52. Essen: Klartext Verlag, 2007.

Perks, Robert, and Alistair Thomson. "Advocacy and Empowerment: An Introduction." In *Oral History Reader*, ed. Perks and Thomson, 183–89. New York: Routledge, 2003.

Perz, Bertrand. "Labour and Extermination of the Workers Chamber." Presentation at the Holocaust Studies Congress, Vienna, 27 July 2007.
Pető, Andrea. *Hungarian Women in Politics 1945–1951*. Boulder: East European Monographs, 2003.
– *To Look at Life through Women's Eyes: Women's Oral Histories from the Former Soviet Union*. New York: Open Society Institute, 2003.
Peto, Andrea, comp. *Zhenskaia Usnaia Istoriia: Gendernye Issledovaniia*, vol. 1. Bishkek: Tsentr Izdatelskogo razvitia, 2004.
Piege-Gro, Nathalie. *Vvedenie v Teoriiu Intertekstualnosti*. Trans. Georgij Kosikov. Moscow: Izdatelstvo LKI, 2008.
"Polacy, Niemcy a Solidarnośc – Dyskusja." *Biuletyn Instytutu Pamięci Narodowej* 7–8 (2005): 4–17.
Poleszak, Sławomir. *Podziemie Antykomunistyczne w Łomżyńskiem i Grajewskiem (1944–1957)*. Warsaw: Oficyna Wydawnicza "Volumen," 2004.
Poleszak, Sławomir, and Rafał Wnuk. "Zarys Dziejów Polskiego Podziemia Niepodległościowego 1944–1956." In *Atlas Polskiego Podziemia Niepodległościowego 1944–1956*, ed. Rafał Wnuk, Sławomir Poleszak, Agnieszka Jaczyńska, and Magdalena śladecka, XXII–XXXIV. Warsaw / Lublin: Instytut Pamięci Narodowej, 2007.
Polian, Pavel. "Die Erinnerungen an die Deportationen während der Deutschen Besatzung in der Sowjetunion." In *Zwangsarbeit im Europa des 20. Jahrhunderts. Bewältigung und vergleichende Aspekte*, ed. Hans-Christoph Seidel and Klaus Tenfelde, 59–74. Essen: Klartext Verlagsges, 2007.
– "'Ne-pe-re-no-si-mo!' Malenkie Ostarbaitery – Ugnannye Deti." In *Na Zadvorkakh Pobedy*, by Roza Soloukhina-Zasedateleva, and *Malenkii Ostarbeiter*, by Nikolai Karpov, ed. Pavel Polian and Nikolai Pobol, 272. Moscow: Rossiiskaia politicheskaia entsiklopediia, 2008.
– *Zhertvy Dvukh Diktatur: Zhizn, Trud, Unizhenie i Smert Sovetskikh Voennoplennykh i Ostarbaiterov na Chuzhbine i na Rodine*. Moscow: ROSSPEN, 2002.
Polischuk, Tamara, comp. *"Stolytsia Vidchaiu": Holodomor 1932–1933 na Kharkivshchyni Vustamy Ochevydtsiv. Svidchennia, Kommentari*. Kharkiv / New York / Lviv: Berezil, 2006.
Popa, Maria Raluca. "Understanding the Urban Past: The Transformation of Bucharest in the late Socialist Period." In *Testimonies of the City: Identity, Community, and Change in a Contemporary Urban World*, ed. Richard Rodger and Joanna Herbert, 159–86. Aldershot and Burlington: Ashgate, 2007.
Portelli, Alessandro. *The Battle of Valle Giulia: Oral History and Art of Dialogue*. Madison: University of Wisconsin Press, 1997.

– *The Death of Luigi Trastulli and Other Stories: Form and Meaning in Oral History.* Albany: SUNY Press, 1990.

– "Oral History as Genre." In *Narrative and Genre*, ed. Mary Chamberlain and Paul Thompson, 23–45. London and New York: Routledge, 1998.

– *The Order Has Been Carried Out: History, Memory, and Meaning of a Nazi Massacre in Rome.* New York: Palgrave Macmillan, 2003.

– *L'ordine è Già Stato Eseguito. Roma, le Fosse Ardeatine, la Memoria.* Rome: Donzelli Editore, 2001.

– Presentation at the Oral History Association Annual Meeting. Pittsburgh, 15–19 October 2008.

– "Smert Luidzhi Trastulli: Pamiat i Sobytie." In *Khrestomatiia po Ustnoi Istorii*, ed. and trans. Marina Loskutova. Saint Petersburg: Izd-vo Evrop. un-ta v S.-Peterburge.

– Personal communication with Marta Kurkowska-Budzan. In *Historia mówiona. Elementarz*, ed. Andrzej Drobik, Marta Kurkowska-Budzan, Ewelina Szpak, Marcin Jarząbek, and Marcin Stasiak, 21. Warsaw: Narodowe Centrum Kultury–Stowarzyszenie "Artefakty," 2008.

Prybytkova, Iryna. "Metamorfozy Kolhospnoho Selianstva" (2005). Accessed 30 July 2015 at http://i-soc.com.ua/institute/metamorfoz.pdf.

Pushkareva, Natalia. "Feministskii Vyzov Noveishei Etnologii i Antropologii." *Etnograficheskoe Obozrenie* 4 (2004): 39–51.

Raleigh, Donald. *Soviet Baby Boomers: An Oral History of Russia's Cold War Generation.* Oxford and New York: Oxford University Press, 2011.

Rathkolb, Oliver, Karl Fallend, and Christian Gonsa. *NS-Zwangsarbeit: der Standort Linz der Reichswerke Hermann-Göring-AG Berlin, 1938–1945.* Vienna: Böhlau, 2001.

Reznikova, Anna. "Presenting Life in Captivity: Oral Testimonies of Former Forced and Slave Labourers from St Petersburg and the Russian Northwest." In von Plato, Leh, and Thonfeld, *Hitler's Slaves*, 286–95.

Ries, Nancy. *Russian Talk: Culture and Conversation during Perestroyka.* Ithaca: Cornell University Press, 1997.

Riese, Nancy. *Russkie Razgovory: Kultura i Rechevaia Povsednevnovst Epokhi Perestroiki*, trans. Viktoriia Gulida and Nataliia Kulakova. Moscow: Novoe literaturnoe ovozrenie, 2005.

Ris, Nensi. "'Profil Burzhuaznosti': Novaia Elita o Sebe." *Semeinye Uzy. Modeli Dlia Sborki. Sbornik Statei*, ed. Sergei Ushakin, 392–419. Moscow: Novoe literaturnoe obozrenie, 2004.

Rogozina, Taisia. Interview by Irina Osipova. *Finskaia Okkupatsiia Karelii*, ed. Alexey Golubev and Alexandr Osipov. *Ustnaia Istoriia v Karelii*, vol. 3:

Sbornik Nauchnykh Statei i Istochnikov, 134–6. Petrozavodsk: Petrozavodsk State University Press, 2007.

Rosaldo, Michelle. "The Use and Abuse of Anthropology: Reflections on Feminism and Cross-Cultural Understanding." *Signs* 5, no. 3 (1980): 389–417.

Rosenthal, Gabriele. "Biographical Research." In *Qualitative Research Practice*, ed. Clive Seale, Giampietro Gobo, Jaber Gubrium, and David Silverman, 48–64. London and Thousand Oaks, CA: Sage, 2004.

– *Erlebte und Erzaehlte Geschichte. Gestalt und Struktur Biographischer Selbstbeschreibungen*. Frankfurt am Main: Campus Verlag, 1995.

– "Reconstruction of Life Stories." In *The Narrative Study of Lives*, ed. Ruthellen Josselson and Amia Lieblich, 59–91. Newbury Park, CA: Sage, 1993.

– "Reconstruction of Life Stories." *Narrative Study of Lives* 1, no. 1 (1993): 59–91.

Roszkowski, Wojciech. *Najnowsza Historia Polski 1980–2002*. Warsaw: Świat Książki, 2003.

Rozhdestvenskaya, Elena. "Narrativnaia Identichnost Kak Produkt Avtobiograficheskogo Rasskaza v Interviu." *Sotsiologiia: Metodologiia, Metody, Matematicheskoe Modelirovanie* 30 (2010): 5–26.

Rud, Mykola. Interview by Albert Venger. Village of Zhovtneve, Sofiivka district, Dnipropetrovsk *oblast*, Ukraine. 28 February 2008.

Rudnev, Yevgenii. Interview by Tetiana Pastushenko. Kyiv, Ukraine. 22 April 2005.

– "Plenennoe Detstvo: Vospominaniia Byvshego Ostarbaitera." *Kievskii Telegraf*, 13 April–13 May 2004.

Rüsen, Jörn. "Krizis, Travma i Identichnost." In *"Tsep Vremen": Problemy Istoricheskogo Soznaniia*, ed. Lorina Repin, 38–62. Moscow: Institut vseobshhej istorii RAN, 2005.

– "Utrachivaia Posledovatelnost Istorii (Nekotorye Aspekty Istoricheskoi Nauki na Perekrestke Modernizma i Diskussii o Pamiati)." *Dialog so Vremenem. Almanakh Intellektualnoi Istorii* 7 (2001): 8–26.

Savranskaya, Svetlana, Thomas Blantion, and Vladislav Zubok, eds. *Masterpieces of History: The Peaceful End of the Cold War in Europe, 1989*. Budapest: Central European Press, 2010.

Scherbakova, Irina. "The Gulag in Memory." In *Oral History Reader*, ed. Robert Perks and Alistair Thomson, 235–46. New York: Routledge, 2006.

– "Oral Testimonies from Russian Victims of Forced Labour." In von Plato, Leh, and Thonfeld, *Hitler's Slaves*, 262–75.

Schiffrin, Deborah. *Approaches to Discourse*. Oxford and Cambridge: Blackwell, 1994.

Schölzel, Christian. "Of Silence and Remembrance: Forced Labour and the NDH, and the History of Their Remembrance." In von Plato, Leh, and Thonfeld, *Hitler's Slaves*, 151–65.

Schütze, Fritz. "Biographieforschung und narratives Interview." *Neue Praxis* 3 (1983): 283–93.

– "Kognitive Figuren des autobiographischen Stegreiferzählens." In *Biographie und Soziale Wirklichkeit*, ed. Martin Kohli and Günther Robert, 78–117. Stuttgart: Metzler, 1984.

– "Prozessstrukturen des Lebensablaufs." In *Biographie in Handlungswissenschaftlicher Perspektive*, ed. Joachim Matthes, Arno Pfeifenberger, and Manfred Stosberg, 67–156. Nürnberg: Verlag der Nürnberger Forschungsvereinigung, 1981.

Schwarze, Gisela. *Kinder, die nicht Zählten: Ostarbeiterinnen und Ihre Kinder im Zweiten Weltkrieg*. Essen: Klartext-Verlag, 1997.

Seppälä, Helge. "Finlandiia kak Okkupant." *Sever* 4–5 (1995): 96–113; *Sever* 6 (1995): 108–28.

– *Suomi Miehittäjänä 1941–1944*. Helsinki: Painovuosi, 1989.

Shanin, Theodor, "Istoriia Pokolenii i Pokolencheskaia Istoriia Rossii." Public lecture, Project "Public lectures Polit.ru," Moscow, 17 March 2005. *Polit. Ru*. Accessed 12 April 2010, at http://www.polit.ru/lectures/2005/08/09/shanin/.

Shcheglova, Tatiana. "1950-1970-e Gody: Ustnaia Istoriia 'Bezmolvstvuiushchego Bolshinstva' v Period Ukrepleniia Kolkhozov i Likvidatsii Neperspektivnyh Sel." In *Derevnia I Krestianstvo Altaiskogo Kraia v XX veke: Ustnaia Istoriia*, by Tatiana Shcheglova, 400–511. Barnaul: Izdanie Pedagogicheskogo Universiteta, 2008.

Shchepanskaia, Tatiana. "Antropologiia Professii." *Zhurnal Sotsiologii i Sotsialnoi Antropologii* 1, no. 21 (2003): 139–61.

Sheridan, Dorothy. "Women and Life History Work in East Central Europe." *Oral History* 19 (1991): 63–7.

Shinkareva, Elena, ed. *Zhenskaia Usnaia Istoriia: Gendernye Issledovaniia*, vol. 2. Bishkek: Tsentr Izdatelskogo razvitia, 2005.

Shipova, Ekaterina. Interview by Yelena Rozhdestvenskaya. Pskov *oblast*, Russia. July 2005.

Shostak, Natalia (Khanenko-Friesen). "Local Ukrainianness in Transnational Context: An Ethnographic Study of a Canadian Prairie Community." PhD diss., University of Alberta, 2001.

Sihvo, Hannes. *Karjalan Kuva. Karelianismin Taustaa ja Vaiheita Autonomian aikana*. Helsinki: Suomalaisen kirjallisuuden seura, 1973.

Silchenko, Olga (mathematician). Interview by Natalia Pushkareva. Moscow, Russia. 12 February 2005.

Skultans, Vieda. "Arguing with the KGB Archives." *Ethnos* 66, no. 3 (2001): 320–43.

– *The Testimony of Lives: Narrative and Memory in Post-Soviet Latvia.* London and New York: Routledge, 1998.

– "Theorizing Latvian Lives: The Quest for Identity." *Journal of the Royal Anthropological Institute* 3 (1997): 761–80.

Słodkowska, Inka. *Społeczeństwo Obywatelskie na Tle Historycznego Przełomu Polska 1980–1989.* Warsaw: Instytut Studiów Politycznych Polskiej Akademii Nauk, 2006.

Smith, Anthony. "Chosen Peoples: Why Ethnic Groups Survive." *Ethnic and Racial Studies* 15, no. 3 (1992): 436–56.

Sommaruga, Claudio. "Cifre Della Resistenza Degli Ufficiali Italiani Internati Nei Lager Nazisti." *Quaderni di storia contemporanea* 6 (1986): 21–38.

Spoerer, Mark. *Zwangsarbeit unter dem Hakenkreuz.* Stuttgart–Munich: Deutsche Verlags-Anstalt DVA, 2001.

Stanisław K. Interview by Marta Kurkowska-Budzan. Konarzyce, Poland. 2 May 2007.

Stanisław O. Interview by Marta Kurkowska-Budzan. Jedwabne, Poland. 27–28 October 2000.

Stebliuk, Yustyna. Interview by Oksana Khymovych. Village of Babychi, Radekhiv district, Lviv *oblast*, Ukraine. 9 February 2008.

Strassberg, Barbara. "Changes in Religious Culture in Post World War II Poland." *Sociological Analysis* 48, no. 4 (1988): 342–54.

Streit, Christian *Keine Kameraden. Die Wehrmacht und die sowjetischen Kriegsgefangenen 1941–1945.* Stuttgart: Verlag J.H.W. Dietz, 1978.

Strękowska-Zaremba, Małgorzata. Interview by David Curp. Warsaw, Poland. 27 March 2010.

Subtelny, Orest. *Ukraine: A History*. Toronto: University of Toronto Press, 1988.

Sulimin, Sergei S., I. Truskinov, and N. Shitov. *Chudovishchnye Zlodeianiia Finsko-Fashistskhikh Zakhvatchikov na Territorii Karelo-Finskoi SSR.* Petrozavodsk: Gosudarstvennoie izdatelstvo KFSSR, 1945.

Suomen sota 1941–1945, vol. 6: *Toim. Puolustusvoimien pääesikunnan sotahistoriallinen toimisto*. Helsinki: Kivi, 1956.

Suutari, Pekka, and Yury Shikalov, eds. *Karelia Written and Sung: Representations of Locality in Soviet and Russian Contexts.* Helsinki: Aleksanteri Institute, 2010.

Svetlana (medievalist). Interview by Natalia Pushkareva. Moscow, Russia. 7 January 2005.

Svetlana K. Interview by Janina Lavrenko. Pinsk, Brest *oblast*, Belarus. 12 September 2009.

Szostkiewicz, Adam. "Linia Michalika." *Polityka*, 28 August 2010.

Szpak, Ewelina. "Robotnice czy Chłopki, Czyli o Zyciu Codziennym Pegeerowskich Kobiet." In *Historia Zwyczajnych Kobiet i Zwyczajnych Mężczyzn. Dzieje Społeczne w Perspektywie Gender*, ed. Dobrochna Kałwa and Tomasz Pudłocki, 73–82. Przemyśl: PWSW, TPN; Kraków: Instytut Historii UJ, 2007.

Sztompka, Petr. "Sotsialnoe Izmenenie kak Travma." *Sotsiologicheskie Issledovaniia* 1 (2001): 6–16.

Tamara D. Interview by Irina Romanova. Obchin, Luban district, Minsk *oblast*, Belarus. 8 July 2009.

Tamara Sh. Interview by Pavel Shevelev. Baranovichi, Brest *oblast*, Belarus. 10 October 2009.

Tatiana (economist). Interview by Natalia Pushkareva. Moscow, Russia. 5 February 2005.

Tatiana (ophthalmologist). Interview by Natalia Pushkareva. Moscow, Russia. 29 January 2005.

Tatiana G. Interview by Irina Makhovskaya. Pruzhany, Brest *oblast*, Belarus. 11 July 2009.

Tatiana T. Interview by Maria Saygutina. Cheliabinsk, Russia. 10 November 2008.

Taylor, Charles. *A Secular Age*. Cambridge, MA: Harvard University Press, 2007.

Terekhova, Liubov. Interview by Yelena Rozhdestvenskaya. Pskov *oblast*, Russia. July 2005.

Teresa C. Interview by Andrzej Drobik. Goniądz, Poland. 7 August 2008.

Ther, Phillipp, Tomasz Królik, and Lutz Henke, eds. *Polski Wrocław jako Metropolia Europejska. Pamięć i Polityka Historyczna z Punktu Widzenia Oral History*. Wrocław: Oficyna Wydawnicza ATUT – Wrocławskie Wydawnictwo Oświatowe, 2006.

Thomson, Alistair. *Anzac Memories: Living with the Legend*. Melbourne: Oxford University Press, 1994.

– "Four Paradigm Transformations in Oral History." *Oral History Review* 34, no. 1 (2007): 49–70.

Thompson, Paul. *Golos Proshlogo*. Trans. Maksim Korobochkin, E. Krishtof, and G. Bljablin. Moscow: Ves mir, 2003.

– *The Voice of the Past: Oral History*. Oxford: Oxford University Press, 1978, 1988.

Thonfeld, Christoph. "Former Forced Labourers as Immigrants in Great Britain after 1945." In von Plato, Leh, and Thonfeld, *Hitler's Slaves*, 324–38.

"Three Autobiographies of Lev Scherba." Fond 770, Op. 1, D. 1. P. 1–9, Archive of Russian Academy of Sciences, Saint Petersburg.

Tichenor, Veronika. "Status and Income as Gendered Resources: The Case of Marital Power." *Journal of Marriage and the Family* 61, no. 3 (1999): 212–21.

Tonkin, Elizabeth. *Narrating Our Pasts: The Social Construction of Oral History*. Cambridge: Cambridge University Press, 1995.

Toranska, Teresa. *Them: Stalin's Polish Puppets*. New York: HarperCollins, 1988.

Tóth, Eszter Zsófia. "The Cultural Identity of Semiskilled Women Workers in Socialist Hungary." In *Testimonies of the City: Identity, Community and Change in a Contemporary Urban World*, ed. Richard Rodger and Joanna Herbert, 45–72. Aldershot and Burlington: Ashgate, 2007.

Tsvetaeva, Nina. "Praktiki i Tsennosti v Epokhu Peremen (Analiz Biograficheskikh Materialov Konkursa 'Zhyt v Epokhu Peremen')." Federalnyi Obozrevatelnyi Portal JeSM. Accessed 19 September 2010, at http://www.ecsocman.edu.ru/images/pubs/2008/02/19/0000321152/010_Tsvetaeva_137-146.pdf.

Uehling, Greta Lynn. *Beyond Memory: The Crimean Tatars' Deportation and Return*. New York: Palgrave Macmillan, 2004.

Ukkone, Alexey. "Kak Zashchititsia ot Sotsialnoi Zashchity." *Karelia*, 31 May 2001.

– "Uzniki Chuzhoi Sovesti." *Izvestiia*, 13 February 2003.

Valentina A. Interview by Salavat Bayazitov. Cheliabinsk, Russia. 30 April 2005.

Valentina K. Interview by Irina Romanova. Soligorsk, Minsk *oblast*, Belarus. 27 August 2009.

Valentina L. Interview by Irina Romanova. Luban, Minsk *oblast*, Belarus. 16 July 2009.

Valentina M. Interview by Irina Makhovskaya. Slutsk, Minsk *oblast*, Belarus. 12 September 2009.

Valevskii, Aleksei. *Osnovaniia Biografiki*. Kyiv: Naukova dumka, 1993.

Vanêk, Miroslav. "The Development of Theory and Method in Czech Oral History after 1989." *Oral History Forum (Forum d'histoire orale)* 28 (2008). Accessed 17 June 2011 at http://www.oralhistoryforum.ca/index.php/ohf/article/view/25.

Vanêk, Miroslav, and Pavel Urbasek, eds. *Vítězové? Poražení? Politické Elity a Disent v Období tzv. Normalizace. Životopisná Interview. 2 Svazky*. Prague: Prostor 2005, 1970.

Vansina, Jan. *Oral Tradition as History*. Madison: University of Wisconsin Press, 1985.

Vasil'eva, Anna. "Zhenshchiny v Nauke I Obrazovanii (Beseda s Matematikom Galinoi Iaroshevskoi)." Informatsionnyi Portal OWL. http://www.owl.ru/win/womplus/1999/science.htm.

Vehviläinen, Olli. *Finland in the Second World War: Between Germany and Russia.* New York: Palgrave, 2002.

Verdery, Katherine. *What Was Socialism, and What Comes Next?* Princeton: Princeton University Press, 1996.

Vilanova, Mercedes. "Work, Repression, and Death after the Spanish Civil War." In von Plato, Leh, and Thonfeld, *Hitler's Slaves*, 37–46.

Vladimir B. Interview by Salavat Bayazitov. Cheliabinsk, Russia. 27 April 2006.

Vladimir Sh. Interview by Inna Simonova. Mariina Gorka, Minsk *oblast*, Belarus. 18 August 2009.

Vladimir T. Interview by Irina Romanova. Rechen, Luban district, Minsk *oblast*, Belarus. 25 July 2009.

von Plato, Alexander. *"Der Verlierer Geht Nicht Leer Aus": Betriebsräte Geben zu Protokoll.* Berlin & Bonn: Verlag J.H.W. Dietz, 1984.

– "'Wirtschaftskapitäne': Biographische Selbstkonstruktionen von Unternehmern der Nachkriegszeit." In *Modernisierung im Wiederaufbau: Die Westdeutsche Gesellschaft der 50er Jahre*, ed. Axel Schildt and Arnold Sywottek, 377–91. Bonn: Dietz, 1993.

– "Victims Competition?" *International Journal on Audiovisual Testimony* (December 1998): 7–14.

– "Zur Geschichte des Sowjetischen Speziallagersystems in Deutschland. Einführung." In *Sowjetische Speziallagerin Deutschland 1945 bis 1950, Band 1: Studien und Berichte*, ed. Alexander von Plato, 19–75. Berlin: Akademie Verlag, 1998.

– ed. *Sowjetische Speziallager in Deutschland 1945 bis 1950, Band 1 Studien und Berichte.* Berlin: Akademie Verlag, 1998.

– "'Entstasifizierung' im öffentlichen Dienst der neuen Bundesländer nach 1989: Umorientierung und Kontinuität in der Lehrerschaft." In *Jahrbuch für Historische Bildungsforschung, Bd* 5, ed. Peter Derek, Hanno Schmitt, und Heinz-Elmar Tenorth, 313–42. Bad Heilbrunn: Klinkhardt, Julius, 1999.

– "Opferkonkurrenten?" In *Eine Offene Geschichte. Zur kommunikativen Tradierung der nationalsozialistischen Vergangenheit*, ed. Elisabeth Domansky and Harald Welzer, 74–92. Tübingen: Ed. diskord, 1999.

von Plato, Alexander, and Almut Leh. *Ein unglaublicher Frühling. Erfahrene Geschichte im Nachkriegsdeutschland (Dokumente und Analysen).* Bonn: Bundeszentrale für politische Bildung, 1997.

von Plato, Alexander, Almut Leh, and Christoph Thonfeld. "Einleitung der Herausgeber." In von Plato, Leh, and Thonfeld, *Hitlers Sklaven*, 9–24.

– eds. *Hitlers Sklaven: Lebensgeschichtliche Analysen zur Zwangsarbeit im Internationalen Vergleich*. Vienna: Böhlau, 2008.

– eds. *Hitler's Slaves: Life Stories of Forced Labourers in Nazi-Occupied Europe*. New York: Berghahn Books, 2010.

Wacquant, Loïc. "For a Socio-Analysis of Intellectuals: On 'Homo Academicus' – Interview with Pierre Bourdieu." *Berkeley Journal of Sociology: A Critical Review* 34 (1989): 1–29.

Wallace, Brandon. "Reconsidering the Life Review: The Social Construction of Talk about the Past." *Gerontologist* 32, no. 1 (1992): 120–5.

Walz, Loretta. *Und dann kommst du dahin an einem schönen Sommertag: Die Frauen von Ravensbrück*. Munich: Verlag Antje Kunstmann, 2005.

Westernman, William. "Central American Refugee Testimonies and Performed Life Histories in the Sanctuary Movement." In *Oral History Reader*, ed. Robert Perks and Alistair Thomson, 224–35. New York: Routledge, 2003.

White, Hayden. *Metahistory: The Historical Imagination in 19th-Century Europe*. Baltimore: Johns Hopkins University Press, 1973.

– *Metaistoriia. Istoricheskoe Voobrazhenie v Evrope XIX veka*. Trans. Elena Trubina and Vladimir Kharitonov. Yekaterinburg: Iz-dvo Uralskoho universiteta, 2002.

Wiesinger, Barbara. "'If You Lose Your Freedom, You Lose Everything': The Experiences and Memories of Serbian Forced Labourers." In von Plato, Leh, and Thonfeld, *Hitler's Slaves*, 166–76.

Wiścicki, Tomasz. Interview by David Curp. Warsaw, Poland. 7 December 2009.

Witeska-Młynarczyk, Anna. "Landscapes of Polish Memory: Conflicting Ways of Dealing with the Communist Past in a Polish Town." PhD diss., University College London, 2010.

Władysława K. Interview by Marta Kurkowska-Budzan. Przytuły Las, Poland. 26 June 2003.

Wnuk, Rafał. "Polityczne i ideowe oblicze podziemia antykomunistycznego w Polsce." In *Aparat represji a opór społeczeństwa wobec systemu komunistycznego w Polsce i na Litwie w latach 1944–1956*, ed. Piotr Niwiński. Warsaw: Instytut Pamięci Narodowej, 2005.

Woloszyn, Jacek Witold. *Chronić i Kontrolować. UB wobec Sródowisk i Organizacji Konspiracyjnych Młodzieży na Lubelszczyznie (1944–1956)*. Warsaw: Instytut Pamięci Narodowej. Komisja ścigania Zbrodni Przeciwko Narodowi Polskiemu, 2007.

"Wytyczne Dyrektora Departamentu IV MSW Dotyczące Form I Metod Działań Operacyjnych Departamentu IV I Jego Odpowiedników w Terenie." In *Metody Pracy Operacyjnej Aparatu Bezpieczeństwa Wobec Kościłów I*

Związków Wyznaniowych 1945–1989, ed. Adam Dziurok, 620. Warsaw: Instytut Pamięci Narodowej, 2004.

Yarshin, Vladimir. Interview by Alexandr Osipov. *Finskaia Okkupatsiia Karelii*, ed. Alexey Golubev and Alexandr Osipov. *Ustnaia Istoriia v Karelii*, vol. 3: *Sbornik Nauchnykh Statei i Istochnikov*, 83–91. Petrozavodsk: Petrozavodsk State University Press, 2007.

Yelena L. Interview by Salavat Bayazirov. Cheliabinsk, Russia. 15 April 2005.

Yulia U. Interview by Daria Antonova. Cheliabinsk, Russia. 5 November 2007.

Yurchak, Alexei. *Everything Was Forever, Until It Was No More: The Last Soviet Generation*. Princeton: Princeton University Press, 2005.

Załęcki, Paweł. "Between Spontaneity, Institutional Church, and State Politics: The Oasis Movement in Poland." *Polish Sociological Review* 110, no. 2 (1995): 83–91.

Zapf, Wolfgang. *Wandlungen der deutschen Elite: Ein Zirkulationsmodell Deutscher Führungsgruppen 1919 bis 1961*. Munich: Piper, 1965.

Zaremba, Marcin. *Komunizm, Legitymizacja, Nacjonalizm. Nacjonalistyczna Legitymizacja Władzy Komunistycznej w Polsce*. Warsaw: Wydawnictwo Trio, 2001.

Zaryn, Jan, and Grzegorz Majchrzak. "Ofensywna Antykościelna i śmierć Księdza Jerzego." *Instytutu Pamięci Narodowej* 10 (2004): 49–53.

Zaslavkaja, Tat'jana. Interview by Boris Doktorov. "From Childhood It Was Known for Me That the Most Interesting Profession Is to Be a Scientist." UNVL Centre for Democratic Culture. http://cdclv.unlv.edu//archives/Interviews/zaslavskaya_07.html.

Zaitsev, Nikolai. Interview by Yelena Rozhdestvenskaya. Pskov *oblast*, Russia. July 2005.

Zdravomyslov, Andrei. "Troistvennaia Interpretatsiia Kultury i Granitsy Sotsiologicheskogo Znaniia." *Sotsiologicheskie Issledovaniia* 8 (2008): 3–18.

Zenon Z. Interview by Marta Kurkowska-Budzan. Łady Borowe, Poland. 2 September 2007.

Zhukov, Georgii. *Vospominaniia i Razmyshleniia*. Moscow: Izdatelstvo agentstva pechati "Novosti," 1969.

Zhuravlev, Vadim. "Narrativnoie Interviu v Biograficheskikh Issledovaniiakh." *Sotsiologiia* 4 (1993–4): 34–43.

Zieliński, Ariel. "Nowe Ruchy Religijne a Nowe Ruchy Społeczne." *Przypadek Katolickiego Ruchu Charyzmatycznego Societas/Communitas* 2, no. 4 (2007–8): 231–51.

Zieliński, Zygmunt. *Kościół w Polsce 1944–2007*. Poznań: Wydawnictwo Poznańskie, 2009.

Zofia K. Interview by Marta Kurkowska-Budzan. Konarzyce, Poland. 1 May 2007.

Contributors

Rozalia Cherepanova holds PhD in history from Cheliabinsk State University, Russia, and is currently an assistant professor (docent) in the department of Russian History as well as a researcher at the Oral History Centre at South Ural State University, Cheliabinsk, Russia. She is the author of more than fifty scholarly articles published in *Neprikosnovennyi Zapas, Obshchestvennye nauki i sovremennost, Vestnik Evrazii, Studies in East European Thought, Novaia i noveishaia istoriia*, and other academic journals and of a monograph *The Russian Way and Its Prophets: The Idea of a "Special Path" and the Messianic Mood in Russian Social Thought in the Second Quarter of the Nineteenth Century* (2007). Academic interests include study of intellectual history, historical anthropology, and oral history.

David Curp holds a PhD in history from the University of Washington and is an associate professor of history at Ohio University, where he teaches contemporary history of Eastern Europe and the Balkans. Currently he is researching grass-roots Catholic religious life in Poland with a primary focus on the work of the Light-and-Life Movement. Dr Curp is also a member of the American Association for the Advancement of Slavic Studies as well as the Polish Studies Association. His publications include the monograph *A Clean Sweep: The Politics of Ethnic Cleansing in Western Poland, 1945–1960* (2006) and articles published in *The Polish Review, European Studies Quarterly*, and *Nationalities Papers*.

Gelinada Grinchenko is an historian and a professor of History at the Department of Ukrainian Studies (Faculty of Philosophy, V.N. Karazin Kharkiv National University, Ukraine). Grinchenko is the founding member and the Inaugural President of the Ukrainian Oral History Association (since 2006). Currently she is editor of the academic peer-reviewed journal Ukraina Moderna, and member of the European research network COST "In Search for Transcultural Memory." Grinchenko's main areas of research include oral history, war and post-war politics of memory, and Holocaust Studies. She has edited several books and journals, and published many chapters and peer-reviewed articles in her areas of research. Her latest authored book is *An Oral History of Forced Labour: Method, Contexts, Texts* (2012).

Alexey Golubev is a PhD candidate in history at the University of British Columbia, Canada, and assistant professor at the Institute of History, Political Science, and Sociology, Petrozavodsk State University, Russia. He specializes in Soviet social and cultural history, as well as history of Northern Europe and transnational history of Finnish diaspora. He is a co-author of *The Search for a Socialist El Dorado: Finnish Immigration to Soviet Karelia from the United States and Canada in the 1930s* (2014, with Irina Takala). He also co-edited several volumes, including *The Barents History: A Transnational History of Subarctic Europe* (PAX, 2015, with Lars Elenius et al.) and four volumes of the academic series *Oral History in Karelia (Ustanaia istoriia v Karelii*, 2006–8).

Natalia Khanenko-Friesen holds a PhD in anthropology and Ukrainian Folklore from the University of Alberta and is an associate professor of Anthropology and the head of the Department of Religions and Culture at St Thomas More College, University of Saskatchewan. She previously taught at the University of Toronto and Harvard University. A former Director of the Prairie Centre for the study of the Ukrainian Heritage, she established and coordinates the Centre's Oral History and Personal Archives Program. Khanenko-Friesen's research interests include diasporic identities and communities, post-socialist transition, labour migration discourse, oral history, and Ukrainian culture. Among her various publications are four books including the two monographs, *Ukrainian Otherlands: Diaspora, Homeland and Folk Imagination in the 20th Century* (2015) and *The Other World or Ethnicity in Action: Canadian Ukrainianness at the End of the 20th Century* (2011). Khanenko-Friesen serves as an inaugural editor of Canada's *Engaged Scholar Journal: Community-Engaged Research, Teaching and Learning*.

Marta Kurkowska-Budzan is assistant professor at the Institute of History at Jagiellonian University, Kraków, Poland. Her recent research concerns methodology of oral history, historical anthropology of everyday life in Polish People's Republic, the presence of history in contemporary mass culture. She is the author of the book *Anti-communist Armed Resistance in the Bialystok Region: The Analysis of Contemporary Symbolisation of the Past* (2009). She is a founding member of Historical Anthropology Group at Historical Sciences Committee of Polish Academy of Sciences, Polish Oral History Association and Center for Historical Anthropology Research at Polish Historical Association.

Irina Makhovskaya is associate professor at the Department of Ethnology, Museology and Art History, Faculty of History, Belarusian State University, Minsk, Belarus. Makhovskaya holds PhD in History from the Krapivy Institute of Art Criticism, Ethnography and Folklore of the National Academy of Sciences of Belarus. Makhovskaya's research interests include Belarusian traditional culture, Slavic mythology, oral history, everyday history. Among her numerous publications, she co-authored (with Irina Romanova) a monograph *Mir: The History of Town as Told by Its Citizens* (2009).

Alexander von Plato is an internationally recognized authority on oral history and one of Germany's leading oral historians. In 1993 he founded the Institute for History and Biography at the Fernuniversität Hagen, Germany's first oral history centre, and later the German oral history journal *BIOS*. During the 14 years he served as the institute's director, he completed 37 research projects, including two ground-breaking studies of former Nazi slave workers and of the Mauthausen concentration camp. He is also a founder and former secretary and vice president of the International Oral History Association. Von Plato has taught at the universities of Essen, Hagen, Vienna and Voronezh. His various monographs include *The End of the Cold War? Bush, Kohl, Gorbachev, and the Reunification of Germany* (2015). The book *Hitler's Slaves* (2010) is an important study on forced labour during the Second World War.

Natalia Pushkareva holds PhD in Russian history from Moscow State University and is a full professor and a Leading Research Fellow at the Institute of Ethnology and Anthropology (Russian Academy of Sciences) where she is head of the Women's and Gender Studies Department. Pushkareva is a chief editor of the yearbook *Sotsialnaia istoriia* (Social History), Standing Representative of Russia in the International Federation for Research in Women's History, the President of Russian

Association for Research in Women's History. Her publication record includes, among other books, *Women in Medieval Rus* (1989), *Women in Russia and in Europe at the Dawn of the Modern Age* (1996), *Women in Russian History from the 10th to the 20th century* (1997), *"There are our sins…": Sexual Culture in Russia from the 10th to the XIXth c.* (1999), *Gender Theory and Historical Knowledge* (2007), *Russian Everyday Life in the Mirror of Gender Relations* (2013).

Irina Romanova is a professor at the European Humanities University, Vilnius, Lithuania. In her research, Romanova focuses on the modern history of Belarus (twentieth century), oral history, rural history and everyday culture. Together with Irina Makhovskaya she co-authored a monograph, *Mir: The History of Town as Told by Its Citizens* (2009).

Yelena Rozhdestvenskaya holds a degree of Doctor of Sociology and is a Professor of Sociology in the Faculty of Social Sciences in National Research University Higher School of Economics HSE, and the Leading Researcher in Institute of Sociology Russian Academy of Sciences. Rozhdestvenskaya's research interests span qualitative sociology, biographical method, war-studies, memory-studies, and gender sociology. Among the books she has authored, co-authored and edited are *Biographical Method: History, Methodology, Praxis* (1994), *Window to the Russian Private Life* (1999), *Oral History and Biography: Women's View* (2004), *Biographical Method in Sociology* (2012) (all in Russian), and *Marriages in Russia* (1999).

Anna Witeska-Młynarczyk received her PhD from the Anthropology Department at the University College London. She is a grantee of the Wenner-Gren Foundation (Dissertation Fieldwork Grant), the UCL Graduate School, the Visegrad Fund, and the Open Society Institute. She studied at the Central European University (Budapest, Hungary) and at the Sabanci University (Istanbul, Turkey). She currently is a lecturer at the Department of Ethnology and Cultural Anthropology at the Adam Mickiewicz University in Poznań (Poland).

Index

www.ingramcontent.com/pod-product-compliance
Lightning Source LLC
LaVergne TN
LVHW090150080826
844660LV00013B/744/J

* 9 7 8 1 4 4 2 6 3 7 3 8 2 *